# CANOES

# CANOES

## A Natural History in North America

Mark Neuzil *and* Norman Sims

*Foreword by* John McPhee

UNIVERSITY OF MINNESOTA PRESS

MINNEAPOLIS · LONDON

A grant from the Andrew W. Mellon Foundation supported the publication of this book and the creation of an online resource companion, which includes archival and multimedia materials. The companion can be accessed at http://minnesota.fulcrumscholar.org.

FRONTISPIECE  William English canoe, model 21 (see page 128). Photograph by Ralph Nimtz.

Published by the University of Minnesota Press
111 Third Avenue South, Suite 290
Minneapolis, MN 55401-2520
http://www.upress.umn.edu

ISBN 978-0-8166-8117-4

A Cataloging-in-Publication record for this book is available from the Library of Congress.

Printed in Canada on acid-free paper

The University of Minnesota is an equal-opportunity educator and employer.

22 21 20 19 18 17 16          10 9 8 7 6 5 4 3 2 1

# Contents

# Scenes from a Life in Canoes

*John McPhee*

The following passages, appearing here as a form of foreword, are from one writer's life in canoes. He is John McPhee, who has written for *The New Yorker* since 1963. His work, all nonfiction, has been highly varied in theme, but, even so, canoes and canoe trips run through it all with surprising frequency—out on the water with a spectrum of people from Euell Gibbons on the Susquehanna to Jimmy Carter on the Apalachicola when he was governor of Georgia. In 1999, the Pulitzer Prize for General Nonfiction was awarded to John McPhee's *Annals of the Former World*, his five-volume work on the geology of North America. He has written twenty-eight books, all in his style of literary journalism. Now in his eighties, he owns five canoes—two chocolate-brown Mad Rivers and three Old Towns. The headnotes and the passages here are all from John McPhee.

— *Mark Neuzil and Norman Sims, 2016*

◁ Julian A. Dimock, *Canoe in Pass, Marco, Florida,* 1907.
American Museum of Natural History Library, image 48519.

*Actually, I gave one of the chocolate canoes to the author Richard Preston not long ago, but I still technically own it because he hasn't paid me the one dollar he owes me for it. Preston paddles as much as I do, makes beautiful wooden kayaks, and will rebuild the canoe. Which brings us to a basic question: What am I doing with five canoes?*

I grew up in a summer camp—Keewaydin—whose specialty was canoes and canoe travel. At the home base, near Middlebury, Vermont, were racks and racks of canoes, at least a hundred canoes—E. M. Whites and Old Town Guides, mainly. They were very good wood-and-canvas keeled or keelless canoes, lake or river canoes. We were in them every day wherever we were, in and out of Vermont. We were like some sort of crustaceans with our rib-and-planking exoskeletons, and to this day I do not feel complete or safe unless I am surrounded by the protective shape of a canoe.

Now and again, Keewaydin let us take our canoes not so much onto the water as into it, during swim period. We went swimming with our canoes. We jounced. Jouncing is the art of propelling a canoe without a paddle. You stand up on the gunwales near the stern deck and repeatedly flex and unflex your knees. The canoe rocks, slaps the lake, moves forward. Sooner or later, you lose your balance and fall into the water, because the gunwales are slender rails and the stern deck is somewhat smaller than a pennant. From waters deeper than you were tall, you climbed back into your canoe. If you think that's easy, try it.

After three or four splats, and with a belly pink from hauling it over gunwales, you lost interest in jouncing. What next? You sat in your canoe and deliberately overturned it. You leaned hard to one side, grabbed the opposite gunwale, and pulled. Out you went, and into the water. This was, after all, swim period. Now you rolled your canoe—an action it resists far less when it is loaded with water. You could make your canoe spiral like a football inside the lake.

And before long you found the air pocket. Having jounced and spiralled to the far end of your invention span, you ducked beneath the surface and swam in under your upside-down canoe. You rose slowly to miss a thwart—feeling above you, avoiding a bump on the head—and then your eyes, nose, mouth were in air, among chain-link streaks of white and amber light, the shimmers of reflection in a quonset grotto. Its vertical inches were few but enough. Your pals got in there with you and your voices were tympanic in the grotto. Or you just hung out under there by yourself. With a hand on a thwart, and your feet slowly kicking, you could breathe normally, see normally, talk abnormally, and wait indefinitely for a change of mood. You were invisible to the upside, outside world. Even more than when kneeling in a fast current, you were one with your canoe.

Kneeling in a fast current. Once in a while, we went to what is now called Battell Gorge, north of Middlebury, to learn to deal with really fast, pounding, concentrated flow. Otter Creek, there, undergoes an abrupt change in physiographic character. After meandering benignly through marshes, woodlots, and meadows of the Champlain Valley, it encounters a large limestone outcrop, which it deeply bisects. By a factor of three or four, the stream narrows and the water squeezes into humps, haystacks, souse holes, and standing waves as it drops ten feet in a hundred yards. Then it emerges from the high limestone walls and the darkness of overhanging hemlocks into the light of a pool so wide it seems to be a pond.

Like horse people, we showed up some distance above the head of the gorge with trailers—racked trailers that each carried seven canoes. The gorge was a good place to learn how to deal with canoes in white water because it was violent but short. In that narrow, roaring flume, you didn't have to choose the best route—didn't have to look for what the voyageurs called the *fil d'eau.* There was pretty much one way to go. But you got the sense of a canoe flying in three dimensions; and the more you did it the slower it seemed, the shoot separating itself into distinct parts, as if you were in a balloon rising in sunlight and falling in the shadows of clouds.

One time, when I was about twelve, I went into the gorge in a very old Old Town Guide that was missing its stern seat. (We didn't take the better boats there.) Two of us were paddling it. I was kneeling against the stern thwart, which was so far back it was only eight or ten inches from gunwale to gunwale, the size of my young butt. My right knee was on the canoe's ribs, and my right leg extended so far back that my foot was wedged in the V of the stern when the bucking canoe turned over. Billy Furey was my partner, and we were doing all we could to keep things even, but whatever we did wasn't good enough, and we flipped near

the top of the gorge. Billy was ejected. Among the countless wonders of the simple design of the native American canoe is the fact that it ejects its paddlers when it capsizes.

This one could not eject me, because my foot was stuck. I struggled to pull the foot free, but it wouldn't come. Upside down in billows of water, I could not get out. Understand: I have a lifelong tendency to panic. Almost anything will panic me—health, money, working with words. Almost anything—I'm here to tell you—but an overturned canoe in a raging gorge. When I was trapped in there, if panic crossed my mind it went out the other side. I had, after all, time and time again been swimming with canoes. There was purpose in letting us do that—a thought that had never occurred to me. After I realized I was caught and was not going to be coming out from under that canoe, I reached for the stern quarter-thwart, took hold of it, and pulled my body upward until my eyes, nose, and mouth were in the grotto. There, in the dancing light, I rode on through the gorge, and when the water calmed down at the far end I gave the canoe half a spiral and returned to the open sunlight.[1]

*Here is something of a footnote to that piece.*

At Vassar College a few decades ago, I read to a gymful of people some passages from books I had written, and then received questions from the audience. The first person said, "Of all the educational institutions you went to when you were younger, which one had the greatest influence on the work you do now?" The question stopped me for a moment because I had previously thought about the topic only in terms of individual teachers and never in terms of institutions. Across my mind flashed the names of a public-school system K through 12, a New England private school (13), and two universities—one in the United States, one abroad—and in a split second I blurted out, "The children's camp I went to when I was six years old."

The response drew general laughter, but, funny or not, it was the simple truth. In addition to ribs, planking, quarter-thwarts, and open gunwales, you learned to identify rocks, ferns, and trees. You played tennis. You backpacked in the Green Mountains on the Long Trail. If I were to make a list of all the varied subjects that have come up in my articles and books, adding a check mark beside interests derived from Keewaydin, most of the entries would be checked. I spent all summer every summer at Keewaydin from age six through fifteen, and later was a counselor there, leading canoe trips and teaching swimming, for three years while I was in college.[2]

*The following fragment, chosen, like everything else, by Norman Sims and Mark Neuzil, may seem to have little to do with canoes. But a dam has a lot to do with canoes if the canoes have to be carried around the dam, if the immemorial river has been turned into a cadenza of pools.*

In the view of conservationists, there is something special about dams, something—as conservation problems go—that is disproportionately and metaphysically sinister. The outermost circle of the Devil's world seems to be a moat filled mainly with DDT. Next to it is a moat of burning gasoline. Within that is a ring of pinheads each covered with a million people—and so on past phalanxed bulldozers and bicuspid chain saws into the absolute epicenter of Hell on earth, where stands a dam. The implications of the dam exceed its true level in the scale of environmental catastrophes. Conservationists who can hold themselves in reasonable check before new oil spills and fresh megalopolises mysteriously go insane at even the thought of a dam. The conservation movement is a mystical and religious force, and possibly the reaction to dams is so violent because rivers are the ultimate metaphors of existence, and dams destroy rivers. Humiliating nature, a dam is evil—placed and solid.[3]

*So it is a reasonable assumption that a person in a canoe, coming upon a dam, will prefer that the dam not be there. Sometimes, in some places, something is done about it.*

With John McPhedran, I carried a canoe around a ballfield in Waterville, Maine, and on into woods. The terrain fell away there sharply. The boat was heavy, but its skin was indestructible and we dragged it, bumping on roots. So much for the loving care reserved for canvas, bark, and Kevlar canoes. This one had no need of it. Its makers promote its type with pictures that show one being thrown off the roof of their factory in Old Town. So we twitched it downhill like a log. On the threshold of the year 2000, this was just one of the countless ways of saying farewell to the nineteenth century.

A few days earlier, we would not have had to choose a model so tough. We put it into Messalonskee Stream, which carried us into the Kennebec River, which, in this stretch, had suddenly lost about five million tons of water as a result of deliberate demolition. Fifteen miles downstream, in Augusta, a dam two stories high and more than nine hundred feet wide had been breached on the first of July.

There were rapids at the mouth of Messalonskee Stream, but they had been there in pre-Columbian time. Just above the dam's impoundment, they suggested what its depth had concealed. A blue heron tried to lead us through the rapids, or seemed to, in a series of short, nosy flights down the left bank. A kingfisher watched. The Augusta Water Power Company blocked the river in the year that Martin Van Buren replaced Andrew Jackson as President of the United States. It was the year of the Panic of 1837, when real estate collapsed, banks failed like duckpins, and homeless people died in the streets. The first steam railroad was nine years old. Oberlin, the first coeducational American college, was four years old. If you could afford Buffaloe's Oil, you used it in your hair to fight baldness. In Augusta, primarily thanks to the new dam, some people could afford Buffaloe's Oil. The dam powered seven sawmills, a gristmill, and a machine shop. Incidentally, it had a fish ladder.

Beside the second rip we came to was a sofa bed, its skirts showing the stains of fallen water. We expected more of the same. We expected grocery carts. This, after all, was not Township 13, Range 11, of the North Woods, where nearly half the State of Maine consists of nameless unor-ganized townships. This was settled, supermarket Maine, but in the fifteen river miles upstream of Augusta we would see one beer can, no grocery carts, and three tires. Now we saw a mallard, a pewee, goldfinches. We heard song sparrows, a wood thrush, a veery. I wouldn't know a veery from a blue-winged warbler, but John McPhedran is acute on birds. I've known him since he was seventeen, seventeen years ago. Since then, he has become a botanist, a general field naturalist, and a freelance water-quality consultant who works for the Maine Department of Transportation. We saw sticking up from a large and newly emergent river boulder an iron bolt fully an inch and a half in diameter and capped with a head like a big iron mushroom. I knew what that dated from—the log drives of the Kennebec, which began in Colonial times and came to an end in 1976. Put a chain around that bolt and you could stop a raft of logs.

We saw no white pines, very long gone as the masts of ships. Or spruce, for that matter. We saw deciduous trees. In fall, the river's walls would be afire in oranges and reds, but now, in summer, the leaves seemed too bright, too light for Maine. Among them were few houses—in fifteen otherwise uncivilized miles, a total of three nervous houses peeping through narrow slots in the trees. This seemed to report a population that had turned its back on the river, which it had, for the better part of a century, because the river was cluttered with the debris of log drives, becessed with community waste, spiked with industrial toxins. Square-rigged ships once came up into the fresh Kennebec to carry its pure ice down the east coasts of both Americas and around

Cape Horn to San Francisco, and even across the Pacific, but by the nineteen-forties and fifties the Kennebec had developed such a chronic reek that windows in unaircon-ditioned offices in the Capitol of Maine—six hundred yards from the river—were kept tight shut in summer. After the Clean Water Act, of 1972, the Kennebec, like so many American rivers, steadily and enduringly cleared, and the scene was set for the dam destruction of 1999 and the resto-ration of this part of the river.[4]

⁓

*I have a 13½-foot Kevlar canoe with a 39-inch beam,*
*and it is so stable that I can cast standing up over flat water.*
*A fast-running river is something else, though, and my*
*center of gravity remains a great deal lower.*

Sometimes, wearing knee-high boots and not waders, I look for a submerged, flat-topped rock, and get out of the canoe so I can cast standing up. In breeze or current, the anchored canoe will swing on its rope, and before long move upstream in the eddy below the rock. It bumps gen-tly against my leg. It bumps again. Too much of that and I give it a shove, to put it out of my way. I cast, concentrate. At the end of the swing, I bring in the line and cast again. The canoe has returned, and is nuzzling my leg.

One afternoon, I was fishing in this manner from a big rock covered with not much water and situated almost in the middle of the river—in effect a small submerged island. Deciding to leave and fish elsewhere, I pulled up the anchor and set it in the canoe. I had meant to change lures before leaving, and had forgotten to do so before lifting the anchor,

so I sat down on the bow seat with my feet on the rock in the water. I removed a shad fly from the leader, and tied on a 1/32-ounce dart. I stood up with the fly rod to try out the dart, and forgot all about the anchor. Slowly, while I cast, the canoe turned and drifted away. I was too late when I realized what was happening. The shad net fell off the canoe and stood upright under water, buoyed by the air trapped in its hoop. The canoe drifted past the shad net and on to-ward Cape Henlopen. What to do? I was marooned on a mid-river rock, in fifteen-inch rubber boots with deep fast water around me. This was embarrassment on a new scale. The dart on the fly rod was extremely small. I cast it into the canoe and made a slow retrieve. The dart maddeningly slid over everything—over the tackle bag, over the life vest, over the paddles, over the stern painter. It somehow missed a tote bag and even a large wire fish basket, as it climbed each thwart and dropped on the other side and made its way through the whole canoe. Coming over the gunwale, it fell into the river. I cast again. The dart missed the ca-noe. I cast again. The dart landed in the bow. Gingerly as I stripped it in, it hopped, skipped, slid over everything, and went back into the river. The canoe was gaining momen-tum and was almost out of range. I cast again, landed where I hoped to, but failed to connect. How can fishhooks get hung up on every twig and pant leg while this one inter-sected nothing? There might be space and time for one more cast, and that would be all she wrote, hoss. I stripped out more line, backcast twice, and sent the dart on its way. It landed in the canoe. As it made its way toward the stern, its barb lodged in the coiled painter. The painter came over the side of the canoe and steadily straightened. A great deal of tension developed against that tiny dart but I couldn't just stand there, I had to pull. Ever so slowly, the canoe began to move upstream, and a little less slowly when at last it felt the draw of the eddy. In the end, it bumped against my leg. On the way downstream, I picked up the shad net with the blade of a paddle.[5]

⌒

*The St. John River rises in Maine and flows north until it intersects Canada, where it turns east toward the Maritimes as the international boundary. In canoes in the North Maine Woods, it's best to go down the river right after ice out, when the rapids are full, as I did one year with John Kauffmann, a National Park Service planner, and half a dozen other people ranging in age from college to quasi-octogenarian. A dam had been proposed at a place called Dickey, and sliding down the wilderness river we had a sense that we were somewhere inside a reservoir that did not yet exist.*
*Forty years later, at this writing, it still doesn't.*

Toward five in the morning, there is a veil of mist from sky to river and in it hangs the moon. Half gone now, gradually eclipsing itself, it tells us how long we have travelled. Half a moon.

Breakfast at six. Strong tea. "Sheep dip" was what the lumberjacks called their tea. We need it. The air is just above the freeze point. We do not eat light. Trout. Fried potatoes. Sourdough pancakes. Big red boiled "logging berries"—the lumberjacks' term for beans.

Tom Cabot returns from a walk in the woods. "I just saw a cow moose," he says. "I looked up, and there was the ass of a moose."

By nine, the sky is blue around big clouds. The day looks good on the river. Easing through the morning, we drop ten miles—Schoolhouse Rapid, Fox Brook Rapid, Poplar Island Rapid—and hunt around for a place to have lunch. For Dick Saltonstall, as guide, any old sandspit will not do. He looks over a brook mouth fringed with alders, crinkles his nose, and keeps paddling.

"Why didn't we stop there?"

"He didn't think it was aesthetic enough, and, being an aesthete, he thought we had better move on," Cabot explains.

Tom is part aesthete, part Wall Street, and he can take his scenic settings or leave them alone. He knows both sides of the wilderness argument, and he is not always with nature in its debate with man. He has seen Lake Powell in Utah, the result of the dam in Glen Canyon, and while he knows what was lost in Glen Canyon, he is (for reasons of public recreation) not sorry the lake exists. Glen Canyon is sometimes brought into discussions about the St. John, because Glen Canyon was remote and few people knew it was there until it wasn't there anymore.

Saltonstall finally picks a luncheon site under three big white pines—symbols of Maine, the Pine Tree State. There were far-reaching stands of them here once, throughout the north Maine woods. They were cut for the masts of navies. These above us are among the few left. Old-growth eastern white pine, they're up there a hundred feet—their kind the tallest trees in Eastern America. If the lake fills over this point in the riverbed, these pines will reach up like masts from a shipwreck, and even their skysail branches will be twenty-five fathoms down.

The Big Rapid is three miles below. We move toward it with everything trebly lashed. Mike Moody and I have the eighteen-foot Grumman, and have again been designated by the guide to go first. If we find trouble, our problem will suggest alternatives to the others. We are the refectory slaves, testing the food of kings.

The four canoes stop on the left bank, and we study the rapid. It does not look forbidding or, for the most part, fierce. It will not be like crossing a turnpike on foot. It is a garden of good choices. Overwhelmingly, it is a spectacular stretch of river—big and white for a full mile before, continuing white, it bends from view. The river narrows here by about a third, pressed between banks of rock, but it is still hundreds of feet wide—big boulders, big submarine ledges, big holes, big pillows, big waves, big chutes, big eddies. Big Rapid. About two-thirds of a mile down, on the left shore, a lone birch leans crazily toward the river. Below the birch, there appears to be a bankside eddy. Shouting above the sound of the rapid, we form our plan. Moody and I are to get into that eddy, and bail, and wait there for everybody else.

"Are you ready?"

"What did you say?"

"All set?"

"Yes, it's lovely here. Possibly we could stop here for another lunch."

"Get going, you sarcastic bastard."

"See you there."

And so we're in it. We make choices, and so does the river. We shout a lot, above the roar. Words coordinate the canoe. My eye is certainly off the mark. I underestimated the haystacks. They are about as ponderous as, for this loaded canoe, they can safely be. I look steeply down at Moody in the bottoms of the troughs. But the route we picked—generally to the left, with some moves toward the center, skirting ledges—is, as Kauffmann would say, solving the problem. We are not playing with the Big Rapid. We are tiptoeing in and hoping it won't wake up. Under the slanting birch, we swing into the eddy and stop. Two. Three. Four. Everybody home, and we bail many quarts.

The river now bends almost ninety degrees to the right, and we can see around the bend to another anchorage, under an isolated maple with an ovate crown.

The run this time is more difficult—the bow kicking high into the air and returning to the surface in awkward slaps. We dig for momentum, sidestep rocks, but not nimbly, for the canoe is sluggish with shipped water. Anxious to get into the calm below the maple, I try a chute that is just about as wide as the beam of the canoe. It's a stupid and almost unsuccessful move, and I get out of the canoe and climb up on a boulder to wave the others around the chute.

We bail a few gallons. Everybody is dry. We relax and joke and look down the rest of the rapid. Less than a mile below we can see flat, and much wider, water. We're so full of ourselves now it's as if we were already there. We do and do not want to be there, for after the end of the rapid the run is smooth and short to Allagash and the end of the wilderness

Winslow Homer, *Canoe in Rapids*, 1897. Watercolor over graphite on off-white wove paper, 35.4 × 53.3 cm (13¹⁵⁄₁₆ × 21 inches).

*Harvard Art Museums/Fogg Museum, Louise E. Bettens Fund, 1924.30. Photograph: Imaging Department. Copyright President and Fellows of Harvard College.*

river. The St. John after that is another river—a border-land, farmland, potatoland river—and then a Canadian, developed river, and not what we think of when we think of the St. John. So we look back upstream, at the whiteness of the river here in big display, coming out of a hundred miles of forest.

A canoe appears, bouncing in the waves. Half a mile above us, it rolls over and begins to wash down. Tom Cabot grabs a rope and runs up the bank, jumping from ledge to boulder, boulder to ledge. Everybody follows, but as we get nearer to the capsized canoe we realize there is nothing we can do. It is near the middle of the rapid. We can't throw a rope two hundred feet. The two paddlers are afloat and hanging on, but the canoe—a fifteen-foot Grumman—is broadside to the current and they are on the downstream side. They are missing rocks, fortunately, but they are apparently oblivious of the danger of being caught between a rock and the canoe. We shout at the top of our lungs, "Get on the other side! Get on the upstream side!" But they don't look around. They can't hear us.

We watch them helplessly, and we return to our canoes. Because the water in the river is little more than ten degrees above freezing, the two in the river could have a greater problem with cold than with rock. When they reach our level, Kauffmann and Cabot move into the rapid in their canoe, Moody and I in ours. Cabot throws them a rope. One of them appears to be shaking but assures us that he is all right. Back-paddling, we wash along with them until the force of the rapid begins to decline, and then we haul in tandem and bring them and their canoe ashore.

One is tall, bearded, and, so it seems, physically unaffected. Relief is the last thing he is about to feel. It has apparently not crossed his mind that the river could have kept him. Instead, he shows fury, frustration, disappointment—like an athlete who has had his big chance and blown it. All the way to the north woods he has come, and has paddled a hundred miles downriver to dump in the Big Rapid, and, kneeling by his canoe, he pounds fist into palm in disgust, saying, "Damn! Damn! Oh, God damn!"

The other paddler is short and thin, and is shaking deeply from cold. He minimizes it, tries to be nonchalant, but does not seem disappointed to be standing on the bank. His T-shirt is dark gray, and above the left breast are small black letters—"YALE."

Tom Cabot questions him about the shirt, asking if it means that he's a student there.

"Yes, I'm there now."

"And how far along are you?"

"I'm '78."

Over Tom's face comes a small-world smile, and he says, "How about that! I'm seventy-eight, too."[6]

*I was seventy-eight once. Yes, as young as Tom was on the St. John River in 1974, when I thought of him as an old man growing younger. Now in my middle eighties, I don't have time for such romantic ruminations, because I have to concentrate on fishing.*

Fishing from a canoe in the Delaware River, I like to ship the paddle and let the boat go where it will. I watch the stony bottom, which flies by under fast-moving water. This is not Philadelphia. This is two hundred river miles above Philadelphia, where the stream-rounded rocks are so clear they look printed. Shoving the rocks, anadromous lampreys have built fortress nests, which are spread around the river like craters of the moon. Mesmerized, I watch the rocks go by. Fly casting for bass, I see golf balls.

From shallows in the Merrimack in Manchester, New Hampshire, I once picked up a ball that bore the logo of a country club two and a half miles upstream. If the river brought it there, the ball had come through deep water and then over the Amoskeag Dam. In the Connecticut River above Northampton, Massachusetts, I've seen golf balls by the constellation—too deep to reach and too far from any upstream golf course for their presence to make sense unless people hit them off their lawns. Compulsions are easy to come by and hard to explain. Mine include watching for golf balls, which I do with acute attention, the fact notwithstanding that I quit golf cold when I was twenty-four. These days, my principal form of exercise is on a bicycle, which I ride a good bit upwards of two thousand miles a year. I go past golf courses. How could I not? I live in New Jersey, which has a golf-course density of five per hundred square miles, or twice the G.C.D. of Florida, which has more golf courses than any other state. Moreover, the vast undeveloped forests of the southern part of New Jersey tend to shove the densities toward and beyond Princeton, in whose environs I ride my bike. The woods that lie between public roads and private fairways remind me of the dry terrain between a river levee and the river itself. In Louisiana along the Mis-

sissippi, this isolated and often wooded space is known as the river batture. If you're in Louisiana, you pronounce it "batcher." From my bicycle in New Jersey, if I am passing a golf-links batture, my head is turned that way and my gaze runs through the woods until a white dot stops it, which is not an infrequent occurrence. I get off my bike and collect the ball.

The Delaware is less accommodating. When you are flying along on fast current, you don't just get off your canoe and prop it up on a kickstand in order to pick up a golf ball. Over time, seeing so many golf balls in the river was such a threatening frustration that I had to do something about it. Research led to the telephone number of a company then in Michigan. A real person answered and was even more than real. She understood me. She knew what I was asking and did not call 911. Instead, she had questions of her own: What was the speed of the current? What was the depth of the river? Was the bottom freestone? Sand? Clay? Silt? After completing the interview, she said, "You want the Orange Trapper."

"The Orange Trapper?"

"The Orange Trapper."

It came in various lengths. I said I thought the nine-footer would do. The nine might be stiffer in the current than the twelve, fifteen, eighteen, twenty-one, or twenty-four. Besides, nine (actually 9.6) just felt right. It was the length of my fly rods.

What came in the mail was only twenty-one inches long, with an orange head, a black grip, and a shaft that consisted of ten concentric stainless tubes with a maximum diameter of 0.68 inches. You could conduct an orchestra with it. It was beautiful. The orange head was a band of industrial-strength plastic, as obovate as a pear and slightly wider than a golf ball. A depression in its inside top was there to secure one side of a ball, but the genius of the device was in a working part, a beveled "flipper" that came up through the throat and would waggle into place on the other side of the ball. The Orange Trapper worked two ways. It had no upside or downside. You could surround a golf ball with either side, then lift it up as if you were playing lacrosse with no strings. You could turn the head over—a hundred and eighty degrees—and the ball would generally stay put. But flip the thing over once more and the ball would always roll free. Made by JTD Enterprises, it could have been designed by Apple.

Even so, finesse was required to trap a ball in shallow current. After seeing one, and swinging around, and going hard upstream, and shipping the paddle, you had about five seconds to place the head of the Trapper over the ball. I missed as often as not. It wasn't the Trapper's fault. My average would have been higher chasing humming-birds with a butterfly net.[7]

*In thirty-eight consecutive Octobers, at this writing, I have been fly casting for pickerel with my friend George Hackl in an acreage of lily pads in Lake Winnipesaukee, each of us in his own canoe, close by an undeveloped island owned by George's wife. In 1984, on returning home, I learned that my father had suffered a severe, paralyzing stroke. In his hospital room, I told him about the fishing, although he seemed to hear nothing. Twenty-five years later, I ended a piece called "The Patch" with this description.*

In a small open pool in the vegetation, about halfway down The Patch, there had been, this year and last, a chain pickerel that was either too smart or too inept to get itself around an assemblage of deer hair, rabbit fur, turkey quill, marabou silk, and sharp heavy wire. The swirls had been violent every time, the strike consistently missing or spurning the fly, and coming always from the same place on the same side of the same blue gap. In the repetitive geometries of The Patch, with its paisley patterns in six acres of closed and open space, how did I know it was the same gap? I just knew, that's all. It's like running a trap line. You don't forget where the traps are; or you don't run a trap line. This gap in the lily pads was thirty yards off the mainland shore between the second tallest white pine and a granitic outcrop projecting from Ann's island. As I was getting back into the story, again speaking aloud in the renewed privacy of the hospital room, I mentioned that I had been fishing The Patch that last morning with my father's bamboo rod, and it felt a bit heavy in the hand, but since the day he had turned it over to me I had taken it with my other rods on fishing trips, and had used it, on occasion, to keep it active because it was his. Now—just a couple of days ago—time was more than close to running out. Yolanda was calling from the island. "John, we must go! John, stop fishing! John!" It was time to load the canoe and paddle west around some islands to the car, time to depart for home, yes; but I meant to have one more drift through The Patch. From the northwest, a light breeze was coming down over the sedge fen. I called to Yolanda that I'd "be right there," then swept the bow around and headed for the fen. Since I had failed and failed again while anchored near that fish, I would let the light breeze carry me this time, freelance, freeform, moving down The Patch like the slow shadow of a cloud. Which is just what happened—a quiet slide, the light rustle on the hull, Yolanda calling twice more before she gave up. Two touches with the paddle were all that were needed to perfect the aim. Standing now, closing in, I waved the bamboo rod like a semaphore—backcasting once, twice—and then threw the line. Dropping a little short, the muddler landed on the near side of the gap. The pickerel scored the surface in crossing it, swirled, made a solid hit, and took the tight line down, wrapping it around the stems of the plants.

"I pulled him out of there plants and all," I said. "I caught him with your bamboo rod."

I looked closely at my father. His eyes had welled over. His face was damp. Six weeks later, he was dead.[8]

# Introduction

WHAT IS THE CULTURAL MEANING of a North American canoe? Such meaning would vary with people, time, and place, of course, as we can imagine the distinction between a courting canoe from the 1920s as compared to a Montreal freighter piloted by eighteenth-century voyageurs. Some meanings, or at least some uses, cut across boundaries for a most basic form of water transportation on the continent. Its design is an example. Should a pre-white-settlement Native from one of the tribes in the northeastern part of the continent show up today, he or she would immediately recognize the silhouette of a twenty-first-century canoe and know what it was for and

how to use it. Few other original Native artifacts, other than the snowshoe, have survived the passage of time with less fundamental change.

Every culture that has lived or worked near water has created craft to meet its needs. Native peoples on more than one continent or island created boats that were long and skinny and propelled with paddles—boats that might be thought of as canoes. The oldest known tools that could have been used to carve dugouts are from 20,000 years ago; sails have existed for 7,000 years.[1] In North America, Natives refined the design over centuries. Few other watercraft have been put to as many uses. Canoes have been used for gathering food, migrations of families, transferring freight, and for pure pleasure. "The variety of such canoes was enormous and depended as much on the use and

◄ Canoeists paddle a Wenonah Kevlar canoe above a rapid in the Boundary Waters Canoe Area.   *Courtesy of Wenonah Canoe, Inc.*

Tom Thomson (Canadian, 1877–1917), *The Canoe*, 1914, spring or fall. Oil on canvas, 17.3 × 25.3 cm (6$^{13}$/$_{16}$ × 9$^{15}$/$_{16}$ inches).

Canoeists in a birch-bark canoe near Steamboat Rock, Wisconsin Dells.

*Photograph by H. H. Bennett. Courtesy of the Wisconsin Historical Society, WHS-7797.*

waters for which they were intended—cargo, passengers, or warfare; lakes, streams, or rapids—as on their makers," writes maritime historian Lincoln Paine.[2] The canoe is relatively easy to build and simple to fix, tough, fast, cheap, transportable, maneuverable—and it comes in different sizes, too. Builders used readily available material, whether it be birch bark from the northern forests, cedar from the West Coast, or the latest twenty-first-century petroleum-based plastics or industrial fibers. Children can be taught

to paddle (and steer) from a young age; many a summer camp visit has been highlighted by a canoe race across a golden pond or a portage in the wilderness.

Today's canoes, while the same basic shape, may differ from their predecessors in their construction material: birch-bark construction is a fading skill and dugouts are a very small percentage of the fleet, as wood has been replaced by modern materials such as carbon fiber and other industrial composites. Beautiful and expensive wood and

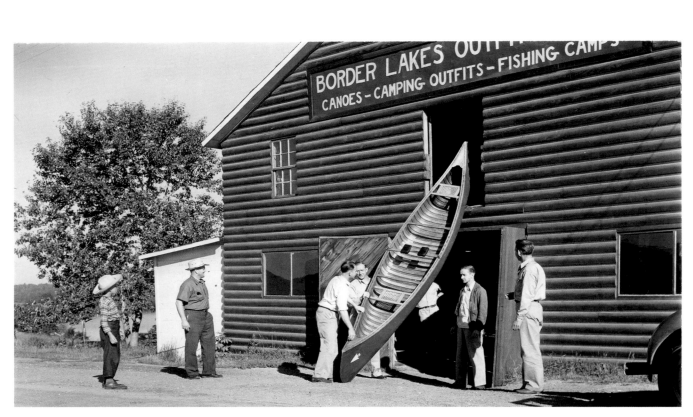

Sigurd Olson's Border Lakes Outfitting Company supplied paddlers with the necessary gear during the 1940s. Here a canoe is retrieved from the company warehouse, April 4, 1940.

*Photograph by Leland J. Prater. Records of the Forest Service, National Archives at Chicago, USFS Negative 400545.*

wood-and-canvas canoes have devoted followings, while cheap plastic boats can be had for a few hundred dollars from national retail chains. But no matter the material, all canoes can provide the same satisfaction, not to say joy, as did the boats of the Ojibwe, Cree, or Beothuk.

For many, like the authors, the satisfaction of paddling a canoe and the enjoyment of a range of experiences from joyful to terrifying contribute to a love of the history of the craft, including the canoe's role in many of the local cultures of North America. In telling a history of the canoe, we have attempted to narrate cultural stories and open a window into their significance. The evolution of the canoe, combined with its basic simplicity, allows paddlers to decide for themselves their level of engagement, from intense and long-lasting to a passing childhood fancy. The best of these relationships can be deeply personal, connected to a time or a place or a friend. Often these meanings begin with a single moment, an event, a day on the water, or even the glimpse of a boat. Both authors have had these experiences; we have built canoes, have taken long canoe trips with good friends, and have spent short outings on small ponds, alone.

One of the authors, Mark Neuzil, lives in Minnesota, a popular place for boats. Eighteen percent of Minnesotans use a canoe or kayak in a given year, according to the Coast Guard,[3] and the Land of 10,000 Lakes includes some of the most popular canoeing destinations on the continent, including the renowned Boundary Waters Canoe Area Wilderness and a national park named after the most famous commercial canoeists: Voyageurs. Every canoeist has a story, and for Mark, as for many, it begins with a childhood memory.

I started canoeing in Iowa at about age ten, back in the 1960s. My father had purchased an all-wood 14-foot Army surplus dinghy for fishing on the lake where we lived, but he, my Uncle Jerry, and I were caught in a bad Midwestern thunderstorm and ran it up on some rocks (if a heavy boat powered by a Sears Ted Williams four-and-one-half-horsepower motor can be said to "run up on" anything). Anyway, the dinghy sank like a stone, and Dad, ever the early adopter, moved on to a fiberglass canoe. That purchase began a lifetime of

adventures in a series of canoes for me, including a stint as a U.S. Forest Service–licensed guide in northern Minnesota.

One of those adventures began in 1999, when a straight-line wind called a *derecho* blew down as many as 25 million trees in the Boundary Waters Canoe Area and on nearby lands along the U.S.-Canadian border. Many of them were white cedars; some of them were salvaged from private property and left outside to dry. A few of *those* were straight enough and long enough to make a cedar-strip canoe. Eleven years after the blowdown, I took my white cedar-strip canoe back to the BWCA, completing the circle back home for the trees.

My coauthor, Norm Sims, talked me into building that canoe, so he gets credit/blame. Five and a half months from the day I started, the boat emerged from my garage in St. Paul.

"As long as it's done before the snow flies, so we can use the garage for the cars again," was my spouse's condition.

Thank you, warm September.

Norm, who can tell the bow of a B. N. Morris from an E. H. Gerrish at a glance, wasn't my only influence. Thomas Schrunk, an internationally known artist in Minneapolis, lent me his forms for a Prospector, from the Chestnut Canoe Co., of New Brunswick, Canada. "You're gonna need some clamps," Schrunk said, as he handed me a box full. Turns out I also needed to buy every spring clamp

Francis Lee Jaques, *Picture Rock at Crooked Lake (Return of the Voyageur)*, 1947. Oil on canvas, 83.8 × 106.6 cm.

*Courtesy of the Minnesota Historical Society, Gift of Frank Hubachek, 60179.*

Myron Nickerson, a former employee of canoe builder J. Henry Rushton, appears on the far right in this 1894 photograph. Nickerson's livery on the Grasse River in Canton, New York, offered rentals of Adirondack guideboats, Rushton-style pleasure rowboats, small skiffs, and canoes. *Courtesy of the Adirondack Museum, P021483.*

at the nearest hardware store and then every spring clamp at the next nearest hardware store. I asked for clamps for my birthday and Father's Day.

The questions come frequently when you are working in your garage all summer in an alley: "How long will it take?" "What kind of wood is that?" "Are you crazy?"

The most-asked question was "How do you bend the wood?" Much of the wood is so thinly cut it bends on its own, but the keels needed to be steamed and bent. I did not own a wood steamer, so

I went to Goodwill and bought a $3 plastic coffee pot, percolator-style, complete with flower-power decal. Another $4 at the hardware store fetched a long piece of PVC pipe. Fill the pot with water, put the pipe on the spout, slide in the wood, and stuff a rag in the end. Plug it in and . . . problems.

The thermostat in the coffeepot turned off the boil before it got up a good head of steam. I bypassed it and then thought of calling my father-in-law, expert on many things electrical. Ever helpful, he said, "Don't burn down the garage."

The futziest part of cedar-strip canoe building is fiberglassing the hull. Even with plenty of advice, it was still a sticky, smelly mess. If I ever got the urge to do it again, I'd lie down until the feeling went away.

About two hundred hours and $900 later, I had a canoe. You build them upside down, on forms, one strip at a time. The strips are cut to ¼-inch thick by ¾-inch high and glued and clamped to each other. It takes a quarter-mile of strips to make a 16-foot boat. It is an old technique—the Canadian explorer David Thompson was said to be among the first Europeans to build a canoe from strips of wood, perhaps as early as 1811.

I have to say completing the canoe, after three coats of varnish, was anticlimactic. I guess I expected something like the description from the French explorer Samuel de Champlain, who wrote, "I cried out to God and began to pull my canoe toward me."[4]

Norman Sims's life in canoes also began in the Midwest, although he now lives in the Northeast, home of some of America's finest writers on canoes and canoe tripping and home, too, of the original wood-and-canvas canoe companies in Maine and around Boston. His story has origins in Illinois, with a good friend and fellow canoeist.

One day in the mid-1970s, I was jogging in Champaign, Illinois, where I was in grad school. I noticed a wood-and-canvas canoe upside down on low racks in a neighbor's backyard. Sneaking a look inside, I saw something different. The ribs tapered as they approached the gunwales, which were strange indeed. That canoe profoundly affected my life, but not for a number of years.

At the time, I was building wood-strip and fiberglass canoes with Todd Bradshaw, who was co-owner of an outdoor store, an artist, a musician, a knowledgeable fellow about fiberglass and woodworking, and later the author of a book on sailing canoes. We learned strip building from David Hazen's book *The Stripper's Guide to Canoe-Building,* which gave us the technical information we needed. Practice taught us the rest.

First we built the hardest boat in Hazen's book, an 18-foot-long Nanaimo two-person kayak that required two perfectly built hulls that fit together lengthwise to form the kayak. If we could build the hardest one, we could build anything, or so we figured. Todd, being the longer and skinnier of us, crawled inside the hull with strips of fiberglass and resin that sealed the two pieces together. It was a beautiful boat, made of Sitka spruce and redwood, but Todd decided never to use fiberglass in a closed environment again. After that experience, we stuck to building open boats: a 22-foot-long fur trade canoe with lines taken from Edwin Tappan Adney and Howard I. Chapelle's great book *The Bark Canoes and Skin Boats of North America*; then a racing canoe; and a 14-foot solo canoe.

The backyard wood-and-canvas canoe up the

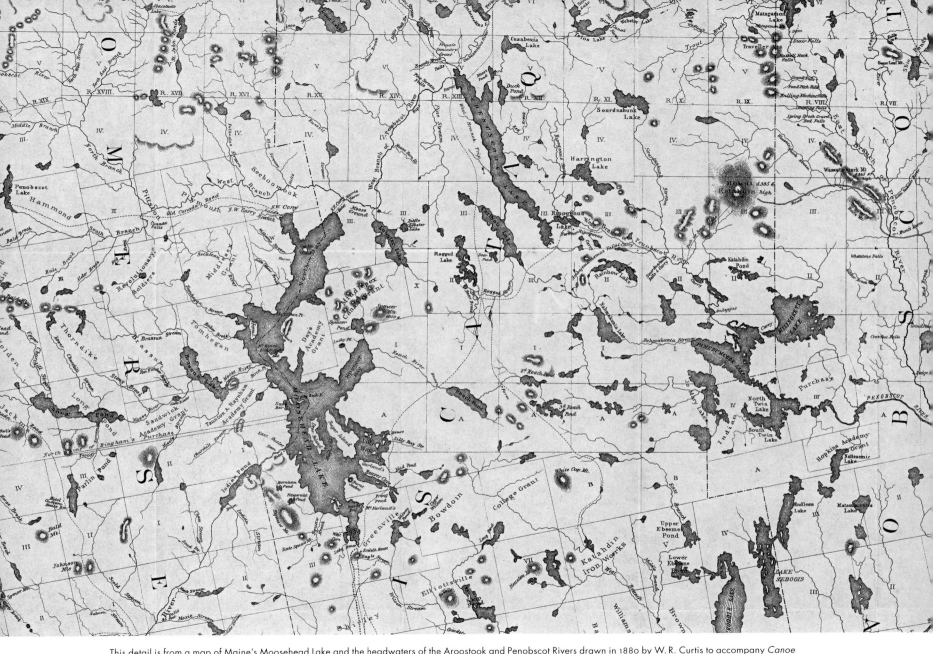

This detail is from a map of Maine's Moosehead Lake and the headwaters of the Aroostook and Penobscot Rivers drawn in 1880 by W. R. Curtis to accompany *Canoe and Camera*, a book by Thomas Sedgwick Steele. It was one of the first maps prepared expressly for canoeists. *Courtesy of the Avery Collection, Maine State Library.*

street intrigued us. The owner said he had $90 in the canoe and had been meaning to fix it up, but that never happened. Ninety dollars later, we carried the boat away. Adney and Chapelle showed that the closed gunwales were similar to what the Indians used on birch-bark canoes.

A strange decal on the front deck said, "B. N. Morris, Canvas Canoes, Row Boats, and Equipments, Veazie, Maine." In the days before Google, it took some searching to find Veazie, which proved to be near Old Town. A letter to the Old Town Canoe Company brought a response from company president Deane Gray, who said Bert Morris built canoes in Veazie until his factory burned down around World War I, after which he worked for Old Town. OK, World War I. So we figured the canoe was from around 1917, which is old, but it was only a backyard boat. We restored it that summer and named it *Bert's Boat*. It remains the best all-purpose open canoe I've ever paddled, both in the lakes of the Boundary Waters and Quetico Parks and in whitewater.

Many rivers later, and after a number of Class 3+ whitewater runs in *Bert's Boat*, I met Kathy Klos through the Wooden Canoe Heritage Association. The leading expert on Morris canoes, Kathy's email signature says, "'Please tell me about your Morris,' she implored, batting her eyelashes." Kathy later wrote *The Morris Canoe: Legacy of an American Family*. She explained that my backyard canoe was

actually one of Morris's earliest ones, dating from about 1896. That news ended the whitewater career of *Bert's Boat*. What had been an enjoyable hobby, including about thirty years of whitewater boating, turned into the madness of an aging collector. I now own five Morris wood-and-canvas canoes and an unidentified 13-foot solo canoe, originally all-wood, that also dates from the 1890s.

My experiences in canoes accidentally reflected in jumbled fashion the evolution of canoe materials, except that I've never paddled a dugout or a sailing canoe.

At Boy Scout camp in Decatur, Illinois, we paddled wood-and-canvas canoes, probably made by Old Town. The first canoe I owned was an Alumacraft made in Minnesota that my ex-wife and I paddled up the Onakawana River to the Abitibi River to the Moose River to the village of Moosonee at the southern tip of James Bay, which attaches to Hudson Bay. We watched with envy as motorized wood-and-canvas freighter canoes shot past us and glided effortlessly toward Moosonee and Moose Factory. Thirty years of serious whitewater paddling followed—in fiberglass open and decked canoes and in Old Town ABS boats, but mostly in plastic, decked solo canoes—in New England, West Virginia, North Carolina, Georgia, Colorado, Idaho, Utah, Oregon, and in the Grand Canyon. And Todd Bradshaw and I built wood-strip and fiberglass canoes, including the fur trade canoe.

Mark Hamel, *Crossing the Shallows, Snake River*, 2014. Oil on mounted ➤
linen, 40.64 × 50.8 cm. *Reproduced with permission of the artist.*

Canoeing became a popular pastime in the twentieth century after the establishment of several national parks throughout North America. Here, two paddlers are photographed in 1952 at Banff National Park in Alberta, Canada. *Photograph by Gar Lunney, National Film Board of Canada Collection, Library and Archives of Canada, R1196-14-7-E.*

from an ecosystem of sorts. Technologies and materials have changed, but European immigrants and modern design have not altered the fundamental form.

This book provides a narrative of historic and modern canoes, some of the people who built them, and the stories of their tribulations and adventures. Canoes have features of technology, industry, art, survival, and cultural history swirling around them.

We begin with the history of dugouts, those incredibly meaningful artistic and cultural expressions made with great difficulty from the most basic of materials—a single tree. The story continues through birch-bark canoes, the boat most often remembered in modern culture as the "original" canoe, with its strong connections to Native Americans and voyageurs. The voyageur story is told, followed by a discussion of all-wood and wood-and-canvas canoes and the transition from working craft to pleasure boat and modern recreation.

Industrial processes brought more changes in materials, including aluminum, fiberglass, and other synthetics after World War II. A surge in leisure time, along with an increased interest in environmental issues and a modern back-to-nature movement, positively affected canoeing in the United States. The importance of canoes is reflected in our literature. Travelers, essayists, and journalists have thought and written about the significance of the craft for several generations. Henry David Thoreau has been credited with saying, "Everyone believes in something. I believe I'll go canoeing." This book goes canoeing, telling those stories and more.

Now, the history of such canoes seems important to us. Canoes allow us to engage closely and quietly and intimately with our environment, and, like the natural world itself, canoes have different adaptations. They emerge

## CHAPTER I

# Dugout Canoes

N HIS SECOND VOYAGE to the New World, Christopher Columbus made first landfall on Dominica in November 1493. The lush Caribbean island near Martinique contained rain forests where huge *gommier* trees could be felled and made into dugout canoes. Columbus and his crew—who knew semi-modern building techniques and metallurgy—were as startled by the long dugout canoes that met them as were the Natives by the European sailing ships.

When North American Natives created dugout and birch-bark canoes, they took their designs from the aquatic conditions they faced and from the tools and resources they had at hand. Edwin Tappan Adney and Howard I. Chapelle,

in *The Bark Canoes and Skin Boats of North America*, vividly demonstrate how varied Native canoes could be, depending on whether they were needed as oceangoing craft, river boats, rice harvesting canoes, or cargo craft. In the Caribbean and the Pacific Northwest—and elsewhere, as it turns out—Natives built large dugout canoes worthy of ocean travel.

There is no evidence that native Carib and Taino peoples used sails on their canoes prior to contact with Europeans.[1] In the fifteenth century, Columbus had never seen canoes. In a letter describing his first encounters, Columbus says:

> They have in all these islands very many canoes
> like our row-boats; some larger, some smaller,
> but most of them larger than a barge of eighteen

◅ Lee Moorhouse, *Log Canoe on the Columbia River*, c. 1900.
*Courtesy of the Lee Moorhouse Photograph Collection, PH036-6172,*
*Special Collections and University Archives, University of Oregon, Eugene.*

seats. They are not so wide, because they are made of one single piece of timber, but a barge could not keep up with them in rowing, because they go with incredible speed, and with these canoes they navigate among these islands, which are innumerable and carry on their traffic. I have seen in some of these canoes seventy and eighty men, each with his oar.

*Modo di navigare nel Mare di Tramontana* (Navigating into the north wind). Woodcut. This illustration of a Taino dugout canoe first appeared in Girolamo Benzoni's *La Historia del Mondo Nuovo* in 1562.

Courtesy of the James Ford Bell Library, University of Minnesota.

The "oars" were different, Columbus explains. The canoes "are worked along with paddles formed like a baker's peel or the implement which is used in dressing hemp. These oars or paddles were not fixed by pins to the sides of the canoes like ours; but were dipped into the water and pulled backwards as if digging."[2]

## THE MADNESS OF OPEN WATER

It's an anthropological curiosity to consider how those Native peoples got to the islands thousands of years before Columbus's arrival. The arc of the Caribbean Islands made island-hopping in canoes from the South American mainland possible, but it required the madness of paddling into open ocean water with no land in sight.

Svante Pääbo of the Max Planck Institute for Evolutionary Anthropology in Leipzig, Germany, has reconstructed the Neanderthal genome and studies what made them different from modern humans. He told Elizabeth Kolbert, a *New Yorker* magazine writer, that Neanderthals evolved in Europe and western Asia, but whenever they reached open water, their migrations stopped. He feels this is one basic difference with modern humans, who would cross open water without land in sight. He said:

> It's only fully modern humans who start this thing of venturing out on the ocean where you don't see land. Part of that is technology, of course; you have to have ships to do it. But there is also, I like to think or say, some madness there.

You know? How many people must have sailed out and vanished on the Pacific before you found Easter Island? I mean, it's ridiculous. And why do you do that? Is it for the glory? For immortality? For curiosity? And now we go to Mars. We never stop. . . . We are crazy in some way.

Pääbo said that modern humans may possess a special bit of DNA that enables this madness. Doing something as crazy as paddling a dugout with low freeboard in the open ocean in pursuit of the unknown, according to Pääbo, separates us from Neanderthals and "changed the whole ecosystem of the planet and made us dominate everything."[3]

On his first voyage to the New World, Columbus's crew might have worried about never making landfall. Columbus shared that madness with the Native peoples he encountered who had been building and paddling their dugout canoes for thousands of years in the Caribbean.

The jump from the southern tip of Florida to Cuba is roughly 90 miles, a trip that would require the madness of exploration with no land in sight. The chain of islands in the Bahamas is about an equal distance east of Florida. But apparently the Natives in Florida did not make that journey, nor were their dugouts capable of ocean travel. Instead, those on the Orinoco River and delta in northeastern South America were apparently responsible for settling the Caribbean Islands.

Maritime historian Lincoln Paine writes, "Research over the past few decades has overturned long-held views that Amazonia was inhabited by primitive forest tribes content to subsist on the jungle's low-lying fruit. The people who lived along the major river systems of tropical South America, notably the Amazon, Orinoco, and their tributaries, are now seen as masters of their environment who planted tropical orchards, built curbed roads up to fifty meters wide as well as causeways, bridges, dikes, reservoirs, and raised agricultural fields."[4]

The Maya in southern Mexico also used dugout canoes, which may have been made from the giant *ceiba* (pronounced "SAY-ba") trees that stood more than 200 feet high. Ceiba was the tree of life for the Maya. When archaeologists in 1952 opened the tomb of Pakal at Palenque in Yucatan, they found the ruler's sarcophagus covered by a stone slab that is one of the finest of Mayan symbolic representations. The carved images encapsulate the Mayan cosmology in the ceiba tree. Pakal rests midway up the tree, which has its leaves in heaven and its roots in the underworld. Many great Mayan cities, such as Yaxchilán on the Usumacinta River between Mexico and Guatemala, and Tulum on the Yucatan coast, were located either on rivers or near the Atlantic Ocean. Artifacts found in the Mayan ruins indicate a lively and extensive trade that reached out great distances. In terms of their skills, the Maya are considered the most advanced of the peoples that Columbus met.

The Maya understood time and the movement of celestial objects in the night sky. They laid down substantial gravel highways that ran straight as an arrow through the jungles for a hundred kilometers. Among only a handful of ancient civilizations, they achieved the most difficult

The Timucua people of Florida used dugout canoes to transport produce to storehouses built of mud and stones.
This 1591 engraving by Theodor de Bry is based on drawings from a manuscript by Jacques le Moyne de Morgues,
who accompanied the 1564 Huguenot expedition to Florida. *Courtesy of the John Carter Brown Library at Brown University.*

and the greatest of human inventions: a written language. Dating from as early as 1,900 years ago, through their peak civilization from about 500 to 800 AD, and until the Early Postclassic period from 1000 to 1250, they built large cities and traded by canoe with inhabitants of the Caribbean rim.

With their navigational skills, the Maya might have been equipped to enter the open ocean and for their descendants to eventually encounter Christopher Columbus, a European with a similar madness. But maybe they weren't that crazy. Paine says the Mayans may not have populated Cuba and may have engaged only in short-range coastal navigation. "The only instance of long-range maritime trade known from the east coast of Mesoamerica was

Dugout canoes are still used in daily life throughout the Americas. This contemporary dugout was photographed at Playa de San Mateo del Mar near Oaxaca, Mexico.

*Courtesy of Enriqueta Flores-Guevara and Lon Brehmer.*

maintained by the Putun Maya between the thirteenth and fifteenth centuries. . . . Putun Mayan mariners may have raided coastal settlements in Guatemala and Honduras; but neither they nor anyone else from Mexico or Central America seem to have sailed east to the Greater and Lesser Antilles of the Caribbean."[5]

Navigating in the Caribbean presented problems similar to those faced by the Norse explorers who sailed to Iceland, Greenland, and North America. Norse sailors probably reached North America when they missed the tip of Greenland in the fog.[6] Like other early peoples, the Caribbean Natives learned to navigate their dugout canoes using stars, wave patterns, winds, and by observing the presence of birds and the directions of their flight. Paine says, "At the most basic level, the essential elements are shared by navigators everywhere: observation of heavenly bodies (celestial navigation), reading the wind and water, and tracing the behavior of birds, fish, and whales. . . . Some of these techniques are common to other maritime traditions—following birds that feed at sea but nest on land, noting where different species of fish or sea mammals are found, looking for smoke generated by natural fires, or discerning changes in water color over reefs."[7] Columbus followed birds to his first landfall in the New World on an island he called San Salvador.

The major Caribbean migration route for the largest populations in the islands was from the south. Anna McCanse writes that the early inhabitants of Dominica "arrived in dugout canoes from the Orinoco River region of South America from as far back as 3000 BC." At about 1200 AD, the Kalinago people, later called Carib, arrived and displaced the Arawak farther north.[8] Paddlers coming

Inscriptions from the Late Classic Era Mayan burial site at Tikal (c. 800–c. 1000 AD) document Mayan canoe transport.

*Drawing by Linda Schele. Courtesy of the Los Angeles County Museum of Art. Copyright David Schele.*

A fresco featuring Putun dugout canoes adorns the interior walls of the Temple of the Warriors at Chichén Itzá. The maritime trading empire along the west coast of the Caribbean was established by the Putun, a group of Chontal Maya from the Gulf Coast of what are today the Mexican states of Tabasco and Campeche. *Copyright 2016 World History Archive/fotoLibra.*

out of the Orinoco River in present-day Venezuela found the Lesser Antilles stretching in a reachable arc to the north and east from South America, including Trinidad and Tobago, Grenada, Barbados, St. Lucia, Dominica, and eventually the larger islands of Puerto Rico and Cuba. According to anthropologist Marshall McKusick, "There is no evidence that ocean voyages were undertaken directly across the central Caribbean. Although voyages frequently took place beyond sight of land, these were between the islands or between islands and adjacent mainland areas. The picture that emerges is one of considerable maritime activity in the fringes of the Caribbean where the islands furnished landmarks and landings with relatively short channel distances to be crossed."[9]

Caribbean fishermen repair their nets on a beach in Martinique, 1959. Their dugout fishing boats are made from massive *gommier* trees native to the islands of the region.   *Photograph by Charles Allmon/National Geographic Creative.*

Columbus found the Lesser Antilles populated by the Carib people. The Greater Antilles islands of Hispaniola, Jamaica, Cuba, and Puerto Rico were inhabited by Arawaks. "One and all they make war on all the other neighbouring islands," Columbus wrote, "and they go by sea in the many canoes which they have and which are small *fustas*, made of a single piece of wood, a hundred and fifty leagues to make raids."[10] (A *fusta* is a light, narrow ship of shallow draft.)

The Arawak and Taino languages have died out, but English retains their original word for those boats that Columbus called *fustas*. The word was *canoe*, originally *canoa*. (We also adopted their words *hammock, guava, barbeque, manatee, hurricane,* and *tobacco,* "which was actually their word for pipe."[11])

Had Columbus tried to explain to the Natives he met exactly how to build one of his ships, the whole process would have seemed impossibly difficult. The Natives had made their sleek and speedy oceangoing dugouts using stone tools, fire, and remarkable building innovations that seem equally extraordinary.

### THOUSANDS OF DUGOUTS

Ancient records of dugout canoes are found not only in the Pacific Northwest and the Caribbean but also in what is now Minnesota, in parts of the southeastern United States, and in Mexico. Dugouts were present along the New England coast as well, although watercraft artifacts are yet to be recovered.

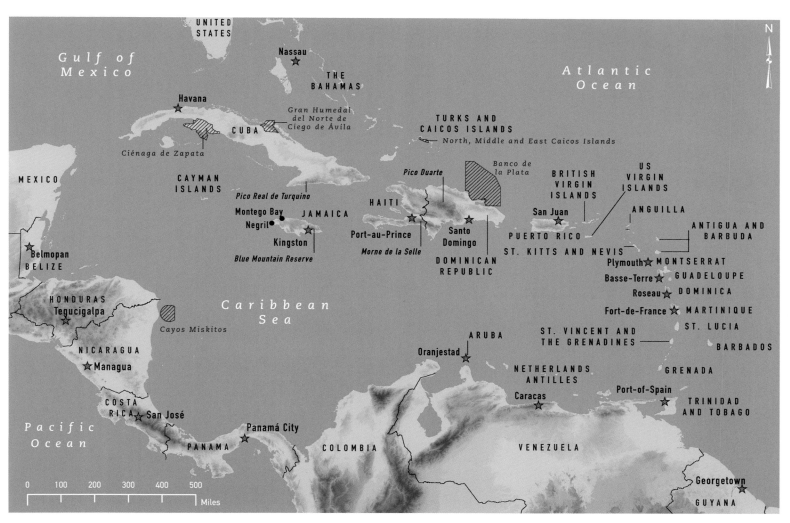

The major migration routes by oceangoing canoes were probably up from Venezuela along the arc of islands toward Dominica, and possibly east from the Mayan empires in Mexico to Cuba.   *U.S. General Services Administration, Office of Citizen Services and Innovative Technologies.*

## ❧ Napolean Sanford

"They were making larger ones," Emmanuel "Napolean" Sanford says of the early Caribs. "Longer ones. Sixty feet. The huge ones were very wide. They could go from island to island. They were naturally deeper. They put fire in them and burned them to hollow them."[1]

Napolean Sanford makes modern dugout canoes. He pronounces the word *canoe* as *canoa*—the original Carib Indian word that Columbus heard. That makes perfect sense, considering his Carib heritage.

Sanford lives in the village of Salybia on the island of Dominica in the West Indies. Salybia is in Carib Territory, a 3,700-acre reservation and the only land set aside for the Caribs in all of the Caribbean. Located near Martinique and St. Lucia, Dominica was Columbus's first sighting of land on his second journey to the New World in 1493.

The early peoples of the Caribbean Rim built dugouts from *gommier* trees that might have lived two thousand years in the rain forests. Sanford still uses the long, straight, fine-grained wood of the *gommier*. A tree more than one hundred years old is large enough to build a 16- to 20-foot dugout. Many such trees exist, Sanford says, but it's a longer trek through the bush to find them than it was when he first learned how to carve dugouts.

### HURRICANE DAVID

When Sanford was nine years old, in 1956, he learned to build canoes from his father, who built them as a hobby. After felling a tree, his father would "dress" it in the forest, removing as much interior and exterior wood as possible. "When I was approximately eighteen years old, I went into the bush with him, seeing what he was doing," Sanford says. "At that time, the way I saw him building the boats, I said to my mind, 'I won't take that hobby.' The man would handle an axe all day. Not chain

Contemporary canoe maker Napolean Sanford builds dugout canoes on the island of Dominica.

*Photograph by Norman Sims.*

saw. Axe. He was alone in the bush with that thing. I said, 'I will not take that trip.' Too heavy. Too hard."

When Hurricane David devastated Dominica in 1979, everything changed. "Today, you still hear the adults talk about Hurricane David and how it affected them," writes former Peace Corps member Anna McCanse.[2] The hurricane surprised Dominicans with 175 miles per hour winds that destroyed the water supply, crushed houses, killed thirty-seven, injured five thousand, and left three-quarters of the population homeless. "The fragile banana trees, the source of Dominica's income, collapsed in unison," McCanse notes.

Sanford remembers the disaster. There was no way to make a living. The fishing boats had sunk or blown away.

"I took another young man I knew and I said, 'What should we do?' We could go to the bush and build a couple boats," Sanford recalls.

"I went to town and I bought one axe for him. And I had one. I had my father's old one because in 1974 he died. We went to the bush. We logged down that tree. I couldn't remember how to dress the boat, so we asked two other fellows that knew. We asked them to come and dress it for us. They dressed it for us and then we brought it out. After this, we couldn't trim the boat because we didn't have an adze. A small one. So we had to call the guys again, who came and helped us carve out the inside of the boat. We asked them to put in the ribs. We could do it, but we didn't know where they should be.

"So that was it. We went to the forest and we started to build boats. I've been doing it till now, since 1979."

Napolean Sanford with a work in progress next to the Carib Council House in Salybia, Dominica.   *Photograph by Norman Sims.*

## A BETTER TREE

After selecting a *gommier* tree in the forest, Sanford tests it for soundness. "I listen for the hard sound. I pick a good tree. When a tree is old, it's usually a better tree." Then he waits until his lucky day, generally a Tuesday or Wednesday, to cut it down. Sometimes a dark phase of the moon is involved, though not necessarily for superstitious reasons. Insects are the biggest danger to the log. "If pests attack the outside of the boat, it comes dark and you have a lot of holes in it now. But when you cut the wood in the proper month, the insects aren't there." Sanford points to the dugout at his feet and says, "Like this one. No pests or nothing."

After felling the tree, Sanford hollows it and shapes the bottom with modern tools, such as chain saws. He drills holes with an auger for ropes in the bow and stern and "man-powers" it out of the forest. The hull can weigh 300 to 350 pounds, which makes the long haul a job for a group of friends. When they reach a road, they truck it to Salybia.

He works outdoors next to the Carib Council House with the wind rustling through the leaves, roosters crowing in the village, and jungle birds singing overhead. Here he does the finer work of shaping the hull with axe and adze. As with the cedar canoes of the Pacific Northwest, the dugout must be spread.

"Stones and water," he says. "It sits there for a week or two weeks and the sun hits it. I use heat when I'm ready. But until I'm ready, it sits in the sun and the sun does the work. When I'm ready, if it's not the way I want it, then I build a fire on the outside. When it is hot, you give it water and it goes out slowly, slowly, slowly, slowly. You just use the rocks. Sometimes when you build a fire, it will just go by itself."

At this point, modern Caribbean dugouts diverge from those of Sanford's ancestors. The ancient logs, once spread, were deep enough for journeys on the ocean.

*Gommier* trees grow to enormous size in the rain forests of Dominica.
*Courtesy of Mark and Sarah McGuire.*

Sanford's 16- to 18-foot-long dugouts, made from younger trees, have little freeboard. They become seaworthy when he adds "borders."

For more than a century, Dominican dugout builders have added side planks, or borders, to increase the freeboard by 12 to 14 inches. Ribs support the borders and a "tie"—as in necktie—or a gunwale caps them off. Seats rest on stringers running along the ribs.

## CHANGING TRADITIONS

Widely used in the islands for fishing, these boats can be paddled, rowed, or propelled by outboard motors. Most of Sanford's business comes before the Dive Fest holiday in mid-July, when the traditional Carib Canoe Races are run.

Lifestyles in the Carib Territory are changing. Several Carib residents said they were not happy about the lack of ambition in young people. They are not learning how to build boats, farm, or fish. But then, when Sanford was a young man, he did not want to build boats until Hurricane David made it a matter of survival. Now he has been successful enough to send some of his children to college.

"What they used before was fish and manioc," Sanford says. "That was their food. For the Carib people, this was the traditional way of living. They go to the rivers or they go to the sea. They used the land, the sea, and the rivers. Now I can go to the shop and buy meat, but they went to the river and caught crayfish or they went to the sea. That was an easy way to live, more easy than you, probably. It still happens with a lot of people. We use our own natural forest, or we use our garden, or I go fishing. I catch fish for the whole week."

Dugout fishing canoes on the beach at Belle Fontaine, Martinique, West Indies, 1947.
*Photograph by Carleton Mitchell. Copyright Mystic Seaport, Carleton Mitchell Collection, 1996.31.5998.21.*

Napolean Sanford uses a colorful dugout canoe called *Storm Petrel* for fishing in the waters off Dominica.

*Photograph by Norman Sims.*

Today young people rarely take up the dugout craft. They can build fiberglass fishing boats more easily. As one fisherman in a small, remote village said, "That's easier than dragging a dugout canoe out of the rain forest." Sanford charges $3,000 to $5,000 in East Caribbean currency for a fishing boat, which equals roughly $1,100 to $1,800 US. That's a lot of money in Dominica.

"The important thing is you and the wood," Sanford says. "I go to the forest. I cut my tree. I love it. I build everything from scratch. I build good boats. I build good boats."

The manner of their fishing.

John White, *The Manner of Their Fishing*, 1585–93. Drawing.
The word *Cannow* is written on the hull of the boat. The Algonquin of
North Carolina used dugout canoes to harvest fish from February to May.

Natives fishing in late summer on Monhegan Island and along midcoast Maine used dugout canoes when hunting large swordfish and cod in the ocean. The Red Paint People of coastal Maine moved among the islands approximately 4,000 years ago, leaving behind evidence of stone tools for woodworking and harpoons for taking large fish. "The frequent co[-]occurrence of adzes and gouges suggests that they were used together in wood-shaping tasks, likely including dugout canoe construction—the gouges for hollowing out the inside and the adzes for shaping the outside," writes archaeologist Bruce Bourque. "Their size ranges suggest different scales of utility. One can imagine the larger ones were used to shape a dugout canoe while the smaller ones were used to carve decorations on it."[12]

After being harpooned, swordfish had a habit of attacking watercraft, which made the birch-bark canoe unsuitable for ocean fishing. "Of course, you can't go swordfish hunting with a birch bark canoe," says Dr. Arthur Spiess, an archaeologist with the Maine Historic Preservation Commission. "If you listen to the stories from old swordfish hunters, they'll rip the boat apart. So these guys were using dugout canoes."[13] Bourque estimates the dugouts were made from large white pines with a diameter of more than 4 feet that were found in Maine forests, large enough to create oceangoing craft. No actual birch-bark or dugout watercraft have been discovered from that era, although Bourque feels that "some may actually be found in the future, however, perhaps deep in the wet peat of the salt marsh that flanks the Turner Farm [on North

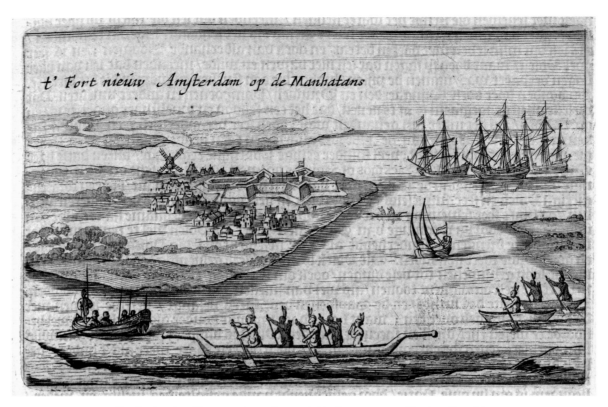

Kryn Frederycks, *t' Fort nieuw Amsterdam op de Manhatans*, c. 1626. Woodcut. One of the earliest views of New York, this scene depicts Native dugouts amid European sailing vessels.

*Courtesy of the Miriam and Ira D. Wallach Division of Art, Prints, and Photographs, New York Public Library, 55679.*

Haven Island], which began to accumulate at least 4,300 years ago."[14]

When Europeans arrived along the Maine coast, they encountered both birch-bark and dugout canoes. Samuel de Champlain in 1607 noted dugouts in use along the Maine coast.[15]

Culturally, the creation and use of oceangoing dugouts may have produced a social stratification among the Red Paint People with the boat captain as hero. Bourque says, "The power of this high-status or powerful chief emerges from hunting dangerous animals in the sea."[16]

In areas of North America where good birch bark was

The oyster industry of the East Coast relied on dugout canoes to navigate the rivers of Connecticut during the nineteenth century. This 1872 photograph depicts a dugout next to an oyster house near New Haven.

*Copyright Mystic Seaport, 1990.50.54.*

not readily available, the dugout thrived. Chapelle, of the Smithsonian Institution, writes that Atlantic Coast Indians also used dugouts for gathering food in ocean bays:

> Until the appearance of the early sharpies [sailboats], dugout canoes built of a single white pine log had been used at New Haven for tonging [gathering oysters with tongs]. The pine logs used for these canoes came mostly from inland Connecticut, but they were obtainable also in northern New England and New York. The canoes ranged from 28 to 35 feet in length, 15 to 20 inches

Julian A. Dimock, *Frank Tiger and Henry Clay pole through the Everglades*, 1910. Dugout canoes are a typical watercraft used by the Seminole tribe of southern Florida. *American Museum of Natural History Library, image 48519.*

in depth, and 3 feet 6 inches in beam. They were built to float on about 3 or 4 inches of water. The bottoms of these canoes were about 3 inches thick, giving a low center of gravity and the power to carry sail in a breeze.[17]

Dugouts have been found from central Canada to the Adirondacks and southward, even in areas where birch was available. Reginald Drayton, who lived in the nineteenth century near Rice Lake in the Peterborough region of Ontario, describes the canoes that he saw.

In 1871 the Indians all used dugout canoes which they made themselves out of basswood or pine or cedar logs about 15 feet long. These were hewn to as good a shape as they could and then the wood was dug out by means of axes and hollow adzes and the sides were made from an inch to rather less at the top where the gunwale was nailed on. The bottom was always left two inches thick; these canoes were not hard to paddle and on account of their weight did not stop the moment the paddle was taken from the water, as is the case with a birch bark or cedar built canoes.[18]

A family was building a dock in Lake Minnetonka in Minnesota during a prolonged drought in 1934 when they encountered a submerged log that proved to be a dugout canoe. Eighty years later, carbon dating showed that the boat was more than 1,000 years old.[19] The species of tree used to make it has not been determined. Other dugout canoes were made of pine in Florida and of white oak in Ohio.

In the age of Columbus, hundreds, and likely thousands of dugouts traveled on Florida's waters. As late as the early twentieth century, Seminole Indians poled dugout canoes in the Everglades to continue their practice of hiding, to the extent possible, from the European cultures.[20] According to Chapelle, "The dugout canoe of the Seminole Indian is very different from all other canoes of the North American continent." The Seminole dugouts, carved from cypress logs, ranged from 18 to 30 feet in length, with a seat in the stern. Canoes were not widened, as was done in the Pacific Northwest, so the boats were narrow and unsuited to the ocean. Paddles were seldom used. Chapelle says, "A canoe for use in the saw-grass-matted streams of the 'Glades' must pole easily, be stable and strong, and must not bunch the floating grass under the bow. The Seminole dugout fulfills all the above conditions."[21]

In 2000, a drought in Florida lowered the level of Newnans Lake, 6 miles from Gainesville.[22] What initially looked like old logs in the shallow lake turned out to be dugout canoes. Donna L. Ruhl, the North Florida Archaeology Collections manager at the Florida Museum of Natural History, helped catalog and preserve the canoes. More than one hundred were recovered. Forty-one canoes date from 2,300 to 5,000 years before the present. Some had thwarts. Long and narrow, they averaged 23 feet in length, and around 2 feet in width. The dimensions of the canoes and upward-sloping ends suggest the craft

Archaeologists Ray McGee, Melissa Memory, and Donna Ruhl examine a dugout canoe found during a drought in 2000 at Newnans Lake, Florida. The canoe is one of the longest and better-preserved dugouts from the lakebed. More than one hundred dugouts have been discovered, ranging in age from 500 to 5,000 years old.

*Photograph by Jeff Gage/Florida Museum of Natural History.*

were built for "speed and light loads, sacrificing stability."[23] Most were fire-hollowed from southern hard pine or cypress logs.

Canoes a thousand or more years old have been found in other locations in Florida as well. Early-twenty-first-century droughts in Florida have exposed 334 canoes at 198 sites. The Newnans Lake canoes "represent the single largest cache of prehistoric watercraft known in North America and possibly the world," according to Ruhl and another researcher from the University of Florida.[24]

In ancient times, Native Americans' canoes were important in Native cultures and trade. Ryan Wheeler writes, "[L]ike the ubiquitous stone tools and ceramics that are readily identified with native Florida cultures, the canoe was a tool of central importance in an aquatic-oriented culture . . . the canoe was not only significant for transport and subsistence activities, but may have held an archetypal role in native Florida society and cosmology."[25]

### THE SEA OTTER

The encounter of technologically sophisticated Europeans like Columbus with Natives was repeated on the Pacific Coast of North America. On the West Coast, Russians preceded the arrival of Europeans, and the meetings had similar outcomes.

Captain James Cook was the first European to arrive on the Northwest Coast—after a journey as difficult then as are trips to the moon today. In 1768, Cook sailed westward from Great Britain and eventually reached the

John Webber, *Tereoboo, King of Owyhee, Bringing Presents to Capt. Cook*, c. 1773 – 84. This watercolor depicts the distinctive "crab-claw" sail of the Owyhee (now Hawaiʻi) Island double-hull canoes. Artist John Webber traveled with Captain James Cook's third voyage to the Pacific in 1776 – 80.

Pacific. Cook made three voyages to the Pacific and was killed by Natives in Hawaii in 1779. In Hawaii, he found Natives paddling sophisticated double-hulled dugout canoes. "Double canoes were the largest and most important vessels used in the colonization of the Pacific. In addition to being more stable, the deck spanning the hulls created more space and protection from the elements for crew, passengers, and cargo. Captain Cook observed double canoes carrying between 50 and 120 people and measuring up to twenty-one meters long and nearly four meters across," according to Paine.[26]

The original twin-hull dugout canoes of the Polynesian inhabitants of Hawaii were like floating farms. Between 900 and 1100 AD, or even earlier, they "settled the Marquesas and other islands including Hawaii," completing the colonization by 1250.[27] These journeys—covering thousands of miles between Tahiti and Hawaii out of sight of land and sailing against the trade winds—far exceeded the length and risk of those made by the Caribbean paddlers. The Polynesians brought with them new plants, such as taro and sweet potato, and animals, including dogs, pigs, and the distinctive red-and-black jungle fowl that resembles a chicken and still thrives on the island of Kauai. Unlike the dugouts in the Caribbean, these craft used a distinctive triangular sail that artist John Webber documented on Cook's voyages. They navigated by cracking the codes of the water, reading the weather, the rising and setting of stars on the horizon, and other signs, such as the direction of ocean swells.[28]

In early 1778, Captain Cook and his men visited the coast of Oregon aboard two sailing ships, *Resolution* and *Discovery*. Near Vancouver Island at the end of March, Cook said, "A great many canoes filled with the natives" met his ships, and they began trading for the furs of bears, raccoons, and sea otters in exchange for knives, buttons, and nails.[29]

The Europeans on the East Coast quickly copied birch-bark canoes for travel up the Hudson and the St. Lawrence Rivers.[30] On the East Coast, fur traders recognized the value of lightweight birch-bark canoes for reaching distant trading partners in the vast interior. On the West Coast, however, most European explorers did not imitate the First People's dugout canoes. The Europeans on the West Coast could wait in port on the vast coastline while Natives in dugouts brought furs, which had been harvested nearby along the coast. Thus adopting canoe technology for interior exploration was not as important to the European newcomers.

Early European sailors on the West Coast counted many canoes. Hilary Stewart in her book on the cedar tree writes:

When Capt. George Vancouver was anchored near Yaculta, on Quadra Island,[31] he recorded that 18 canoes came out to meet his ship, leaving 70 still on shore. At a village on the west coast of Vancouver Island, Capt. James Cook estimated that 500 people occupied the 80 canoes that swarmed around his vessel for trading, while Jewitt described a raiding party that consisted of 40 vessels carrying 10 to 20

John Webber, *"Resolution" and "Discovery" in Ship Cove, Nootka Sound*, 1778. Watercolor, pen, and ink on paper, 58 × 147 cm. Surrounded by dugout canoes, Captain Cook's ships reached Vancouver Island in March 1778.

warriors each. The factor at Fort Langley, on the Fraser River, recorded the daily passing of canoes going home from the fishing grounds after the salmon run, and entries such as "150 Cowichans [*sic*] families stopped at the wharf" and "200 canoes of Whooms stopped alongside" or "100 more canoes passed" are frequent. In the Queen Charlotte Islands, in 1791, Captain Barnet recorded that the staggering number of 600 Haida canoes surrounded his trading ship in Cloak Bay.[32]

Martine Reid estimates that, by the late 1800s, "some ten thousand canoes were plying the West Coast, with families traveling to sell their baskets or to find work in the hop fields of Puget Sound."[33]

The luxurious sea otter fur on the West Coast proved even more valuable in trade than the beaver fur that was responsible for the exploration of eastern Canada. The Chinese cared little for the manufactured goods the European ships carried, except for gold and silver, which made it difficult to trade for valuable Chinese porcelain and furniture. Sea otter furs, however, could be traded in China, "where they were deemed the royal fur, valued more than any other by the rich and powerful, used to trim robes and capes, and to make hats and winter coats."[34] After the American Revolution, sea otter fur became

Dugout canoes line the beach at Songhees Reserve in Victoria, British Columbia, 1868.

*Photograph by Major James Skitt Matthews. Courtesy of the City of Vancouver Archives.*

almost an American monopoly as a three-cornered trade developed. Boston goods were taken around the globe to the Pacific Northwest and traded for fur. After exchanging the pelts in Canton and elsewhere, the ships returned to Boston with coveted Chinese goods.[35] The great profits made by outside traders seem unfair in terms of what they paid the First People. John Ledyard, an American trader in the 1780s, said "the skins which did not cost the purchaser six pence sterling sold in China for 100 dollars."[36] Captain Robert Gray in 1790 "once obtained two hundred otter skins for only one iron chisel apiece."[37] Captain James King, who sailed with Captain Cook, reported that sea otter furs were eagerly exchanged for metal trinkets of trifling value. "In Canton, however, the furs took on a startling new value. One sailor sold his store for $800; altogether Captain King . . . estimated that the men realized £2,000 sterling, a considerable sum for the day."[38]

Sea otters can weigh up to 100 pounds and have a dense, thick fur that made their pelts valuable in the fur trade with China.
This engraving, made after a drawing by John Webber, was published in Captain Cook's narrative *A Voyage to the Pacific Ocean* in 1780.
*Courtesy of the Library of Congress Rare Book and Special Collections Division.*

Emily Carr, *Tzartsiseucomy (Haida Village)*, c. 1912. Watercolor on paper, 54.7 × 75.7 cm.

*Gift of Dr. and Mrs. Max Stern. Copyright McCord Museum of Canadian History, M981.118.*

The First People may have seen the transactions differently, as did their East Coast brethren. Modern historians view the transactions as more balanced than once thought.[39] The value of a metal axe or chisel, for example, was much higher to a Northwest Coast resident living in a vast landscape of giant cedar trees than it was to a European aboard a wooden sailing ship. "Among the riches the newcomers brought were the scarce and prized metals copper and iron, the latter being the rare and invaluable metal that would stimulate woodcarvers' art to new heights, as chiefs, enriched by the lucrative fur trade, required more ritual paraphernalia and accoutrements to demonstrate their status and acquire more wealth," writes Reid.[40]

Before the traders arrived, sea otters had not been heavily hunted by Natives. Otters proved relatively easy to harvest, and trading the fur for metal tools saved months of labor in carving dugout canoes. Along with trade goods, unfortunately, came alcohol and imported diseases that had a similar effect on the West Coast as on the East.

Relationships between traders and Northwest Coast Natives were marred by exploitation and violence, at which the Russians were perhaps the worst. Professional hunters from the Siberian region, known as *promyshlenniki*, started the sea otter trade even before Cook arrived. Rather than harvesting the pelts themselves, writes Eric Dolin, they

> usually forced the natives, or Aleuts, as they
> dubbed them, to do it for them by taking some of
> them hostage and threatening their lives unless

the remaining members of the tribe returned with pelts. This particularly savage form of extortion worked particularly well for the *promyshlenniki,* who were more than willing, and at times almost eager, to slaughter the Aleuts if they disobeyed. When the Aleuts rose up in defiance, bloodbaths ensued.[41]

The American, European, and Russian fur traders insatiably slaughtered sea otters like wolves slaughtered sheep in a pen. Between 1790 and 1830, sea otters were reduced to near extinction, as would also happen with the American bison and even the beaver. A *Wall Street Journal* article reported that a population of 400 million beaver—"America's first commodity animal"—was reduced to 100,000, mostly in Canada. "By 1894, the largest forest left in the eastern U.S., the Adirondacks, was down to a single family of five beavers."[42] Sea otter populations on the West Coast are still recovering.

The human participants hardly fared better. After sailing for seven to nine months and more than halfway around the world through dangerous waters, the European and North American traders seemed to feel it was their right to take immediate advantage of the Native people. When the sailing ship *Boston* arrived in Nootka Sound in 1803, the ship's captain insulted the village chief, Maquinna. The captain failed to treat his Native business partners with proper respect. The next day, with friendly gestures, the Natives deceived the crew into splitting into two parties. All but two of the crew were killed, and

A Kwakiutl family is shown navigating the waters of Quatsino Sound on Northern Vancouver Island in the early 1900s. Korpreno Tom (Sealing Tom) demonstrates how to throw a double-pronged sealing spear. *Photograph by Ben W. Leeson. Courtesy of the Vancouver Public Library Special Collections, VPL14059.*

As this sea otter trade declined early in the twentieth century, the dugout canoe as an element of tribal art and culture was nearly forgotten except for some anthropological attention.

### BILL REID AND THE DUGOUT REVIVAL

Sometimes when people hear the term "dugout canoe," a couple of thoughts flash through their minds. First, perhaps, a general feeling that dugouts belong to the ancient past. Second, an image of the beautiful oceangoing dugouts made from huge cedar trees by the Native peoples of the Pacific Northwest. Both thoughts have validity, but things are more complicated. As we have seen, dugouts were not built solely on the Northwest Coast, nor have they died out.

The classics were the spectacular Pacific Northwest cedar canoes like the ones that met Cook's sailing ships. The people of the Northwest expressed their culture for more than seven thousand years through carvings and pictorial works of art. Among those works of art was the canoe.

For most of the twentieth century, Northwest Coast Indian art was considered a "primitive" art form and was not well regarded in the artistic community. Such opinions changed slowly. Between 1896 and 1927, the anthropologist Franz Boas published several documents about the art and design of Northwest Coast Indians, and in the 1950s and 1960s anthropologist Bill Holm did the same.[44] Their scholarly work prepared the ground for French anthropologist Claude Lévi-Strauss, who in the 1970s classified

their heads posted on stakes. The two survivors were held captive for two years and later told the tale. Past injustices stood behind the killings. As Dolin writes, "In fact the history of the Pacific Northwest coast fur trade is littered with examples of white men, and certainly not just Americans, behaving atrociously and brutalizing the local Indians."[43]

British botanist and ethnographer Charles F. Newcombe photographed this newly hewn Haida dugout canoe at the village of Kasaan, Alaska, along the Northwest Coast, c.1900. *Courtesy of the Royal BC Museum and Archives, image PN00987.*

Northwest Coast Indian art as "among the four or five great artistic traditions of human history."[45]

Bill Reid (1920–1998), an artist whose mother came from the Haida tribe in British Columbia,[46] is celebrated today for deepening interest in the living artistry of the First People of the Pacific Northwest. At the same time, Reid's reputation was controversial among the First People because of his modernism and partial European heritage. Nevertheless, with one foot in a traditional culture and the other in the modern world, he helped revive the construction of Northwest Coast dugout canoes.

One of several crowning achievements of his artistic career was a beautiful dugout canoe displayed at the University of British Columbia Museum of Anthropology. Another achievement, Reid's huge wooden sculpture *The Spirit of Haida Gwaii—the Jade Canoe*, greets passengers when they arrive at the Vancouver airport.

Reid understood the ceremonial and cultural role of dugouts in the Northwest. The boats served the purposes of trade and survival but also provided for social interaction and artistic expression. "Western art starts with the figure," Reid says. "West Coast Indian art starts with the boat."[47]

Creating such a craft was a monumental task for pre-contact Natives and for Reid, too. In 1985, Reid supervised Gary Edenshaw (Guujaaw) and Simon Dick as they created the 24½-foot dugout on display at the Museum of Anthropology.[48] It was a prototype for a full-size, nearly 50-foot-long ocean-going canoe named *Lootaas* (Wave Eater) that he and his associates carved from a single cedar log at Skidegate, a Haida community in Haida Gwaii (formerly the Queen Charlotte Islands) of British Columbia. Both crafts were displayed at the 1986 World Exposition in Vancouver. *Lootaas* carried Reid's ashes to his mother's ancestral village when he died in 1998, at age seventy-eight;

Pioneering dugout canoe builder Bill Reid with a bentwood box, c. 1865 (left), and one of his drawings of its design, *Master of the Black Field No. 1* (right), in 1967.
*Photograph by Ross Kenward,* The Province.

Three cedar canoes on the beach at the Haida Heritage Centre, Skidegate, British Columbia, 2008.
The canoe on the left is *Lootaas* (Wave Eater), carved by Bill Reid.    *Photograph by Ron Caves.*

the canoe is now displayed at the Haida Heritage Centre at Skidegate.

Western red cedar was *the* canoe tree—the tree of life for the Northwest Coast Natives. "It will make houses and boats and boxes and cooking pots," writes Reid. "Its bark will make mats, even clothing. With a few bits of sharpened stone and antler, with some beaver teeth and a lot of time, with later on a bit of iron, you can build from the cedar tree the exterior trappings of one of the world's great cultures."[49]

Old-growth cedar trees are immense and can provide the materials for several boats. In this photograph, four different canoes are being hewn from one red cedar log at Olympic Loop, Queets River, Washington, c. 1930.

*Photograph by Dale O. Northrup. Courtesy of Quentin Mackie.*

An elbow adze similar to those used to create dugout canoes. This example from the Stikine Tlingit people dates from 1876.

*Courtesy of the Burke Museum of Natural History and Culture, University of Washington, purchased from George T. Emmons, catalog number 1876.*

Metlakahtla Indians use elbow adzes to hollow out a dugout canoe on the banks of the Skeena River in British Columbia, early 1900s.  *Courtesy of the Royal BC Museum and Archives, image C-08103.*

In ancient times, one giant log 300 feet high and 10 feet in diameter could be used to carve three or four dugout canoes.[50] "Red cedar became the perfect material for canoe building" because it was rot-resistant, straight-grained, and lightweight, according to Martine Reid, Bill's widow.[51]

Using modern tools such as an elbow adze, Bill Reid and his assistants began hollowing the log for the shorter dugout in 1985, leaving an even thickness on the sides and shaping the bow and stern lines. Smaller adzes, axes, and chain saws made the work easier than that of their ancestors, who used fire, stones, and shells instead of metal tools.

"Think of the time it would take to fall a big cedar by burning through its base with a slow controlled fire, or felling it with a stone blade with your time divided equally between chopping and sharpening, to say nothing of the days it took to make the tool before you could begin," Bill Reid writes. "Then to shape the log into a canoe, and hollow it by more burning and scraping, and then to steam and shape it and fit it out."[52] Typically, trees aged four hundred to eight hundred years were used to make dugouts of this size.

The next step for Reid and his colleagues was to use a

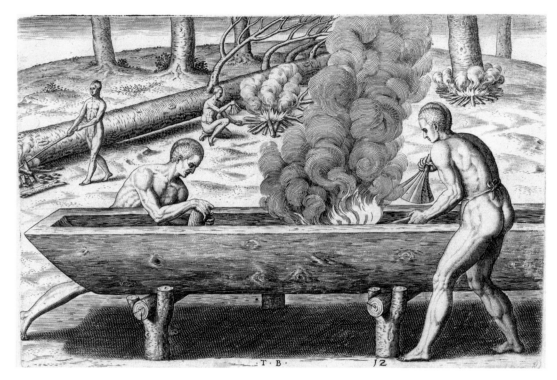

Theodor de Bry, *The manner of makinge their boates*, 1590. Engraving. The ancient process of making a dugout canoe includes felling a tree using fire at the base and hollowing the log.

*Courtesy of the John Carter Brown Library at Brown University.*

technique discovered by ancient builders that made dug-outs seaworthy. Hollowed logs would roll and ship a lot of water in the ocean, except for a step in the building process that spread the sides of the hull and created additional stability and flare. After the log was hollowed, the ancient builders partially filled it with water and added stones heated in a fire. Placing hot stones in the boat brought the water to near boiling. As the hull softened from this internal steam-bending, spreaders were inserted to push the sides outward. Extending the sides caused the ends to rise, giving the craft a greater ability to deflect and ride over waves. Northwestern dugouts resemble modern canoes in the flare of their sides and their rocker, or lift, in the bow and stern. Reid used hot water with the same effect. The end result was a traditional craft capable of long journeys on the open ocean.

Large dugouts decorated in classic Northwest Coast motifs were used in transportation, warfare, fishing and whaling, seal hunting, for trade with other peoples, and in ceremonies such as weddings and burials. They came in different sizes depending on need, with the Haida building the largest for ocean trade. The canoes themselves became valuable trade items and a symbol of wealth. Sometimes oceangoing craft had a plank added to increase the freeboard. Planks could be stripped from a straight-grained cedar log fairly easily and then sewn to the canoe using cedar rope or roots.[53]

For Reid, as for the ancestral builders of dugouts, the canoe was much more than a means of transportation. Canoes represented the knowledge of their makers and contained ritualistic and mythical elements. "Northwest Coast canoes were metaphors for different sets of ideas, including wealth and property, exchange and gift, war, marriage and death," writes Martine Reid.[54] Late in his artistic career, Bill Reid found a fusion of form and function in the dugout canoe. He said:

> The cedars grew tall and straight in the rainforests of the north, but it took the experience of generations of skillful men to change their trunks into seagoing boats, sometimes seventy feet long. The log was shaped and hollowed, and then, in the supreme example of primitive genius, the whole thing was steamed by partly filling it with water

In 1985 Bill Reid and his associates created a dugout canoe at the Museum of Anthropology in Vancouver. An important step is steaming the hull to spread the sides and provide a bit of lift at the ends. The floor and sides of the canoe are covered with brush so that the hot stones put into the water do not touch the wood of the canoe.
*Photograph by Bill McLennan. Courtesy of the UBC Museum of Anthropology, Vancouver, Canada.*

A Haisla dugout canoe carved and painted by David Shaw in 1934 in Kitamaat, British Columbia. In 1967, the canoe was
over-painted by Bill Reid in a Haida design of a killer whale with its head and dorsal fin on the prow and the body and tailfins on the stern.

*Courtesy of the UBC Museum of Anthropology, Vancouver, Canada, A1535.*

and adding hot rocks until the water boiled, so it could be spread to the proper beam. This gave the beautiful flaring curve to the sides, and the rough seas dictated the high bow and stern. And so, as always, perfect function produced perfect beauty.[55]

"Canoe-making was not a dead art when Bill Reid decided to construct one in the early 1980s," writes Maria Tippett.[56] But only a few canoe builders and painters remained in the tribes. The last of the great Northwestern seagoing dugouts had been built early in the twentieth

century. Reid had watched a Haida canoe being carved in 1956, according to Tippett, and was aware of some of the other builders. Research and practice over many years taught him how to carve the log so the lines would finish straight after the hull was spread using boiling water. *Lootaas* began as a 200-foot-tall cedar that was 8 feet in diameter. When finished, it was 2 inches thick at the gunwales, 1 inch along the body, and 3 inches at the keel. Steaming the boat for two hours caused the hull to expand by 20 inches. The 50-foot-long *Lootaas* is a remarkable 71 inches (nearly 6 feet) wide at its midpoint.[57]

Graham Herbert (Hornby Island, British Columbia), *Sacred Escort*, 1994. Watercolor on paper, 36.83 × 52.07 cm.

*Reproduced with permission of the artist.*

Edward S. Curtis, *Into the Shadow*, 1910. Clayoquot Sound, British Columbia.

Courtesy of the Edward S. Curtis Collection, Library of Congress Prints and Photographs Division, LC-USZ62-136568.

His collaborator, Gary Edenshaw (Guujaaw), says, "We had an old canoe blueprinted because we were trying to figure out how to build one ourselves. The shipwright that we retained was astonished to realize not only the beauty of the design but also the accuracy of the craftsmanship, which he said wouldn't be surpassed in any conventional wooden boat. At every scale, from the canoes to the spoons, the workmanship was inspiring."[58]

Since the 1980s, the construction of traditional dugout canoes has revived in the Pacific and in the Northwest. Several groups all over North America have been building canoes out of birch bark and wood as a way of preserving the cultures of First People. The Swinomish tribe in La Conner, Washington, began hosting annual Tribal Journeys events in 1989 that feature traditional art, culture, and food and always involve oceangoing voyages in dugout canoes. In this way, the dugout builders have joined other Native American tribes from the birch-bark regions in preserving old methods of canoe building.

Marilyn Wandrey of the Suquamish tribe, speaking of the modern Tribal Journeys event, says, "The canoe is just like our big houses, our long houses. It also carries our culture. The canoe was our life blood. It took us to our neighboring bands and villages where we would be able to have these kinds of celebrations with our relatives and our friends. It also meant that we could travel to those places where our resources were at. It's been very vital to our life."[59]

"Building upon the success of Tribal Journeys, which grew operations from 13 traditional cedar canoes in 1989 to now more than 100 canoes and 10,000 participants from the United States, Canada (First Nations), Hawaii, New Zealand, Japan and the Philippines, the One People Canoe Society adopted protocols like the Tribal Journeys' *Ten Rules of the Canoe*, a kind of life lesson plan that offers guidance on respect, trust, support, adaptability and charity; and launched new traditions such as their paddle workshops," according to a 2016 *Smithsonian* magazine article. " 'The thing I really love about the canoe is that you always have to work together no matter what. If you're not paddling together, you can always feel it . . . ,' says Wilbur Lkoowagoon Brown of the Killer Whale Clan from the House that Anchored the Village in Sitka."[60] Many of the journeys are made without modern navigational tools.

Peg Deam, another member of the Suquamish tribe, describes how "Each canoe is extremely different. They're like people." In a pre-industrial society, even when similar building techniques were used, every dugout and birch-bark canoe was an individual creation. "You cannot assume anything about a canoe," she says. "They all have different teachings. They all have different personalities. They all have different things to teach us."[61]

And teach they do. Bill Reid discovered his heritage in art and dugout canoes. So, too, have members of other tribes and cultures—using different canoes—learned the craft as they let the canoes speak to them.

CHAPTER 2

# Birch-Bark Canoes

ERIK SIMULA, a Minnesotan born near the shores of Lake Superior just a couple days' paddle from the fur-trading center of North America, may be one of those fellows who came into this world two centuries too late. "Living in the bush," as he calls it, has been his way of life for more than two decades, and birch-bark canoes have been at the center of it.[1]

Simula builds bark canoes in the traditional way as much as he can—wandering into the woods in the late winter or early spring, looking for suitable birch, cedar, and spruce trees, cutting with hand tools, hauling his own water, and using a woodstove or campfire for heat. He made his living guiding fishermen in the Boundary Waters and Quetico wildernesses and running dogsled teams, while selling his handmade snowshoes. He learned from Ojibwe boatbuilder Bunky Fairbanks of Ball Club, Minnesota, and Russ Merritt, a snowshoe maker from Cohasset, Minnesota, who was looking for an apprentice. Eventually his income came from demonstrating bark-canoe making for visitors at Grand Portage National Monument and teaching at the North House Folk School in Grand Marais, Minnesota.

In 2009, to mark his daughter Anna's graduation from high school, he paddled more than 1,000 miles from near Grand Portage to Grand Rapids, Minnesota, in one of his 14-foot, 45-pound bark canoes, with only a sled dog named Kitigan as company. "Maybe this happened because

*Birchbarks at Batchewang*, 2012. Canoes built and photographed by Ferdy Goode of Arbor Vitae, Wisconsin. *Courtesy of Ferdy Goode.*

Contemporary birch-bark builder Erik Simula working on a bark canoe in 2009.  *Photograph by Layne Kennedy.*

of the birch-bark canoe," he said. "I had no time limits. If I wanted to explore, or stop and spend an extra day, I did." By 2012, Simula had moved to rural Finland, Minnesota. The years of living in the bush, building boats by hand and hauling water and wood, have taken their toll on his body, particularly his back. But he manages, and as he puts it, "I can't live in town."

Simula is among a line of birch-bark builders that stretches back to the Ojibwe and earlier, a line that includes twenty-first-century artists such as Henri Vaillancourt of New Hampshire, David Gidmark of Ontario, Steve Cayard of Maine, and Ferdy Goode of Wisconsin, as well as Native American experts such as the late Anishinabeg Algonquin master William Commanda and his nephew, Daniel "Pinock" Smith, and Barry Dana of Penobscot heritage. The modern builders of traditional bark boats can credit French explorers with wholly adapting Native designs for trade and transportation, beginning a relationship that linked the Indian cultures of North America with the Europeans who arrived on their shores.

Considering that Canada contains more lakes and inland waters than any other country in the world,[2] it is not surprising that canoes made there were ingrained into the daily lives of the Natives, including their theology. The Slavey and Chipewyan peoples of northwestern Canada believed that, upon death, the soul of the deceased boards a stone canoe for a slow paddle across a large, long lake; a good soul makes it safely to the other side, where game and firewood are plentiful. An evil soul sinks like a stone

Erik Simula's canoe *Nama* and his dog Kitigan at Mountain Lake in the Arrowhead  ➤
region of Minnesota.  *Photograph by Erik Simula, Arrowhead Wilderness School.*

A solitary paddler sits in a birch-bark canoe at Moose Factory, Ontario, in the 1880s.
Moose Factory is at the outlet of the Moose River into James Bay, the far southern tip of Hudson Bay.

*Photograph by R. Bell, Geological Survey of Canada (22491). Courtesy of the Canadian Canoe Museum.*

Toronto newspaper columnist Roy Mac-Gregor.[5] Our birch-bark story begins on these many miles of Canadian waterways.

French captain Jacques Cartier sailed to the northeastern coast of North America and the region of the St. Lawrence River in 1534 with an idea of what he would find. Although Cartier is sometimes considered the European "discoverer" of what is now Canada—indigenous peoples having lived there for thousands of years, of course—other European explorers, including Leif Eriksson, John Cabot, and the Florentine Giovanni da Verrazzano, had already reached Canadian waters. Verrazzano wrote a sparse account of his 1524 travels, but Cartier, who made three visits to the region over an eight-year period, was a far better chronicler of his adventures—or at least he is credited with writing three accounts; some scholars question their authorship.[6] His notes on the Native population, language, hydrology, landscape, and other experiences have been considered nearly definitive for almost a half a millennium.

Cartier was detailed and thorough about specifics important to a sea captain, such as soundings, shoals, and in the canoe, spending eternity in the cold depths of the black water.[3] Gidmark notes how often "canoe" shows up in a grammar book written by missionaries in the nineteenth century.[4] "What could be more Canadian than the purely Canadian First-Nations invention that made Canada possible? The canoe *made* Canada," writes longtime

Jean Antoine Theodore Gudin, *Jacques Cartier Discovering the St. Lawrence River*, 1847. Oil on canvas, 142 × 266 cm.
Gudin, who finished this painting more than three hundred years after the event, was a well-known French painter of naval scenes.

*Copyright Château de Versailles, France/Bridgeman Images.*

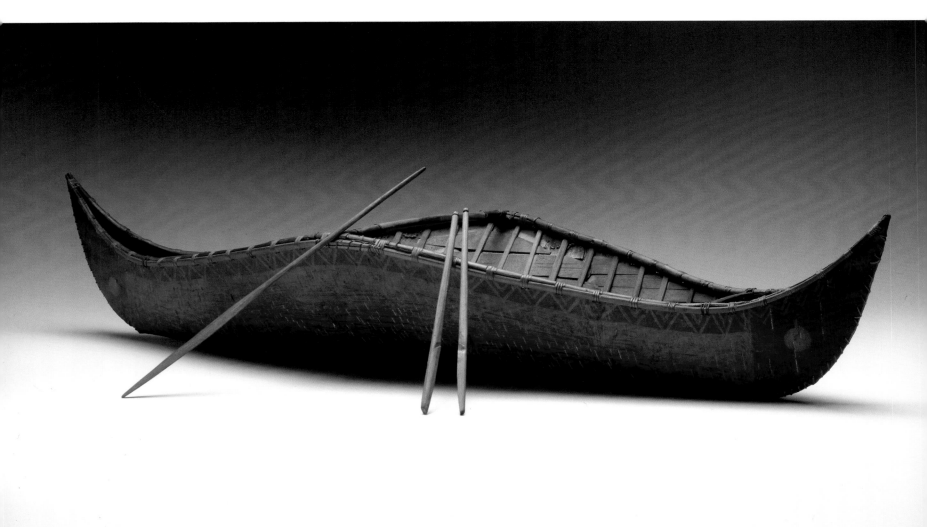

Edwin Tappan Adney's model of a Beothuk canoe illustrates the unique shape of the gunwales, rising amidships, that would permit the boat to be heeled at an extreme angle (as when hauling aboard game or large fish in coastal waters). A regularly designed canoe would swamp at such an angle. The Beothuk people lived in Newfoundland until the early nineteenth century.

*Courtesy of the Mariners' Museum, Newport News, Virginia.*

shorelines—although he never mentions the names of his two ships—and as such he took note of the birch-bark canoes that served as Native watercraft. He is credited with being the first European to describe birch-bark canoes (Verrazzano mentions only dugout canoes), although he was not the first to see them and, unfortunately, he was disappointingly spare in his description. Nonetheless, brief observations are better than none.

In the book of his first voyage, in a section dated Friday, June 12, 1534, Cartier mentions birch-bark canoes for the first time. The reference is part of his initial observations on a tribe, possibly Beothuks, hunting for seals in the region of Blanc-Sablon (now in far eastern Quebec). "There are people on this coast," he writes, "whose bodies are fairly well formed, but they are wild and savage folk.[7] They wear their hair tied up on the top of their heads like a handful of twisted hay, with a nail or something of the sort passed through the middle, and into it they weave a few bird's feathers."[8] After a brief comment on their clothing, Cartier moves to their transportation. "They have canoes made of birch bark in which they go about, and from them they catch many seals. Since seeing them, I have been informed that their home is not at this place but that they come from warmer countries to catch these seals and to get other food for their sustenance."[9] The Beothuks were great seal hunters; it is also possible that the Blanc-Sablon canoeists were an Iroquoian tribe from the St. Lawrence Valley.

Thus the first mention is made in Western literature of a sophisticated boat that had been developed over the previous five thousand years by the aboriginal peoples of North America. As mentioned in chapter 1, the word *canoe* probably comes from a West Indian word of similar sound that stood for a log used as transportation. The Arawak, expert dugout builders in the Caribbean, called their boats *canaoua*, which Christopher Columbus shortened to *canoa* in Spanish; the French translated that as *cannowa*, then *canot*, and finally *canoe*.[10]

Cartier mentions canoes a few more times in his accounts and even named a small waterway Canoe River, where they had seen Natives crossing the river in their canoes.[11] On July 4 of his first visit, Cartier and his men encountered a fleet of forty or fifty canoes, probably Micmac or Hurons, and three weeks later another forty canoes, possibly Iroquois, fishing for mackerel. The bark canoes were about the only item of value the Indians possessed, he writes, since "the whole lot of them had not anything above the value of five *sous*, their canoes and fishing-nets

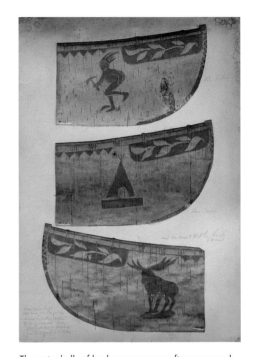

The outer hulls of bark canoes were often engraved with symbols, animal silhouettes, and geometric shapes. Bark collected in the winter is better for such etchings than summer bark. Edwin Tappan Adney drew these designs on birch bark from a canoe built in Old Town, Maine, and exhibited at the New York Sportsman's Show in 1897.

*Courtesy of the Mariners' Museum, Newport News, Virginia.*

excepted."[12] Cartier also notes the use of the boats as a shelter: "They have no other dwelling but their canoes, which they turn upside down and sleep on the ground underneath."[13] At Natashquan Point on the northern shore of what is now the Gulf of St. Lawrence, the wind kept Cartier offshore, and two six-passenger canoes, probably Montagnais, paddled to meet him. A few days later, he returned to France.

Cartier had taken note of a watercraft that was employed by more tribes than the few that he encountered; all used the same skin-and-plank bark construction, although with distinct differences in style. The canoe had existed for thousands of years in the northern part of the continent as the primary transportation for Indians, much of whose existence was defined by water. It was the only way to get any distance in the spring after ice-out, in the summer, and in the fall before freeze-up.

As a daily transport, the bark canoe was a sensible craft, built of local materials over a span of two or three weeks. Some were made for large inland lakes; others were smaller and more maneuverable for use in swift rivers; while still others were shaped for ocean travel. Shorter versions were light enough to be carried by one person from waterway to waterway or around dangerous rapids. Should a canoe be torn in an encounter with a sharp rock, a trip to the nearest woods for repair materials was in order. Paddlers faced forward, unlike Europeans in their rowboats, and were able to propel their lightweight crafts at a rapid rate. Cartier noted how the Micmac chased and caught his longboat with remarkable speed and little effort.

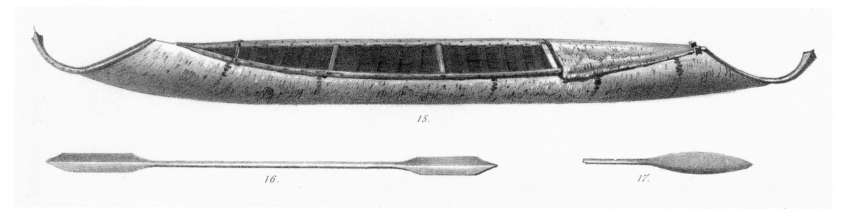

*15.*

*16.*    *17.*

Boats from the Amur River valley region of Asia share similarities with Kutenai-Salish canoes across the sea in Canada, which has led to speculation about the transfer of the design from one culture to another, or its independent development for similar needs. Is this evidence of a long-gone land bridge?

*From the collections of the Ernst Mayr Library and Archives of the Museum of Comparative Zoology, Harvard University.*

Phyllop Peter and his wife paddle a Kutenai canoe on Kootenay Lake in 1922. In British Columbia and elsewhere on the west coast of North America, these boats (also called sturgeon-nose canoes) were designed to cut through the bulrushes easily in areas where ducks' eggs could be harvested and muskrats could be trapped. They were fast, but unstable in rapids.

*Courtesy of Touchstones Nelson, Museum of Art and History, Nelson, British Columbia, TN_HunterAlbum1.050b.*

The Native canoes were also built with an artistic touch. Scenes and symbols were often painted or etched into the bark on the hull. Individual makers could add personal flair with a style of stitching or the curve of a bow.

Much of what we think we know about the earliest birch-bark canoes is speculation, of course, because they were quickly used up, discarded, and recycled back into the earth. None of the craft from pre-white settlement has survived to the present.[14] Did the design come from Asia? Evidence of bark craft from the Amur Valley region in Siberia shows a look similar to those made by the Kutenai people in the Pacific Northwest, for example. It is possible that, as was the case with other engineering successes, bark canoes were developed independently in different parts of the world as a solution to the same problem. It is also possible the technology migrated from Alaska to Russia.

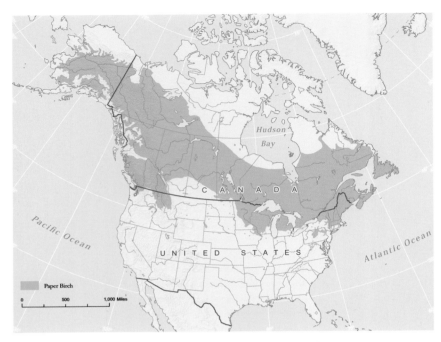

The range of the paper birch (*Betula papyrifera*) in North America. The tree is sometimes called canoe birch. *Map by Charles Rader.*

### THE BIRCH TREE

The aboriginal peoples of North America used the local flora and fauna to serve a variety of needs, from food to shelter to transportation. Among the most important plant species for those who lived in the forests of the northern and northeastern part of the continent was the paper birch, *Betula papyrifera*.[15]

Many tribes regularly used the paper birch (also called canoe birch, silver birch, or white birch) because its six varieties had a vast range, from the northern limits of the forest—as far north as any deciduous tree—near the Arctic, as far west as Alaska, east to Nova Scotia and south and west to the edge of the Great Plains.[16] In the early seventeenth century, Captain John Smith reported that the Nanticoke people in the Chesapeake Bay region traveled up the Susquehanna River to trade for birch bark.[17] One scholar of early ships and shipbuilding, James Hornell, writes that the best habitat for birch was from 45 degrees (present-day Minneapolis and Bangor, Maine) to 60 degrees latitude (the northern tip of Newfoundland and Labrador) in North America: "In this region bark canoe construction attains the perfection of its art."[18]

A relatively short-lived, shallow-rooted deciduous tree (few last more than 140 years), the paper birch grows to 70 or 80 feet at maturity with an average diameter of a foot or so, although larger members of the species can be 3 or 4 feet around or more, and those are the ones the canoe builders coveted.

Paper birch can grow on a mountain, along the border of a swamp, up through a moraine, or on an open hillside. Soil texture doesn't seem to matter: sandy soils in glacial areas, peat bogs, river silt, or even gravel will host a tree, so long as the soil is fairly well drained. It doesn't like a lot of shade, but the tree can be happy with its neighbors in a mixed forest. It's also among the first colonizers after a forest fire.

A partial list of the items crafted by Indians from the tree's pale, easily worked hardwood includes bows, arrows, spears, quivers, and, of course, firewood. Sleds, snowshoes, and poles for housing frames were made by builders who took advantage of the wood's combination of strength and

The birch forest stretches across Alaska, Canada, and the northeastern part of the United States. This stand of trees was photographed at Bognor Marsh near Georgian Bay off Lake Huron.   *Photograph by Robert Hart/sevenacres.ca.*

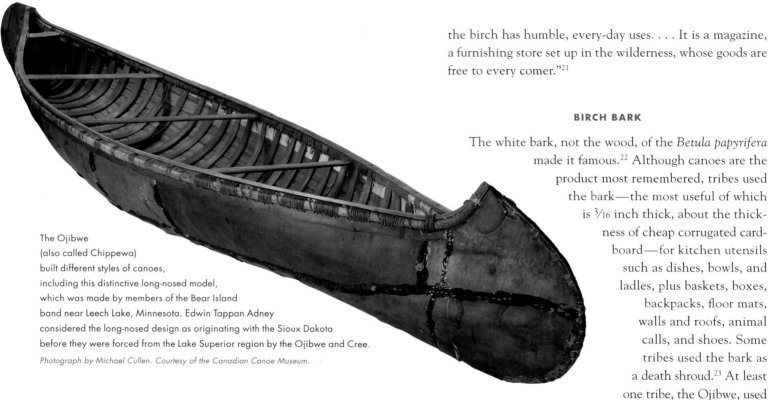

The Ojibwe
(also called Chippewa)
built different styles of canoes,
including this distinctive long-nosed model,
which was made by members of the Bear Island
band near Leech Lake, Minnesota. Edwin Tappan Adney
considered the long-nosed design as originating with the Sioux Dakota
before they were forced from the Lake Superior region by the Ojibwe and Cree.

*Photograph by Michael Cullen. Courtesy of the Canadian Canoe Museum.*

the birch has humble, every-day uses. . . . It is a magazine, a furnishing store set up in the wilderness, whose goods are free to every comer."[21]

## BIRCH BARK

The white bark, not the wood, of the *Betula papyrifera* made it famous.[22] Although canoes are the product most remembered, tribes used the bark—the most useful of which is ³⁄₁₆ inch thick, about the thickness of cheap corrugated cardboard—for kitchen utensils such as dishes, bowls, and ladles, plus baskets, boxes, backpacks, floor mats, walls and roofs, animal calls, and shoes. Some tribes used the bark as a death shroud.[23] At least one tribe, the Ojibwe, used bark for scrolls.[24] "Birch is not a large tree," write Clifford and Isabel Ahlgren. "It did not dominate the landscape, but its bark provided transportation and shelter for both the Indian and European."[25] A historian writes that the bark was more valuable than the wood: as evidence, the Ojibwe would roll up the bark from their wigwams and move on, leaving the frames behind.[26] Birch bark was used well into the twentieth century; R. M. Patterson reports

flexibility. Sap provided medicine and a low-sugar-content syrup; its bracket fungus, *Fomes fomentarius*, the brittle, feathery material that grows on the bark, is excellent tinder and has various medicinal uses.[19] The chemical compound betulin in the resin contains elements that could be used to treat poison oak, insect bites, and rashes.[20] "This tree has great stay-at-home virtues," notes nature writer John Burroughs. "Let the somber, aspiring, mysterious pine go;

Paul Kane, *White Mud Portage, Saulteaux*, c. 1851–56. Oil on canvas, 47 × 75.2 cm. The Natives are from the White Mud Band of Salteaux. The portage was a short one, less than two-tenths of a mile.

that in 1927 he found birch baskets used to hold berries at an abandoned camp in Canada. The containers were discarded after the harvest—they weren't important enough to pack up and transport to the next stop—"they would make new ones and not bother carrying these."[27]

Geologist Lucius L. Hubbard, writing of a trip to Maine in 1881, uses "birch" as a synonym for canoe throughout his book *Woods and Lakes of Maine*; his admiration for the tree and Native uses of it are captured in a fanciful section:

Should the human race ever come to a "wooden age," and the iron in our axe and knife [be] replaced by birch, for example, we shall see the Indian coursing down streams in his birch canoe, or impelling it over lakes with his birchen paddle; "calling" his moose with a birch-bark horn, shooting him with a birchen arrow, skinning him with a birchen knife, cutting birch logs with a birchen axe, kindling his fire with birch bark, boiling his birch partridge in a birch-bark pail, eating him from a birch-bark plate with a birchen fork, drinking his birch-twig tea from a birch-bark cup, wiping his mouth with a birch-bark napkin, ornamenting his squaw's dress with birch-bark silhouettes, bringing up his pappooses [sic] with a birchen switch, and, finally, going to bed in a birch-bark wigwam by the light of a birch-bark torch. In fact, his whole life will be birchen, from being rocked in a birchen cradle to being buried in a birch forest.[28]

Folk tales varied across tribes, of course, but birch canoes figured into them in many cultures. At Grand Lake Victoria, northwest of Ottawa, in the 1920s, D. S. Davidson collected the story of why it was so hard for the Indians there to find a straight, tall canoe birch:

When the Indians first learned to use birch bark for canoes and utensils, Meso [the Trickster-Culture Hero] foresaw the possibility of the Indians utilizing all the trees in the forest. He was afraid that if the good building bark could be found on every birch tree, the Indians would become extravagant and would not take care of the things they made. He feared the Indians would throw the things away while they were still useful and that they would make no effort to find those which had become lost. . . . All the trees would soon be cut down and that would mean the end of the forest upon which the Indians and the game were

Birch-bark baskets like this Ojibwe example from Grand Portage are used for winnowing wild rice.
*Courtesy of the Minnesota Historical Society, 6935.20.C.2.*

Birch had a number of uses for Native tribes. Two Ojibwe women, Mary Bigwind and Maggie Skinaway, make birch vessels for maple sap, which could be made into syrup, supplying the tribe with its sugar, c. 1930.

*Photograph by Kenneth Melvin Wright. Courtesy of the Minnesota Historical Society, 4995-A.*

dependent for so much. Meso, therefore, climbed into many of the birch trees and swayed them about until their trunks became crooked and twisted. This he did to protect the forest.[29]

Meso, to finish the job, then took a balsam fir switch and slashed the bark of many of the remaining birches, to ruin them for making so much as a box.

What makes the bark useful and versatile? With a sharp knife and a deft touch, it is relatively simple to slice and peel large lengthwise pieces from a tree, as the bark has a longitudinal grain (like most trees) rather than a traverse grain around the trunk. The pieces can be rolled up and thus transported back to camp. The bark shares the tough and flexible qualities of the rest of the tree, owing to a high oil content, and there is no

Eastman Johnson, *Canoe of the Indians*, c. 1856–57. Oil on canvas, 43.2 × 96.5 cm. Johnson spent the summers of 1857 and 1858 around Lake Superior, near his brother's sawmill. His portraits of Native Americans are considered sympathetic and astute, although the perspective and portrayal of the Ojibwe in this canoe (note their faces) has caused some scholars to wonder if the painting was unfinished.

*Permanent Collection of St. Louis County Historical Society, Duluth, Minnesota, 62.181.11.*

ruinous nasty insect or bacteria that renders it useless. (An attack of forest tent caterpillars or gypsy moths can quickly defoliate a birch forest, but these pests don't often kill the trees or affect the bark.) Further, the bark does not shrink or expand when wet. Boats have been weighted with rocks and sunk in the shallows of a lake for winter storage or hiding, sometimes for months, without damage.

As critical as the paper birch was to the tribes, it seems something of a letdown to say that it wasn't the most important tree for most wildlife. An exception is the moose, which browses on it, as does the white-tailed deer, although deer like it less than moose. Rabbits and squirrels may eat seeds or buds, as do birds, but it's not a particularly critical nesting or cover tree. The saplings get nibbled down, which can result in the multi-trunked versions of the tree that seem to be common.

Attaching one piece of birch bark to another on a canoe was usually done with the roots of another common tree, the black spruce, *Picea mariana*. Black spruce often grows near birch, particularly in swampy areas, and its roots are easily dug up and split.[30] The fast-growing roots grow laterally, usually no more than 8 inches below the surface, and can be pulled up from loose soil in single strands several feet long. The roots (*watap* in Ojibwe) are then split and used as a cord-like binding material that stretches slightly when wet and holds fast, shrinking and tightening, while it dries. The ideal spruce root is about "the diameter of a pencil."[31] The spruce tree also supplied its resin, or gum, to be made into a sealant that coated the seams of the boat. Writing of canoes made of the bark, Grace Lee Nute asks: "What other vehicle could have been so constructed, without nails or other substances than what the forests afforded?"[32]

Crafts as short as 8 feet were known; an 18-footer was a common size among many Native tribes. Canoes were built for many purposes by expert craftsmen and women, including speed, stability, and carrying capacity.[33] Speed was important both on the water and on the frequent portages, where ambushes were set up among warring tribes and the boat's light weight was appreciated. "Part of the time it carries us, and part of the time we carry it," reports one French missionary.[34] A British author may be exaggerating only slightly when he writes, "A 12-foot birch, weighing only 20 pounds or less, may be taken across a portage by simply

The Cree were excellent birch-bark builders, as seen in this boat dating from the period 1875–1900. The boats of the Western Cree, who tended to occupy the region that is now parts of Ontario and Manitoba as well as sections of Alberta and Saskatchewan, resembled the design of their neighbors, the Ojibwe. Birch bark was scarcer farther west, so spruce was sometimes a replacement material, according to Edwin Tappan Adney.
*Courtesy of the Mariners' Museum, Newport News, Virginia.*

thrusting the arm beneath the middle thwart and carrying it as a woman would carry a market basket."[35]

Stability was a requirement in a variety of circumstances, including on tricky rapids and when high winds swept across large, shallow lakes. When the French came,

Black spruce trees, from which roots were grubbed and made into sewing materials, are plentiful in northern and northeastern forests near birch trees. The roots often run for several feet in all directions and are not deeply grounded in the soil, which makes them easy to dig.   *Photograph by Ed Nater.*

longer and longer boats with more capacity came into style, particularly for trade goods; the colonial government limited the number of canoes in its hired fleet, causing the fur traders and their partners to bump up the size of the ones they launched.

The bark of other trees was sometimes used but often found wanting. The Iroquois favored elm, probably the second-best choice, and hickory, cedar, and spruce bark boats were not unknown, especially for short-term use. These pieces of bark tended to be smaller than birch, however, which meant more seams on the canoe, which meant more leaks. Other barks were not as flexible, either.

## ꙍ Elm-Bark Canoes

Not all aboriginal bark canoes were made of paper birch. Elm bark may have been the second-most-used wood, but it was not as useful as birch for a number of reasons, mostly because of questions of workability and availability.

The Iroquois made elm-bark canoes, but those boats were considered inferior to birch in every way. Early references to bark canoes noted the differences; in fact, Samuel de Champlain misidentified the Iroquois canoes as made of oak in the battle on the lake that would carry his name. The baron de Lahontan, one of La Salle's officers, was less than charitable in his descriptions of the elm boats of the Iroquois in 1684, calling them heavy, slow, crude, and poorly designed.[1] The baron did not fear pursuit by the fleet of elm canoes on open water.

Louis-Armand de Lom d'Arce, baron de Lahontan, drew this description of the elm-bark canoes of the Iroquois for a three-volume memoir of his time in New France, which ended in 1693. In addition to discussing canoes, portaging, and paddles, Lahontan's work is a valuable source on flora, fauna, ethnography, and trade in the colony. Elm-bark canoes were considered inferior to the birch-bark models, but elm was the building material most available to the Iroquois.

*Courtesy of the James Ford Bell Library, University of Minnesota.*

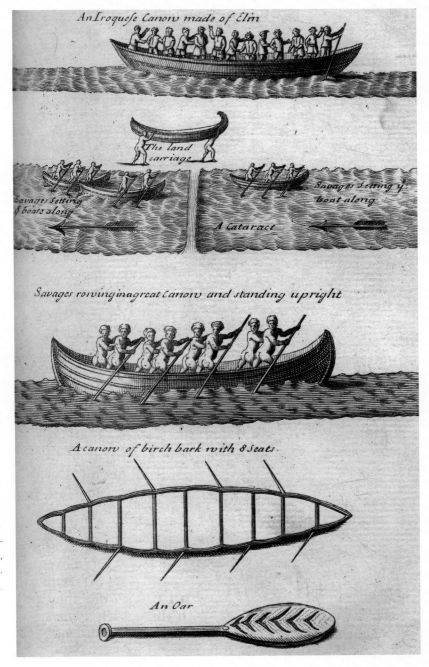

Birch bark was not as abundant for the Iroquois in their home territory. To be fair to the Iroquois, the tribe's craftsmen did not build elm canoes for hostile actions; the Iroquois preferred to make war in the winter, on snowshoes, and used the elm boats for ferry service, only to quickly discard them. Elm canoes were not built for the long haul. On home waters, the Iroquois used dugout canoes as more permanent vehicles, and more than one commentator praised the boat-handling abilities of the tribe despite the poor equipment.[2]

The Iroquois used dugouts on larger lakes where the boats did not need to be portaged.

Adney and Chapelle report that other barks were used, listing spruce, chestnut, hickory, basswood, and cottonwood (spruce being more common in the higher latitudes).[3] These woods required different types of construction, including scraping rough surfaces to make the material thinner and more flexible, and none had the resin contained in paper birch trees that made the latter so useful. Nonetheless, one chronicler from the mid-nineteenth century witnessed a spruce canoe built in two days in the Adirondacks.[4]

The canoe historians note that no elm canoes from the Iroquois period have survived, so any detailed description of how the boats differed from birch craft is speculation. Only the comments of travelers and military officers such as Lahontan remain to offer clues. It appears that white elm was preferred, with red elm also being used. And it was not only Iroquois who used elm bark— a mid-nineteenth-century traveler noted "Chippewas on the River Maitland, Ontario," near Lake Huron, using elm-bark boats for hunting and the fur and syrup trade.[5]

As a canoe material, elm bark was distinctly different from birch, as evidenced by this example built by Rick Nash. Elm canoes tended to be less durable, less flexible, and unsightly. The Iroquois are often associated with elm canoes because of the availability of that species in their home territory.

*Photograph by Evan Holt. Courtesy of the Canadian Canoe Museum.*

## CONSTRUCTING THE CANOE

The individual master canoe makers among the pre–white settlement tribes are lost to history, along with their canoes. It is possible that the Indians of the Old Copper Culture (roughly 4000–1000 BC) around the Great Lakes used birch bark in their boats; certainly, "in a land where to travel at all was to travel by water,"[36] they used boats to reach some islands in the summer, where evidence of their occupation has been found. Perhaps they used dugouts, but no record of any boat exists, although tools needed to make a watercraft—whether birch-bark or dugout or raft—such as awls, knives, adzes, and gouges have been discovered. Settlement patterns of the region around the Upper Midwest and Canada from as long ago as 7000 BC illustrate the Natives' use of and reliance on rivers, lakes, and streams. Observers by the seventeenth century note that fish was a "principal means of subsistence," as well as geese and ducks in the fall and spring.[37]

Until white authors such as Henry Wadsworth Longfellow and his fictional Hiawatha emerged in the nineteenth century, the lack of a written language among the tribes meant that stories of individual Indians and their canoes were less documented; Native societies often tended to emphasize the community over the individual anyway. Aided by a small but intense reinvigoration of the tradition among tribes in the

Setting a frame for a bark canoe involved preparing the ground, driving in stakes, sliding in the bark, and attaching a frame in the general shape of the boat. This photograph was taken c. 1895 at an Ojibwe camp.

*Photograph by T. W. Ingersoll. Courtesy of the Minnesota Historical Society, E97.35 p19.*

mid- and late twentieth century, enough of the methods and techniques of building a birch-bark canoe were passed along through the oral tradition to allow a faithful consideration of how they were put together. An example of that work came from William Commanda (1913–2011),

Splitting the bark from a downed tree took a light touch and patience. A sharp knife or axe was used to make a vertical cut, and the bark was carefully peeled away around the trunk. *Photograph by George L. Waite, 1927. Courtesy of the Wisconsin Historical Society, WHS-41464.*

ing of the traditional way of life of Native peoples. When he died, nearly all of the obituaries made note of his role as a master teacher. Commanda, who met the Dalai Lama and Nelson Mandela, "was the one former prime minister Pierre Trudeau turned to when he wanted his canoe repaired," said a Toronto newspaper.[38]

The original Native materials and designs were so fully functional that, more than two hundred years after their first contact with Cartier and the French strangers, the aborigines' birch-bark canoe remained unchanged.[39] It is not much of an overstatement to say that "Europeans contributed nothing to its design or function."[40] By the mid-1700s, when French boatbuilders in Canada were organized and at work, they used Native craftsmen and even situated their shops near Indian settlements to take advantage of skilled labor nearby.[41]

Birch-bark canoes are a shell construction, in that the frame of the boat is cut to fit the skin; skeleton construction is the other main method, in which the frame is made first and then wrapped with the shell, which is usually made of planking but sometimes made of skin.[42] One of the reasons the Europeans took note of the canoe building of the Indians is that their own ships had been built using both skeleton and shell construction for a number of generations, but they had not built canoes.

Entire families participated in the making of canoes, which began with the collection of the bark in the spring or early summer when the sap flowed and the bark was simpler to remove.[43] When builders chose to add artwork to the hull, winter bark was easier to etch and often dif-

an Algonquin elder from Quebec. Commanda was a highly respected leader who among other honors was made an Officer of the Order of Canada. The passing of his knowledge of the building of birch-bark canoes was of a piece with his experience as a trapper and guide and his understand-

ferent in color. The process might start with the scouting of a suitable tree in the late winter, before the ice was out and the trees sprouted buds. Henry David Thoreau, on an 1857 trip to Maine, described the largest canoe birch that he found as 14½ inches in circumference at 2 feet off the ground, a size small enough to indicate that single birch trees large enough for canoe building had been cleaned out of the area of his travels.[44]

The trees were often, though not always, cut down to get at the bark. Doubtless some had already been toppled by a windstorm. Prior to the introduction of European iron tools, one method for felling a large birch was to burn near the base of the tree to assist in the chopping. A ring of mud was plastered around the tree to prevent the fire from spreading up the trunk and damaging the valuable bark. In some places, where the thin soil was peppered with granite and basalt and the roots were shallow, it was possible to push a tree over.

Two logs were often placed on the ground where the tree would land, outside of the usable bark portion, with some brush or bushes as a cushion to keep the birch from smashing into a sharp object on the ground and spoiling the bark. The builders removing the bark could also reach all the way around the tree if it were propped slightly off the ground. Bark could be removed from a standing tree, and it did not always kill the tree to take the bark in this way, but the challenge was to skin the bark while 20 feet

above ground and lower it gently. (The lower couple of feet of bark were usually too soggy to use.) "The hard part is getting it from the tree to the ground without tearing it," Wisconsin builder Ferdy Goode says.[45]

The ideal tree was straight and tall, with no branches on its lower portion to create knots, the bane of all woodworkers. Care was taken to examine the lenticels (the

Native builders would roll the stripped birch bark into a backpack of sorts, secure it with roots, and carry it back to the canoe-making camp. The individual with the pack is identified as Cheemaun, of an Ojibwe tribe in Wisconsin, in 1927. *Photograph by George L. Waite. Courtesy of the Wisconsin Historical Society, WHS-41465.*

Edwin Tappan Adney took this photograph of Walter Soulier splitting a spruce root for use in binding birch bark in Ontario in 1930. Note the resting axe and folding knife stuck into the log on Soulier's right. The best spruce root was the diameter of a pencil, which was divided into two for sewing.

*Copyright McCord Museum of Canadian History, MP-0000.2141.2.*

girdled the ends and a long vertical slice began its removal. Knives made from antlers or bones were used to spread the bark gently back from the inner ring of cambium (the growth layer), taking care not to poke a hole through it.

Once removed from the tree, the bark was rolled up inside out, tied, and toted back to camp. Usually it was placed in water to keep it moist and flexible. As the really large birch trees became harder to find during the later years of the voyageurs, the making of a canoe from a single tree became more rare. Additional pieces of bark became necessary even for two-person boats, and several pieces might be needed for war or freight canoes that could reach 35 feet or longer. A trade in bark no doubt existed, especially when the larger trees became harder to find.

While the men were away cutting bark, women and children usually had the job of collecting spruce roots. Grubbing in the loose soil under a spruce tree, the worker discovered a root and followed it as far as possible before it got too thin (or thick) to use. Often the roots, which could also be harvested from tamarack, white spruce, jack pine, or basswood, needed to be untangled from each other or another tree, and the job could take

watertight eyes of the bark), as well as the bark's thickness and flexibility. Lengths of an ideal piece of bark ranged from 14 to 18 feet for a versatile-sized canoe, with a tree circumference of 36 to 48 inches. After the birch was dropped, three cuts were made through the bark: two

several hours. The roots were cleaned, stripped of bark, split into two pieces, and then coiled into a hoop that was wrapped and kept moist until needed.

One other vital product for bark canoe construction was the gum of the spruce tree. Spruces secrete gum when the bark is cut; the gum hardens when dry and makes a fine natural adhesive. The gum was simply scraped off the tree, or gashes were made in the tree to produce the gum; it was stored in a birch box, where it could be saved to be heated, mixed with animal fat (to keep it flexible) and charcoal (to help it set), and used as a seam-sealer. The black stripes along the sides of the canoes are created with this sealant. David Gidmark, who learned canoe building by liv-

ing among the Algonquin, notes that pieces of spruce gum could be carried and chewed into a usable wad to patch a hole in an emergency.[46] Goode uses a secret recipe of deer tallow and/or bear grease for his adhesive.[47]

Ribs and planking were often carved with a crooked knife out of white cedar, which grows readily in the north woods, is easy to work with, and is rot resistant. If white cedar wasn't available, other light softwoods such as spruce could be used. Thwarts could be made of a harder wood— ash, maple, or birch—partly because they were carved and not steamed and bent. A steady supply of firewood was also important throughout the building process. Hot water, to make steam for bending boards and keeping the materials moist, and hot coals, for keeping gum soft, were necessary. Rocks were needed for weight. Tools were typically flint knives, bone needles, awls, and drills. Metal tools (and metal nails to replace spruce lashings) came with Europeans in the mid-1500s and sped up the building, but the basic canoe design did not change.

In this 1959 photograph, balsam fir pitch is cooked with ashes as a sealant in bark canoes. By the mid-twentieth century, Native builders were working to pass on their knowledge before skills were lost.

*Photograph by Monroe P. Killy. Courtesy of the Minnesota Historical Society, AV1988.49.229.*

A tray or a pouch made of birch bark was used to carry hardened pieces of specially prepared spruce gum (sap mixed with animal fat and ash), which could be chewed or heated to repair canoes during a trip.

*Courtesy of the Minnesota Historical Society, 1981.70.11.A-I.*

## ❧ The Oldest Birch-Bark Canoe

British soldier John Enys may seem an unlikely character to hold an important place in the history of canoes. The Eton-educated Enys fought with the 29th Regiment of Foot against the colonists in the American War of Independence; his unit fortified the besieged Quebec City and drove the rebels back to Montreal, where British General Guy Carleton's forces defeated them at the Battle of Trois-Rivières in June 1776.[1] When the light infantry company of the 29th was nearly wiped out in October 1777 at Saratoga, Enys was promoted to lieutenant; he eventually made captain before the war ended.

British Army Lieutenant Colonel John Enys.

Enys was called back into active service in 1784 and spent the better part of the next four years garrisoned in Canada and traveling in the United States. An avid fisherman, he sought trout and salmon in the Great Lakes region. When war broke out with France, Enys saw action in several European theaters, retiring as a lieutenant colonel in 1800 after twenty-five years of service. He died in Bath in 1818 at age sixty.

Either in his travels in America or after he returned to England, Enys obtained a birch-bark canoe; it may have been a gift from his regiment. That boat was shipped to England. The canoe, found on the family estate in Cornwall, is one of the oldest-known surviving birch-bark canoes.[2]

The exact origins of the craft are a mystery. A curator at the Canadian Canoe Museum, Jeremy Ward, measured the craft at 20 feet long and dated it between 1776 and 1780. The canoe was in tough shape when it was found in a stone shed. Experts say its style is Malecite or Abenaki, both members of the Wabanaki Confederacy, and probably from what is now the Maritime Provinces of Canada. Ward says the boat shows influence of Malecite and also Beothuk builders.[3] American builder

Curator Jeremy Ward (left) of the Canadian Canoe Museum examines the Enys birch-bark canoe with executive director James Raffan (right) and Curve Lake elder Doug Williams (center). The canoe, discovered in England, dates from the late 1700s and is perhaps the oldest surviving example of birch-bark canoes in existence. *Photograph by Clifford Skarstedt. Reprinted with the express permission of the Peterborough Examiner, a division of Postmedia Network, Inc.*

The Penobscot Canoe, held by the Peabody Essex Museum, is one of the oldest birchbarks in existence and the oldest canoe in one piece. The canoe first appears in the museum's records as being donated in 1826; it was restored in 1947. The boat is slightly more than 19½ feet long with a 37-inch beam and, in the estimation of the museum, was made from the bark of a single birch tree.   *Photograph by Mark Sexton. Copyright 2006 Peabody Essex Museum.*

Henri Vaillancourt examined the craft in 2011 and writes that it was "characterized by a rather high, peaked and undercut bow and stern."[4]

Other clues came from the gunwales, the bark cover, and the pronounced rocker. The thwarts are missing, so precise measurements of the hull were problematic, but the canoe has a fair amount of tumblehome, a beam somewhere between 32 and 35 inches, and a depth of 13 or 14 inches. The boat's skin came almost entirely from a single sheet of bark, but the cedar frame was knotty, perhaps indicating a shortage of cedar at its building site, according to Vaillancourt.

In a journal of his experiences, Enys recorded meeting a fleet of canoes paddling under birch-bark torches on Lake Ontario in 1787. "Curiosity prompting us to see what they were, we soon got up to them and found that they were all Indian Canoes fishing, each containing a man and a woman and some of them a child or two."[5]

The Enys family donated the canoe to the Canadian Canoe Museum in Peterborough, Ontario.

The Peabody Essex Museum in Salem, Massachusetts, holds a birch-bark canoe that is probably from the era of the Enys canoe. The Penobscot Canoe, as it is called, first appears in the museum's records as a gift from the East India Marine Society in 1826. Measuring 19 feet, 7¾ inches long with a beam of 37 inches, it is in better shape than the Enys boat. A 1948 article on the canoe says it "appears to have been in use for some time . . . and was constructed similar to other canoes from the same and adjacent regions."[6] At that time, it was considered the oldest surviving birch-bark canoe, but the Enys canoe is probably older.

Not many other examples of pre-twentieth-century canoes exist: a Malecite birch-bark canoe of similar length, dated 1824, was found in an Irish university collection in 2001.[7]

As the bark rolls were brought to camp, which was often near a shoreline (but not in sand—the stakes wouldn't hold), an area was cleared for the construction site, or bed. Sharp objects were brushed aside or grubbed out, and the ground was raked as flat as possible. The soil needed to be

A crooked knife was an essential tool in the shaping of ribs, sheathing, thwarts, and other parts of the canoe. The knife had a curved handle and was usually drawn toward the holder, slicing off thin shavings of soft cedar and other woods. *Courtesy of the Canadian Canoe Museum.*

deep enough to drive stakes. The sheet of bark was placed on the ground, with the outer bark facing up, so that the inner bark of the tree would become the outside of the canoe. (Fake birch-bark canoes or models often get this detail wrong, showing the white outer bark of the tree on the outside of the canoe.) If the tribe designed canoes with highly raised bows and sterns, more dirt was piled up underneath the ends.

Two pieces of cedar or spruce about as long as the planned canoe and 1½ inches square were lashed together at each end to form an outline of a gunwale. The pieces were spread apart and held with temporary thwarts and then carefully laid on the bark. Hundreds of pounds of rocks were used to hold the frame in place. From a top view, it looked like the outline of a canoe.

A series of tapering gores were sliced into the bark to help it bend up around the gunwale frame, and 3- or 4-foot-long stakes were driven into the ground next to the skin to hold it so it looked, in essence, like a birch envelope. Battens could be run lengthwise across the stakes to help support the bark. Spruce roots were used to sew the bark ends together at the bow and stern. In most boats, a single piece of bark was not large enough to reach the height of the gunwale at the center of the craft, so an additional panel was sewn lengthwise on each side.

The rocks were tossed aside and the frame raised to inner gunwale level. An outer gunwale, of the same material, was carved and fitted to sandwich the bark between the two. All three were stitched together with spruce root. The stakes were then also tossed aside, and the basic

# CONSTRUCTING THE BIRCH-BARK CANOE

*Drawings by Edwin Tappan Adney. Courtesy of the Mariners' Museum, Newport News, Virginia.*

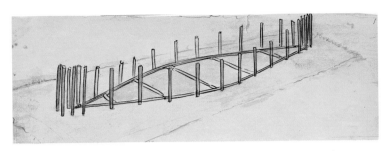

1. Stakes are planted in the general shape of the canoe; a frame in the shape of the gunwale is dropped in, with temporary thwarts attached.

2. A sheet of bark is placed on the ground; the frame is set on it and weighted with rocks; the stakes are temporarily moved aside.

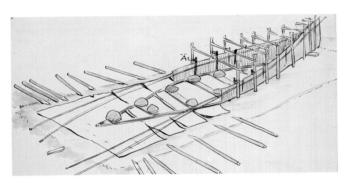

3. The stakes are put back and the bark is shaped inside them. Note that the stakes are now tied at their tops. Long battens are used to strengthen the frame.

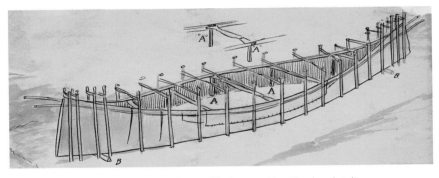

4. The bark is in place and the gunwale frame is lifted into position. The sheer height is shown in cutaway (A). Blocks (B) are placed under the ends to provide the rocker.

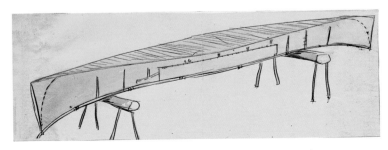

5. Shaping the ends and sewing is done upside down, on sawhorses.

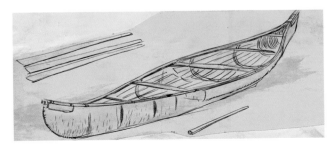

6. Sheathing and ribs are added to give the canoe its final shape.

outline of the canoe was finished. "They [the canoes] were made in the form of a new moon," wrote explorer John Guy from Newfoundland in 1612.[48]

Bow and stern pieces were carved, steamed (or hot water was poured on them), and bent into shape. One of the ways to distinguish the canoes of various tribes was by the outline of the stems in height, construction, and curvature. These were sewn into place, and the bark was trimmed flush. Thwarts were carved and fitted across the beam of the boat, sometimes with a mortise and tenon connection, and the canoe was prepared for planking and ribs.

Cedar planks, as thin as the maker could split and shave them, were installed lengthwise along the bilge and up the sides. These could be most often overlapped slightly or butted edge to edge. The ribs, generally 5 feet long, 2 or 2½ inches wide, and roughly ¼-inch thick, were cut, steamed, and bent over the builder's knee. The rib ends that met each gunwale were trimmed and snugged into place, held

In 1939, Ojibwe tribal members at Grand Portage, Minnesota, near the border between the United States and Canada on Lake Superior, completed a birch-bark canoe in the traditional manner as part of a Works Progress Administration arts program. Here a headboard is installed.

*Courtesy of the Minnesota Historical Society, E97.35 r20.*

by the tension of their curves. The rib-plank design also caused tension on the bark, molding it into its final shape. In later periods, a cap was fitted over the gunwales to protect the spruce root stitching. Some builders did not sand smooth:[49] "I wouldn't want to do that because that would take away all my handmade knife marks," Goode says. "They belong on a birch canoe."[50]

Spruce gum was heated in a basket with holes in it, like a strainer, so the gum could be separated from any bits of bark and dirt. When melted, the gum floated out of the box and was strained off. Animal fat and charcoal were added and the gum was worked into place with a dull knife, spud, or by hand along the seams. The twentieth-century wilderness writer and adventurer Calvin Rutstrum estimates that the formula for a successful adhesive was "six part resins from cone-bearing trees, one part of animal fat, and pulverized charcoal."[51]

The canoe was then slid into the water and tested for

Chippewa Indian kneeling in canoe, c. 1914. Native American canoes typically did not have seats, so paddlers knelt, leaned against a thwart, or sat on their heels. *Courtesy of the Minnesota Historical Society, E97.35 r53.*

leaks. If any were found, the boat was returned to camp, flipped over, and resealed. Because the inner bark of the birch varied in color, the canoes ranged from a dark brown to a light tan and often changed color with use and exposure to the elements. Tribes would often carve or paint distinct figures or symbols on the hulls.

Most traditional Indian canoes did not have seats; they were paddled from a kneeling position, the paddlers sitting on their heels, the inside of their feet, or leaning against a thwart. Paddles were carved from a single piece of hardwood, and each tribe had a distinctive shape of the blade or handle, depending on its needs or artistic vision.

The alert reader will note that no mention has been made of a keel, for the Indian boats typically had none

(Beothuk canoes being one exception).[52] The boats may have seemed a bit tippy to the Frenchmen and the rest of the adventurers who encountered rugged weather for the first time in them. The craft's lack of secondary stability was not what they were used to in their heavy, plank-on-frame European boats. "[L]ike everything wild, [canoes] are timid and treacherous under the guidance of a white man; and, if he not be an equilibrist, he is sure to get two or three times soused, in his first endeavors acquainted with them," writes the artist George Catlin.[53] The birchbarks were remarkably buoyant—more than one writer called them a leaf skittering across the water.

### AN INDISPENSABLE TOOL, AND A BOOK

The canoe was essential to the Native way of life in the northern forests. There were few roads—as Europeans understood them anyway—and for the half-year or so of ice-free waters, boats were needed to move any distance at all. Indian encampments were located next to rivers and lakes for food as well as for transportation. Methodist missionary Egerton Ryerson Young, working in the Hudson Bay region in the nineteenth century, writes: "It is to the Indian denizen here what the horse is to his more warlike red brother on the great prairies, or what the camel is to those who live and wander through Arabian deserts."[54] With the Natives' use of snowshoes, the rivers and lakes were also thoroughfares during the winter.

Basic transportation, hunting, fishing, gathering wild rice, and making war were common uses of the canoe. Pi-loting and skill with the paddle or pole were not gender-specific; women and children bent to the task of propelling their boats as often as men did. "The squaws are very expert in the management of canoes," writes Catherine Parr Strickland Traill, the wife of a government functionary, in 1836, "and preserve their balance with admirable skill, standing up while they impel the little bark with great velocity through the water."[55]

An early and critical resource about the birch-bark canoes comes from an American who spent most of his life in Canada. Edwin Tappan Adney, born in Ohio in 1868, had been trained as an artist when he went to Canada in 1887 on what was intended to be a brief trip. He met Peter Joe, a Malecite, in New Brunswick and started a career as an artist-journalist-ethnographer-collector. The two built a birch-bark canoe, with Adney recording each step, and he published the results in *Harper's Young People* magazine in 1890. That article and a story printed in *Outing* in 1900 form the earliest complete written descriptions of the construction of the craft.[56]

What may have begun as a hobby for Adney became, by 1925, much more than that. Adney spent almost the entire rest of his life among the Indians, building models, drawing plans and sketches, interviewing, and collecting canoes until his death in 1950. He became a consultant to the museum of McGill University and began building models of each type of tribal canoe. Financial and personal problems dogged him throughout his life; he returned to the United States in the 1930s and continued his work, depositing more than one hundred models and reams of

Seth Eastman, *Rice Gatherers*, 1867. Oil on canvas, 80.6 × 103.5 cm. This painting of Ojibwe women harvesting wild rice was one in a series commissioned for the U.S. House of Representatives Committee on Indian Affairs.

*Collection of the U.S. House of Representatives, 2004.040.008.*

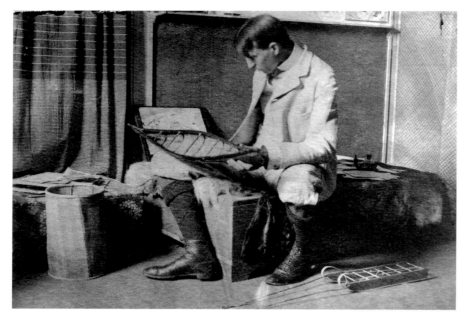

Edwin Tappan Adney, an expert on bark canoes, studies one of his models in 1896.
*Courtesy of the Carleton County Historical Society, Woodstock, New Brunswick.*

*and Skin Boats of North America.* The book has been a rich and essential resource for everyone from scholars of Native American culture to canoe builders and collectors.

Among the conclusions reached by Adney was that differences in canoe design, tools, and materials were based not only on the resources and transportation needs of individual tribes but also on artistic and stylistic touches. "The distinctive feature that usually identifies the tribal classification of a bark canoe is the profile of the ends, although sometimes the profile of the gunwale, or sheer, and even of the bottom, is also involved," write the authors.[57] A low bow profile, for example, often meant the canoe was used in open water because it would catch less wind than a high-bowed boat and would thus be easier to handle. A high bow profile might mean that the canoe was used on a fast river with many rapids, where water could be deflected from shipping over the bow. Even with these practical considerations, the authors note, tribal builders may have retained distinctive shapes or features whether they were fully functional or not.

papers into the Mariners' Museum in Newport News, Virginia, when it became apparent to him that Canadian authorities were not sufficiently interested in his work. His son donated the remaining papers pertaining to bark canoes after his death.

After Adney's passing, Howard I. Chapelle, curator of transportation at the Smithsonian Museum, was given the task of wading through the mountain of paper and canoe parts Adney left behind, producing the definitive published work on the Native crafts in 1964, *The Bark Canoes*

## THE PASSING OF AN ERA

If Cartier was the first European to describe the birch-bark canoe, Samuel de Champlain was the explorer and adventurer most responsible for its wholesale adoption by the French colonizers. Tramping around the St. Lawrence

This row of Têtes de Boule canoes was photographed by Edwin Tappan Adney in the early 1900s.
Adney considered the larger fur trade canoes built by the Têtes de Boule to be of the highest quality, and the tribe
was employed by the Hudson's Bay Company for that purpose. These boats are smaller, possibly hunters' canoes.

*Courtesy of the Mariners' Museum, Newport News, Virginia.*

The crooked canoe was built to turn quickly and handle the sharp bends and dangerous rapids of major river systems. What was gained in maneuverability was lost in carrying capacity; these canoes were not meant to haul a substantial load. The pronounced fore-and-aft rocker design, often associated with the Cree, could rise as much as several inches from midship to the ends.

*Courtesy of the National Anthropological Archives, Smithsonian Institution, GN 7007.*

region in the late 1500s, Champlain realized that, for both trade and exploration, the canoe would work as well for the French as it did for the Indians, although, in his words, the craft is "no small labor to those not used to it."[58] To keep King Henri IV's interest in New France, as the St. Lawrence region was called, arrangements were made for a number of New World gifts for the monarch in 1605. The most striking: a 30-foot birch-bark canoe, stained a bright red.[59] The fur-trading era was ushered in on the gunwales of the Native birch-bark canoe.

≺ Forest rangers needed canoes to travel on the frontier just as Natives, trappers, and explorers did. These rangers at Outlet Bay, Lake Temagami, in northeastern Ontario, are relaxing and doing a bit of boat repair in 1895. A forest reserve was established in the region in 1901.

*Courtesy of Exporail, the Canadian Railway Museum, Canadian Pacific Railway Fonds, NS1178.*

CHAPTER 3

# The Fur Trade

*I*N 1636, **A LARGE GROUP** of Huron leaders traveled to the banks of the St. Lawrence River at Trois-Rivières in what is now Quebec on their annual summer trip to trade and socialize. Likely led by a headman named Aenons, the Hurons were in a particularly mournful mood that spring because two important people were not with them. One was the Huron leader Amantacha, who was lost and presumed captured, tortured, and killed during a raid against the Iroquois. Second, their great ally, trading partner, and

friend Samuel de Champlain had died the previous winter on December 25. At Trois-Rivières, the Huron gave their French partners a series of gifts in Champlain's memory, "presents to cause our French to dry their tears and more easily swallow the bitterness they experienced."[1]

The Hurons weren't the only tribe to praise the French explorer and statesman, now remembered as the Father of New France. The Algonquin, Micmac, Montagnais, and even the Sac and Fox in the Mississippi Valley passed on stories about the man they called the "chief of the French."[2]

In a long and distinguished career, Samuel de Champlain (1574–1635) was perhaps the European most responsible for the acceptance and use of the canoe by white settlers as the principal means of transportation for the fur trade in the New World. From the time of his first visit to

◄ Frances Anne Hopkins, *The Red River Expedition at Kakabeka Falls,* 1877. Oil on canvas, 91.4 × 152.4 cm. This painting was completed seven years after the Red River Rebellion was put down by British officer Garnet Wolseley. Louis Riel, leader of the Métis provisional government, successfully negotiated the colony's entrance into the Canadian Confederation as Manitoba, but Wolseley's soldiers forced him to flee to the United States.   *Courtesy of the Frances Anne Hopkins fonds, Library and Archives of Canada, R5666-0-8-E.*

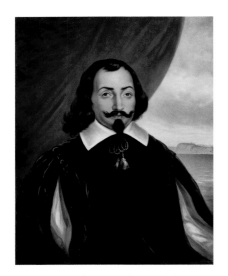

Théophile Hamel, *Portrait de Samuel de Champlain*, 1870. Oil on canvas, 66 × 86 cm. Hamel's work, painted 235 years after Champlain's death, is a guess as to what his subject looked like. No known portrait of Champlain from his lifetime exists.

*Copyright House of Commons Collection, Ottawa.*

the St. Lawrence region in 1603, Champlain, eventually chief administrator of the colony and the founder of Quebec and two other successful settlements, realized the critical importance to be played by canoes in the commercial foundation of New France's economic survival. Not until the British gained long-term control of Canada some 150 years later did the canoe begin to be replaced, slowly, with European-designed boats, and then only on the larger bodies of water.

Champlain is closely identified with the second wave of European fur trading in the New World. Commerce between Europeans and the Natives had been going on for decades before he arrived in 1603, mostly along the Atlantic coast and the St. Lawrence River. And the locals, of course, had been trading among themselves for centuries. But at least two critical differences existed between Champlain's era and the one that preceded it.

First, in the period following French explorer Jacques Cartier's visits, Indians held the job of trapping and transporting beaver, mink, marten, and other furbearers from the interior of the continent to waiting French ships. Tribes such as the Montagnais, Nipissing, Algonquin, and Huron served as middlemen, buying furs from farther north or inland and reselling them to the French. The Natives were in charge of labor, wholesaling, and distribution. Upon the European acceptance of the canoe, French-Canadian traders eventually replaced the tribes as middlemen, traveling to the source to buy furs directly from the Indian trappers.

Second, and certainly related to the first: attempts at permanent settlements by Cartier and others had failed, often spectacularly (Cartier's interest was not in the fur trade, but in finding a route to China). The French companies that held fur-trading rights thus relied on Indians to collect and deliver products. Furs were moved into the holds of waiting sailing ships anchored in the most convenient harbor. The ships then returned to Europe before winter weather made the Atlantic crossing problematic. Champlain's permanent settlements organized and stabilized the system by establishing regular locations for trading and for the longer-term storage of furs and trade goods.

Champlain and his contemporaries also took a different approach to their relationships with the Indians. Instead of capturing and enslaving the local population, as the Spanish had done in Mexico, or driving them inland, as the British did in New England, the early-seventeenth-century French explorers led by Champlain began a partnership based on trade carried in tribal canoes. Both sides benefited economically.

In the course of his thirty-year career, Champlain wrote frequently and extensively on canoes; he traveled thousands of miles in crafts of all sizes in the inland waters. His writings contain detailed descriptions of their construction and use, beginning with his first trip to the Caribbean in 1599, where he saw the dugouts of the island people near the coast of South America. There he took note of some three hundred canoes carrying slaves who were forced to dive for pearls and mussels. The mistreatment of the Caribbean slaves stuck in Champlain's memory, and he was generally well liked for his respect of and admiration for the Native tribes in New France.

Champlain and his party first landed in the northeastern part of the North American continent in what is now Canada at Tadoussac, where they encountered what he estimated as one thousand Indians, many of them Montagnais, and two hundred canoes celebrating a coalition victory over the Iroquois. He quickly noted that the canoes could outrun his well-manned shallop, a light sailboat used as a tender. "Two do only the work of propelling the boat, a man and a woman. Their canoes are some 8 or 9 feet long, and a foot or a foot and a half broad in the middle, growing narrower towards the two ends," he wrote.[3]

As he made his way inland, Champlain's encounters with dangerous rapids near present-day Montreal and in the larger tributaries of the St. Lawrence quickly convinced

George Henry Millar, *A View of the Pearl-Fishery*, c. 1785. Copper etching, from John Hamilton Moore, *A New and Complete Collection of Voyages and Travels*. French explorers witnessed the pearl-diving industry in the Caribbean, where the newcomers got a glimpse of the Native dugouts used in the activity.

*Courtesy of the John Carter Brown Library at Brown University.*

George Agnew Reid, *The Arrival of Champlain at Quebec,* 1909. Pastel on wove paper, 62 × 43 cm. Artists worked from written accounts describing the moment of contact with Native tribes and Champlain's ship. This study for an oil painting used Champlain's images of the Natives and their crafts. Reid, noted for historic works such as this, was president of the Royal Canadian Academy of Arts and a longtime proponent of the arts in Canada.

*Courtesy of the George Agnew Reid fonds, Library and Archives of Canada, R11283-0-7-E.*

him of the value of the canoe as being fast, light, and maneuverable yet capable of carrying freight. He made his first mention of a ride in a canoe near Verchères,[4] where his party explored the small islands filled with fruit trees and bushes on the southern shore. Later, his party tried to navigate rapids in their skiff but repeatedly became stuck, while the canoes shot through the whitewater easily.[5]

At the head of navigation on the St. Lawrence, which Champlain eventually named the Lachine Rapids, the only way past was to walk around. A skiff was too heavy, so "any one desiring to pass them should provide himself with the canoe . . . which a man can easily carry." His own boats, Champlain wrote, were unfit for the journey. "But in the canoes . . . one can go without restraint, and quickly, everywhere, in the small as well as the large rivers. So that, by using canoes . . . it would be possible to see all there is, good and bad, in a year or two."[6] Many Frenchmen who came later confirmed Champlain's analysis of the utility of the canoe. The Reverend Paul Le Jeune, a Jesuit, lived for many years among the tribes along the St. Lawrence. On a trip to meet the Hurons, his small birchbark encountered high winds, and "as I have already found, by experience, . . . our Ships are not as safe or as swift, if the wind is not fair, as the little Bark canoes of the Savages."[7]

Of the birch-bark canoes themselves, Champlain wrote: "They are very liable to turn over if one does not understand how to manage them, for they are made of the bark of trees called *bouille,* strengthened inside by little ribs of wood strongly and neatly made."[8] At the hands of skilled craftsmen, bark canoes were relatively fast, cheap to construct, and easy to repair. On the other hand, the dugouts of Native construction that he found farther south near what is now Massachusetts were "very liable to upset unless one is very skilled."[9]

## A FUR-TRADE ECONOMY

Champlain realized that it was not enough simply to trade with the Indians, as his predecessors had done; instead it was necessary to engage in a full partnership by what his biographer David Hackett Fischer calls "combining the economies of two cultures."[10] His permanent settlements were not mere trading posts but *colonies commerciale,* established for long-term and two-way commerce with France based on mutual interests.

It was not a get-rich-quick plan. The scholar Harold Adams Innis, in his landmark work on the Canadian fur trade, concludes that the economy of New France grew slowly because the fur-fish industries were so steadily profitable for two hundred years; investments that might have been made elsewhere (and grown more quickly) were funneled into the fur trade, which had a smaller short-term yield but greater long-term results.[11]

While the French were struggling with the establishment of an efficient trading system in what is now Canada, the English attempted to take advantage of the fur markets farther south. Settlements at Jamestown and Plymouth were founded in part on a model that financed them with animal skins shipped to British markets. And in the geographic middle, along the Hudson River, the Dutch were

Samuel de Champlain, *Map of New France*, 1632. This last, great map that Champlain produced summarized the locations of most of his travels. He later revised it by adding a mountain range near Cape Breton.

*Courtesy of the General Map Collection, Library and Archives of Canada, 4153517.*

busy figuring out how to meet their own economic goals. Eventually the British would shift to a market system more heavily dependent on tobacco than fur, but the French continued to chase after animal skins in canoes for several generations. By the eighteenth century, Shelagh Grant writes, the French were actually operating the fur business at a loss, but they were keeping up trade and good economic relations with the tribes in order to keep the British hemmed in to the south.[12]

In Europe, the wearing of fur had long been a symbol of the upper classes.[13] One scholar of French dress notes that "Versailles was an insatiable system of conspicuous consumption, on which thousands of livelihoods depended, like the annual fashion shows in Paris and Milan today."[14] Formal portraits of the royals, for example, often featured them wearing the skin of an exotic furbearer such as sable or ermine. A 1779 portrait commonly thought to be of Marie-Antoinette features her wearing a hat of black beaver with white ostrich plumes.[15] Royals often dressed their entourages in furs. The Empress Maria Theresa of Hungary dressed her Noble Life Guards in "the most splendid uniform in Europe," including a fur cap, a white egret aigrette, and a leopard skin tossed over the shoulder.[16] A few European leaders wrote statutes forbidding poor people from the wearing of certain furs.[17]

The fur most important to the New World trade was that of the beaver, and the fur of the beaver was best suited for hats. For nearly two hundred years, from the late 1500s to the 1700s, fine beaver hats were stylish and expensive. Descriptions of King James, in 1605, and his son Henry,

After Hyacinthe Rigaud, *Portrait of Louis XIV*, after 1701. Oil on canvas, 289.6 × 159.1 cm. The demand for exotic furs from the New World was driven in part by European royalty, who wore (and were painted in) clothing made from the pelts of animals. Shown here are the Sun King's coronation robes, made from ermine, the white winter coat of a stoat, a species of weasel with a black-tipped tail.

The Cataract of NIAGARA, some make this Water-Fall to be half a League while others reckon it no more than a hundred Fathom

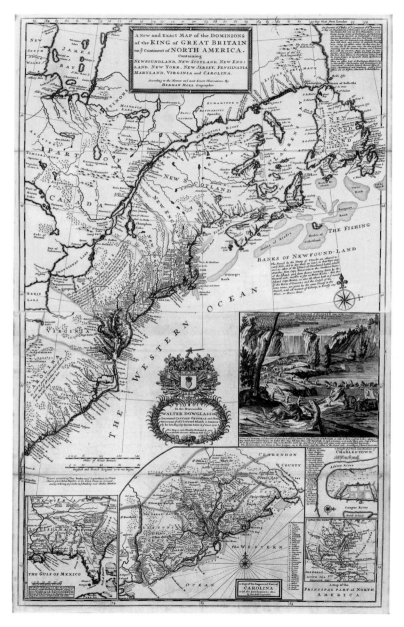

John Bowles, Thomas Bowles, and Herman Moll, *A New and Exact Map of the Dominions of the King*, 1731. This work is known as the "beaver map"—credited as the work of Moll—because of the image of the animals at work near Niagara Falls (above). At the time, this was the most detailed and largest-scale map of British possessions in North America, but it was criticized as a plagiarism of the work of earlier cartographers. First issued in 1715, the map went through seven different issues to 1736.

*Courtesy of the David Rumsey Map Collection, 9729.010.*

in 1608, showed beaver-made clothing of many colors and adornments costing 3 to 6 pounds each.[18] The British clerk and diarist Samuel Pepys paid 4 pounds for a beaver hat later in the seventeenth century, when the average annual earning of a Londoner was less than 100 pounds.[19] The desirability of beaver hats was partly caused by scarcity; in the early 1500s, the last beavers had been trapped from the British Isles, rendering them extinct in England.[20]

Not so across the Atlantic. By at least one count, the beaver was the most widely dispersed mammal on the North American continent in the pre-Columbian period.[21] Furs from the northern lands or higher elevations were particularly prized because the colder weather made thicker pelts. An average adult beaver is about 4 feet long and weighs perhaps 50 pounds; its tail was considered a delicacy, and a yellowish secretion called castoreum was used in medicines and, later, perfumes. Usually chestnut brown in color (although sometimes black, reddish brown, and very rarely white), the animal's hair consists of two types: an outer layer of coarse, longer guard hair and a denser, softer undercoat. To make a hat, the hair was turned into a silky felt by a process of shearing, wetting, agitating, rolling, and compression at a specific high temperature.

Beaver do not migrate far; they also have a low reproduction rate. Those two factors meant that an efficient trapper could clear a wetland of all its beaver relatively quickly. Overharvesting cleared the eastern coasts of North America, and trappers had to travel farther and farther inland to find new beaver habitat. Historian Conrad Heiden-

John James Audubon, *Castor Fiber Americanus, Linn. American Beaver*, 1845–48, in *The Viviparous Quadrupeds of North America*, vol. 1, no. 10, plate 46. Audubon is better known for his images of North American birds but also painted other wildlife, such as these two beavers working on a tree. In this volume he wrote, "The sagacity and instinct of the Beaver have from time immemorial been the subject of admiration and wonder." Courtesy of the University of Michigan Special Collections Library, 29377_0049.

reich suggests that, at the time of Champlain's death, the Hurons were running out of beaver; their problems were made worse by smallpox making its deadly way through the tribe.[22] The impact of the fur trade on Indian societies is beyond the scope of this book, but it is important to note that the trade of European goods—spear points, utensils, guns, and alcohol—began a cycle of dependency that,

Beaver pelts were used in making felt, which could be turned into a top hat, such as the one shown here with its case. This example is from the late 1800s, by which time silk had replaced beaver as the material of choice for the upper classes. *Courtesy of the HBC Corporate Collection.*

The process of making hats from the pelts of beavers is partially illustrated in this 1858 artwork from Charles Knight, produced by the London Printing and Publishing Company. *Courtesy of the Science, Industry, and Business Library, New York Public Library, Astor, Lenox and Tilden Foundations, 109640.*

among other social concerns, caused the tribes to hunt and trap more intensively in order to meet market demands.[23] Even some prairie-based tribes became expert canoeists to trade with the French.[24]

### COUREURS DE BOIS AND VOYAGEURS

By the late 1620s, Champlain had established permanent settlements along the seaway and recruited interpreters and traders to keep commerce flowing. Fifteen to twenty thousand furs made their way to France each year, almost all of them beaver. Hurons used their canoes for long-distance trading and fishing; their major villages were near one another and connected by foot trails through the woods. There were "no roads as understood in civilized lands," wrote one Methodist missionary.[25] The French went along in the canoes, but the Huron usually made the Europeans remove their hard-heeled boots so as not to puncture the hulls. Jesuit missionaries, who were usually not required to paddle, also joined many trips. Officials supplied the priests with material for sails to give to the Indians as compensation for their labor-free ride.[26]

But the French began to lose control over the labor market when hundreds of young men from settlements across the frontier joined in trips to Indian country. These men were the coureurs de bois—trappers and independent traders—and they followed the animals that they hunted, trapped, and traded across the continent and down the Mississippi Valley as far as Louisiana. Eventually the fur trade rode on the backs of these free-trading French,

Cornelius Krieghoff, *Coureur de Bois*, c. 1855. Oil on canvas, 43 × 38 cm. Images of the fur trade and its colorful workers have been popular in North American culture almost since they began paddling on the frontier, or "in the bush," in the popular lexicon. A coureur de bois was often a freelance (unlicensed) adventurer/trader of French or French-Indian heritage.

*Courtesy of New Brunswick Museum–Musée du Nouveau-Brunswick, www.nbm-mnb.ca, W6746.*

Abby Fuller Abbe, *The Voyageur*, c. 1860. Oil on canvas.
The voyageur's knit cap kept him warm during the cold nights
on the trail. The pipe in this painting is probably clay; the voyageurs
took hourly breaks, during which they smoked. They often measured
distances based on the number of pipe breaks between points.

*Courtesy of the Minnesota Historical Society, Gift of Miss Abby A. Fuller, 36846.*

Métis, Scots, and scores of other settlers and vagabonds, working with the clerks, bourgeois, and sailing captains to supply the European market.

A system of *congés*, or licenses, to control the market was eventually put in place by the French; a congé served as something like a passport to leave a French settlement. Many coureurs de bois held a license, but probably half did not. The investor whose capital financed the expeditions was called a *bourgeois*. The men whom he hired were the famous voyageurs, or travelers. (It was also a general term for all the workers in the system, but essentially a voyageur was an indentured servant.) Among the voyageurs were several social strata of employees, including the seasonal workers called *mangeurs de lard* (pork eaters) and the *hivernants*, longer-term employees who wintered in the hinterlands. Freemen were former voyageurs who left their servitude and stayed in the *pays d'en haut* (upper country) independently, often settling down with Native wives and families.

Like many nationalistic stereotypes, a stereotype about the voyageurs, particularly in Canadian culture, involves some glamorization. The popular image is of a pair or more men in a canoe, small clay pipes clenched in determined teeth and red toques flying in the wind, crashing through dangerous rapids as lightning crackles across an ominous sky. Singing, drinking, brawling, and living off the land— the harsher elements of indentured servitude are usually glossed over in favor of an imagined freedom offered by the unbroken horizon.

To the south and west, on the North American prairie,

Arthur Heming, *The Voyageur*, 1915. Oil on canvas, 76.7 × 102.2 cm. Heming became known as "the chronicler of the north."
His output is all the more remarkable because of his color-blindness; as a result, he often painted in black and white.

Frederic Remington, *Radisson and Groseilliers,* 1905. Oil on canvas, 110.2 × 194.3 cm. The American artist Frederic Remington captured the explorers
Pierre-Esprit Radisson and Médard Chouart, sieur de Groseilliers, in this painting, a rather unusual portrayal of a bark canoe in calm, shallow waters.
Radisson and Groseilliers were brothers-in-law who in the seventeenth century established the trading routes that were later used by the Hudson's Bay Company.

perhaps a similar stereotype is that of the cowboy; in this picture, the cowboy's horse replaces the voyageur's canoe. Although the traditional stereotypes have similarities—male, outdoors, controlling animals, great hats—a comparison of voyageurs and cowboys is not as strong as one might think, partly because the stereotypical cowboy could be a loner and the canoeist needed at least one partner to be most effective. Perhaps a better comparison group would be lumberjacks, who also worked in teams in rugged country and in a nearly completely masculine environment, or sailors, who spent months and years away from their families, also near water.

What was the reality? As historian Carolyn Podruchny notes in her excellent analysis of the voyageur life, very little evidence written by the voyageurs themselves survives; almost all of the historical record from the period comes from their bosses or from missionaries, who tended to praise the voyageurs in heroic pentameter.[27] One reason little written material exists is that literacy was not a requirement of the trade.

Podruchny found only a single document written by a voyageur in her search of the archives. His name was John Mongle (also known as Jean Monde); the document, probably dictated to a clerk, was a letter written to his wife in 1830.[28] The document survived in the Hudson's Bay Company archives because his wife submitted it as evidence that her husband had been an employee. The unfortunate Mongle was drowned in the Columbia River on October 25, 1830, a few months after he wrote home. His spouse, Marie, was attempting to collect his back pay.

Mongle, who was from Maskinongé, Quebec, joined the North West Company in 1816 at about age fifteen; he signed with the Hudson's Bay Company in 1821 upon the merger of the two companies. He left, then rejoined the HBC in 1829, and, because of his previous experience, was hired as a *boute* (steersman) for slightly higher pay.[29] On April 12, 1830, he crafted this letter:

> My very dear Wife
> It is with a deep longing that I awaited the occasion which presents itself by the voyageurs going to Montreal, to let you know the state of my health, which is very good so far, thanks be to God. I pray God that the present letter will find you enjoying the same happiness, I think that there is nothing more painful than to be separated from someone as dear as a wife, Also I assure you that nothing can delay my return once my time is up. I would be obliged to know whether you received my letter last autumn by Pierre Delard, and at the same time if you received the letter please tell me if you have withdrawn 3 louis[30] from the offices of the Hudson's Bay Company, and if you have received it please let me know in your letter so that I can take it into consideration, and I left for you, in the hands of Mr. Châtelain, 12½ shillings to give you. Let me know if you received it. I cannot send you any this year since my account is not here and the bourgeois cannot do it without seeing my account. But you can be sure for next year because I will

take my precautions early on. I would be obliged to know if you are in the same place where I left you and if by any chance you have not left, I would be pleased if you could stay until my return. On my return, the master of the house will be compensated for the pains he will have taken in your care. My respects to my sister and sister-in-law, and all those who ask for me, wishing you perfect health and that God preserves you while waiting for the pleasure of seeing you

    I am your affectionate and tender spouse

        John Mongle

    Mr. Pierre Bruneau gave me a letter for Mr. Kittson but I had the bad luck to lose it on the way and for that reason he is just as informed as I am. Your friend Payette

      MARIE ST. GERMAIN, MASKINONGÉ[31]

Clearly Mongle missed his wife very much; he was also concerned about her financial support. The HBC archives show that Mongle was a valuable man, working various construction jobs around Fort Colvile in what is now Washington State. On the fateful day of October 25, he and four men from the post joined four "heavily laden" boats that were shorthanded from lack of experienced *boutes* on the dangerous waters of the Columbia River. Below the Okanagan Falls, disaster struck. Three of the boats made it through the rapids below the falls, but the fourth capsized in a whirlpool. Seven men were drowned;

six were newcomers and the other was Mongle, who, as an experienced *boute*, may have been in the bow. Three men were saved, including another steersman, who could swim and made it to shore, and two who clung to the bottom of the boat and were rescued by their colleagues.[32] By 1832, his wife believed the rumors of her husband's death and pursued her claim.

From the 1680s to the 1870s, voyageurs such as Mongle provided much of the labor for the economic system of the continent. At its pre-1821 peak, perhaps three thousand voyageurs were at work, moving tons of goods in their canoes and on their backs. The dominant commercial entity was the Hudson's Bay Company, which had been chartered by King Charles II in 1670 to exploit the lands that drained into that far northern bay at the request of two disillusioned Frenchmen, Pierre-Esprit Radisson and Médard Chouart, sieur de Groseilliers, who had been punished by French authorities for trading without a license and signed up with the British.

After the Treaty of Paris ended the Seven Years War in 1763 and tossed control of much of the region to the British, the fur trade was reorganized at Montreal under their management. Merchants created a syndicate in the 1770s that became the North West Company, the great rival to HBC. The two firms skirmished for two generations as game supplies dwindled and business expenses rose until, under pressure from the British government, they merged in 1821; by then Montreal was no longer the undisputed center of the fur trade (St. Louis, not nearly as dependent on canoes, was founded as a fur trade center in 1764),

George Caleb Bingham, *Fur Traders Descending the Missouri*, 1845. Oil on canvas, 73.7 × 92.7 cm. The fur trade extended farther south into the United States as the decades passed and game became harder to come by in the northern climates. At the time of this painting, Bingham was living in St. Louis, which had become a trading center in America. He originally titled it *French Trader, Half-Breed Son* (which recognized the fact that some trappers married Native women), but the title was thought controversial, and the painting was renamed when it was first exhibited. *Courtesy of the Metropolitan Museum of Art, Morris K. Jessup Fund, 33.61.*

and other products were bought and sold alongside the beaver.[33] The French moved south into what is now the United States but soon found that the Mississippi River system was not as amenable to canoes, and the flatboat was developed as a freight handler. John Jacob Astor's American Fur Company gained control of the Great Lakes trade by the 1820s, and it introduced steam power to the Missouri River system, further replacing the canoe brigades as haulers.[34]

By the 1830s, silk hats, made with raw material acquired in the China trade, began to replace beaver at the fashionable end of the European market; and Captain James Cook had traded with Natives in dugout canoes laden with valuable sea otter fur on the Northwest Coast in 1778, opening the clothing market to another fur.[35]

### THE CANOES

The largest of the three main trading canoes in the time of the voyageurs was the *canot de maître* (Montreal canoe), used to move goods from Montreal to posts on the western end of Lake Superior at Grand Portage and Fort William. Although the size of a canoe varied with the individual builder, the Montreal canoes were roughly 36 feet in

Nicholas de Fer, *Le Cours du Missisipi*, 1718. De Fer was a French cartographer, engraver, and publisher not necessarily known for his accuracy. He published more than six hundred maps, including a 1698 map of North America that Herman Moll allegedly plagiarized seventeen years later in his famous "beaver map."

*Photograph courtesy of the Newberry Library, Chicago, Ayer 133 F34 1718.*

## ꙮ The Algonquin Fur Trade

When the casual canoeist thinks of a birch-bark boat, the profile that comes to mind is likely an Algonquin model. The graceful, high-ended shape, with the gunwales climbing into a bow often squared off at the top, came to represent birch-bark canoes in the popular imagination. Other tribes made canoes, and some made them just as well if not better, but perhaps none were as beautiful.

The modern American builder Henri Vaillancourt, one of the acknowledged masters of bark building, constructs his canoes after the Algonquin style. He notes that the swept-up bow with the rounded or square top was designed not for utility—it seems to serve no unique purpose—but simply for aesthetics.[1] As such, building a canoe in this way required more time and skill than simpler patterns. The canoes, which sport a fine cutwater—the forward edge—are 14 to 16 feet long, have slightly flared hulls and a beam of about 34 inches, and can be easily portaged by one person.

Early French fur traders often bargained and bought from the Algonquins; their canoes became the models for the larger fur-trade canoes built in the decades to come. French traders employed Native craftsmen, who also made snowshoes and sleds, as boatbuilders at the posts. Canoe scholars Edwin Tappan Adney and Howard Chapelle divided the Algonquin models into old forms and newer forms, with the old forms having higher ends and more sheer in the gunwales.[2] When the sportsmen's market grew in the late nineteenth century, some newer Algonquin boats, called *wabinaki chiman*, tended to be assembled quickly, with fewer features or techniques and designs borrowed from other tribes.[3] When a canoe was needed as a gift for the Prince of Wales in 1860, the Algonquin birch-bark style was the logical choice.

The Algonquin tribe, which practiced agriculture in the summer and followed game in the winter, originally lived in the Ottawa and Upper St. Lawrence river systems in what is now Quebec and Ontario. As the first tribe upriver from

This Algonquin canoe is held by the Canadian Canoe Museum. The tribe primarily resided in the Ottawa River region. Many Algonquin boats were used for hunting; the craft were considered to be well built and easy to paddle.

*Photograph by Michael Cullen. Courtesy of the Canadian Canoe Museum.*

*Birch-Bark Canoe Presented to His Royal Highness the Prince of Wales by the Governor of the Hudson's Bay Company* (Illustrated London News, February 9, 1861). British royalty visiting Canada have often been given canoes, such as this gift in 1860. Many were built in the Native style, or by Native craftspersons.

William Armstrong, *Indian Encampment*, c. 1860. Watercolor on paper, 29.8 × 42.2 cm. This watercolor depicts an Algonquin village with typical dwellings. Armstrong, born in Dublin, was an early important artist around Toronto. He was part of the Wolseley Expedition to the Red River Colony in 1870, documenting the effort needed to move the army through the wilderness under difficult circumstances.

Montreal, the Algonquins (who called themselves Abenaki) became the most important consistent trading partner of the French. In addition to the fur the tribe trapped and hunted, they sold corn and furs from interior tribes to the Europeans. Many skirmishes and a few full-scale wars were fought with nearby tribes, including the Iroquois Confederacy, as the Algonquins struggled to maintain their hold on the trade market.

In the late sixteenth or early seventeenth century, when the Algonquin began trading regularly with the French, the population totaled about 6,000. One hundred fifty years later, the British estimated the Algonquin population at 1,500. Today, in the early twenty-first century, the majority of Canada's 11,000 Algonquins live on nine reserves in the province of Quebec and one reserve in Ontario.[4]

length, with a 5-foot beam and a 2-foot depth. In 1750, the canoe factory at Trois-Rivières, Quebec, produced twenty Montreal canoes of 36 feet in length.[36] The French favored larger boats than the Indians for cargo-hauling reasons, and the size of the boats grew with the reduction in the number of licenses the government issued.

At around 600 pounds unloaded, the Montreal canoes were not built to be portaged, although several voyageurs could wrestle one where it needed to be. The boats could hold 8,000 pounds of cargo—a typical partial outbound bill of lading included 600 weight of biscuit and 200 weight of pork, plus 3 bushels of peas, sail, axe, kettle, tarp, sponge, line, gum, bark, and roots. "A European on seeing one of these slender vessels thus laden, heaped up and sunk with her gunwale within six inches of the water, would think

that his fate is inevitable in such a boat, when he reflected on the nature of her voyage; but the Canadians are so expert that few accidents happen," wrote the explorer Alexander Mackenzie in 1801.[37] A crew of up to sixteen men manned these big-water boats. Crossing a wide stretch of open water or the mouth of a big bay was called a traverse—although the voyageurs avoided cutting straight across Lake Superior. Instead, they worked the northern shoreline, out of the wind, until they reached the western end.

The *canots de nord* (north canoes) were smaller, perhaps 300 pounds unloaded, and used for paddling inland rivers and larger lakes. These boats were roughly 25 or 26 feet in length, with a crew of eight to ten and a cargo capacity of 2,000 to 3,000 pounds. The cargo from the Montreal canoes was shifted into the north canoes at the Lake

J. Halkett, *"Canot du maître" Carrying Two Officers*, 1822. This watercolor from the Manitoba Museum's Hudson's Bay Company Collection illustrates a Montreal canoe, which was among the largest in the fleet, as shown by the sixteen passengers in this one. It is unclear whether the credit for the painting should go to John Halkett, a Hudson's Bay Company officer (and brother-in-law of Lord Selkirk of Red River settlement fame) with no lasting record of work as an artist, or if Halkett is one of the men in top hats in the middle of the boat.

*Courtesy of the Hudson's Bay Company Archives, Archives of Manitoba, HBCA 1987/363-C-11A.*

Adam Sherriff Scott, *Chief Trader Archibald McDonald Descending the Fraser, 1828*, c. 1942. Oil on canvas, 81.28 × 63.5 cm. This is a twentieth-century painting of a voyage taken by Hudson's Bay Company trader Archibald McDonald on the Fraser River in 1828. After the Hudson's Bay merger with the North West Company in 1821, McDonald was sent to the Columbia River basin to trade. He rose to be the chief trader at several forts and served as deputy governor of the Red River colony.

*Courtesy of the HBC Corporate Collection.*

Superior posts for trips inland. Also used for this purpose was the *bâtard* (bastard), which was neither Montreal nor north (thus the name), sized in between the other two at 28 to 32 feet long, and often considered the most pleasing to the eye.

Natives made canoes in more than three sizes, of course, including one-person boats that the whites called the Indian or "light canoe" of 10 to 14 feet in length.[38] Some canoes had seats, but men usually sat on bedrolls, kneeled, or leaned against a thwart.

Several authors have noted that, although certain voyageurs were expected to be canoe repairmen (some were paid extra for maintenance duties on the routes), few of them became expert canoe makers; instead, the Native tribes were relied upon to supply the companies with boats.[39] Indian boatbuilders set up shop in Montreal and Trois-Rivières to meet the market; tribes also built and sold canoes near the main posts at Grand Portage and Fort William as well as other heavily used settlements. Trois-Rivières in particular was a canoe-building center for nearly two hundred years, with the de Maitre family as the principal builders.

### THE CREW

The man in the bow was the *avant de canot,* or *ducent,* or *devant*; the steersman was the *gouvernail*; and the middlemen were the *milieux*. The men at either end were also called *boutes*. Captains were appointed for each brigade of five to thirteen canoes and, like captains on the ocean, had complete authority once the trip was under way. Crew members, like people in other jobs, were in socially stratified roles and paid as such. Places in the canoe itself were used to mark class distinctions. The trader Alexander Ross describes one circumstance:

> The bourgeois is carried on board his canoe upon the back of some sturdy fellow generally appointed for this purpose. He seats himself on a convenient mattress, somewhat low in the centre of his canoe; his gun by his side, his little cherubs fondling around him, and his faithful spaniel lying at his feet. No sooner is he at his ease, than his pipe is presented by his attendant, and he then begins smoking, while his silken banner undulates over the stern of his painted vessel.[40]

Each propulsion job had its own tool in the form of differently shaped paddles and setting poles. The need for light weight, constant use, and steering dictated the design. The *milieux* paddles were the shortest and narrowest, perhaps only 2 feet long and a few inches wide. The *gouvernail* had a longer, wider paddle that could also serve as a rudder, and the *avant*'s paddle was larger as well. Setting poles were used to muscle the boats through low water, marshes, and swamps. Europeans compared the paddles to the "oven peele" used by bakers to move bread around.[41]

Voyageurs provided their own paddles and poles, usually custom-made for their size and the job ahead. In addition, the men were allowed a personal ditty bag of 40 pounds.[42] One-third of their wages was paid in advance, including a blanket, shirt, trousers, two kerchiefs, several pounds of twisted tobacco, and a few other items, including

Frederic Remington, *Voyageur with Tumpline*, c. 1890s. This drawing of a voyageur struggling with his load illustrates the use of a tumpline across the top of the head to help distribute the weight more evenly. "Tumpline" is based on the Algonquian word for line.   *Courtesy of the Wisconsin Historical Society, WHS-30348.*

winter clothing.[43] Contracts were for three to five years, with wages from 80 to 100 pounds per year.[44]

The unfortunate Mongle aside, the historical record is nearly empty of biographies of the voyageurs; more material exists about those involved in the management of the fur trade, such as the bourgeoisie. A very few men started as voyageurs and moved up. A bit of the character of the men and their work can be gleaned from four careers noted in the *Dictionary of Canadian Biography* (which, tellingly, does not have an entry for "voyageur"). These men were working in a period of transition in the trade, when the French influence was on the wane and wars with Britain and with the encroaching Americans caused upheavals in the market.

Laurent Ducharme (1723–1787?), a fur trader with family connections in the business, was law abiding, religious, and hard working.[45] Born in Montreal, he moved to the western fur-trading village of Michilimackinac (now Mackinaw City, Michigan) on the Lake Superior route. He experienced Indian attacks, put up with garrisoned British soldiers, and participated in the American Revolution on the British side. He was licensed to take trade goods from Montreal to the interior, and he traded in Milouaqui (Milwaukee) and La Baye (Green Bay, Wisconsin).

As a merchant, a trader, and a Roman Catholic, Ducharme was distressed by the profane culture at the trading post, and he and other merchants petitioned for a missionary in 1778 to bring piety to the impious. He pledged 18 pounds in currency per year to pay the churchman, a modest sum that suggests his annual income was not enough to make him wealthy. He also pledged 7,500 pounds in currency (called half a canoe load, which illustrates the

Fur-trade routes and trading posts: The voyageurs plied the North American frontier for generations, often leaving from Montreal, York Factory, or Lake Winnipeg on their long-distance trading journeys and not returning for many months, sometimes years. *Map by Charles Rader.*

value of the canoes' payloads) in 1779 in a general store partnership. Eventually dividing his home between Montreal and Michilimackinac, Ducharme wintered with his fur-trading partners to get better prices.

Jean-Baptiste de Couagne (1720–1795?), although born into a prominent Montreal fur-trading family, became a voyageur and as such was sent wherever his bosses needed him.[46] An indentured servant, he was shipped to the Illinois country (where he was captured by Cherokee and escaped), then assigned to Detroit and in 1749 to Lake of the Woods, due west of Lake Superior. He eventually cast his lot with the British at Fort Edward, New York, and he lived nearby among the Iroquois at the Six Nations. He ended his career as an interpreter for the British but lost his eyesight and retired to Montreal by 1780.

René Bourassa (1688–1778) worked on the illicit side of the fur-trade industry, at least for a while.[47] Born at La Prairie, Quebec, Bourassa had taken notice of the British black market in furs by the 1720s. He entered into the smuggling of pelts between Montreal and Albany, New York, but was caught and fined 500 *livres* in July 1722. Following in his father's footsteps to the western market, he wound up in a partnership in Green Bay but was known to carry "letters" to New England, often a cover for illicit fur trading. He sold wine to the French and Indians and bought slaves to manage his lands at Michilimackinac.

The frontier dangers for a fur trader, even one not working the black market, were real and frequent. In June 1736, Bourassa and his party of four were returning to Michilimackinac when they were captured by one hundred Sioux warriors, who claimed the French were arming their enemies. All five men were to be burned at the stake before Bourassa's Sioux slave girl made a dramatic and successful plea for his life. He and his crew subsequently escaped.

Francois-Jean-Daniel d'Ailleboust de la Madeleine (1702–1793) was born into Canadian nobility but saw limited chances for advancement and limited income from a lack of property, so he turned to the fur trade.[48] Such a move allowed him to retain his class status while taking a chance on building wealth in the business; he did not make his fortune but did lead an adventurous life as a voyageur and a bourgeois. He directed at least ten trading trips to the Great Lakes, hiring crews of *mangeurs de lard* to make summer runs to the western posts after he obtained trade goods on credit. In and out of a number of partnerships, La Madeleine joined the army at age forty in order to advance his career and social standing but kept an economic foot in the fur-trading business, which tied him to the western country, and he did not rise in the service.

**THE TRIP**

Men such as La Madeleine and their canoes usually left Montreal each May. The brigades had only five months or more of ice-free travel in which to complete their trading. At the westernmost point of Montreal Island, the canoes passed St. Anne's Chapel. The travelers adopted St. Anne, mother of Mary and grandmother of Jesus, as their patron, and the chapel was the men's last house of worship for

## ✆ Frances Anne Hopkins

Frances Anne Hopkins (1838–1919) had every reason not to like Canada, the fur trade, or even the birch-bark canoe. Two of her five children died at very young ages on the Canadian frontier, and her husband's commercial career came after the glory years of the North West and Hudson's Bay Companies. Yet Hopkins created paintings of fur traders, Native peoples, voyageurs, bourgeois, and the world of the nineteenth-century wilderness with a realism, eye for detail, and scenery that left her legacy as one of the most important artists in the nation's history. "More than any other artist, she recognized and interpreted accurately the demanding skills of canoe handling," says the *Dictionary of Canadian Biography*.[1] Further, "[m]eticulous in her drawing and thoroughly capable in her painting, she treated numerous Canadian subjects but her special achievement is the vividly convincing pictorial record of the canoes and paddlers of the nation's first great transportation system. In these works she rose to a level of colourful realism."[2] Her paintings are frequently used by historians and others as a valuable research source in their fine details of such special items as the sailing rigs used on fur-trade canoes.

Hopkins traveled with her husband by large canoes

Frances Anne Hopkins at age twenty-five, in 1863.

*Photograph by William Notman, copyright McCord Museum of Canadian History, I-8275.1.*

on at least three long trips with Mohawk voyageurs after 1858, from which much of her inspiration came.[3] Her painting *Canoe Manned by Voyageurs Passing a Waterfall* (Ontario) is among her best works and, along with other details, shows the birch-bark canoe used by the company to transport officials and spouses to visit trading posts on the frontier. She showed particulars such as buttons on a coat and a coffeepot nested in the boat. Records show that among the places visited on her travels were Manitoulin Island in Lake Huron and Kakabeka Falls near Lake Superior.[4]

She was the daughter of British Rear Admiral Frederick William Beechey, an Arctic explorer and painter, and granddaughter of English portrait painter Sir William Beechey, and studied under both. She married Edward Martin Hopkins, secretary to Sir George Simpson of Hudson's Bay Company, at age twenty. (One of her husband's nephews was the poet and Jesuit priest

Frances Anne Hopkins, *Canoe Manned by Voyageurs Passing a Waterfall*, 1869. Oil on canvas, 152.4 × 73.7 cm.
Hopkins inserted herself into this image as she traveled with her husband, Hudson's Bay official Edward Hopkins, and
voyageurs. She journeyed extensively with her husband by canoe along the company's trading routes in 1864, 1866, and 1869,
and perhaps on a fourth trip in 1870. *Courtesy of the Frances Anne Hopkins fonds, Library and Archives of Canada, R5666-0-8-E.*

Gerard Manley Hopkins.) Edward, who took charge of
the company's interests in Canada upon Simpson's death
in 1860, had three sons by his first marriage. The couple
settled first in Lachine, then Montreal. The fur trade was
winding down by the 1860s, and the couple left Canada
in 1866, returning only once, in 1869, before settling in
London in 1870 and then Oxfordshire.

Part of the phenomena of governors' wives travel-
ing and painting (Elizabeth Simcoe; Amelia Cary,
Vicountess Falkland; Hariot Georgiana Hamilton-
Temple-Blackwood, Marchioness of Dufferin and Ava)
or military officers' or other diplomats' wives (Millicent
Mary Chaplin, Katherine Jane Ellice, Amelia Frederica
Dyneley), Hopkins alone made travel paintings a career.
Her first major exhibit was at the Royal Society of British
Artists in 1867; later her work was shown at the Royal
Academy and in numerous commercial galleries. Hop-
kins, by all accounts a savvy businesswoman, remained
active in the art world well into the twentieth century.
She died in London on March 5, 1919, at age eighty-one.

months, if not years. At St. Anne's Rapids on the Ottawa River, the voyageurs would petition the saint with caps, hats, and other clothing tossed overboard in exchange for a safe journey.[49]

The trip from Montreal to Grand Portage, on the western end of Lake Superior, could take eight weeks, but wind and weather greatly affected travel times. Often brigades would meet at a halfway point—one from Montreal, the other from Grand Portage—and exchange loads before re-turning home. The Montreal canoes were not always fully laden on Lake Superior so more freeboard could be gained to navigate its rough waters.

In the interior, the canoes departed from their Lake Superior posts in July for points as far distant as the Atha-basca region (in present-day Alberta), the Pacific Coast, or the Arctic, 2,000 miles away. One main route started with a trip to Rainy Lake, while the Lake Superior–to–Lake Winnipeg journey was also a thoroughfare. Brigades

Frances Anne Hopkins, *Canoes in a Fog, Lake Superior, 1869*, 1869.
Oil on canvas, 68.6 × 121.9 cm.   *Collection of the Glenbow Museum, Calgary, Canada, 55.8.1.*

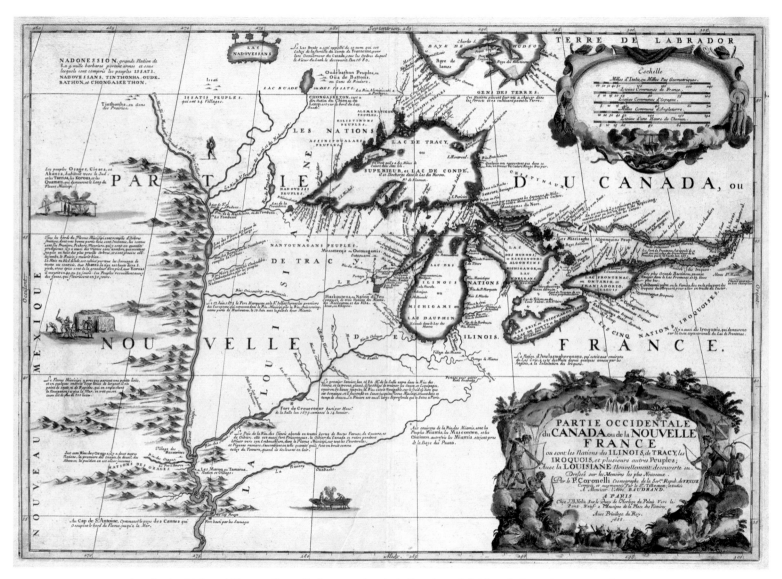

Jean-Baptiste Nolin and Vincenzo Coronelli, *Partie occidentale du Canada ou de la Nouvelle France* (Paris: J.-B. Nolin, 1688).

Nolin and Coronelli's map is the first printed map to focus on the Great Lakes and Upper Mississippi region.

Much of the information for the map came from French missionaries of the late seventeenth century.

*Courtesy of the James Ford Bell Library, University of Minnesota.*

from the Superior posts consisted of five to thirteen canoes, with four to seven men in each boat; the fleet divided as the trip lengthened.[50] Podruchny notes that it was not unheard of for aboriginal wives and children of the voyageurs and bourgeois to accompany the interior brigades in their own canoes, sometimes serving as translators, hunters, and gatherers.[51]

Scholars debate how far the voyageurs traveled in an average day; surely each trip was different depending on several factors. Broken canoes, bad weather, injured men, or encounters with hostile Indians or trading rivals could delay trips for days. Desertions occurred, weakening the crew, and deserters were rarely caught; the rivalries between the two main companies made labor fluid, valuable, and competitive. Replacements were hired along the way; crews were split and reassigned as needed.

Nonetheless, estimates of 75 to 100 miles per day are given at the upper end; others say the average trip was closer to 50 miles per day.[52] Certainly travelers on the trip between Lake Superior and Lake Winnipeg, with its difficult and frequent portages, did not progress more than one or two dozen miles in a day.

### PORTAGES

The portages[53] were trails through the woods that connected bodies of water. Most had been there for centuries, beaten into a path first by animals and then by the Native tribes. Portages combined three features: they were the shortest distance between navigable waters, at the lowest elevation, and (usually) away from soft ground. Their locations became well known, and the most difficult acquired their own names. The longest portage east of the Canadian Rockies was the 13-mile Methye Portage in northwest Saskatchewan, called Portage La Loche by the French. Both names mean the same thing: *methye* is Cree and *la loche* is French for burbot, an edible freshwater fish very high in oil and other nutrients. The Lake Superior drainage held the greatest number of difficult portages, but to the northwest, on the route from Rainy Lake to Winnipeg, twenty or thirty portages awaited travelers, depending on the water levels.

Slippery rocks and steep slopes were not the only danger on a portage. They were places of ambush for the Indians, especially the Iroquois.[54]

Even though some of the portages had been in use for perhaps ten thousand years, finding them on a foggy morning or in a storm-wracked canoe was not a sure thing. To help, a chunk of the bark of a tree was sliced off (blazed) to mark the end of a portage, but that mark wasn't always visible from a distance. To fix that problem, lob trees were used. These were prominent trees along the route whose lower branches were trimmed (lobbed) to make the tops stand out against the skyline. Some of the prominent lob trees, like the portages, received names.

Were individual canoes named, like naval vessels or merchant ships? Sometimes they were, by Jesuits who would bless a trading fleet (similar to the religious custom of blessing a fishing fleet). The priests would paint a saint's name in red on the canoe to ask for protection for its crew.[55] Most canoes were not named because they were so

Paul Kane, *The Mountain Portage*, 1849-56. Oil on canvas, 64 × 51 cm. Kane felt the falls of the Kaministikwia River at Kakabeka surpassed those at Niagara in beauty and romance. The massive nature of the cut of the river dwarfs the voyageurs struggling under heavy loads on the portage.

fragile, lasting only a year or two, and numerous: seventy canoes were built for the North West Company per year at the height of the Winnipeg–Grand Portage trade.[56]

Trimming lob trees and blazing their bark weren't the only ecological effects of the voyageur on the portage. Plantains, small herbaceous plants with oval leaves that love compacted soil, were tracked in by the French; the Indians began calling the invasive species "white-man's foot," because they "noticed it appeared everywhere whites walked" on the heavily used portages.[57] Plantains, more properly *Plantago major*, became one of the few non-native woody plants to become naturalized, along with wild plum and Virginia creeper, in the harsh climate of the northern forests.

Weight was of constant concern to the voyageur on the portage—the weight of the packs (called *pieces* in French, usually 90 pounds each), canoes (50 to 100 pounds or more), paddles, their personal gear (40 pounds), and other stores—because everything needed to be carried. A north canoe might have thirty to thirty-five *pieces* in it. Each voyageur carried two packs—180 pounds—stacked on his back, and some could carry four. (Not surprisingly, hernias were a common injury.) On the trip from Montreal, the packs contained the materials for barter, such as guns, ammunition, liquor, blankets, cloth, beads, flour, and kitchen utensils. On the way back, the packs were furs smashed into bundles. On the longer portages, the voyageurs dropped the packs every third of a mile and ran back to get the next load.

The ends of the portages were also places to eat and camp. By the late nineteenth century, one traveler, Robert

A lob tree was an evergreen, often like this white pine, trimmed of lower branches and smaller trees and brush around it to mark the head of a portage or a campsite. With its neighbors cut away, the lob tree could more easily be seen from a distance. This pine, on the Kawishiwi River in Minnesota, was probably a survivor of logging and fire when a young Arthur Carhart, working for the Forest Service, took this photograph in 1919. Carhart became one of the leading voices for wilderness preservation in North America.

*Courtesy of the Forest History Society, Durham, North Carolina, R9_152967.*

H. A. Ogden, *At the Portage*, from George Monro Grant, ed., *Picturesque Canada*
(New York: Belden Brothers, 1882). Hudson's Bay Company employees are shown
in this engraving from the late nineteenth century. The sheer size of the 90-pound
packs, boxes, and barrels to be transported in the canoes can be appreciated.

*Courtesy of the Archives and Special Collections, University of Minnesota Libraries.*

E. Pinkerton, noted that the habit of drinking tea on
the part of the Indians and voyageurs left evidence on
the path. "In the north country, there is invariably one
distinguishing feature at each end of every portage—the
tea stick. . . . [S]hould there be no blaze or trail to mark
the take-off of a portage, the traveller should look for the
blackened sapling thrust into the ground or propped across
a rock."[58] The drink could be made from the leaves of
nearby shrubs, including a *Rhododendron* commonly called
Labrador tea (though it is called Indian tea in Labrador).

### TRADING POSTS

Trading posts varied in size. The larger posts, such as at
Grand Portage, were transportation hubs; medium-sized
posts lasted a few years but were not well-staffed or visited
often. The smallest posts had only a couple of traders and
were usually set up for a season; they were at great distances
from the major routes.[59] The arrival of a brigade (a fleet of
canoes) at a trading post was a notable event. A daily record was kept in a "provision book" of the goods shipped
in and out at the posts as well as the comings and goings
of the boats. In addition to long lists of freight and furs,
these books, much like a ship's log, contain records of
weather and wind direction as well as births, deaths, and
marriages, Indians arriving and departing, and firewood
gathered. Many of the entries simply say "all the same
as yesterday."

This could lead to some misinterpretation. Henry John
Moberly was a factor (boss) of the Hudson's Bay Company

Colin Fraser Jr., a trader at Fort Chipewyan, held the job of sorting furs to prepare them for a trip to market in the 1890s.
His father, Colin Fraser Sr., had been a longtime Hudson's Bay man who ran the second Jasper House—the gateway to the
Athabasca and Yellowhead Passes in the Canadian Rockies—for fifteen years and was called "the forefather of the mountain Métis."

*Courtesy of the Library and Archives of Canada, C-001229.*

and in its employ for thirty-three years, beginning in the 1850s. One of his entries from the Lac La Biche post read: "All hands chopping cordwood. Mrs. Bellerose was delivered of a fine girl." For the next thirteen days, the entry was "All the same as yesterday." Moberly wryly noted, "So it would appear that the wood-chopping had included Sunday [a day of rest] and that poor Mrs. Bellerose had become the mother of fourteen children in as many days, which is rather hard to credit."[60]

A brigade, or fleet, could be anywhere from a few boats to thirty. An English doctor named John Jacob Bigsby, observing a fleet of fur-trade canoes early in the nineteenth century, describes the landing at a portage this way:

> When a brigade of fur-trading canoes, 10, 20, or
> 30 in number, are compelled to land suddenly, it
> is done one by one in rapid succession. The first
> makes a dash at the beach. Just as the last wave is
> carrying the canoe on dry ground, all her men jump
> out at once and support her; while her gentlemen
> or clerks hurry out her lading.[61]

The beach crew then seized the next canoe in line and repeated the process until all were unloaded. If any women were aboard, they were carried off piggyback style. Stopping the canoe short of the shore prevented it from knocking against a rock or rubbing it thin on sand or gravel shorelines.

Trading posts were places of great importance, if only for the interaction with people other than those in your boat. As such, there were cultural ceremonies associated with the posts, including firing guns upon the arrival of important visitors. First-time visitors got sprinkled with water from a cedar branch, while "giv[ing] certain promises, such as never to kiss a voyageur's wife without her consent."[62]

Problem-solving was an important skill at the posts, where the work included construction, repair, growing and hunting food, chopping firewood, and, of course, traveling and trading. Moberly used the skins of moose to have his men make canoes, "the seams being sewed with sinew and rubbed with tallow."[63] His moose-skin canoe held eight men besides himself, as well as the cook and a load of furs and provisions—eighteen packs of 90 pounds each.

Moberly mined the tar from the Clearwater River by Methye Portage on warm days, digging it and cutting it with a knife. After boiling the tar to concentrate it, the HBC used it to repair its boats. And Moberly used whatever boats happened to be available, not just canoes. His memoirs list scows, dugouts, birchbarks, skin canoes, and other boats, as well as steamboats for the big waters.[64]

### A DAILY ROUTINE

On the leg from Montreal, there was no time to hunt or fish, so the men ate food prepared by the company. Dried peas, salted pork, and biscuit were the staples, and when those were exhausted a corn–and–pork-fat mush or sagamite—a cornmeal stew sometimes flavored with animal brains—landed on the plate. When all the provisions provided by the company were eaten, the men bought food

George Franklin Arbuckle, *The Spring Fur Brigades Leave Montreal for the West*, c. 1946. Oil on canvas, 77.47 × 78.74 cm. "Archie" Arbuckle was a mainstay on the cover of *Maclean's* magazine in the 1940s and 1950s, often illustrating men and women at work. Hockey players, farm families, oil drillers, railroad men, and even voyageurs populated his images, which were inspired by both historical and current events.

*Courtesy of the HBC Corporate Collection.*

Frances Anne Hopkins, *Canoe Party around Campfire*, c. 1870. Oil on canvas, 90.2 × 151.8 cm.
Canoes could be used to shelter a fire from the wind or to sleep beneath on a wet night.

*Courtesy of the Frances Anne Hopkins fonds, Library and Archives of Canada, R5666-0-8-E.*

from the Indians—some tribes such as the Cree and Assiniboine, which had served as middlemen in the fur trade, switched to the work of provisioners and supplied food as well as canoes.

Pemmican, which is dried and pounded buffalo mixed with hardened fat and berries, was among the items on the menu in the interior.[65] (It was high in protein and calories and kept for years.) The men preferred meat over fish and wild game over farmed, perhaps because of their reputation as voyageurs who lived off the land. Game birds and small mammals were likely the most-often-eaten meat, with the occasional deer, bear, or moose thrown in. Farther south, traders on the prairie ate buffalo.

Whitefish, salmon, pike, and other species were regularly available fish. Most of the voyageurs were Roman Catholic and respected the church's dietary restrictions regarding fish on Fridays, for example. One exception was the church's allowance of beaver meat during Lent. Since the animal spent more time in the water than on land, the church considered it more fish than not.

Breakfast and supper were eaten on the portages; longer, steeper portages earned the men lunch as well. Crews rose early and traveled for three to five hours before breakfast. The young men would paddle, in time, from forty to sixty strokes per minute over the course of a 12- to 15-hour day or more, with regular 10- to 15-minute breaks to smoke (the stops were called *pipes*) and rest. Powering a canoe without sitting in a seat can be a difficult task; Pierre

Radisson summed it up neatly, after traveling several hours with voyageurs, by noting "the feare in ye buttocks."[66] On a breezy day, their speed could reach 6 miles per hour or more if they used a sail.

In 1818, a bourgeois named Robert Seaborne Miles left a travel journal from a trip from Lachine to Lake Athabasca. He described two typical days on the Ottawa River in June:

[DAY ONE]

| | |
|---|---|
| 2:30 A.M. | The crew left their encampment |
| 7:30 A.M. | Went ashore to breakfast for an hour |
| Mid-morning | At Portage du Canard, the men hauled the canoe and cargo up with the line and walked over |
| 1:40 P.M. | Went ashore to eat |
| 2:30 P.M. | Resumed paddling |

[DAY TWO]

| | |
|---|---|
| 5 A.M. | Set out |
| 7 A.M. | Portaged and breakfasted |
| 8 A.M. | Set out again |
| 1:15 P.M. | Reached Portage de Roche Capitaine, crossed it, ate |
| 3 P.M. | Resumed journey |
| 8:40 P.M. | Stopped and set up camp at Little River[67] |

Frederic Remington, *Voyageurs in Camp for the Night*, c. 1890s. Music played an important role in the daily life of the voyageurs, from songs to help keep time while paddling to ballads for entertaining each other at the end of a long workday. Many of the tunes survive today, including the popular "Shenandoah," which may have originated with traders traveling "across the wide Missouri." *Courtesy of the Wisconsin Historical Society, WHS-3776.*

The fragile nature of the wooden canoe is evident in this old campaigner, found near the Takhini River in the Yukon in 1995 by the Lake Laberge Archaeology Project. Thought to date from the early twentieth century, this dugout canoe from a cottonwood tree was found cached in dense bush. The canoe, 14½ feet long and 3 feet across, was cached upside down on two logs, which kept it from rotting entirely. Patches of red ochre paint could still be seen on the hull, and paddles were stashed underneath.

*Photograph courtesy of Government of Yukon.*

A voyageur was sometimes paid a bonus for a fine singing voice.[68] Music was used to keep time while paddling, remember home and family, honor fallen colleagues, and kill time when bored. The songs reflected the danger and loneliness of the work. Many of the songs were stories set to music, tales of brave men, beautiful women left behind, and feats of great strength and endurance. A few songs survive to the present, including "The Little Rock," about the hero Jean Cadieux, who sacrificed himself to save his crew from the Iroquois.[69]

The Minnesota writer Sigurd Olson tells the story of "two old voyageurs" in the twentieth century, when their careers—and way of life—had ended. They were still left with a faithful canoe but did not have the heart to burn it or leave it in the woods to rot. They considered sending it through the rapids, unmanned, as a final symbolic act, but could not bring themselves to part with it. Finally, one of them picked up a saw and sliced the canoe across its beam; each took one half home and made a bookcase out of the pieces.[70]

CHAPTER 4

# All-Wood Canoes

HE EVOLUTION from Native craft to modern North American canoes occurred during the great era of wooden canoes, stretching from about 1865 to the onset of World War II. Three geographical areas played the largest roles in this transition because they were home to active and successful commercial builders: Peterborough, Ontario; Canton, New York; and Old Town, Maine.

This era saw two waves of popular recreational interest in canoes, the first generated by all-wood paddling and sailing canoes, and a larger second wave created by the arrival of affordable wood-and-canvas canoes. Design

A cedar-strip canoe made in Peterborough, Ontario, on exhibit at the Antique Boat Museum in Clayton, New York, 2005.

*Photograph by Barry Cunningham.*

evolved as new construction techniques were invented and patented. Hull shapes and canoe types changed as well, from double-paddle canoes (which today might be thought of more as kayaks) based on John MacGregor's original 1865 *Rob Roy*, through cruising canoes that could be both paddled and sailed, to open "Canadian" canoes propelled with single-bladed paddles.

The factories and shops that turned out these canoes set the stage for organized canoe groups such as the American Canoe Association. They enabled widespread recreational and romantic uses of the canoe, drawing thousands of paddlers to the waters of Boston, Detroit, and Minneapolis, for example. Graceful Native American designs were adapted and preserved by builders who understood both the qualities of a great canoe and the nature of modern marketing. Today we look at the beautiful surviving canoes from this era as works of art.

### THE PETERBOROUGH ALL-WOOD CANOE

Peterborough, a small industrial city located above Lake Ontario an hour and a half northeast of Toronto, still shows signs of its vibrant past.

At the turn of the last century, Peterborough had thriving factories making woolen fabrics, paper, tents and sails, stoves, carriages, harnesses and saddles, lumber, pumps and agricultural implements, sawmill equipment, and locks. Ovaltine, Quaker Oats, and Canadian General Electric had factories there. The areas around the industrial core of the town were home to substantial working-class neighborhoods (as well as the original home of the Canadian Canoe Museum). Railroads shipped the factory goods across Canada, and via the Great Lakes and the St. Lawrence River to the rest of the world. Peterborough grew from around 3,800 people in 1862 to about 15,000 in 1900, which was the primary era of its canoe innovations.[1]

The Otonabee River flows through the city from Lakefield and Stoney Lake on the north to Rice Lake on the south. "It's a fertile crescent of canoe building more or less along the Otonabee River," says John Summers, former general manager of the Canadian Canoe Museum in Peterborough.[2]

Unlike the later development of wood-and-canvas canoes, which were modeled after Native American birch-bark canoes, the Peterborough all-wood canoes evolved primarily from Native dugouts.

When the Europeans designed their own dugouts, the shape of the hull and stems changed and the thickness of the walls lessened. "You begin to see a boat that is a little higher sided than First Nations' dugouts," Summers says. "They're a little more gracefully shaped, certainly the ends are finer. These are pretty finely carved." Summers, who has been a museum curator, boatbuilder, and watercraft historian, grew up in Vancouver. He has been general manager of the Canadian Canoe Museum in Peterborough, Ontario, and has worked at the Antique Boat Museum in Clayton, New York, the International Yacht Restoration School in Newport, Rhode Island, and at the Marine Museum of Upper Canada in Toronto. He mentions that the Europeans had metal tools such as adzes, axes, chisels, and planes that could create walls no more than $5/8$ or $1/2$ inch thick, as compared to an inch or more on some Native or First Nations' dugout canoes.

In the mid-1800s, canoe owners duplicated their favorite dugouts by using them as forms for wide-board or planked canoes. "At some point, again we don't know exactly, somebody decided to take a dugout—perhaps one they were particularly fond of because of its shape—and use it as a pattern for another boat," says Summers. "This was using an inverted dugout as a mold on which to build a boat. This is the real genesis of what became the Peterborough area method of production. This is quite distinct from the wood-canvas tradition that had its origins in the northeastern U.S. and places like Maine." Ribs and

A trapper's dugout canoe constructed of basswood. The end decks, deck caps, and wide outwales on this canoe echo what would become the best-known features of Peterborough-area all-wood canoes. This dugout dates from the early twentieth century and was used by its maker, Sherman Hill.

*Courtesy of the Canadian Canoe Museum.*

planks were nailed directly onto the dugout. "If you were inside the dugout, this would look like the Iron Maiden with all these fastenings sticking into you," he says. The hulls had to be pried off the form and the protruding nails clinched, or folded over, by hand.

The early Peterborough canoes were made with three or four wide planks on each side. The origins of this design have been credited to several early builders, including John Stephenson, Thomas Gordon, and Dan Herald in the 1850s, and William English. The British-Canadian fur trader and explorer David Thompson may have created a wide-board or lapstrake canoe as he traveled the Columbia River to the Pacific Ocean in 1811, though it had no direct relationship to Peterborough-area construction techniques.[3]

John Stephenson (1831–1920), a Peterborough resident with experience as a blacksmith, shingle maker, stove maker, and lumber manufacturer, told a story about going on a canoe trip around 1856 with three other men in a dugout canoe that weighed 200 pounds. After carrying the boat twice on a 3-mile portage, Stephenson swore to produce a lighter canoe for the following fall's hunting trip. As he started making board canoes to replace the dugout, sportsmen bought them as fast as he could produce

This beautiful cedar-strip canoe was built by the Lakefield Canoe Works of Peterborough, c. 1925-30.
The canoe uses three wide boards as planking on each side.   *Photograph by Anne Evans.*

them. He had no time for hunting that year. Stephenson later operated three canoe shops in the Ashburnham section of Peterborough, held patents on the cedar-rib and longitudinal strip–building techniques, and sold his designs to the new Ontario Canoe Company in 1883.[4]

The William English Canoe Company catalog in 1903 gave credit to Stephenson for the board canoe. The catalog said the early Stephenson canoes were 16 to 18 feet long and 28 to 32 inches at the beam. "The late Mr. William English soon after followed Mr. Stephenson's lead, as did all the other builders," the catalog stated.[5] William English (1840–1891) operated a long-lasting canoe factory in Peterborough. Along with other builders in the area, English made rib-and-batten canoes over a form, which was the classic Peterborough method. English became an active member of the American Canoe Association in the 1880s.[6]

Family stories claimed that Thomas Gordon (1833–1916) of Lakefield, Ontario, built the first so-called board canoe; his company merged with Strickland and Company in 1904 to become the Lakefield Canoe Works. Dan Herald (1833–1890), who shipped out of County Down in Ireland sometime between 1840 and 1845 and settled in Gore's Landing on Rice Lake, started building canoes in 1862.

According to historian Ken Brown, the original invention hardly matters:

Stephenson, English, Gordon, Herald. They were all both builders and inventors who initially built solid wood, wide-board canoes. All contributed in some way to new and better designs. All operated canoe-building businesses for their livelihood. All exhibited and sold canoes internationally. Together they laid the foundation for the businessmen who operated the factories of the Ontario, Peterborough, and Canadian Canoe Companies—businesses that maintained Peterborough as the canoe building capital of the world into the 20th century.[7]

John Stephenson, one of the early innovators of canoe design in Peterborough.

*Courtesy of Ken Brown.*

The industrial evolution of the Peterborough canoe began with those same builders, whose canoe shops "participated in the evolution of all-wood canoes from wide board to cedar-rib and longitudinal strip construction," writes Brown.[8]

The various techniques require some explanation.

All-wood construction techniques involved considerable skill in boatbuilding. With canoes made of wood, as with any watercraft, the first problem was keeping water out.

In 1871, Herald used a novel waterproofing technique. He sandwiched a white lead–soaked canvas sheet between two layers of cedar planking. His "double-cedar" canoe had interior vertical and exterior horizontal layers

Employees of the William English Canoe Company pose with a giant war canoe built in the factory on Charlotte Street in Peterborough, Ontario. The factory operated from as early as 1861 to 1915 at that location. In 1918, English offered a 30-foot club canoe, 46 inches wide and 18 inches deep, although this boat may be larger. *Courtesy of Jim English.*

of cedar. No ribs were needed, making the canoe smooth-skinned inside and out.[9] This technique did not catch on because it was labor-intensive and produced a relatively heavy canoe and also, as Summers said, because the canvas worked "until it didn't," and then the canvas in the sandwich could not be replaced without disassembling the hull. Herald's company later merged with the Rice

Lake Canoe Company. Subtle designs, fine craftsmanship, and relatively low production make Herald's canoes rare and highly sought-after today.

Stephenson patented a design for a "cedar rib" canoe, a unique construction in which tongue-and-groove ribs ran vertically from gunwale to gunwale and were supplemented with strips of wood called battens that ran

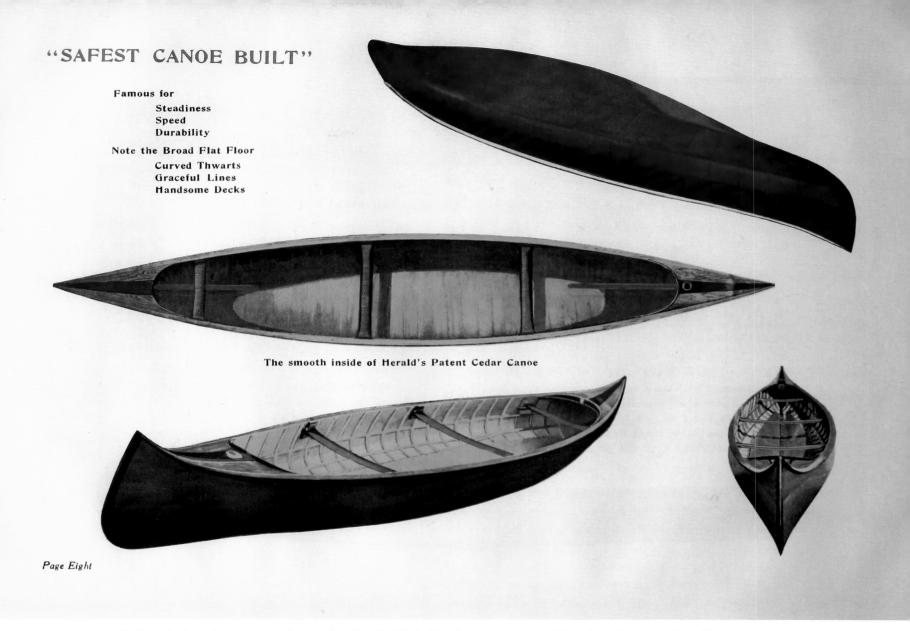

# "SAFEST CANOE BUILT"

Famous for
- Steadiness
- Speed
- Durability

Note the Broad Flat Floor
- Curved Thwarts
- Graceful Lines
- Handsome Decks

The smooth inside of Herald's Patent Cedar Canoe

*Page Eight*

The Rice Lake Canoe Company catalog from 1900 listed Dan Herald's double-cedar canoe (center), which had a layer of canvas sandwiched between two layers of cedar planking. The canoe was smooth-skinned inside and out but difficult to repair. It was invented in 1871 near Peterborough, Ontario.

*Courtesy of the University of Toronto Library.*

A restored William English canoe, model 21, which was listed as 16 feet long, 31 inches at the beam, and 12 inches deep. The English catalog of 1918 described it as "a good pleasure canoe and fairly fast to paddle." All-wood canoes such as this were paddled solo using a double-bladed paddle, as shown, or tandem with single-bladed paddles.   *Photograph by Ralph Nimtz.*

lengthwise inside the canoe. In effect, the ribs served as both ribs and planking. Peterborough-area companies continued to build in this style well into the twentieth century.

Stephenson also developed a "rib-and-batten" technique for his wide-board canoes. Three or four wide planks about a quarter-inch thick ran lengthwise on each side. They were fitted together for a smooth hull, and the seams between the planks were waterproofed with battens along the inside. The battens could stand proud on the inside of the planking, in what was known as "raised-batten" construction, or be let into the inside of the planking, which was known as "flush-batten." Small ribs running from gunwale to gunwale every 4 to 6 inches provided support, with the battens forming a grid on the interior of the canoe. Several builders used similar wide-board techniques.

The most popular design, and the one that became synonymous with the Peterborough-style canoe, proved to be the "longitudinal strip" model. Often referred to today as "cedar-strip" construction, it should not be confused with contemporary wood-strip and fiberglass building. According to Summers, "Longitudinal strip construction is the Peterborough method. It's long strips with some kind of lapping on the edges. It started out as tongue-and-groove—I think the patent actually mentions tongue-and-groove—but later on it was shiplap. Shiplap was simpler. The most typical way, which requires a fair bit of machining, is to shiplap the edges to make a sealed shiplap joint." Thin planking only about an inch wide ran lengthwise on the canoe, with a rabbet cut into the edge—a recess or groove allowing two pieces to fit snugly together. Unlike the planking on wide-board canoes, which had to be custom fitted, the longitudinal strip–planking technique needed only three or four shapes per canoe, so planking could be premanufactured in large quantities and quickly applied by relatively unskilled workers. The canoes typically had narrow, half-round ribs running vertically from gunwale to gunwale on the inside. Usually floorboards of thin planking stock were added to make kneeling more comfortable for paddlers and to protect the ribs and planking.

Large factories in the Peterborough region made canoes and eventually merged with one another. The first big shop, the Ontario Canoe Company (OCC), was organized by a group of businessmen in 1883 and had John Stephenson supervising construction. James Z. Rogers, the owner of a planing mill that made storm-sash doors, sashes, and blinds, became president and general manager of the OCC,[10] which employed twenty-five men by 1892. "Once you had a couple of canoe companies, you started to build a work force," says Summers.

A lot of this was piece work. People would float from one company to another, get hired, dehired, rehired, and get together. These companies were located on opposite sides of the street. At one point—depending on how you count because some were one-man shops that only built a few boats—there were twelve or thirteen in existence in this arc from Lakefield to Rice Lake. The biggest were places like Peterborough and the Canadian Canoe Company, occupying three- or four-story factories. These were by the 1880s significant industrial-scale establishments. Their letterheads and billheads featured those classic "happy smokestack" engravings with the coal smoke of prosperity coming out of the chimney and railroad sidings and workmen bustling and piles of lumber and piles of canoes. It all looks very grand and prosperous.

A cedar-strip all-wood canoe (right) at the Canadian Canoe Museum.
A double-cedar canoe, with a layer of canvas between the planking, is at the left.

*Photograph by Ray Goodwin.*

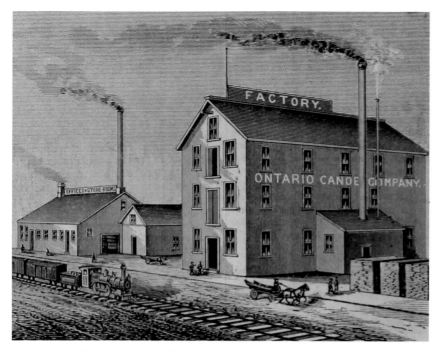

This drawing shows the Ontario Canoe Company factory adjacent
to the railroad tracks in Peterborough in the early 1880s.

*From Canadian Forest Industries, 1884. Courtesy of the University of Toronto Library.*

Our contemporary viewpoint treats these all-wood canoes as beautiful objects. "We forget that these were mass produced, manufactured objects," Summers says. "They were made under very constrained building circumstances. These guys were doing this to make a living. They were doing it to enrich shareholders, not because it was beautiful. It's fine to appreciate it as a beautiful ob-

ject, but I think it does more service if that's underlain by some understanding of the circumstances that gave rise to that form of canoe."

Company owners earned a nice return. "All told, Felix Brownscombe earned $45,838, a 35-year compound return of 22.32 percent on his initial investment in the Canadian Canoe Company in 1892, which was $760. Even investors who came on board in 1893–1894 and missed out on the very early profitable months earned a compound return of 18 percent on their investment through to the company's liquidation in 1928," writes Brown.[11] The wages of laborers were a different story. Workers earned $.30 to $.75 an hour for nine-hour days in 1919. In that year, they went on strike, seeking increased wages with a minimum of $.50 an hour. The request would have provided slightly higher wages than average, but was turned down by the two major canoe companies.[12]

In the 1880s, the first wave of recreational interest in canoes saw the organization of the American Canoe Association (ACA), increased tourism in areas such as the Adirondacks in upstate New York and the Thousand Islands region of the St. Lawrence River, and a rising market for Canadian-style open canoes in Great Britain. Rogers marketed OCC canoes in England and through distributors in Canada. The rival Strickland Canoe Company had exported six hundred canoes to England by 1898. "Rogers and his initial staff of three builders were able to offer a wide product choice in the 'preliminary catalogue' of 1883," writes Brown. "There were six sizes of 'patent cedar rib' canoes available, painted or varnished, at prices from $35 to $70. And the same six sizes of 'patent longitudinal rib canoes' were offered for $5 less (from $30 to $65), perhaps because this was the newer, untried design." Brown notes, "The canoe was something of a luxury item in the 1880s and 1890s. Consider that, at the time, the annual salary of a young bank clerk was less than $100."[13]

On May 9, 1892, a fire destroyed the OCC factory. Shortly before the fire, Rogers had participated in the sale of the OCC to a new company that became the Peterborough Canoe Company (PCC).[14] The PCC would become the dominant canoe manufacturer in Canada but faced stiff competition from another maker that was also located in Peterborough.

Arthur Tebb, a former employee of the OCC, founded the Canadian Canoe Company (CCC) in 1892 about three months after the Ontario Canoe Company building burned. Tebb set up shop in the old office and sales outlet of the OCC and actually began production before the PCC could manufacture its first canoe.

The first Canadian Canoe Company factory stood on Water Street in Peterborough from 1892 to 1904 near the rail office, from which all the canoes made in town were shipped. *Courtesy of Ken Brown.*

The several builders around Peterborough, including Strickland in Lakefield and William English, competed to build the most beautiful and the fastest all-wood canoes. They would also custom-build canoes to a racer's specifications. Peterborough craftsmen built some of the fastest open canoes and sailing canoes that were raced at American Canoe Association gatherings.

Meanwhile, the residents who lived in the "fertile

The building department at the Canadian Canoe Company factory, late nineteenth century. *Courtesy of Ken Brown.*

Sawdust and shavings litter the floor of the workshop at the Canadian Canoe Company factory as builders fashion canoes in distinctive shapes.  *Courtesy of Ken Brown.*

crescent of canoe building" along the Otonabee River and its lakes celebrated their boating heritage in annual regattas. They dressed in style, often in white, and paddled their all-wood canoes in races, which included classes for women before the ACA held such races.

In the early 1900s, a new technique arrived that would transform canoe building. In New Brunswick, the Chest-nut brothers, William and Henry, started selling the new wood-and-canvas canoe. The company opened in 1904 making canvas canoes "built after the Morris model," which was an early wood-and-canvas canoe made in Maine. Not many canoes were being built, according to the local newspaper, because "there are no experienced canoe builders in this city and . . . the men all have to

A coat of varnish, applied in a dust-free environment, was one of the final steps in canoe construction at the Canadian Canoe Company factory. *Courtesy of Ken Brown.*

learn the business."[15] In 1904 William Chestnut went to Old Town, Maine, where he hired several canoe builders to train local workers. His aggressive tactics resulted in a lawsuit filed by the Old Town Canoe Company, which initially won; however, the case was overturned on jurisdictional issues with no regard to the merits of the original case.[16] Old Town had made its point. The Chestnut company also attempted to patent the building process for wood-and-canvas canoes in 1905 and ended up in court again, this time against the Peterborough Canoe Company. That case ended without resolution, although Peterborough correctly argued that many manufacturers had been making wood-and-canvas canoes before Chestnut came into existence.[17]

After Chestnut and the PCC merged in 1923, Peterborough continued to build all-wood canoes and "Chestnut concentrated on the canvas-covered canoe market and supplied Peterborough with canoes to sell under their own label," writes Ted Moores.[18] According to Brown, "Canvas-covered canoes came in to Peterborough from New Brunswick by the boxcar load—locally, employees peeled back the burlap wrapping to put on the appropriate company sticker."[19] The last Chestnut canoe was made in 1978 or 1979.

The PCC and CCC became the major manufacturers of all-wood canoes in Canada. In 1915, the PCC acquired the William English Canoe Company.[20] In 1928, the PCC and CCC merged to become part of a larger holding company, Canadian Watercraft Limited. After this merger, their catalogs showed a full range of all-wood canoes, al-though fewer and fewer were sold by then. The Chestnut Canoe Company, part of the larger corporation, made the popular wood-and-canvas canoes. By 1934, even the conservative American Canoe Association—whose members had been customers of the all-wood canoe companies in Peterborough—had recognized the wood-and-canvas canoe as its own class.[21]

## RUSHTON'S CONNECTIONS AND HIS CANOES

J. Henry Rushton started building boats—probably skiffs or guideboats—in a barn in Canton, New York, in 1873. Within three years, he had added canoes; he founded the Rushton Canoe Company around 1875.[22] Rushton's canoes gained notoriety in the 1880s because of an adventurous man of small stature who in his sixties paddled canoes around the near-wilderness of the Adirondacks in upstate New York.

George Washington Sears wrote about his trips under the pen name Nessmuk in his book *Woodcraft* (1888) and in *Forest and Stream* magazine, the leading American outdoor publication of the time.

Nessmuk witnessed the transformation of the isolated Adirondacks into a destination for outdoor tourism. Paddling in the Fulton Chain and the Moose waters in 1880, Nessmuk said, "The weather was perfect, the banks thickly studded with trees, mainly spruce and balsam, and I caught frequent glimpses of beaver meadows, with the light, graceful foliage of the tamaracks showing beautifully as a background to the dark, sombre evergreens of the river banks."[23] By that time, the shorelines were also home to substantial camps and boathouses, such as the Moose River Hotel and the Forge House, that served the tourist trade. The Blue Mountain Lake House, one of three hotels lined up on that shoreline, could host 150 guests.[24]

Nessmuk advocated self-guided and self-contained travel rather than professionally guided trips. "All the waters in the western and northern portions of the wilderness are 'essentially damned,'" he wrote. "As to the short-sighted policy that has caused this, time will show."[25] The Adirondacks had been opened. The "sports" and their expensive guides were everywhere. "You meet them in the most out of the way places, just where you expected to be

George Washington Sears wrote under the pen name Nessmuk in *Forest and Stream* magazine about his canoe trips in the Adirondacks. It was said that he taught America how to camp.

*Courtesy of the St. Lawrence County Historical Association.*

Dr. Arpad Gerster, a prominent New York surgeon, vacationed with his family in the Adirondacks during the 1890s. Here, Gerster portages a Rushton pack canoe at Camp Oteetiwi, Big Island, Raquette Lake.

*Photograph by Alonzo L. Mix. Courtesy of the Adirondack Museum, P009669.*

alone, and always the breech-loader and fly-rod which they hang to like grim death," he wrote.[26] The tourists ate trout and venison harvested from the waters and woods. The situation could not last. "The days of the hermit hunter have passed away forever so far as this wilderness is concerned. The deer are disappearing rapidly and the trout are being thinned out at a deplorable rate."[27]

Nessmuk danced across the lakes and portages in small, quick canoes that permitted solo travel. Because he was only 5 feet, 3 inches tall and 105 pounds, he sought lightweight canoes that made easier work of the lengthy portages, called carries, between Adirondack lakes. In his popular magazine articles, he extolled the virtues of all-wood canoes made by J. Henry Rushton, who himself weighed only 108 pounds. Nessmuk's traveling gear included an extra shirt and pair of socks, a small oilcloth knapsack, a 9-ounce fishing rod, a hatchet and two knives, a blanket roll, a small tent, two nesting cooking pots made of tin, and a few days' supply of tea, butter, bacon, and sugar.[28] On breaks from his long paddles, he also took advantage of the lodging and food available at the Adirondack camps and hotels.

The Adirondacks underwent serious changes in Nessmuk's time. Casual tourists found the former wilderness much more accessible. "By 1886," Hallie Bond writes, "visitors could board a northbound train in New York in the evening, dine and sleep while rumbling up the Hudson valley, and arrive in North Creek, the end of the line for Thomas Clark and William West Durant's Adirondack Railroad, in time for an early breakfast. At 7:00 A.M. they

Leah and J. Henry Rushton around 1884. Leah Rushton was active in community affairs around Canton, New York, and also made sails for Rushton sailing canoes. *Courtesy of the St. Lawrence County Historical Assocation.*

Arthur Fitzwilliam Tait, *A Good Time Coming*, 1862. Oil on canvas, 50.8 × 76.2 cm. This painting depicts the artist's own camp on Raquette Lake, New York. Tait moved to Raquette Lake in 1860 after other areas became crowded with resort hotels. Currier & Ives published this image as a hand-colored lithograph in 1863, which helped attract sportsmen to the Adirondacks.

*Courtesy of the Adirondack Museum, Gift of Harold K. Hochschild, 1963.37.1.*

boarded a stagecoach for the ride to Blue Mountain Lake, theoretically finding themselves at the Prospect House in time for a late lunch."[29] Such tourists tended to stay close to the hotels, as compared to the hunters and anglers who were led from lake to lake by professional guides. Canoes became popular for day trips from the hotels and liveries.

Nessmuk paddled Rushton-built canoes in the Adirondacks. *Wood Drake*, or *Nessmuk No. 1* (as it was later called),[30] was 10 feet long and weighed less than 18 pounds. *Susan Nipper* was 10½ feet long and weighed

16 pounds. *Sairy Gamp*, built in 1882 and named after the character of a drunken nurse who took no water in Charles Dickens's novel *Martin Chuzzlewit*, was the last and the lightest of his canoes and the only original that survives. Nine feet long and 10½ pounds, *Sairy Gamp* belongs to the Smithsonian Institution and is on long-term loan to the Adirondack Museum in Blue Mountain Lake.

After building *Sairy Gamp* in 1882, Rushton wrote to Nessmuk, "It looks as if it might float a hundred pounds,

The Hotel Ampersand looms over an Adirondack guideboat on Lower Saranac Lake, c. 1890. The increased development of hotels and lodges led writer George Washington Sears to despair for the future of the Adirondacks.

*Photograph by Seneca Ray Stoddard. Courtesy of the Library of Congress Prints and Photographs Division, LC-USZ62-74086.*

at least I mean to try 108 in it when done. If it goes busted I will build another one. Now you must *stop* with *this* one, don't try any smaller one. If you get sick of this as a *Canoe* use it for a soup dish."[31]

Later that month, Rushton told Nessmuk that he had *Sairy Gamp* hanging in the rafters of his shop where visitors could see it. "W. W. Durant, son of Durant of Adirondack R.R. was here the other day, he saw the 'Sairy.' He is near six ft and 170# (guess). I had hard work to keep him from ordering a duplicate, as it was he ordered a 'Nessmuk.' No, I go for light weights, but never thought to get down to 10 1/2#." In that same letter, Rushton wrote something prophetic: "If she takes you through the woods safely I think she will be as deserving of honor as the 'Rob Roy' or the Paper Canoe."[32]

While future president Theodore Roosevelt was in the Adirondacks nursing his asthma in July 1883, Nessmuk was picking up his newest canoe nearby in Booneville. "Sears must have smiled when he saw her for the first time, saw the graceful flare at bow and stern, the beamy waist, the shallow depth amidships," writes Christine Jerome. "Beneath coats of oil and shellac, her lapstrake siding, three-sixteenths of an inch thick, seemed recklessly delicate, but her maker had known what he was doing. . . . The lightest boat J. Henry Rushton had ever produced, she was so small that Sears could lift her with one hand."[33]

The *Sairy Gamp* on display at the Adirondack Museum in Blue Mountain Lake, New York.

*Photograph by Jared Beck.*

# FEATHER-WEIGHT CANOES.

## NESSMUK.

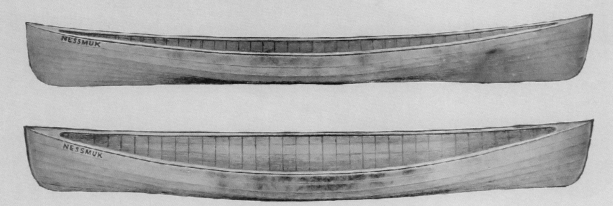

DIMENSIONS—Length, 10½ feet; beam, 27 inches; depth at ends, 15 inches; depth amidships, 9 inches; weight about 20 to 22 pounds.

MATERIAL—Keel and stems, oak; planking, white cedar, 3–16 inch thick; gunwales, spruce; decks, white cedar; ribs, red elm.

CONSTRUCTION—Lap streak; ribs very light and spaced 3 inches; very short decks; no inside floor; no inwales.

FITTINGS—One ash folding seat and one double blade paddle with drip cups.

PRICE—$29.00.

Where cash does not accompany order, our charge for packing the above canoe in burlap and excelsior, will be $1.00; for crating, $1.50; for both, $2.50.

J. Henry Rushton listed the Nessmuk model in his 1907 catalog under the heading "Feather-Weight Canoes."

*Courtesy of the Winterthur Museum Library.*

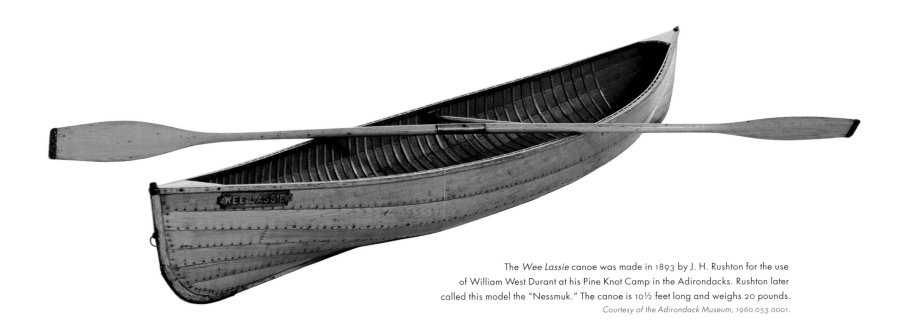

The *Wee Lassie* canoe was made in 1893 by J. H. Rushton for the use
of William West Durant at his Pine Knot Camp in the Adirondacks. Rushton later
called this model the "Nessmuk." The canoe is 10½ feet long and weighs 20 pounds.
*Courtesy of the Adirondack Museum,* 1960.053.0001.

Nessmuk wrote about the first of his Rushton canoes in an 1880 *Forest and Stream* article: "She is ten feet long, twenty-six inch beam, with eight inches rise at center; and, propelled by a light double paddle, with a one-fool power in the middle, gets over the water like a scared loon. . . . She was built by J. H. Rushton of Canton, N.Y., and is by several pounds the lightest canoe ever made by him."[34]

Nessmuk's popular book and magazine articles "taught America how to camp"[35] and also gave Rushton free tes-timonial advertising to his target audience. Rushton used modern business practices, such as cost accounting and national marketing, but nothing beats free. Rushton wrote to Nessmuk in 1882 that his magazine articles "*advertise* me as a builder and *that* is so much *cash* to me."[36]

Nessmuk paddled *Sairy Gamp* 266 miles in the Adirondacks on the 1883 trip that proved to be his last. "I have brought the *Sairy* home without a check in her frail siding," he wrote. "She sits lightly on a shelf, where I can rest my eyes on her."[37]

The Grasse River sweeps by the Rushton Boat Shop, the white building at back left, during a flood in 1885.

*Courtesy of the Adirondack Museum, P036125.*

Rushton's home base was in Canton, New York, about 18 miles southeast of Ogdensburg, which is on the St. Lawrence River. In 1890, Canton had a population of about 2,500. Ample water power from three dams on the Grasse River made Canton home to several industries, including a grist mill, a sash and blind factory, a sawmill, and makers of axes and scythes, shoes, carriages, furniture, and caskets. Ice breakup and spring floods had a habit of damaging the factories arrayed near the falls on the river. Rushton's three-story canoe factory stood near the corner of State Street and Water Street (now Riverside), slightly uphill and only a couple hundred feet from the river.

Rushton's original canoes were all-wood lapstrake boats, and many were decked sailing canoes. In lapstrake construction, such as in the *Sairy Gamp*, the edges of the planks overlap and are usually nailed together with short tacks. "Early in his career he developed practices of constant experimentation, attention to quality, and innovative marketing which eventually made him the best-known canoe-builder in America," writes Bond.[38]

Rushton based his sailing canoes on the English Rob Roy model rather than on Indian designs.[39] John MacGregor, a Scottish sportsman who was introduced to the canoe during a trip to the United States and Canada in 1858, had created the Rob Roy canoes. He told of his journey through Europe in *A Thousand Miles in the Rob Roy Canoe*, a best seller in 1866, the same year he founded the British Royal Canoe Club. At the time, such a watercraft was known as a "double-paddle canoe." Although equipped with a small sail, the Rob Roy was primarily paddled. It lacked lateral plane and could only be sailed downwind.

Decked sailing and cruising canoes—paddled with a double paddle—became popular in North America following MacGregor's writings. The first boat design in the recreational expansion of canoeing in North America was based on the Scottish sportsman's decked Rob Roy. Although MacGregor's exact inspirations for the design

Rushton's version of the famous Rob Roy canoes of John MacGregor was the American Traveling Canoe model, a lapstrake canoe that could be paddled or sailed with a main and a mizzen, or one sail only. This 14-foot craft, with the name *Keego,* was built c. 1881–83 and is probably the oldest American-built decked sailing canoe in existence.

*Courtesy of the Adirondack Museum, 1999.007.0001.*

Frederic Remington donated this drawing to J. Henry Rushton for use in his catalogs. It shows a
Rushton American Traveling Canoe, which, like the Rob Roy canoes, could be paddled or sailed.

*Drawing: Private collection. Photograph courtesy of the Frederic Remington Art Museum, Ogdensburg, New York.*

A decked sailing canoe dated 1882–85 owned by the Adirondack Museum. This 14-foot canoe is similar to MacGregor's *Rob Roy*, with an all-wood lapstrake hull, pin-and-lateen sail rig, and watertight cargo hatch. It may have been built by J. H. Rushton, or it simply may have used Rushton hardware.

*Courtesy of the Adirondack Museum, 1963.166.0001a.*

of *Rob Roy* are not known, he had traveled in North America and had seen both open canoes (commonly called Canadian canoes) and kayaks.

Nathaniel H. Bishop, an American who paddled his canoe *Maria Theresa* 2,500 miles in 1874–75 and was a founder of the ACA, had less love for *Rob Roy*. Bishop wrote:

> It is not many years since Mr. McGregor, of London, built the little Rob Roy canoe, and in it made the tour of interesting European waters. His example was followed by an army of tourists, and it is now a common thing to meet canoe voyagers in miniature flotillas upon the water-courses of our own and foreign lands. Rev. Baden Powell, also an Englishman, perfected the model of the Nautilus type of canoe, which possesses a great deal of sheer with fullness of bow, and is therefore a better boat for rough water than the Rob Roy. The New York Canoe Club have adopted the Nautilus for their model. We still need a distinctive American type for our waters, more like the best Indian canoe than the European models here presented. These modern yacht-like canoes are really improved *kyaks* [sic].[40]

In addition to boatbuilding, Rushton helped organize the American Canoe Association, which provided a social structure for canoeing. He built racing canoes on demand

Rob Roy, Nautilus, and Maria Theresa canoes, as illustrated by Nathaniel Bishop in his *Voyage of the Paper Canoe*, published in 1878. Bishop paddled 2,500 miles in his *Maria Theresa*.

*Courtesy of York University Libraries, Toronto.*

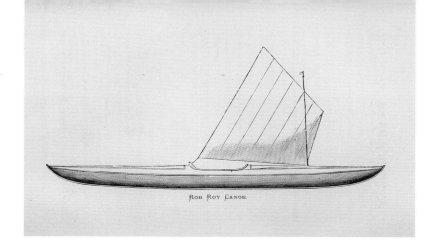

ROB ROY CANOE.

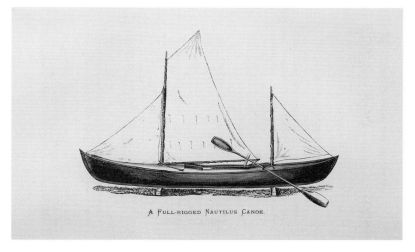

A FULL-RIGGED NAUTILUS CANOE.

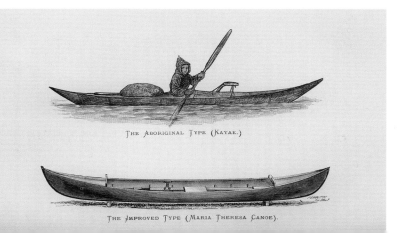

THE ABORIGINAL TYPE (KAYAK.)

THE IMPROVED TYPE (MARIA THERESA CANOE).

This Rushton pack canoe, displayed at the Wisconsin Canoe Heritage Museum, was one of many lightweight small boats he made for hunters and sportsmen.   *Photograph by Eric Lawson.*

for ACA members and took full advantage of the resultant publicity. He was closely connected with paddlers in New York City who were frequent visitors to the Adirondacks near Rushton's home and factory.

### ORGANIZATION OF THE
### AMERICAN CANOE ASSOCIATION

Founded in 1880, the American Canoe Association joined similar clubs, fraternal organizations, foundations, and charities in the age of the industrial robber barons. Hikers, climbers, and boaters from the Massachusetts Institute of Technology also formed the Appalachian Mountain Club in Boston in 1876. Such organizational memberships became wildly popular at the time. According to Bond, at that time nearly half the men in America belonged to fraternal organizations of one sort or another.[41] Bicycling in particular competed for membership and would eventually overtake canoeing, although bicycles could not match canoes as vehicles for romance. Many of these organizations, the ACA included, provided opportunities to dress up and get together with like-minded individuals of a similar social class. "Cruising canoeists were the same social class of men who went on sporting excursions in the Adirondacks," writes Bond of the ACA members. They were "largely professional men, with a sprinkling of business men, and some mechanics," wrote a participant in the 1892 gathering.[42]

Two dozen noted canoeists founded the ACA, including Nathaniel H. Bishop, author of *Voyage of the Paper Canoe*, who proposed the organization; William Alden; Robert J. Wilken; J. Henry Rushton; noted New York boat designer W. P. Stephens; and Lucien Wulsin, who had paddled a decked Rushton canoe to the headwaters of the Mississippi River in 1879.[43]

The ACA held annual summer gatherings, first on Lake George in New York, then on Grindstone Island in the St. Lawrence River, and at other locations, such as Peconic Bay on Long Island, Lake Champlain, the Hudson River, and Chatham on Cape Cod. The assemblies on Juniper Island at Stoney Lake near Peterborough, Ontario, starting in 1883, were instrumental in introducing Peterborough-area builders and paddlers to the larger organization. Canadians joined the Northern Division of the ACA. From 1903 onward, meets were held on Sugar Island, which is still owned by the ACA.[44] Sugar Island sits in Canada near the line of the border that zigzags through the Thousand Islands of the St. Lawrence River. Usually the gatherings lasted for two weeks. These events combined a social quality and camaraderie with intense competition in all-wood cruising and racing canoes that were often made by the best builders in Canada and by Rushton.

In the Thousand Islands region of the St. Lawrence, the ACA paddlers seemed a bit woodsy when compared to the yachting crowd, according to Emmett Smith, curator at the Antique Boat Museum in Clayton, New York.[45] The yachtsmen's money came from the manufacturing fortunes of the day, such as the Singer Sewing Machine Company. The era of the robber barons saw an astonishing accumulation of wealth in a few hands and a display of conspicuous consumption that advertised this wealth to the public. The yachting folks built castles along the St. Lawrence—literally, their mansions were designed to look like castles. They hired naval architects who built long, sleek, high-speed racing motorboats that cost tens of thousands of dollars around the turn of the century. Compared

with them, the ACA outings devoted to canoes seemed quaint.

Though canoes from this period were referred to as "the poor man's yacht," "poor" was a relative term, as canoes represented a considerable expenditure at the time. It might be more appropriate to refer to them as "the poor yachtsman's yacht."

ACA members were mostly middle and upper middle class. Members could afford two weeks and sometimes a month of vacation at a time when most workers were granted no vacation time at all. They raced their expensive Rushton and Peterborough canoes and camped out in style. "The 'poor man' paddling a 'poor man's yacht' was only poor in comparison to the blue-water yachtsmen who competed for the recently-instituted America's Cup. In 1882 Rushton's Princess model cruising canoe cost $120 complete with rig, which might have seemed steep to a carpenter earning $2.25 per day, but cheap to a man considering the expense of berthing and maintaining even an eighteen-foot catboat," writes Bond.[46]

Women attended the ACA summer gatherings but could not become ACA members or hold office. Bond says, "Women remained excluded from full membership until the middle of the next

The St. Lawrence Canoe Club tent at the American Canoe Association meeting on Grindstone Island in 1886. J. H. Rushton is the short, bearded man standing in the center; his wife, Leah, is seated in front of him.

*Courtesy of the Adirondack Museum, P036205.*

An 1881 gathering of canoeists on Canoe Island in Lake George, New York. The three canoes in the foreground include, from left to right, a decked canoe paddled with a double-bladed paddle, a decked sailing canoe, and a Canadian-style all-wood open canoe.

*Photograph by Seneca Ray Stoddard. Courtesy of the Adirondack Museum, P015453.*

A woman races in a solo open canoe class in 1922 at a regatta in Chemong Park just north of Peterborough.

*Courtesy of the Peterborough Museum and Archives, Balsillie Collection of Roy Studio Images, 2000-012 (32-1).*

century."[47] In 1944, the West Coast chapter pressured the national club, and, by a 9–3 vote of the Executive Committee, women became full members in the ACA.[48]

### THE SAILING CANOE

Competition at ACA gatherings produced rapid changes in sailing canoe design. John Summers, who has done extensive research on the history of canoes for a book manuscript about sailing canoes and canoe sailing, says,

"The earliest models of canoes became eponymous. An 1880s report from, say, the Toronto Canoe Club would say something like, 'Eight members signed up for building a clubhouse and we're raising money by subscription. In our boathouse, we have two Rob Roys, three Model 1 Nautiluses, two Shadows and a Pearl.' Those are all particularly early designs that had become types. Shadow was William Alden's traveling canoe model. Nautilus models were the work of Warington Baden-Powell, whose brother Robert started the Boy Scouts. Pearl was another model of English canoe built by Walter Stewart. To an early canoeist, those all meant distinct types. These early canoeists were men of property and education. They were writers and thinkers and polemicists and organizers, as well as sportsmen. Early on they began to compete with each other."[49]

Sailing canoes quickly evolved, or degenerated, depending on your perspective. "Racing being what it is, as soon as you race something you start this accelerated evolution," Summers says. The ACA assigned classes to canoes for racing, depending on whether they were primarily paddled or sailed, or a combination of the two. "As you sail

Walter Stewart sails *Pearl* at the American Canoe Association meeting in 1886. Stewart was an admirer of American-built canoes.

*Photograph by Seneca Ray Stoddard. Courtesy of the Chapman Historical Museum, 1977.218.5169.*

Bob Lavertue in command of the late-nineteenth-century all-wood sailing canoe *Pretty Jane* at the Wooden Canoe Heritage Association assembly at Paul Smith's College, New York, in 2012. *Photograph by Brad Chamberlin.*

American Canoe Association founding member William Alden and his original canoe *Shadow* at the ACA gathering on Lake George in 1881. *Shadow* was a dual-purpose paddling/sailing canoe from the years before racing produced more specialized craft. She had only a shallow external keel and lacked the centerboards and elaborate hardware of true sailing canoes such as *Vesper* or *Nautilus*.    *Photograph by Seneca Ray Stoddard. Courtesy of the New York State Museum, Albany, H-1972.84.84.*

a canoe, you realize first of all that the more lateral plane you have, the more effectively you can go to windward," says Summers.

The early traveling canoe like Alden's *Shadow* had an inch and a half external keel and that was it. He might have been on a broad reach on a good day. But by and large it was an off-, cross-wind, or downwind tool. He certainly wouldn't have been going upwind at 15 degrees off the

wind or something like the America's Cup boats. So you start to add some lateral plane, which needs a trunk. Right away, canoes become more complicated. There's a centerboard that has to go up and down in a trunk. You have to put it somewhere inside the boat and build some structure for it. That means you can sail more effectively. Then the rigs start to get bigger. This was the point where the English and the American traditions started to diverge.

The British built heavier boats for seagoing sailing in which the sailor sat in the bottom of the canoe, while the American canoes were lighter and designed so the sailor could lean over the side for balance. "This difference in techniques became apparent the first time the British came over to sail at the ACA meet," says Summers. "In the 1880s, Warington Baden-Powell brought a number of expeditions over to sail at the meet. Surprise, surprise. When they brought their heavy, ballasted British canoes over and sailed them sitting down, the Americans sat up on the side deck and they cleaned the floor with them. There were lots of discussions that this was not sporting; this was not fair. But you're racing to win."

Seeking advantage, sailors put larger and larger sails on their canoes. Expecting to capsize, they designed self-draining cockpits. "All through this time, sail areas are getting bigger and bigger, to the point where a canoe that was 16 feet long and 30 inches beam with a sliding seat might have had 130 or 140 square feet of sail area. An astonishing amount of sail. Even the winner in a race would capsize four or five or six times," Summers says. Some rule-making had to take place.

As early as 1892, J. Henry Rushton wrote, "To-day the Racing Canoe, like the race horse, is good for little else."[50] Summers says, "Though Rushton built his early business on the racing success of canoes such as Robert Gibson's Vesper, racing sailors had moved on to other builders such as [W. P.] Stephens and [Joshua] Slocum by the early 1890s and Rushton never did build completely decked-over sailing canoes."

"There was a period of really crazy experimentation," Summers says.

People showed up with three-masted rigs, one-masted rigs. But what eventually emerged was a typical size of boat about 16 feet long, about 30 inches beam, and about 85 to 100 square feet of sail. That seemed to be the best all-around combination. These boats still had a very strong element of skipper skill involved. These boats became known as 16/30s because those were the relevant principal dimensions. By 1910 or so, this is what the racers are sailing. By this point, this canoe bears only a tangential resemblance to the cruising canoe. The 16/30s will not stand up. When you launch them, they fall over like a bicycle. As you ride it, it gets steady.

The cruising guys think this is the end of the universe as we know it. They get decried as hopeless, freakish racing machines, dangerous to life and limb, good for nothing else. The guys who sail them are having a grand old time racing around the buoys. The cruisers have harrumphed off and gone back to cruising boats and are actually doing more paddling in Canadian-style canoes.

In 1915, designer Hilding Froling proposed a change in the ACA rules. Froling said, "The present rules for decked canoes produce a craft useless for anything but a few hours of racing."[51]

In this photograph, titled *The Canoe, the Cup and the Captor*, R. W. Gibson poses with the International Challenge Cup, which he won in the Rushton Vesper that he had designed in 1886. This Vesper was a decked sailing canoe 15 feet, 6½ inches long by 30½ inches wide. *Photograph by Seneca Ray Stoddard. Courtesy of the Adirondack Museum, P036295.*

The sailing canoe had evolved into a racing canoe. Besides a mast or two, these canoes had a sliding seat and a centerboard or daggerboard trunk that didn't start until the cockpit bottom. They were completely decked with a footwell as a cockpit. "A 16/30 is an enormous pain in the ass to launch, to rig, and to get away from the dock. To sail it, it's brilliant. But it's more than a pain in the ass otherwise. You wouldn't want that to be your only boat. It's not good for much except around-the-buoys high-speed racing," Summers says.

The British eventually took their revenge. "A guy named Uffa Fox comes on the scene," Summers says. "Uffa Fox was many things—commando, incredibly brave man, eclectic inventor, a very good sailor, sailing instructor of the royal family—taught Prince Charles how to sail. Also a keen technician."

Fox found a solution to the problem of the displacement hull. Displacement hulls are supported by buoyancy, but because they displace water their speed is limited by waterline length. Planing hulls rise out of the water, decreasing the wetted surface. They can move much faster than displacement hulls. Fox created the planing hull that broke out of the formula of speed in a displacement hull being a function of the square root of the waterline length. In 1933, Fox won the Admiralty Trophy and also the decked sailing canoe challenge race at the ACA meet on Sugar Island.[52]

"He took the canoe into planing dinghy territory," says Summers. "That boat survives today in the international 10-square-meter canoe, which is 17 feet long and 40 inches wide, has a 7-foot-long sliding seat, and carries about 108 square feet of sail. Until some of the foil-borne [or hydrofoil] dinghies like the *Moth* came along, it was the world's fastest sailing monohull. It could go 25 knots under sail and it planes upwind. It is wicked fun to sail."

The cruising canoe situation was also complicated. According to Ted Moores, the Peterborough canoe builders "were aware of the developments in Maine," but "they failed to take the canvas-covered canoe seriously."

. . . The American sporting press and American Canoe Association (ACA) were also slow to accept the cedar-canvas canoe; they did not acknowledge it until 1910, when the cedar-canvas canoes were flooding the market. The ACA did not officially recognize the wood-canvas canoe as a class until 1934. American recreational paddlers were members of the elite, gentlemen who liked to think that they had nothing in common with the class of people who used the canoe as a working tool. At the time, the ACA even looked down on the open Canadian canoe because they thought it couldn't compete with their sailing and double paddle canoes.[53]

## NEAR DISASTER FOR RUSHTON

At the Rushton factory in the early 1880s, business was thriving. In 1884, Rushton wrote to Nessmuk that the U.S. Department of Agriculture had offered to place the

⊰ An all-wood decked sailing canoe with a double sail rig on display at the Antique Boat Museum in Clayton, New York.  *Photograph by Brandon Hatcher, drivedivedevour.com.*

Rushton and his staff pose for a photograph outside the three-story boat shop in Canton, New York, 1880s. *Courtesy of the Adirondack Museum, P036132.*

*Sairy Gamp* on exhibition in New Orleans and then in Washington. At that time, Rushton's shop was building about 250 boats a year worth around $18,000.[54] He told Nessmuk, "The decked sailing canoes have taken the lead. Prospects are good for next year. There is very little doubt but the meeting of the A.C.A. will be held in '85 at the same place as '84. This will help me. I have now an order from the Commodore elect for a new and fine canoe for next season and am in correspondence with many more to the same end. You like the feather weight and the backwoods. So do I if I could leave my business for any time, but as a matter of business and to make the builder known abroad the decked sailing canoes are the ones I have to look after."[55] Rushton's catalogs joined the Sears Roebuck and Montgomery Ward catalogs in the mail. Twenty men worked in his factory by 1887.

Two Nomad decked sailing canoes under construction at the Rushton boat shop, c. 1900.

*Courtesy of the Adirondack Museum, P036173.*

J. H. Rushton poses with his Stella Maris model canoe outside his new boat shop in 1882. *Courtesy of the St. Lawrence County Historical Association.*

In 1892–93, Rushton exhibited his canoes at the World's Fair in Chicago, known as the Columbian Exposition. To do so, he went into debt, which proved an untimely business decision when a nationwide depression began in 1893. "In the spring of 1893 a wave of bankruptcies destroyed major firms across the country, and stock prices fell to all-time lows," writes Bond. "In the resulting panic 600 banks and 15,000 businesses failed. The depression that followed lasted until 1897. It was the deepest the nation had known because never before had the fortunes of industry, labor, and farmers been so interdependent."[56] Many small boatbuilders who relied on local clients survived, but Rushton's wider marketing efforts temporarily fell on hard times.

It was an unhappy summer for Rushton, according to Atwood Manley. Orders were scarce and the display of ten boats in Chicago did little to stimulate business. Rushton's son, Harry, said the debt under which his father labored as a result of the investment in the Columbian Exposition "hung like an anchor about his neck for years," Manley wrote. "The Columbian Exposition and the depression reduced Rushton to near-poverty for a period of five years, causing worry and occasional irritability.

"But he weathered hard times with less damage to morale than hundreds of thousands of other Americans, and at the turn of the century, he was in the market with a popular new canoe."[57] Rushton's best seller would conflict with his emotional attachment to all-wood canoes.

Bert and Charlie Morris from Veazie, Maine, also had an exhibit at the Chicago World's Fair, but they weren't as damaged as Rushton by the expenses. Their less-expensive wood-and-canvas canoe business was on an upswing with a recently constructed factory.

A postcard advertising the J. H. Rushton canoe exhibit at the Columbian Exposition in Chicago, 1893.
The expenses of mounting the exhibit and the arrival of a serious economic depression the same
year almost put Rushton out of business.    *Courtesy of the St. Lawrence County Historical Association.*

## ✍ Jule Fox Marshall

*"I was born out of a canoe and moved into one to stay."*
—JULE FOX MARSHALL

In the spring of 1980, I (Norman Sims) stood in a single-car garage looking at a 12-foot-long birch-bark canoe named *Babishe*, deeply darkened with age, alongside a sixty-year-old all-wood Peterborough open sailing canoe with a ⅝-inch black stripe below the gunwales. Suspended on the wall was a red wood-and-canvas Chestnut canoe lightly faded from only a dozen years of life.

A friend and his grandfather stood next to the birch-bark canoe. The ninety-year-old man extended his hand.

"I'm Jule Marshall," he said. I shook his hand and introduced myself. Nodding toward the bark canoe, I said, "So, this is your discovery?" But he had not released my hand. I pulled back, but he held tight and stared straight into my eyes.

"When two canoeists meet," he said, "there is immediately a certain bond between them."

I stopped pulling against his firm grip and squeezed his hand in return. "I'm glad to meet you, Jule."

Jule Fox Marshall was once canoe editor at *Forest and Stream* magazine, the leading outdoor magazine of the 1920s and the official publication of the American Canoe Association. He was active in racing open paddling and sailing canoes at the ACA summer gatherings. He and his wife, Mae, paddled on wilderness trips sponsored by Dr. William Bruette, editor of *Forest and Stream*.

Marshall looked back on canoeing in the twentieth century from the perspective of the canoeing culture

Jule and Mae Marshall. *Courtesy of the Marshall family.*

of the New York City metropolitan area. When Marshall was eight years old, in 1898, his father bought him an all-wood Rushton canoe. "The canoe was 10 feet long, clinker built, narrow ribs, weighed 22 pounds, and the width was 28 inches," he said.[1] When he was twelve, he paddled this canoe, named *Seminole*, from his home base in Whitestone, New York, on the western end of Long Island, to New London, Connecticut, a distance as the gull flies of roughly 100 miles. Later that year, he paddled *Seminole* all the way around Long Island. Accompanying him on the trip was another boy, Ed Davis, in a similar canoe. The trip took eleven days. It's impossible to measure their exact route, but the trip would have been at least 280 miles.

Jule Fox Marshall with *Babishe*.    *Courtesy of the Marshall family.*

His parents let him go wherever he wanted. "They put no restrictions on me at all. So I explored the Long Island Sound, which was my saltwater lake and is one of the most beautiful spots in the world. We couldn't get away from it. We went to live on the other side of the sound at Greenwich, Connecticut. I spent twenty-five years there. I was born out of a canoe and moved into one to stay."

His father had been in the export-import business. His mother was an amateur artist. His father "saw to it that I had all kinds of equipment for growing up as a boy. Archery equipment. Tennis. We had our own tennis court, a clay court. A canoe, as soon as I could swim. Oh, and fly rods particularly. Golf clubs, but I didn't take any interest in it. I liked the water and stayed with that."

Marshall attended college at Pratt Institute, where he studied design, engineering, and draftsmanship. He designed a felt countertop display mat for a cigar manufacturer, which ordered a half million copies. After that event, the American Felt Company hired Marshall to work in New York, Philadelphia, Cincinnati, and Chicago. Eventually he became a member of the board of directors, and "from then on the rest of it was a long easy parade into success." He retired as a vice president of the company in 1958.

As a member of the same socioeconomic class as his father, Marshall was able to order customized all-wood open racing canoes, which were built by Peterborough and the Canadian Canoe Company. "I parted with *Seminole* only to purchase *Squaw* next," he said. *Squaw* was a Rushton Indian Girl canvas-covered canoe. "I disposed of *Squaw* only to acquire the first all wood V-bottom, flush skin 16-foot by 30-inch, 58-pound racing canoe built by Peterborough and available in a class developing at Brooklyn Canoe Club, Gravesend Bay in lower N.Y. Harbor. Named *Terrapin*." From 1914 to 1916, he owned a 17-foot B. N. Morris canoe for use on rivers and streams in Pennsylvania.

He used his education as an engineer to customize canoes after he joined the ACA in 1908, at age eighteen, and the Inwood Canoe Club of New York the following year. Marshall said the main reason to attend the two-week gatherings at Sugar Island in the St. Lawrence River was for the pleasure of the company, but the canoe races were also an opportunity to compete and innovate. At first, Marshall raced *Terrapin*.

"Up to 1917," he wrote, "when we left for the West, the summer regattas and camps were most attractive. We camped with fine outfits and got to know each other, *really*. I joined the Inwood C. C. of N.Y.C., 40 members. Truly a fine group of young business men, excellent canoeists. I met Mae—she came with her brother, a member of a rival group, the Port Washington C. C. of New Jersey. The canoes were almost 100% Peterborough, or Deans, Wm English, Chestnut, all Canadian types, 16' × 30" with beautiful underwater design and handsome profiles above. All wood. These wood canoes were for racing by paddle or sail, one

Jule Fox Marshall, sketch of canoe racers at an American Canoe Association gathering, 1920s. *Courtesy of the Marshall family.*

leeboard, no rudder, and also used for flat water cruising."

Pictures of Marshall at this age show a man of short stature with strong arms. All that paddling on the Sound paid off. Mae's brother, Tom Zuk, proved to be his stiffest competition in ACA sailing races. Tom and his son, Larry, later became commodores of the ACA and were canoe racers.

"As the 1914 season opened, I had a desire to win some of the important historic trophies at the ACA encampment," Marshall said. "I ordered a V bottom Dean 16 foot, 30-inches wide, 10-inches deep, and 40 pounds, made in Toronto. When I arrived at Sugar Island, I found the *Terrapin II* had to be supplemented by another canoe for fishing, exploring and general purpose use so I went to the Gananoque C.C. Livery and acquired a Canadian #16 for $8.00. That later became *Turtle Dove #1*. After much study for a sailing canoe trial, it became a winner in its class and the model for the sizable 'Lady Bug' sailing class, which I named after the 'Lady Bug' trophy originated at Brooklyn Canoe Club." The Lady Bug class, which began in 1907, was an open cruising canoe division where the boats were steered with a paddle rather than a rudder and the lateen sail was limited to about 40 square feet.[2]

Jule Fox Marshall, c. 1926.   *Courtesy of the Marshall family.*

Jule Fox Marshall won the Admiralty Trophy, which was for cruising-type canoes, in 1920. He won the trophy again in 1928, 1930, and 1931. He won the Manhattan Trophy for Tandem Paddling in 1914 (with W. A. Bartholomew) and in 1920 (with J. W. Kempson). He won the Cruising Trophy, awarded as the Open Sailing Trophy since 1907, in 1928. Marshall won the George W. Gardner Trophy, awarded since 1914 (no exact type of race indicated), in 1930 and 1935. In 1916, 1920, and 1925, he won the Wilderness Trophy, presented by *Forest and Stream* since 1914. And in 1928 and 1930, he won the All Outdoors Trophy for open sailing canoes.[3]

His brother-in-law, Thomas Zuk, won the Paddling Championship Trophy in 1913, the Admiralty Trophy in 1921, the Cruising Trophy in 1920, and the All Outdoors Trophy for open sailing canoes in 1926.

"I never built a canoe," Marshall said, "but I knew what I wanted and I got other people to do that."

Marshall ordered custom canoes from Peterborough, modifying the design a little bit each time until he got the boat he was looking for, such as by requesting shagbark hickory gunwales. "Considering that it was confined to 16' 6" and 30-inch width, I wanted to find the right length in there. Most of them were as close to 16 as possible to keep the weight down. I reasoned that 16' 3" was the right approach to the entry of the water. It seemed to me the smoothest contour design." He had four more canoes built before he got the right one. "The rig and the design for sailing was my own thinking on that. I used the thinnest amount of wood I could for the leeboard, and the paddle was used for steering. The sail was probably my own design. I stayed right with it. I couldn't go into Olympic training. I didn't have the time to devote and the pain that goes with that, paddling thousands of miles and paddling every day. I couldn't do it. Up to that point, I did the best I could.

"My last Peterborough was 16' 3" by 30" with a 2" bottom line rake at each end away from normal 12" depth—the end profiles were perfect as I designed them." His last open sailing canoe, sitting in the garage of that home in 1980, was built by the Canadian Canoe

Mae Marshall.  *Courtesy of the Marshall family.*

*Turtle Dove V*, built in 1926.  *Courtesy of the Marshall family.*

Company in 1926 to match ACA requirements and named *Turtle Dove V*. "At Inwood, all canoes had a red turtle at the bow," Marshall said. "My *Turtle Dove* indicated that I was a sailing turtle." On a tag affixed to that canoe, Marshall wrote, "It is probably the fastest 'cruising' canoe ever built."

He knew several canoe designers. In a letter, Marshall said, "I knew W. P. Stephens, N.Y.C., Drake Sparkman, Larchmont, N.Y., Hilding Froeling, Lubec, Maine (best of all). All gone. Also know Max Andersson, Västerås, Sweden, (tops on Olympic canoes now)."

In his later years, Marshall saw some things that disappointed him. Aluminum canoes were stacked in the parks and camps, but he didn't see anyone paddling them. People didn't seem to know how to paddle the right way, nor did they enjoy themselves the way he and his acrobatic friends had at the ACA gatherings— walking on gunwales and thwarts, tilting at each other in novelty events, and comparing boat designs. Even the ACA had changed. "It's a sorry situation. It doesn't have the class of people in it, the professional people. Sorry to say."

## CHAPTER 5

# Wood-and-Canvas Canoes

OTHING KEPT J. Henry Rushton's Boat Shop afloat better than the Indian Girl wood-and-canvas canoe.

At the turn of the twentieth century, the first wave of recreational interest in the all-wood decked canoe receded. A new market emerged for open wood-and-canvas canoes at the tail end of the depression of 1893, and we can understand why. Wood-and-canvas canoes were cheaper.

In 1903, Rushton's all-wood cruising sailing canoe models, such as Wren and Vesper, cost $100 and included only the mast tubes, plates, and hatch fastenings; add rudder and centerboard and the cost went to $170; and

◄ Wood-and-canvas canoes built by the B. N. Morris Company of Veazie, Maine, among other builders, were made to order for paddlers overseas. This highly prized Morris canoe is owned by Tim Rowe in Great Britain, where several clubs collect the Canadian-style canoes built in North America.

*Courtesy of the Wooden Canoe Heritage Association, UK Chapter.*

with a mast and sail it could hit $200. His all-wood open Canadian-style canoes, such as the Ugo model, cost $85 for a top-grade 16-footer. At the same time, an Old Town HW model 16-foot wood-and-canvas canoe in top grade cost $38, and only $30 in the medium grade. Rushton's 16-foot Indian Girl wood-and-canvas canoe, introduced in 1902, in top grade cost $39, which put the Indian Girl in direct competition with the Maine builders.[1] In 1901, a 16-foot B. N. Morris Indian Model Extra Beam wood-and-canvas canoe made in Veazie, Maine, sold for $42.[2] For canoe paddlers in the second wave, who might be comparing the cost of a bicycle to that of an all-wood canoe, the price differences for wood-and-canvas canoes were significant.

Building "rag canoes" was a market decision, possibly forced upon Rushton by his Columbian Exposition debts

Planking is applied to a pair of Indian Girl canoes
in the Rushton Boat Shop, early twentieth century.

*Courtesy of the Adirondack Museum, Po36211.*

Rushton Indian Girl canoes in the sanding room, c. 1908. After the bare
wood hulls were sanded, canvas was stretched over the hulls and filled with
a special compound.  *Courtesy of the St. Lawrence County Historical Association.*

and by serious competition from the Maine builders, such as E. M. White, B. N. Morris, and the recently formed Old Town Canoe Company. In his 1902 catalog, Rushton announced that he had hired "a skilled builder from Maine, a man with fourteen years' experience." This was probably Melvin F. Roundy, who was in Ogdensburg, New York, for the census of 1900 but had also lived in Maine.[3] According to Dan Miller, it was a naval architect named Fred Martin, who had worked at Racine, Wisconsin, and moved to

Clayton, New York, who designed the Indian Girl. Roundy constructed the Indian Girl in 1901. He may have built boats for a company such as the Spaulding St. Lawrence Boat Company in Ogdensburg in 1900, as well as building canoes in Maine.[4] In 1903, the Rushton catalog acknowledged the origins of canvas-covered canoes: "To the several builders of this class of work in the 'Pine Tree State' [Maine], belongs most of what credit there is in the production up to nearly the present time."[5] Miller estimates

# CANVAS COVERED CANOES—INDIAN GIRL.

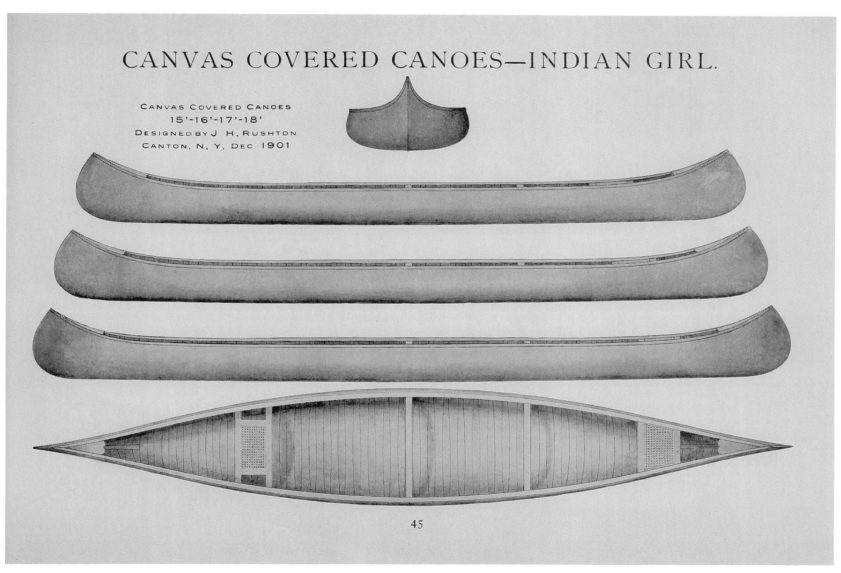

CANVAS COVERED CANOES
15'-16'-17'-18'
DESIGNED BY J. H. RUSHTON
CANTON, N. Y, DEC. 1901

45

Rushton's Indian Girl canoe could be ordered in sizes ranging from 15 to 18 feet. The stern seat and decks are distinctive markers of the Indian Girl.

*Courtesy of the Winterthur Museum Library.*

Workers at the Rushton Boat Shop in 1905. J. Henry Rushton stands at lower left. *Courtesy of the St. Lawrence County Historical Association.*

that about 5,500 Indian Girl canoes were made in total. The model set sales records in Rushton's shop. Production ended in 1916, and the Indian Girl remains one of the most coveted wood-and-canvas canoes.

Rushton stood by the lapstrake all-wood canoe. "I am a staunch believer in the Cedar Canoe without the canvas cover, and no less so now than heretofore," he wrote in the 1903 catalog, "but I cater to the wishes of many, and among the number are those who prefer the canvas covering."[6] He assigned construction of the Indian Girl to Roundy, and in 1904 began to pull

A 16-foot, 10-inch, 76-pound Rushton Indian Girl canoe built between 1911 and 1916. In terms of quality, this was an "OI" grade, which was third-best. This Indian Girl came with open gunwales, which were cheaper to produce.

*Courtesy of the Adirondack Museum, 1983.037.0001.*

Nelson Brown, master craftsman, foreman, and the longest-tenured employee at the Rushton canoe factory, shapes a paddle in the wood-and-canvas building room in 1908.

*Courtesy of the St. Lawrence County Historical Association.*

back from the business because of ill health. On May 1, 1906, at age sixty-two, J. Henry Rushton died of Bright's disease, or inflammation of the kidneys.[7]

His son, Harry, took over management of the firm in 1905. When J. Henry Rushton died, the shop had six hundred boats and canoes in stock, most of them Indian Girls.[8] The shop was incorporated as J. H. Rushton, Inc., and that label on any Rushton boat dates it to 1906 or later. After 1911, the shop was managed by Judd W. Rushton, Henry's half-brother. The Boat Shop closed in late 1916 or early 1917 with the onset of World War I, which was responsible for a dramatic decline in recreational canoe sales.[9]

Rushton canoes are justifiably glorified. The Indian Girl was his best-selling canoe, but his all-wood canoes are even more rare and beautiful.

## RISE OF THE WOOD-AND-CANVAS CANOE

In Maine along the Penobscot River, the modern canoe evolved from Native American birch-bark canoes. Builders in Maine and Canada were traveling great distances by the 1880s to find usable canoe birch trees. In the region around Old Town, Maine, all-wood bateaux or skiffs—flat-bottom rowboats used in the lumber industry—were common. When someone wanted a canoe, they bought one from the local Penobscot Indians or built their own using birch bark.

Canvas, however, was readily at hand for use in sails, clothing, and carriages. Several builders in Peterborough, Ontario, started using canvas before it was used in Maine.

A Gerrish canoe at McTrickey Cottage on Madawaska Lake, Aroostook County, Maine, c. 1915.

*Collections of Caribou Public Library, item 13192. Courtesy of www.vintagemaineimages.com.*

Dan Herald tried putting a layer of treated cotton or canvas between two wooden layers. A Peterborough newspaper article in 1878 reported that John Stephenson had built a canoe with the outside "covered with light canvas, treated with various gums and varnishes."[10] Stephenson's 1879 Canadian patent application said, "The second part of my invention relates to the covering of the said Hull with paper or cotton or other textile fabric fastened on with waterproof glue forming a waterproof skin to the wooden hull."[11] Intermittent communication existed between Canadian and American builders, so Stephenson's short-lived experiment with canvas may have been known by craftsmen near Old Town. In wood-and-canvas canoes, however, the canvas is not glued to the hull but instead is stretched and tacked at the gunwales, and thus it can easily be replaced.

The turning point may have come when Evan H. (Eve) Gerrish built a wood-and-canvas canoe over a form. Others may have built such a craft before Gerrish,[12] but we have the testimony of another great canoe builder, Edward M. White, of an encounter in Maine. "I saw a man by the name of Evan Gerrish of Bangor riding in the Penobscot River in a canvas-covered canoe," White said. "I quickly saw the advantages of that kind over my birchbark, which moreover

A Gerrish canoe, c. 1900, serial number 1772, restored by Zachary Smith. Note the reed wrapping at the end of the gunwales, which was a Gerrish feature. *Courtesy of Zachary Smith.*

Ella and Bert Morris (far right) and his brother Charlie (far left) pose with their staff in front of the B. N. Morris storefront, c. 1900.   *Courtesy of Daniel Miller.*

leaked. I examined the canvas canoe closely, and in a short time was able to produce one which was so good someone wanted to buy it."[13]

The key to this evolutionary change was not the canvas, but the use of metal bands on a form for building the canoe and of waterproof filler for the canvas. Another fertile crescent of canoe building—the area along the Penobscot River through Old Town, Veazie, and Bangor, Maine—became a center for the new wood-and-canvas technology in the 1880s and 1890s.

The Big Four original builders in that area were Eve Gerrish, E. M. White, Bert Morris, and Guy Carleton. A historical list at the Wooden Canoe Heritage Association (WCHA) website lists forty-seven smaller companies making birch-bark or wood-and-canvas canoes in Maine prior to 1900.[14]

Bert Morris explained the transition in one of his early catalogs:

The birch-bark canoes built by the Indians years ago were very light and graceful and easily handled, but in spite of the care exercised in their construction they were far from reliable, owing to the lack of forms on which to properly bend the ribs, and lack of proper protection for the bark covering, which was liable to puncture from even a slight contact with a rock or some hidden obstruction. The Indian's ideas of building a light water craft were recognized by the white men as good ideas for a beginning, but it was apparent that owing to the scarcity of suitable bark for the covering it would be necessary to use some other material, and for many years the white man's ingenuity was severely taxed to devise an improvement over the Indian's craft.[15]

Bert Morris and his brother Charlie, carpenters and sons of a carpenter, opened their wood-and-canvas canoe

The B. N. Morris canoe factory in Veazie, Maine. Bert and Charlie Morris started building canoes around 1891 in a shop behind Bert's house, and later in this factory, until a fire in 1919. Only the front-most building survives today.   *Courtesy of the Penobscot Marine Museum.*

This 17-foot B. N. Morris canoe was originally built c. 1912 and has been carefully restored by Rollin Thurlow of the Northwoods Canoe Company in Atkinson, Maine.

*Photograph by Steve Ambrose.*

company around 1891 in a shop behind Bert's house in Veazie, Maine, a small town located between Old Town and Bangor on the Penobscot River. Charlie, six years older than Bert, had been a carriage maker before they started building canoes.[16] The Morris brothers produced fast, stable canoes with tumblehome and a little rocker that were a dream to paddle. They were copied over and over in later years by other builders such as Joe Seliga in Minnesota and the Chestnut Canoe Company in Canada. By World War I, they had a large factory on the edge of town and were successfully competing with the largest canoe builders. Then in 1919 the factory burned to the ground.

E. M. White began building boats in 1889. Guy Carleton had started a boat company in the 1870s, largely building bateaux, and by 1888 was listed in the Maine Register as a builder of wood-and-canvas canoes.

The canoe changed Evan H. Gerrish's life. Born in 1847, he worked as a Maine guide and, as often happened, had difficulty with the somewhat fragile nature of birch. His experiments with canvas apparently led to the first wood-and-canvas canoe, at least in the Penobscot area. He moved to Bangor at age twenty-eight and opened a shop that sold paddles, fishing gear, and wood-and-canvas canoes. By 1878, he was producing about eighteen canoes a year, and six years later the number was up to fifty.[17]

IN THE SHADOW
OF MT. KINEO.

1204

Cornelia "Fly Rod" Crosby fishes from an E. M. White canoe on Moosehead Lake in Maine, c. 1895.
Two years later, she became the first licensed Maine guide. Her presentations and popular syndicated
columns made her a role model for young women and promoted her personal philosophy
of athleticism and independence. *Collections of the Maine Historical Society, item 15315.*

The Maine builders used two important and innovative building techniques.

First, wood-and-canvas canoe builders turned birch-bark building techniques upside down, literally. Bark canoes were made upright, with stakes driven into the ground to outline the shape. All the work was right-side-up, looking down into the canoe. Wood-and-canvas hulls started off upside down over a form. Peterborough builders had used forms created from dugouts as early as the 1850s, but the Maine forms had the advantage of metal bands placed on the form everywhere a rib would be. The ribs were steam bent over the metal bands. Thin cedar planking was nailed through the ribs. The nail tips hit the metal bands and bent back, or clinched, into the rib.[18] The hull could be easily removed from the form. Then canvas was stretched around the hull, tacked in place along the gunwales, filled with special compounds, sanded, and finally painted, sometimes in elaborate patterns.

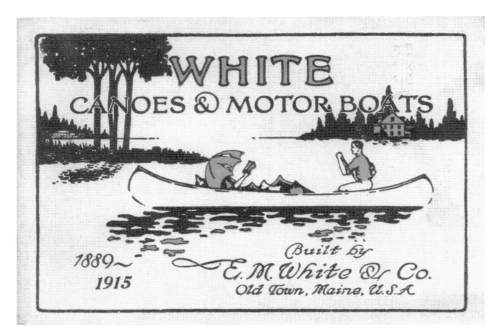

The E. M. White Company catalog cover from 1915 shows a courting canoe.

*Courtesy of Daniel Miller.*

Tom Thomson, *Canoe and Lake, Algonquin Park,* spring 1913. Oil on canvas, laid down on panel, 17.5 × 25 cm.   *Private collection.*

Second, while canvas is a sturdy fabric, it is not water-proof, and paint is too brittle to seal it. After stretching canvas over the hull, builders needed to fill it with a material that would dry hard and waterproof, yet remain flexible. Canvas filler was as important for the new industry as were metal bands on the form.

The filler recipe may have roots in the manufacture of stagecoaches and carriages.[19] In a Veazie catalog, undated but post-1905, Bert Morris described the canvas and filler on his canoes and then commented, "The finished result is a surface as fine as carriage work and equally as durable."[20] Historical records indicate some overlap of canoe builders with carriage merchants (including Charlie Morris), woodworkers, and blacksmiths.[21]

The origins of the filler formula probably reached back to medieval artists who created sizing and gesso to smooth canvas or wood for paintings or carvings. Linen canvas for painting had a sizing of glue or white lead and turpentine. It was filled with a gesso made of glue and a white powder, and then sanded smooth. Often chalk was used, or plaster of Paris, or the highest-quality silica. Artists and craftspeople did not have highly developed chemistry sets; the same basic ingredients, such as linseed oil, silica, and turpentine, were used repeatedly with different additives.

Canvas canoe filler comes in many formulas, which were originally secret. Today there's less secrecy, and fillers can be purchased pre-made. Tom Seavey in New Hampshire rubs the stretched canvas with a compound that he makes from boiled

linseed oil, paint as a binder, lots of silica powder, Japan drier (which helps dry oil-based products), and solvents or thinners. Older fillers included white lead to protect from mildew, but the frequent use of toxic white lead explains why a lot of canoe builders had few children. Rushton's recipe was "5 lbs Silacks [shellac], 1½ qt. Turpentine, 1 qt. oil, 1 pt Japan [drier], 2 lbs white lead."[22] Rushton may have used alcohol or heat to dissolve the shellac flakes. The filler takes from two weeks to two months to cure on the hull, after which it can be sanded smooth and painted.[23]

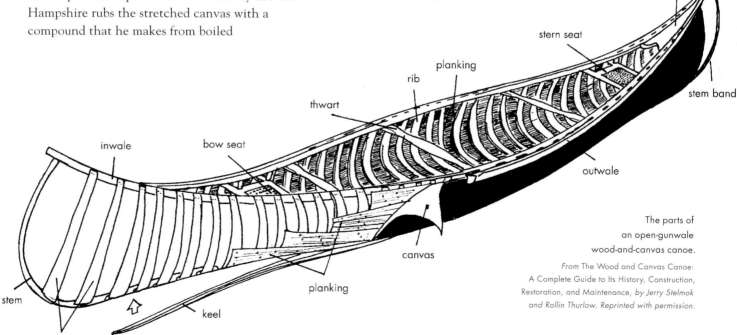

The parts of an open-gunwale wood-and-canvas canoe.

*From* The Wood and Canvas Canoe: A Complete Guide to Its History, Construction, Restoration, and Maintenance, *by Jerry Stelmok and Rollin Thurlow. Reprinted with permission.*

Canvas being stretched over a 1905 Morris Veazie model canoe. Note the tacks at the gunwale that hold the canvas to the boat. *Photograph by Tom Seavey.*

## ❧ Tom Seavey

Tom Seavey, who builds and restores wood-and-canvas canoes, got into the craft with the help of Jerry Stelmok, coauthor with Rollin Thurlow of *The Wood and Canvas Canoe: A Complete Guide to Its History, Construction, Restoration, and Maintenance.*

Seavey had spent years as a professional musician and working in the fine furniture and cabinet refinishing business. He fell in love with restoring canoes after an experience working on an 18-foot 1937 Old Town Guide, during which he consulted Stelmok and Thurlow's book. Then Seavey started attending Wooden Canoe Heritage Association (WCHA) gatherings during the summer.

One night around the campfire, Stelmok heard Seavey singing. "Jerry heard me and said, 'Tom, I didn't know you were such a musician.' I said, 'That's really what I am. I went to school for it and I've been a professional musician for

years.' I told him I'd like to get into this wooden canoe thing more. He said, 'You should come up and just visit sometime.' We started hanging out and visiting and getting to know each other and then realized we're both

Tom Seavey with a 1905 Morris
Veazie canoe that he restored.

*Photograph by Norman Sims.*

completely pathetic. Jerry calls it the Pathetic Bastard Club. We refused to get a real job and grow up. So we clicked. I worked with him, for him, learning a lot about the process."[1]

Seavey says working with Stelmok became a habit. "I refused to go away. We've since been great friends and worked together." Stelmok now builds the boats that Old Town sells as its wood-and-canvas canoes. Seavey helped build the forms and created a honey-amber sprayed finish for the interiors of Stelmok's Millennium Sojourner canoes.

At his shop in Henniker, New Hampshire, Seavey builds new canoes based on two versions of E. M. White boats and restores old wooden canoes. Fifteen years of wood-finishing skills make his work special.

The tangled business of restoring a rotted canoe stem.   *Photograph by Norman Sims.*

"I like taking an old canoe and making it look *not* like it's just been fixed. Making it look like that's the way it's supposed to be. That replaced rib doesn't show. Then the rest of it is canvasing and filling the canvas and leveling it, and leveling it, and leveling it. A lot of great builders do that and take the time to sand it out meticulously so that your final coat really comes out nice. It's a cross between woodworking and auto body. You're leveling out that finish so when the final one goes on it looks really beautiful. Having experience spraying gives me a little edge for laying on that perfect finish." He worked for years on high-end antiques and restoring office interiors, such as for a law firm in Boston with 110-year-old quarter-sawn oak that had to be matched perfectly. "It works great for canoes," he says.

Seavey built his shop as well as the log home where he lives with his wife, Jan. When a canoe arrives for restoration, Seavey first has to decide if it's worth it, or whether the boat is kindling for the burn pile, or a flowerpot. Almost anything can be restored, but it's not always worth the time, effort, and money.

He starts thinking ahead about fifteen steps. "You always think about the physics of what's going on. What's going to happen?

"The ends are always weak. I've only had one canoe in fifteen years that didn't need work on the structural part of the ends. Of all things, it was a 1910 Charles River canoe that was healthy in the stems and the inwales. I'm always chopping down stems and scarfing on and adding inwale ends. Even canoes from the fifties need that."

He scans the boat. The wood looks like old barn boards, gray and worn out, but can come back to golden brown. He talks with the owner. Is the owner happy with the old finish that can look nice if refurbished, or does the owner want it to look like a brand-new canoe?

The most difficult and tedious task can be replacing the inwales. They have to be steam bent and cut to exact lengths. Combine that with replacing a dozen or more ribs, and the old canoe can lose its shape. "I'll do a section at a time with strongbacks on the canoe to keep its shape. You can't hurry because if you take them off too soon and the ribs start bellying out, then you're going to have a bubble in the floor," says Seavey.

Other problems crop up all the time. A fine piece of mahogany gets milled and steamed, but when it's put on the jig for bending, it breaks—ruining a whole day's work and an expensive board. The ribs on a Morris canoe must be tapered and then fitted into the notched inwales. After carefully applying a fine spray finish, a moth might land on the paint. Seavey has seen almost everything that can go wrong, but when something new comes along, he calls Stelmok.

One of his favorite restorations was the Bass family's canoe. John F. Bass was an ambassador who bought a Carleton canoe from Abercrombie and Fitch in about 1910, at the time when the Carleton Canoe Company had just been sold to Old Town. They called it the XX model, which meant that it was experimental and that Old Town didn't quite know what to do with the Carleton forms. "The uncle in the family, who grew up in that canoe as a boy, got to see it again. He was in his late eighties. The restored canoe was delivered. As it was told to me, he stepped into the canoe, pushed off, and he turned around and he had tears in his eyes and a smile on his face," says Seavey.

"I'm finding that a lot of the grandchildren are coming back to restore these canoes rather than the sons. The sons went into the modern stuff—the fifties food and the quick-and-easy—and the wooden canoe, that old thing, got stuck under the porch. But the grandchildren found it and said, 'What's going on with this? I remember being in this.' I've done a lot of canoes for grandkids with Grandpa going out in the canoe. They want it back. They want it back, and I do it for them. It's a killer feeling.

Tom Seavey attaching the extended outwale to the canvassed Veazie canoe.

*Photograph by Norman Sims.*

They're living with it again. It's not a lot of money to have that dream come back. To me, that's really worth it."

Fifteen years into his craft, Seavey relishes calling himself a canoe builder. "I love this whole process," he says. "I love providing this craft. A lot of people convey feelings to me about how magical it is for them to get into their boat and just disappear. Working on them, my daydream becomes: 'I wish I was in one and off and gone.' That's mostly what goes through my head.

"It's the closest thing to a drifting, ethereal spirit because you're not really grounded. And wooden canoes are so beautifully flexible. They're in touch with the oneness of that water." He recalls that on a canoe trip on the Allagash River in northern Maine an eagle landed in a tree above him. "That whole aloneness adds a little bit of scariness to it. You really need to pay attention. You can't screw up with the axe. Everything is careful and thought-out. You're out there alone. My ears get so sensitive. That time I heard that eagle coming, I was alone and I heard this wooosh.

"I have this saying that I dreamed out of my head: *'From a wooden canoe, you see more than just the world.'* If you let go, you actually transcend and see a lot more of yourself, of your personal circumstances, of your loved ones around you. There's a huge reflection that goes with being in a wooden canoe, for me. It's a magical thing."

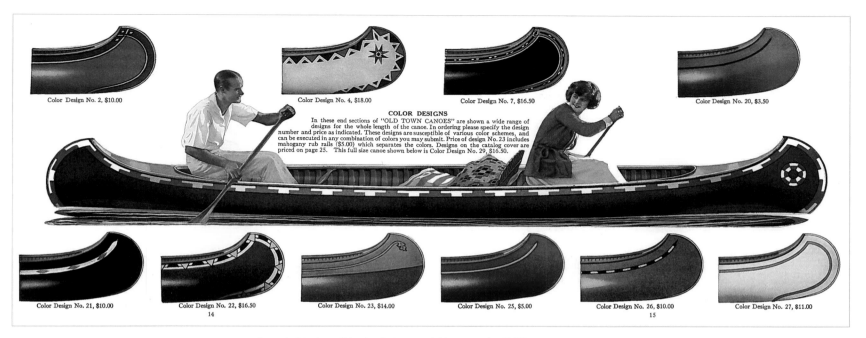

Several of the beautiful color designs available in 1926 for Old Town canoes.

*Courtesy of the Gray Family Collections.*

These two technological innovations—forms with metal bands and canvas filler—produced social and cultural change. Birch-bark canoes were fabulous in design and often graceful in execution, but it took considerable skill to build them. Most didn't travel far from their birthplaces. As was true of the all-wood canoes built in Ontario and New York, few people could own one. Once builders like Morris, Gerrish, White, Carleton, and Old Town in Maine, Rushton in New York, and Canadian builders such as Chestnut started producing wood-and-canvas canoes and sending catalogs through the mail, the second wave of recreational canoeing took shape in North American life.

Canvas did not require constant attention, as did birch bark. It was easily obtained and could be painted in beautiful designs; damaged canoes could be restored or recanvassed. Generally owners replaced the canvas every twenty years, or more frequently if the canoe got regular use.

The rise of the wood-and-canvas canoe coincided with a change in the American view of the outdoors. Settlers, loggers, and farmers who struggled to earn a living

Railroad advertising, such as this 1920 poster by Walter L. Greene, attracted tourists to Lake Placid. An overnight train from New York City brought visitors, rested and fed, to the edge of the Adirondacks.

*Courtesy of the Library of Congress Prints and Photographs Division, LC-USZC4-14976.*

George Washington Sears, who wrote under the name Nessmuk, was an early staff writer at *Forest and Stream*, one of the most popular outdoor periodicals of its day. In the 1920s, thirty years after his death, the magazine was still publishing a regular feature called "Nessmuk's Campfire," which offered reviews of the latest hunting and fishing equipment.

outdoors often viewed nature as an adversary. In the late nineteenth century, however, urbanites started to think of the backwoods as a place to take pleasure in hunting and fishing, as a beautiful quiet landscape, and as a place to affirm oneself against nature's challenges. The increasingly crowded, smoky, noisy, and dirty cities created by late-nineteenth-century factories made the vanishing "wilderness"[24] look better by comparison. As the country recovered from the depression of 1893, a new middle class took up canoeing as a leisure activity.

Theodore Roosevelt, whom Mark Twain called "the most popular human being that has ever existed in the United States,"[25] promoted a "strenuous life" for men. As president from 1901 to 1909, Roosevelt created five national parks and signed the Antiquities Act of 1906 that permitted presidents to designate national monuments. The system of parks grew enormously after 1906, especially after Congress created the National Park Service in 1916.[26] Rampant industrialism made it seem even more important to preserve undeveloped landscapes and for people to go see those landscapes.

The early canvas canoe makers, including Gerrish, White, Morris, Carleton, the Old Town Canoe Company, and later Rushton, mailed their catalogs all over the United States and Canada. Some advertised in the new, large-circulation magazines, creating their own national brands. Benson Gray's research shows how the number of canoe makers grew. "I have found that there were no canoe builders listed in the *Maine Register* from 1856, three in 1887, six in 1891, and 18 in 1913," he writes.[27]

Wood-and-canvas canoes made in Maine factories were carefully packed in straw and burlap and sent on train cars to distant towns. By 1914, the Old Town Canoe Company was selling as many canoes in one year as the total number of Indian Girl canoes built in the history of Rushton's Boat Shop.

## Old Town Canoe Company Sales, 1907–17

| YEAR | OLD TOWN | CARLETON | TOTAL |
|------|----------|----------|-------|
| 1907 | | | 2,101 |
| 1908 | | | 2,000 |
| 1909 | | | 2,450 |
| 1910 | | | 3,100 |
| 1911 | 3,310 | 490 | 3,800 |
| 1912 | 3,541 | 590 | 4,131 |
| 1913 | 4,600 | 600 | 5,200 |
| 1914 | 5,282 | 1,013 | 6,295 |
| 1915 | 5,247 | 672 | 5,919 |
| 1916 | 6,405 | 820 | 7,225 |
| 1917 | 4,868 | 623 | 5,491 |

*Estimated by Benson Gray*

Shipments of Old Town canoes arrived wrapped in straw and burlap at Shenk & Tittle, a sporting goods store in Lancaster, Pennsylvania. *Courtesy of Susan T. Audette.*

Dozens of newly finished canoes were stored on the roof of the
Old Town Canoe Company factory. *Courtesy of the Gray Family Collections.*

The businesses of the innovative individual canoe builders did not last long in the twentieth century. Many of the smaller Canadian companies were absorbed by the Peterborough Canoe Company and the Canadian Canoe Company. In Maine, Gerrish made beautiful boats from American chestnut with spruce root lashings on the bow deck, like the Indian canoes, but he died early in the twentieth century; in 1909 the business was sold to his foreman, Herbert Walton, who produced a few canoes into the 1930s.[28] Guy Carleton's company was sold in 1910 to Old

Town, and the Carleton factory burned in 1911. Old Town produced a wood-and-canvas Carleton canoe until World War II. Bert Morris's factory in Veazie burned in December 1919. Morris did not rebuild but later worked for the Old Town Canoe Company. In New York, Rushton died in 1906, and, though his son and half-brother soldiered on, the firm closed in 1916–17. Only E. M. White's company lasted in one form or another past mid-century. It wasn't necessarily their business practices that doomed the original builders. By the 1920s, the company founders were old or dead and succession didn't work out well. One exception was the Old Town Canoe Company.

### A CURE FOR GALLS AND A MODERN BUSINESS

The Gray family started what became the Old Town Canoe Company beside the Penobscot River around 1900.[29] Although the Grays are no longer owners, having sold to Johnson Diversified in 1974,[30] the company still makes canoes today.

The Old Town Canoe Company was a business built for the twentieth century, as were the Peterborough and Canadian canoe companies in Canada. Old Town's canoes became so universal that today when many people see any wood-and-canvas canoe they call it an "Old Town" as a generic term, like asking for a Coke when you mean a soda, or a Kleenex when you mean a tissue.

Alexander Gray came to Old Town, Maine, around 1834[31] to run a sawmill on the Stillwater side of an island in the Penobscot River, but the dam on the other side of the island controlled all the water, draining his sawmill of power. "He ended up opening a meat market in Old Town to sell lamb and beef that was raised on the farm. It was a booming lumber mill town at that time so the demand was good. It wasn't a fit place to raise a family in his opinion so he stayed on the farm as much as possible," says Benson Gray, who is Alexander's great-great-grandson.[32]

Alexander had three sons, Wilbur, the oldest, George, and Herbert. "They couldn't afford to send Wilbur or George to college," Benson says. "Herbert was the youngest and showed promise so they all were able to save enough for him to get a business college degree from Augusta."

By the 1880s, the family businesses included hardware, meat, and a sample case factory. Later other businesses were added, including logging, lumber milling, the Old Town Ribbon and Carbon Company, and the Old Town Woolen Company.

The successes of the Gray family took an upward turn in 1884 when Abiel Bickmore, who owned a cooperage next door to the Richardson & Gray Hardware Store, used his kitchen stove to cook up a salve for horses. It cured galls, which were sores caused by harnesses rubbing against skin that could put an expensive workhorse out of operation for days. Bickmore's Gall Cure incorporated in 1892 with financial support from Herbert and George Gray and with George Richardson as treasurer. Production started in Herbert's building, where he had been making carbon ink. Herbert marketed the cure up and down the East Coast. By 1896, Bickmore's was selling 1,700 boxes a day and couldn't keep up with demand.[33] Bickmore's Gall Cure

The George A. Gray hardware store of Old Town, Maine, in 1906.
George Gray stands at the far left. *Courtesy of the Gray Family Collections.*

gave the Grays national distribution experience that became important when they opened a canoe factory.

The canoe company formally incorporated on January 16, 1902.[34] It carried a couple of names, first the Indian Old Town Canoe Company in 1900[35] and then the Robertson & Old Town Canoe Company. J. R. Robertson had been building wood-and-canvas canoes since about 1895 in Auburndale, Massachusetts, but his relationship with Old Town lasted only about a year. By January 23, 1903, he was gone, and the name was changed to the Old Town Canoe Company. Old Town relied on builders and designers such as Alfred Wickett and J. R. Robertson in the same way that James Z. Rogers, an owner of the Ontario Canoe Company, had relied on the expertise of John Stephenson.[36]

Sam Gray was in the third generation of Grays in Old

Town. He graduated from Bowdoin College in Maine and returned home in 1903. Perhaps only 1 or 2 percent of the population had a college education then. Sam's uncle Herbert had attended college, but the family couldn't afford to send Sam's father, George. Returning from Bowdoin, Sam thought he might get involved in the wholesale hardware business, make some money, and travel all over the country. His father felt there was plenty to keep a young man busy close to home.[37]

"He appears to have had the summer off after college graduation and his father sent him out to manage a lumber crew in the woods for the winter," explains Benson Gray, Sam's grandson.

It was quite a challenge for a young college kid to manage a large group of older and pretty gruff characters. His father's feeling was probably that learning to handle a woods crew would be a good way to build practical management skills. He survived it, although there were some pretty wild stories like coming back from town on the sleigh with a drunken crew and having to throw the bottle into the woods when he thought that the men didn't need anything more to drink. He survived it, and then came back to work at the canoe company during the next year.

The labels of Abiel Bickmore's salve and powder that cured sores on workhorses. The Bickmore powder, backed in 1884 by Herbert and George Gray, gave the Gray family national distribution experience that they used in marketing canoes.

*Courtesy of the Gray Family Collections.*

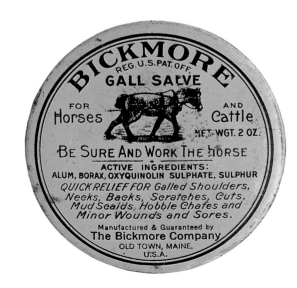

The Old Town Canoe factory. Wrapped canoes await shipment near the railroad.  *Courtesy of the Gray Family Collections.*

## "Old Town Canoe" FACTORY

Here is where "OLD TOWN CANOES" are made. The continuous length of the buildings is over 570 ft. Total floor space is over 150,000 sq. ft. It is the largest Canoe Factory in the world. Continuous production is kept up. This makes trained men skilled in their work from years of application and assures a standardization of workmanship and quality safeguarding an "OLD TOWN CANOE" buyer against an uncertain product.

No outdoor sport is so cheaply available to everyone and none more healthful than Canoeing. The first cost of an "Old Town" and equipment is the only investment for a period of years. "Old Town" popularity can be met only by modern factory methods, and we are proud to be able to market a product made in a plant which has every advantage of newest machinery, approved methods, trained workmen and sprinkler protection against fire—a product as American as the aboriginal American who invented it.

An illustrated view of the Old Town factory in the company catalogs.

*Courtesy of the Gray Family Collections.*

After that winter in the woods, Sam took a leading role in a minor family business. "Look, there's some potential in this canoe company. Do you want to take a run at it?" George asked his son. Sam wasn't alone, but he had the run of the place. "George Richardson was helping and Herbert Gray, George's brother, was there. There were other people around to help him out as need be," says Benson. George was, in effect, saying, "Here's some rope. You can hang yourself or make something out of it."

With typical understatement, Benson says, "The timing turned out to be very good."

### A MORE DEMOCRATIC CANOE

"They had the concept of nationwide sales from the Bickmore Gall Cure," says Benson. "They recognized that the available railroads offered a transportation network that could deliver canoes nationwide or internationally. The Penobscot Valley was the primary source for some of the best boat-building woods in the world. Most of the lumber that built the cities across the Eastern Seaboard came out of Maine. They had access to huge numbers of raw boards and a chance to select the best ones for building canoes. All of the necessary elements were there."

National brands and national distribution were relatively new. "It's always easy to look back on these things and think that their ultimate success was clear from the start. Actually, they were late," he says. "There were a number of other builders that were already well established in the business, including Rushton, Gerrish, Carleton,

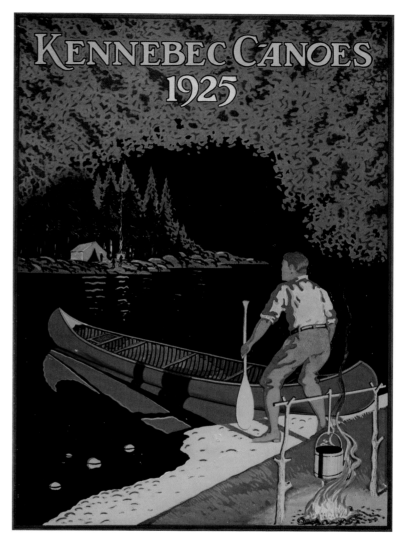

The Kennebec Canoe Company operated in Waterville, Maine, from 1909 to 1941. Some features of Kennebec canoes were similar to Morris canoes. Walter D. Grant, who supervised the building at Kennebec, had worked for the Morris Canoe Company and hired other workers who had learned from Bert and Charlie Morris.

*Courtesy of Daniel Miller.*

Finishing work was done by hand on canoes built at the Old Town factory during the 1920s and 1930s.
*Courtesy of the Gray Family Collections.*

Prior to varnishing, Old Town employees used a vacuum system to remove dirt and debris left over from sanding, c. 1922. *Courtesy of the Gray Family Collections.*

White, Morris, and others. They weren't as late as Thompson, Kennebec, or Penn Yan but they were clearly not the first. However, they managed to pull through."

The Grays brought business expertise to the manufacture of canoes, as did the owners of the Peterborough and Canadian canoe companies. They were not so much designers and builders as they were managers. Their skilled employees handled the details of construction. One of their first builders was Alfred Wickett, who had earlier worked for E. M. White and would later form the St. Louis Boat and Canoe Company.[38]

Construction of a wood-and-canvas canoe in a factory setting required less skill than building an all-wood canoe. The planking, for example, did not have to be shiplapped or shaped as carefully as in an all-wood canoe because the canvas provided waterproofing. Speedier factory construction meant the product could be less expensive.

Although Old Town was a small place with a population of about 5,700 in 1900, the Grays could think beyond Maine. "My impression of White and some of the builders is that they weren't looking that far afield," says Benson. "In fact, I think to a large extent the customers were coming to them. The people were coming to Maine because that was where they knew they could find canoes. They had a huge demand in places like the Charles River [in Boston] and New York." Rushton had a higher-end market in New York for his all-wood lapstrake canoes, but many of those buyers were not in the market for "rag" canoes.

"I think the wood-and-canvas canoe was to some extent a more democratic canoe, if you will, or more wide-spread, more available. It was the common man's canoe," says Benson. "There were still some very fancy wood-and-canvas canoes. But the fanciest wood-and-canvas canoe was probably still less expensive than a lapstrake Rushton, particularly a sailing one that was fitted out with all the nickel-plated hardware they had." Rushton and Old Town pursued different markets despite Rushton's Indian Girl canoe. Old Town sold through some high-end outdoor suppliers in New York, but it also looked to small businesses all over the country, particularly hardware stores, as dealers.

Benson Gray, a historian with the Wooden Canoe Heritage Association, is a member of the family that founded the Old Town Canoe Company.

*Photograph by Norman Sims.*

When this Carleton Canoe catalog cover was published in 1924, Carleton canoes were built in the Old Town factory. *Courtesy of Historic New England.*

"There are a number of questions about why Carleton was purchased in 1910," Benson says. "Carleton had an established name, a dealer network, and good manufacturing capability, but my understanding is that the real value of Carleton was in their timber rights and sawmill. This was Old Town's opportunity to integrate vertically and secure their source of raw material supplies. It also helps explain why the Carleton fire in 1911 was not as devastating as it could have been. They were able to move nearly everything into the Old Town factory and continue their operations. The separate Carleton brand was maintained so they could sell Old Town canoes to Macy's and Carleton canoes to Abercrombie and Fitch. Technically these dealers weren't competing with one another, even though the canoes were coming out of the same factory and the dealers were only a few blocks apart in New York City." As late as 1938, the factory inventory at Old Town listed six Carleton and fifty-one Old Town canoe forms.[39]

Sales figures from the Old Town Canoe Company suggest that solid demand for wood-and-canvas canoes lasted from around 1906 until the onset of the Great Depression in the early 1930s. Perhaps a 50 percent dip in sales occurred during World War I, when the company reported to shareholders, "The year closing Dec. 31, 1918 has been one of keen disappointment for our business due as we well understand to conditions beyond our control and unparalleled in the memory of our years. A steady falling demand for our goods accompanied by steadily rising costs for manufacture produced the inevitable end of doing business without any profit." Immediately after the war, business picked up again.[40]

An ardor for courting in canoes contributed to sales before and after the war, making the canoe a romantic vehicle.

## THE GREAT CANOEDLING CONTROVERSY

The second wave of recreational interest in canoeing featured young men and women paddling as couples on rivers such as the Charles, Detroit, Schuylkill, and Potomac, in other urban areas such as the Chain of Lakes in Minneapolis, and in Canada.[41] Many fancy courting canoes were built in the Charles River area of Boston bearing names such as "Arnold, Nutting, Brodbeck, Kingsbury, Partelow, Emerson, Mather, Shea, Emmons," according to Dan Miller of Dragonfly Canoe Works and editor of the *Wooden Canoe* journal.[42] John Stephenson's son, George, came down from Peterborough around 1885–86 to build all-wood canoes for Robertson's canoe company and in 1887 for the H. V. Partelow Company in Auburndale, Massachusetts, which was one of the earliest Charles River canoe makers, dating from 1884–93.[43]

True courting canoes were designed for the man to paddle from the stern, with the woman seated in the bow facing the man. Some were built lacking enough room for the bow passenger to face forward. The Peterborough Canoe Company in Canada built a "Girling Canoe" with a permanent front seat facing the rear.

This 16-foot Comfort Craft courting canoe was built by the Peterborough Canoe Company in 1904. Also known as the "Girling Canoe," it came equipped with lockers under the side decks for a phonograph and records. The front seat faced the stern of the canoe.
*Photograph by Michael Cullen. Courtesy of the Canadian Canoe Museum.*

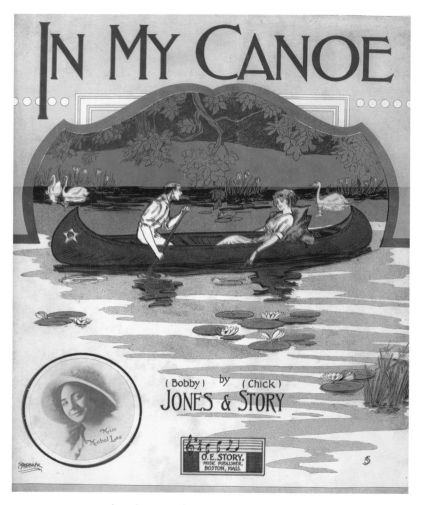

Cover from sheet music for "In My Canoe," a song written by
Bobby Jones and Chick Story, published by O. E. Story in 1913.

*Courtesy of the John Summers Collection.*

This 16-foot canoe included cabinets under the decks for a phonograph and record albums.[44]

With a few pillows, blankets, and rugs, any open canoe could be made comfortable. Fleets of hundreds, sometimes thousands, of canoes filled the Charles River in Boston as couples showed off their stylish dress and watercraft. Other urban areas saw similar turnouts. For example, at Belle Isle in Detroit, a park designed by Frederick Law Olmsted, C. J. Molitor's livery specialized in courting canoes built to exact specifications by B. N. Morris, with long decks made of mahogany. "Molitor was the only Morris dealer who only sold Morris canoes—no other canoe brands, no camping gear or guns—just Morris canoes," says Kathy Klos. The Molitor canoes had distinctive torpedo-shaped stems.

"The boats in Charles Molitor's livery—eighteen feet long, with three-foot bow decks and two-foot stern decks—may very well have set the standard for the liveries on Belle Isle," writes Klos.

The fore and aft decks displayed pennants on foot-long poles. For wooing a lady on a moonless night, there were carbide spotlights, like those used on Ford's Model T, attached to the bow decks of some of the canoes. Paddlers could rent a Victrola, complete with morning glory horn, and rugs for the floor, backrests that propped against the thwarts, and a supply of pillows—some emblazoned with the Belle Isle name. Tasseled roping, draped from bow to stern along the outside of the gunwales, not only added to the canoe's decoration but deflected the

Courting on Grand Canal in Belle Isle Park in the Detroit River, with Detroit, Michigan, on one side and Windsor, Ontario, on the other, c. 1900. Note the Victrola mounted in the canoe in the foreground.

*Courtesy of the Detroit Publishing Company Collection, Library of Congress Prints and Photographs Division, LC-DIG-det-4a19551.*

bumps of other canoes in the canals of Belle Isle, which became crowded as the second decade of the century progressed.[45]

With long decks and specially equipped interiors, including chairs for the women, courting canoes were among the fanciest wood-and-canvas canoes ever built. Some were trimmed entirely in mahogany. In Boston and the suburbs of Auburndale and Newton, couples could rent a canoe for a day's outing from several large boathouses that lined the Charles River. Young people and families in search of diversion and recreation took trolley lines directly from Boston to the amusement center at Norumbega Park, which opened in 1897 in Auburndale. Across

the Charles from Norumbega, the Riverside Recreation Grounds offered a large swimming pool, sporting fields, and, of course, a boathouse. The Metropolitan Parks Commission controlled 6 miles of the Charles River from Newton to Waltham, known as the Lakes District, and encouraged public entertainment with amusement rides, a zoo, a penny arcade, band concerts, outdoor theater, picnic grounds, restaurants, fountains, walkways, scenic vistas, and canoeing.

According to a publication of the Newton History Museum:

The river became a recreational mecca. Norumbega had a boathouse that rented canoes, and soon built

On July 12, 1919, hundreds of canoeists saluted "The Star Spangled Banner" during a band concert at the Riverside Recreation Grounds on the Charles River in Weston, Massachusetts. *Collection of David Kingsbury. Courtesy of the Weston Historical Society.*

another to keep up with demand. . . . The banks of the Charles were soon lined with boathouses. At one time more than 5,000 canoes were stabled in the various boathouses in the "Lakes District," the placid stretch of the Charles between Newton Lower Falls and the Moody Street dam in Waltham. On weekends the river became a bank-to-bank traffic jam. You could walk from Newton to Weston, the joke went, without getting your feet wet, just by stepping from canoe to canoe. The Metropolitan District Commission established its own police force to keep order, and set up a station in a boathouse that included holding cells for the over-exuberant. . . .

In Auburndale around the turn of the century, a young man's first major purchase was likely to be a canoe. The canoe taught responsibility, provided recreation and transportation, and was one of the very few places a young man and a young woman could be together without a chaperon nearby.[46]

When couples went courting early in the twentieth century, there were few opportunities for intimacy. After 1909, darkened nickelodeon theaters exploded onto the urban cultures of the working class and immigrants. Some people attended the movies five times a week.

In addition to nickelodeons, there were courting canoes. Between 1901 and 1912, the number of permits for

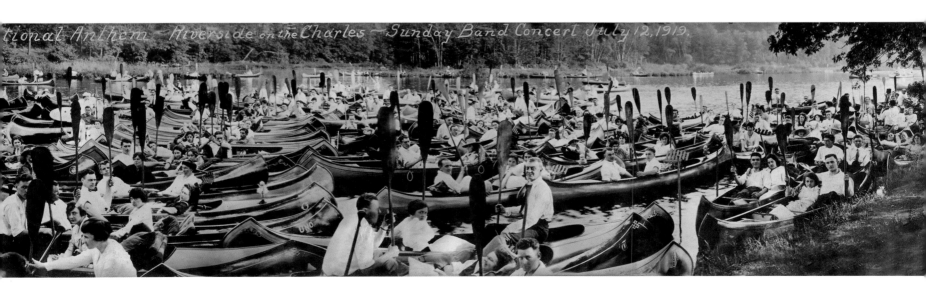

tional Anthem - Riverside on the Charles - Sunday Band Concert July 12, 1919.

A wood-and-canvas courting canoe with mahogany extended decks. The forward thwart served only as a backrest for the woman, who sat facing her man in the stern (and sometimes the other way around). The long decks were handsome and pushed the couple closer together.  *Photograph by Michael Livdahl.*

The Charles River at Newton, Massachusetts, became one of the most popular waterways for "canoedling" among young people during the early twentieth century.  *Courtesy of the John Summers Collection.*

Early postcards documented the scandalous "canoedling" craze that took place on lakes and rivers throughout the Midwest and eastern United States. *Courtesy of the Canadian Canoe Museum, O'Connor Collection.*

storing canoes at lakeside docks in Minneapolis increased from 200 to 1,200 and a midnight lake curfew was enacted, although rarely enforced.[47] The superintendent of the Riverside section of the Charles River Reservation in Boston estimated that the number of canoes owned or rented rose from 700 in 1900 to 3,500 in 1903. The Metropolitan Parks Police added a launch and rowboats to control the crowds.[48]

Puritanical preachers and Progressive Era reformers encouraged the Metropolitan Parks Commission to curb the "craze for pleasure" among the young. In 1903, the commission issued rules for boaters, number 1 of which prohibited gambling, drinking, and "any obscene or indecent act." Kissing and lying together in canoes were punishable offenses.[49] The first arrest came in August 1903. The *Boston Herald* commented: "It may not be wicked to go canoeing on the Charles with young women on Sunday, but we continue to be reminded that it is frequently perilous. . . . The canoeist arrested for kissing his sweetheart at Riverside was fined $20. At that rate it is estimated that over a million dollars' worth of kisses are exchanged at that popular canoeing resort every fine Saturday night and Sunday."[50] A $20 fine was expensive. In 1903, new canoes listed in the Old Town Canoe Company catalog ranged in price from $28 to $48.

A week after the first arrest for kissing in the summer of 1903, canoeists rebelled. Men and women refused to sit upright in the canoes, as ordered by police, and taunted the police by slouching, lying side by side, and singing derisive songs.[51] The *Boston Sunday Globe* on August 23 reported, "Tonight, for some unexplained reason, the vigilance of the Metropolitan park police in the enforcement of the regulations for canoeists at Riverside, put into effect one week ago, was relaxed, and the old time go-as-you-please order of affairs prevailed. Naturally there was much delight among those who thronged the river to enjoy it and the weekly concert." According to another account, "Scores of couples attended, defiantly lying under blankets in their canoes. When the police launch approached the area, it was met with jeers, hisses, and pounding on the canoes. The band struck up the tune, 'Please Go Way and Let Me Sleep.'"[52]

The canoedling controversy proved costly for the parks and boathouses. "Not only was the number of canoeists on the river noticeably small," wrote the *Globe,* "but the trains to Riverside today carried only a fraction of the crowds that usually go out on pleasant Saturdays. At the canoe liveries it was said that less than one-fourth the canoes usually let had been taken out this evening."[53]

In the next two years, thirty-seven couples were arrested for kissing or lying down in canoes. Perhaps more was involved than kissing. An editorial in the *Boston Herald* said that "simply kissing was euphemistic" in the original arrest. This must have required a fine sense of balance.[54]

A Harvard student and his woman friend were arrested on 10 July [1904] "while resting in a shady nook." In August the police apprehended the treasurer of the protest committee that had been organized the previous season to fight the sit-up rule. When the canoeing activist pleaded guilty to a charge of fornication, the police gained a public relations victory.[55]

This "parlor" or "silk cushion" canoeing did not decline, despite the regulations.[56] Young people didn't stop "canoedling." They simply moved upstream to unregulated areas of the Charles River.

After the police suffered a defeat in court in 1905, arrests declined. Between 1906 and 1910, only four couples were arrested for fornication and another three for indecent or immoral acts.[57] An analysis by David Nasaw of the thirty-seven people arrested between 1903 and 1905 showed a mostly native-born and middle-class group with a median age of twenty-two. "Because of the enormous expansion of white-collar work at the turn of the century, young middle-class men and women had more time, energy, and money for recreation than had their predecessors or many of their blue-collar counterparts," writes historian Thomas McMullin.[58] Their canoes tended to be wood-and-canvas, however, not the more expensive all-wood canoes made by Rushton or Peterborough.

In 1911, when future President Dwight Eisenhower was traveling from Abilene, Kansas, to West Point to begin his military education, he stopped off at the University of Michigan to visit his brother. They went canoeing:

> That evening he hired a canoe and we set out on a river—I believe it was the Huron—with a couple of college girls. We took along a phonograph and played the popular songs. Paddling in the moon light, we passed canoe loads of other students enjoying the pleasant June evening. Afterwards, we paid for the canoe and walked the girls back to their dormitories . . . this was, up to that moment, the most romantic evening I had ever known.[59]

Courting in canoes lasted a long time. The construction of fancy courting canoes continued well into the 1920s and 1930s. "The canoes didn't all disappear from the Charles at once, of course, but things changed. The automobile replaced the trolley as a mode of transportation—and it replaced the canoe as a place to be alone with a girl."[60]

Music publishers capitalized on the popularity of courting canoes in the 1920s with songs like "While We Drift Along" by Harry D. Squires. *Courtesy of the John Summers Collection.*

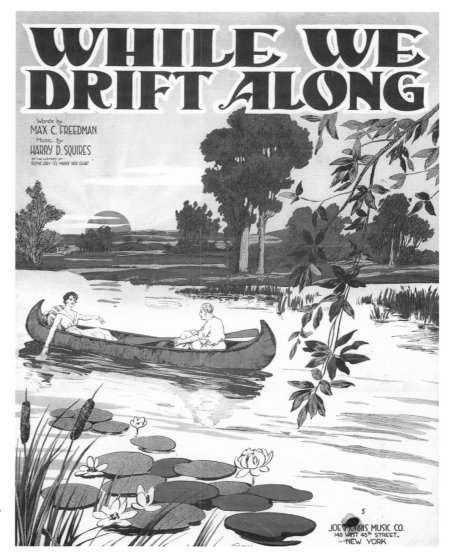

The changing role of women in canoeing became evident on postcards of the early twentieth century. *Courtesy of the John Summers Collection.*

Canoeing Girl

COPYRIGHT 1908 P. GORDON

Between the years of 1917 and 1919, women began to be portrayed as much more active paddlers on the covers of the Morris company catalogs.

TOP *Courtesy of Daniel Miller.*    ABOVE *Courtesy of the Gray Family Collections.*

More important, the role of women in canoes changed. Women were pushing the boundaries of Victorian morality by taking up outdoor recreation such as canoeing and bicycling, and by encouraging what we now call "dating" as opposed to "calling and chaperoning."

We can see evidence of this cultural change in the catalog illustrations of the major canoe companies. Early in the century, catalog covers usually showed women as passengers, generally facing the man paddling in the stern. After World War I, catalogs represented women as paddlers, not passengers. Morris catalog covers switched from a 1917 courting illustration to an energetic outdoor scene with two women paddlers in 1919.

The Old Town Canoe Company led the way in the portrayal of women paddlers. In 1905, 1909, and 1910, catalogs showed women with paddles. The 1919 catalog cover had a military theme, but then came a long run of images showing women paddling in both the bow and stern.[61] Most women stopped reclining on pillows and picked up a paddle. The new battle was over who would control the boat from the stern. "Put the grunt in the front and the finesse in the back" would be spoken many times as the century wore on.

The Old Town Canoe Company celebrated the end of World War I in 1919 with a military-themed catalog cover. *Courtesy of the Gray Family Collections.*

By 1923, images of women paddling canoes, especially from the stern seat, were prominent on the covers of catalogs produced by Old Town and other makers. *Courtesy of the Gray Family Collections.*

One might call the Old Town Canoe Company daring in its catalogs, or very savvy about the national audience for canoes. *Printers' Ink: A Journal for Advertisers* in 1918 identified women as a potential audience. "As there are more women working than ever before, and at much better wages, presumably the feminine half of the nation may also be regarded as a potential market worth thinking about," the article said.[62]

### THE DEATH AND LIFE OF WOODEN CANOES

All-wood or wood-and-canvas canoes are not as fragile as people assume. If treated properly, they don't turn to dust and they don't dissolve in water. As with any wooden product, however, if left in contact with the weather or the ground, they will rot. But if stored inside, wood can last for hundreds of years. Look at all those colonial New England homes, for example, or the interiors of European churches.

In their battle with the forces of nature, early wooden canoes had a short life expectancy. During the nineteenth century, canoes might last for five years. All-wood lapstrake canoes needed lots of tender care to remain watertight. The more expensive boats—Rushtons, and some of the Peterborough and Morris canoes—found storage in their owners' boathouses, at a summer camp, or in a barn.

Wood-and-canvas canoes could be renewed easily, and their era coincided with the age of the automobile garage and the large boathouses, such as those on the Charles River and Belle Isle, where they found shelter.

Time takes its toll. Rivers and lakes are not as much of a threat to a canoe as is neglect. Left outside, canoes begin a slow unwinding that ends poorly. Abandoned in a barn or attic with the canvas removed or the planks gapped, they are eventually thrown away by later generations with no knowledge of their past. The wonderful process that keeps us from being inundated in antiques and makes room for the new also makes for special moments when canoes can be saved and savored.

A wooden canoe can decline like an elegant old house in Detroit. The house may have started as the fine home of an automobile executive but changed hands when the exec moved to the suburbs. When it was converted to apartments a couple owners later, maintenance stopped keeping up with decay. Eventually, everyone moved out and the house was abandoned, at which time all of the copper and metal was stripped. Almost no amount of restoration can restore its original beauty.

Canoes can have a similar descent. In western Massachusetts, a gorgeous 1917 Old Town Ideal canoe with mahogany gunwales and bird's-eye maple thwarts, seats, and 24-inch decks was rescued from a dump minutes before it would have been destroyed. Its previous owner probably thought it was beyond repair, or just didn't care in the rush to clean out Grandpa's barn. Except for a lack of canvas, the canoe was in excellent condition and could be restored to its original luster.

Wooden canoes have an inner tension like a spring. The ribs want to straighten and spread outward. The gunwales and thwarts hold them in place. The gunwales meet at the stems of the boat and attach to each other by the

The gunwales and planking of a canoe await restoration at Dylan and Emily Schoelzel's
Salmon Falls Canoe workshop in Shelburne Falls, Massachusetts. *Photograph by Paul Franz.*

A before-and-after restoration by Tom Seavey of a 1927 Carleton canoe, which was built in the Old Town Canoe Company factory. Using the Old Town "build record," the canoe was restored to the same colors and condition as the original.    *Photographs by Norman Sims.*

decks. The decks and stems hold all the dynamic forces of the wooden spring in place. Unfortunately, stems and decks are the first to rot away when the boat sits upside-down on the ground or is stored outside and attracts moisture. As rot advances, the spring starts to unwind toward flatness. The canoe takes on an earthen shape not worthy of a watercraft.

When an unrestored wooden canoe is discovered, it's a miracle. By one means or another, through accident, fire, neglect, disinterested heirs, gnawing by animals, weathering, or collision with rocks, logs, or the road, most craft did not survive. As everyday objects with a short life span, they came and went like our home computers today. Yet dozens of unrestored wooden and wood-and-canvas canoes are found every year.

Old canoes seem rare. Historian Kathy Klos, for example, estimates that the B. N. Morris company produced roughly twenty thousand canoes between 1891 and 1919. Several years ago, Klos and Denis Kallery started a database of the surviving Morris canoes. In 2015, the database contained about 350 canoes. Assuming the database contains only half of the surviving boats means that only about 3 percent of the originals survive.

Jeff Dean, founder of the WCHA with his wife, Jill, and with Tom and Karen MacKenzie, wrote in the first issue of *Wooden Canoe* magazine in 1979:

> Years ago there were many large manufacturers of wooden canoes in North America. In the United States, only Old Town remains as a producer of substantial numbers of wooden canoes. In Canada, even Chestnut—long a famous maker of fine wooden canoes of many types—has closed its doors. In response to threats to this endangered species, numerous small-scale builders have sprung up, even though labor costs make new wooden canoes quite expensive. The rare birch-bark canoe still is being created by a handful of builders, perpetuating a craft remembered largely in legend but rarely seen on today's waterways.

> My wife, Jill, and I decided to found the Wooden Canoe Heritage Association and publish *Wooden Canoe* in order to preserve these canoes and to serve the people who appreciate their beauty, craftsmanship, and heritage. We thought about starting a wooden-canoe organization for a couple of years before trying it. Then, in the spirit of "nothing ventured, nothing gained," we just stopped thinking and started starting.

That last sentence remains good advice for those thinking of taking on a wooden canoe restoration.

## TOMORROW'S CLASSICS

If you wanted to have original Arts and Crafts or Mission-style furniture in your home, you could shop among antique stores and search the Web in hopes of finding some.

Chestnut canoes continue to be one of the most popular styles among paddlers. Mike Elliot of Kettle River
Canoes in British Columbia restored this Chestnut Bob's Special model.   *Courtesy of Kettle River Canoes.*

Then you would need to restore it and deal with all the issues of old and wobbly furniture, but in the end you would have something beautiful. Paddlers who restore old canoes have similar challenges. Replacing broken ribs and planking, rotten stems, and broken or dry-rotted gunwales can seem like a huge task. Both furniture buyers and canoeists have similar alternatives—make their own or find craftspeople who can build new ones that are just like the old ones.

The graceful forms and beauty of all-wood and wood-and-canvas canoes have generated renewed interest in recent years. Those who appreciate the perfect hull shapes of the old Gerrish, Morris, White, Old Town, Rushton, Peterborough, or Chestnut canoes can now buy a new canoe made on the same lines and using the same materials—in some cases, made on the original forms. In the WCHA, these canoes are known as "tomorrow's classics." Several builders have created their own canoe models, some of which are slight modifications of wonderful old designs.

And women have joined the community of canoe builders.

A young woman contemplating a career building all-wood or wood-and-canvas canoes can look back on successful pioneers. When we asked about potential women builders, everyone said we should talk to Alice Zalonis Brylawski. She had built canoes under the tutelage of Rollin Thurlow, Jerry Stelmok, and Tom Seavey.

Is this a field where women can compete and thrive? This question was addressed first in interviews with a couple of the pioneers.

Pam Wedd has been building canoes in Parry Sound, Ontario, since 1989 and has completed sixty-five boats at her Bearwood Canoe shop.

In the mid-1970s, Wedd worked at a YWCA girls' camp in Toronto. "During slow periods, we chose to fix the wood-and-canvas canoes," she says. "We did some terrible things."[63]

Later she read Ted Moores's *Canoecraft: An Illustrated Guide to Fine Woodstrip Construction* and built several woodstrip epoxy canoes in the mid-1980s. She said, "When Jerry and Rollin's *The Wood and Canvas Canoe* book came out, I read that and knew that my heart was in the more traditional wood-and-canvas canoe." She met Will Ruch and spent some time in his shop learning the basics of canvas canoe building. In 1992, after renovating an old barn to become her canoe workshop, Wedd built her first form, based on the 16-foot Chestnut Pal. Her latest form is based on a late-1800s 14-foot Gerrish. "Building a replica, and particularly one of this vintage, has been a real challenge and a lot of fun," she says.

Originally Wedd spent time both building new canoes and repairing old ones. Now she teaches people to either build or repair their own canoes in her shop classes. "It is a wonderful thing to pass on the knowledge and skills of wooden canoe building," she says.

She says her early canoes had good attention to detail and other builders knew she was serious about the craft. Canoe building was a "good venue to come and learn and be accepted quickly. I never felt unwelcome," she says.

Wedd adds, "In the nineties, canoes didn't have to be

Pam Wedd, owner of Bearwood Canoe Company near Parry Sound, Ontario, paddles a restored Gerrish canoe. *Courtesy of Cody Storm Cooper Photography.*

a replica of anything. But people are older now. They're buying antiques."

Pam Wedd's advice to young Alice Zalonis Brylawski: "Go for it. The more good wooden builders there are, the better to keep the skill alive."

When another pioneer, Emily Schoelzel, first met her future husband, Dylan, he had a keen interest in canoe building. Dylan learned from Jerry Stelmok and worked with Schuyler Thomson in Connecticut. "He wanted to do canoe building and I had just graduated from college as a fine arts major," Emily says.[64] In 2002, they decided to give it a go together. "It was contingent on the relationship coming first. If we couldn't stand working together, we would stop. And I had to like the woodworking."

Now they build or restore about twenty canoes a year in their 1860s barn that serves as a workshop, finish room, and storehouse for their Salmon Falls Canoe shop in Shelburne Falls, Massachusetts. Customers often ask about what Emily does in the shop.

"Well, I do everything that Dylan does," she says. "I can build a canoe. I operate all the machines. I can do all the tasks. We're equal in this relationship and business." When the customers are a married couple, Emily says, "The woman is always surprised that I can work together with my husband. There are few husband-wife duos. We were clear from the beginning that if we couldn't figure out how to do it, we wouldn't."

Her interests formed before she met Dylan. As a girl, she attended a canoe-tripping camp in northern Ontario. Her brothers went to Keewaydin, which then served only boys. At sixteen, Emily took a six-week river canoe trip to Hudson Bay. "It was epic," she says. "It was all girls. Canoe tripping in general has been a major influence on my life and how I found myself. That led me to start the girls' program at Camp Keewaydin in 1999. It was a big transition to have a girls' program."

She remains an assistant director at Keewaydin. The camp has used wood-and-canvas canoes since it was founded in 1893, and now they use some of Emily and Dylan's boats. "I think it's even more fun because our canoes are being used by Keewaydin. We get to talk to the kids about the canoes and repair them when they come back and they've torn the canvas. They take them on long trips. The more kids get a chance to get outside and paddle things that were handmade, the better."

Emily was drawn to this career by the long tradition of wooden canoe building and by the quality and design found in the boats. "The idea of being a boatbuilder is a romantic idea," she cautions. "You can convey images of wood shavings and the sweet smell of cedar in the steam box. You can imagine the varnish glazing up nicely, and it's romantic being on the water. It's not that at all mostly. It's physically challenging work. I wonder how I could do this every day without a partner. Some tasks might be challenging physically. I'm strong but I'm only 5'6".

"The more people who are building and the more information there is, then people will learn that the wood-canvas canoe is superior and the experience is superior, and that's why they've been around for more than a hundred years," she says. "When it comes to manufacturing things

Emily Schoelzel restoring a 1964 Old Town OTCA canoe in the Salmon Falls Canoe shop. *Photograph by Norman Sims.*

Dylan Schoelzel makes wood-and-canvas canoes at Salmon Falls Canoe in Massachusetts along with his wife, Emily. Note the metal bands on the canoe form at left. *Photograph by Paul Franz.*

of high quality, there have been lots of women involved. It just takes some time to talk with people."

Women builders are few, but they have been successful. Jeanne Bourquin has been building and repairing wood-and-canvas canoes since 1984 in Ely, Minnesota. She built a canoe with Jerry Stelmok and took long trips in a wooden canoe on the South Nahanni from the headwaters to Fort Simpson, and from Ely to James Bay. As a teenager, Alice Zalonis was impressed when she watched Bourquin give a demonstration on canvasing at the WCHA Assembly one year. "Here was this woman showing all these guys how to do this," she said.[65] Another woman builder in Atikokan, Ontario, Thelma Cameron, took over her uncle's business at Fletcher Canoes when he retired.

Alice Zalonis Brylawski grew up in a canoeing family. Her father, Mark Zalonis, was an early member of the WCHA, and her mother, Ruth, gives demonstrations at gatherings. In 1989, Mark booked a wood-and-canvas canoe trip with Maine guide Alexandra Conover, who suggested that twelve-year-old Alice come along because Jerry Stelmok's daughter was coming. "It was cold and windy," Alice says. "We waited for the wind to drop and we paddled at night. I was scared to death to complain that my fingers were cold. It was absolutely the most wonderful thing I'd done."

Alice Zalonis Brylawski stands in a dugout canoe at a Wooden Canoe Heritage Association Mini-Assembly at Gifford Pinchot State Park in Pennsylvania in 2012.  *Photograph by Mark Zalonis.*

When she was a freshman in college, Alice decided to build a skin-on-frame kayak. "I had done a lot of sewing, clothing design, and building backpacks," she said.

I didn't know a lot about woodworking. Suddenly I had to learn this entirely new skill set. How to drive dozens and dozens of slotted brass screws, how to scarf wood strips, and so on. I was doing the kind of thing I'd never seen any other girls or women doing. It was new and different, and at that age I was into not being like other people.

You go from a pile of wood that you've been milling and fitting and cutting and trimming, and you put it together and suddenly it looks like a boat. It's more than the sum of its parts. There's something magic about that. Part of me was hooked on that magic moment.

She kept the boat in her dorm room at St. Mary's College of Maryland. Her roommate would help her get it out the window, and she would paddle on the St. Mary's River.

In following years, in Rollin Thurlow's classes, she helped build an Atkinson Traveler and another of his designs, the 13-foot American Beauty, which is her favorite solo canoe. She helped her father build a 16-foot Guide at Jerry Stelmok's shop, and she built a White Light Tripper in Tom Seavey's shop. She owns four boats that float and one that doesn't.

Now some people are hopeful she'll become a "tomorrow's classics" canoe builder.

Not so fast.

Her husband is a biology professor and she manages a lab at the university. "I'm not a professional builder and may not become one because my current job has a retirement plan," she says. "The best answer is maybe. I've done all kinds of things in my life that I didn't think I would get to do. I'm so grateful that I happened to intersect with this great group of people and had a chance to learn from them."

Those who practice this craft usually trace their interest in it back to Jerry Stelmok and Rollin Thurlow and their book, *The Wood and Canvas Canoe: A Complete Guide to Its History, Construction, Restoration, and Maintenance.* As they revived the building of classic wood-and-canvas canoes, some using old forms and some using newer designs, they have been mentors to two generations of canoe builders.

Jerry Stelmok of Island Falls Canoe in Maine builds the wood-and-canvas canoes sold as Old Town Canoes and under the L. L. Bean name; he also has original E. M. White forms.

Rollin Thurlow, owner of Northwoods Canoe Company in Maine, builds reproductions of Morris and Rushton canoes, among others, and his own Atkinson Traveler. Thurlow built his one-thousandth canoe in 2014.

In the mid-1970s, Thurlow and Stelmok were trying to ride the coattails of *Wooden Boat* magazine, which had reached an audience interested in older boats. They were a bit ahead of their time. "We struggled mightily for a few years," Thurlow says.[66] They couldn't pay for advertising, but their books reached people who were interested in

## ๑ Canoe Sails

As an artist, Todd Bradshaw would never allow an errant line in a drawing. As a bass guitarist, he would never allow an improper note on an album from his band, The Ship. He's a bit obsessive about such things. These same qualities make him one of the best canoe sailmakers for the past twenty-five years.

He had paddled perhaps a thousand miles in a canoe before he ever sailed anything. Then his brother moved to the desert and left behind a Sunfish sailboat. Bradshaw remembers thinking, "Hey, this is pretty neat. You just hold a rope and steer. What a concept."[1]

Then the obsession took over. "The sail was pretty bad, so I built a new one out of better fabric and had its shape computer-plotted with the day's most advanced sail-design software. The sail is black, with a hot-pink and lime-green star-cut panel layout. It is probably one of the most high-tech lateen sails ever built and still sails well."[2] Within a few years, he started a company called Addiction Sailmakers in Madison, Wisconsin. He wrote a book on the subject titled *Canoe Rig: The Essence and the Art*, and transformed his living room into a sail loft with an industrial-strength sewing machine fastened to the floor.

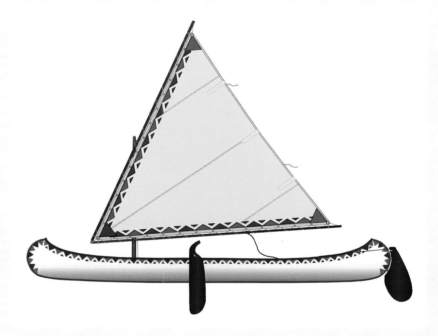

An illustration of a lateen sail design by Todd Bradshaw for an Old Town wood-and-canvas canoe. *Reprinted with permission of the artist.*

A Rushton batwing sailing canoe in front with a lateen-rigged sailing canoe behind it. These canoes were on the water at one of the early Antique Boat Shows held in Clayton, New York. Beginning in 1964, these gatherings were the birthplace of the modern antique boat renaissance. *Courtesy of the Antique Boat Museum Archives.*

Historically accurate sails for old wooden canoes require a bit of research and traditional sailmaking techniques. "The bat wings are almost always Rustons," he says. "Lateens were easy to use in converting a canoe to a sailing boat and they were cheap."

Now Bradshaw uses Dacron instead of the original Egyptian cotton, which is rare and difficult to find in sail quality. "Dacron is more dimensionally stable so the sail will hold its design shape better," he says.[3] "It's far less vulnerable to mold, mildew, and rot. They actually make Dacron for traditional boats in a light cream color or dark brown to mimic the old treated cotton sails. It's very thin and slick and crunchy, but from 10 feet away you can't tell that. It's resin coated and the stiffness helps hold its dimensional shape so the sails don't stretch." Old looms for weaving fabric were of different sizes, so he cuts today's large sheets of Dacron into narrow strips like the original cotton.

"The paneling and the corner reinforcing patches are what make it look right from a distance. For someone who has done a meticulous restoration of the hull, this works better than a modern sail-making process," he says.

Shape is everything. "The 3D shape is the hardest thing," he says. "Sails are three-dimensional. To get the airfoil shape is the most intricate part. We have straight spars on top and bottom, and we make the edge of the sail curved rather than straight. When the curved edge is laced to the straight spar, there is excess fabric that creates the draft, or belly, of the sail. The more edge round we add, the deeper the draft is going to be, and then we have this excess fabric that needs to be positioned in the proper spot. I do that with broad seaming, a matter of the seams being widened as we approach the edge of the sail. It moves the excess toward the middle of the sail rather than the edge."

Much of Bradshaw's work involves educating canoeists about the intricacies of sailing. The racing canoes of the 1880s tended to be over-powered and frequently tipped. "The majority of people I deal with are converting their modern or wood-and-canvas canoe. They want something simple that clamps on or bolts on without major modifications to the boat," he says. Today's canoe sailor needs to figure out where to locate the mast and attach the leeboard on a canoe that would otherwise be paddled.

"It's probably worth noting the vulnerability of open canoes for a conversion," Bradshaw says. "It's not a multi-purpose sailboat. If you dump it in the middle of the lake, you might have a long swim. People learn to pick their weather carefully and work their way up. It'll never be a boat you can sail every day you want."

Rollin Thurlow working in his shop at Northwoods Canoe Company in Atkinson, Maine. Thurlow restores old wood-and-canvas canoes and builds his own Atkinson Traveler canoes along with new Morris, Rushton, and E. M. White boats. *Photograph by Garrett Conover, Aurorashot Photography.*

restoring and building old wooden canoes. At about that time, the WCHA formed and brought together modern builders such as Jack McGreivey in New York and Joe Seliga in Minnesota.

"I really liked the Gerrish, the White, and the Morris canoes," Thurlow says. "I like to build those characteristics in my own boats." As with many in the WCHA, Thurlow has a primary affection for all-wood lapstrake canoes and wood-and-canvas canoes. He says no one has ever asked him to hammer out the dents in Grandpa's aluminum canoe, or restore a fiberglass or ABS canoe.

To this day, Thurlow is surprised every time someone calls about an old wooden canoe. "Every year I think there couldn't possibly be another—and I've thought that for thirty years," he says.

"It would be sad if the next generation weren't interested in wooden canoes. But someone else would discover them again. They'll discover one of these boats and do the research again. People will still want to work with their heads and their hands."

Craft builders restore old boats and specialize in creating new wood-and-canvas canoes and all-wood canoes. Along with Thurlow and Stelmok in Maine, they include Tom Seavey (E. M. White canoes), Geoffrey Burke (lapstrake Rushton canoes), and Kevin Martin (lapstrake Rushton canoes; he also has the original Kingsbury forms for Charles River courting canoes) in New Hampshire; American Traders (Atkinson Traveler designed by Thurlow, and other canoes) in Vermont; Dylan and Emily Schoelzel at Salmon Falls Canoe in Massachusetts; Jeanne

Jerry Stelmok building a classic E. M. White wood-and-canvas canoe. His Island Falls Canoe Company also builds wood-and-canvas canoes sold by the Old Town Canoe Company.

*Photograph by John Patriquin/Portland Press Herald/Getty Images.*

Bourquin in Ely, Minnesota; Dan Miller of Dragonfly Canoe Works in New York (Rushton, and decked sailing canoes); Al Bratton in Pennsylvania; Alex Combe of Knife River, Minnesota (Chestnut and White); Dave Osborn in Wisconsin; Pam Wedd (Gerrish canoes) and Thelma Cameron in Ontario; and many others.

Several builders have built birch-bark canoes: Ferdy Goode in Wisconsin, the late Ted Behne (birch-bark mod-

els) in New Jersey, Henri Vaillancourt in New Hampshire, Erik Simula in Minnesota, Steve Cayard in Maine, Daniel "Pinock" Smith and Barry Dana of Penobscot heritage, and David Gidmark and Tom Byers of Canada.

The WCHA builder page lists dozens of contemporary canoe makers from British Columbia to Nova Scotia in Canada, from Maine to Washington in the United States, and in the United Kingdom.[67]

CHAPTER 6

# Synthetic Canoes

TEPHANIE KWOLEK, a chemist employed by DuPont, nearly threw away a batch of polymers she had mixed on what had started out as a typical workday in 1964.[1] The liquid was cloudy and thin instead of clear and thick, and Kwolek thought the test batch might have been contaminated. Kwolek, in her early forties, was an experienced scientist who would contribute to the usefulness of compounds that would become known by trademarked names such as Orlon, Lycra (spandex), and Nomex.

Kwolek was born into a Polish American family in 1923 in New Kensington, Pennsylvania; her father died when she was ten years old. As a bright, determined stu-

dent, she graduated from Carnegie Mellon shortly after World War II; her degree was in chemistry, but she had plans to attend medical school. Instead, she was offered a job by DuPont in Buffalo, New York, and wound up helping save more lives than a team of doctors, for the compound in that cloudy container was the first hint of Kevlar, the key material in bulletproof vests.[2]

Her career as a chemist was not as unusual as it might seem in the postwar period, especially considering her employer. DuPont was known as a company that hired women; in addition, the war had opened up many traditionally male jobs to women and had broken down some resistance to women in the laboratory. DuPont's laboratories had a record of innovation, including, in 1938, the production of the first commercially successful synthetic polymer,

◄ Canoes in a splash of colors await paddlers on Moraine Lake at Banff National Park in Alberta, Canada. *Copyright Darlene Bushue Photography.*

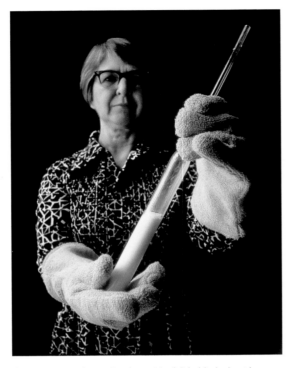

The pioneering chemist Stephanie Kwolek holds the liquid crystal polymer that became Kevlar. Kwolek, working for DuPont in 1964, developed the synthetic fiber that is a key ingredient in lightweight canoes. Kevlar is a registered trademark of DuPont. By 1971, it was made available commercially. *Photograph courtesy of DuPont.*

Kevlar fibers are used in a variety of applications, perhaps most famously in bulletproof vests. The incredible impact resistance of the material has been appreciated by generations of canoeists who have bounced the familiar yellow-gold crafts into sharp rocks. *Photograph courtesy of PRF Composites.*

which was originally marketed for toothbrushes but gained acceptance as the main material in women's stockings: nylon.

By the early 1960s, DuPont chemists were looking for a compound to make automobile tires lighter but stronger and more energy efficient; some experts were predicting a shortage of gasoline, and cars like the Volkswagen Beetle and Ford Falcon were marketed accordingly. Kwolek's liquid was not tossed out; it was set aside in a lab in Wilmington, Delaware, for more testing. A lab assistant ran the murky material through a spinneret, a device used to extrude fibers from polymers, and, much to the surprise of the chemists, the fiber did not snap under a little pressure, as did nylon. More tests followed, and it wasn't long before the chemists knew that they had something special.

Kevlar, which would be used for protective gloves, helmets, boots, cables, and hundreds of other products, represents the post–World War II era of synthetic products that found their way into canoes. Among the other

The Souris River Canoe factory in Atikokan, Ontario, produces several popular canoe-tripping models made of Kevlar fibers and epoxy resin. Other manufacturers use resins of polyester and/or vinyl ester. By tensile strength-to-weight measure, Kevlar is five times stronger than steel.

*Photograph by Debbie Hartmann.*

materials in that line were acrylonitrile butadiene styrene (ABS), fiberglass, polyurethane, and carbon fiber. They all played a part in the manufacture of canoes that for centuries had been made almost entirely from a fairly narrow range of wood from nature's forests.

A boom period in canoe sales came along with twentieth-century materials and the advent of more lei-sure time after World War II. Families who would not have considered boat ownership could spend $175 on an aluminum canoe without breaking the budget; they could also store it outside without harm, and it seemed as though they could pound it into rapids and rocks. Then came plastics. Canoes sold as well as or more rapidly than before, and for less money, too. In Canada alone, canoe ownership went from 123,000 in 1970 to 607,000 in just more than twenty years.[3] The canoe became a familiar recreational vehicle for all classes of society.

### ALUMINUM

The first of the postwar canoes to hit the market successfully in a material other than wood were built of aluminum—not a synthetic material, but not an element with a huge market share in mass-produced boats. Aluminum had

With the Second Industrial Revolution in full swing, boatbuilders began experimenting with materials they hadn't used before, such as aluminum. The French racing yacht *Vendenesse*, built for a count, was one such attempt. Launched in 1894, it had a 2-millimeter-thick skin, and the builder claimed a 40 percent weight savings on the hull. *Illustration from Daniel Charles,* Histoire du yachting.

a brief history with watercraft, full of stops and starts and mostly dead ends.

One of the more ambitious projects came via the French, who in 1894 launched two vessels—the yacht *Vendenesse* and the torpedo boat tender *La Foudre*—with aluminum hulls and other parts. Steel was rejected as not practical because of its weight.[4] The torpedo boat tender, which had aluminum plates on its hull, did not fare well; within two years the hull was damaged by salt water and, because it was not mended or maintained properly, was beyond repair. Only the deck, covered by rubber "cloth" glued to the metal, remained intact.

The *Vendenesse*, owned by Count Jean de Chabannes la Palice, made two trips to sea from the French port at Le Havre but also had problems with deterioration. Paint seemed to delay the degradation of the metal, but the paint inevitably wore away as it rubbed against a pier or was overexposed to the elements. And there were other problems: "The enormous weight of her lead keel and the pitching of the vessel caused her hull to shake violently, and, owing to the sonorousness of the metal, the waves dashing against her sides created a deafening noise inside," according to the *Yachtsman*.[5] In a bit of an understatement, *Scientific American* said the craft "does not present a very encouraging prospect for the introduction of aluminum boats."[6] Among other problems, the uneven quality of processed aluminum alloys at the seams bedeviled the builders.

# ∽ Canoe Patents

At the United States Patent and Trademark Office archives in Washington, D.C., the dreams of men such as Dominicus Parker Tuck of Danforth, Maine; Frederick W. Zeidler of Jersey City, New Jersey; Verplanck Colvin of Albany, New York; William Armstrong of Chicago, Illinois; and Royal L. Boulter of Grand Forks, North Dakota, are on file. These fellows and dozens of others tried, and mostly failed, to invent and sell improvements on the design of the canoe, a design that Native Americans had perfected over hundreds and hundreds of years.

It wasn't for lack of effort. Tuck was among the many who sought to improve the stability of the canoe and "to prevent their sinking if swamped, and to enable them to carry more."[1] His idea was a pair of inflatable sponsons ("rubber or other elastic material") and a couple of clamps, all of which could be "easily stowed away in canoe A or carried in an overcoat pocket."

Inventor Zeidler and his partner, Carl Halpern of Newark, New Jersey, were also interested in balance, or lack thereof, in their canoes. Instead of trying to steady the boat from the outside, the two men came up with a sort of swinging stern seat that kept the paddler more or less upright while the boat rode the waves, "the object

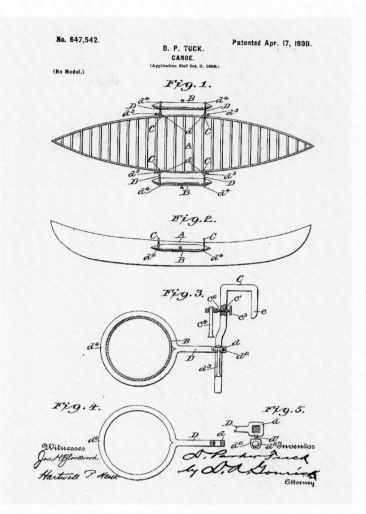

Inventors have struggled for years to make canoes feel more stable. Sponsons, which are essentially buoyant pieces attached to the gunwales, were a common answer, including this attempt by D. P. Tuck from 1900.

*Courtesy of the U.S. Patent and Trademark Office.*

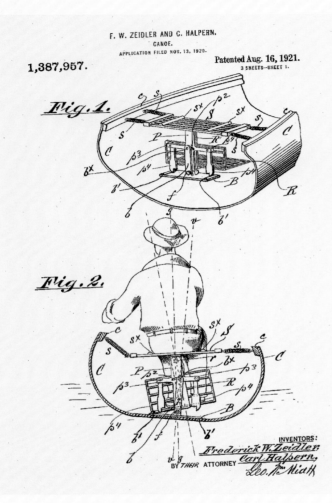

F. W. ZEIDLER AND C. HALPERN,
CANOE.
APPLICATION FILED NOV. 13, 1920.

1,387,957.

Patented Aug. 16, 1921.
3 SHEETS—SHEET 1.

*Fig. 1.*

*Fig. 2.*

INVENTORS:
*Frederick W. Zeidler*
*Carl Halpern*
BY *THEIR* ATTORNEY
*Geo. Wm. Miatt*

Floats projecting from the boat apparently weren't a desirable solution for F. W. Zeidler and C. Halpern, who in 1921 patented a system to rotate the canoeist, rather than add to the exterior of the boat. In terms of catching on, this idea did not.

*Courtesy of the U.S. Patent and Trademark Office.*

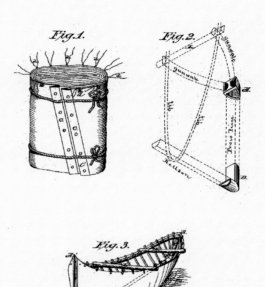

V. COLVIN.
Portable Boats.

No. 155,710.

Patented Oct. 6, 1874.

*Fig. 1.*

*Fig. 2.*

*Fig. 3.*

Attest:
Geo. D. Hill.
Milly Blake

Inventor:
Verplanck Colvin

Stability wasn't the only concern for inventors and shade-tree tinkerers. Portability, which did not seem to be a problem for Native American builders, couldn't be left alone by the mid- and late 1800s. In one of several attempts at a packable canoe, V. Colvin patented a canoe in 1874 that rolled into a giant tube.  *Courtesy of the U.S. Patent and Trademark Office.*

being to stabilize navigation, mitigate lateral rocking, and prevent the capsizing of the boat in so far as possible."[2] We could all agree on his last point, although a more thorough understanding of the dynamics of a well-designed canoe in tall waves would have stopped this project before it started.

Colvin, a noted surveyor and writer in the Adirondack region, bypassed stability in favor of improving another main worry of the paddler: portages. In 1874, he patented a portable canoe (when have most canoes *not* been portable?) that rolled up like a window shade, albeit one the size of a small round bale of hay. Colvin's design was such that the wilderness paddler had to hack thwarts, ribs, and gunwales in the wilderness from "boughs and timber (cut in the first thicket or wood)" and build on the spot.[3] Even for sportsmen used to rugged mid-nineteenth-century wilderness travel, piecing together their own canoe damned near from scratch was more work than they wanted to do, and the idea died.

Six years later, Armstrong addressed the portability issue with a design that also did not catch on, since it seemed to be a cross between an accordion and a large bag of laundry. It also asked for a fair amount of work from the user, not the least of which was sewing the pieces together.[4]

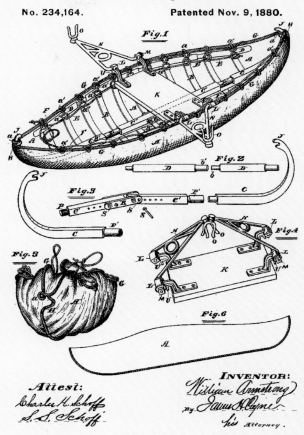

In 1880, W. Armstrong designed a folding canoe that fit in a handy carrying pouch. It also had oarlocks attached to outriggers.

*Courtesy of the U.S. Patent and Trademark Office.*

Boulter's idea was a bicycle boat. Or two boats, actually. A pair of canoes rode side by side with a superstructure resembling a bike, complete with seat, handlebars, pedals, and chain. The chain turned two paddlewheels instead of bicycle wheels. It was not suitable for portaging, needless to say. Buoyancy, as addressed by Tuck and the others, was not forgotten nor, from the looks of the drawings, was it achieved. The boats would "tend to remain in upright positions," which is always sought after in canoeing. "The machine is also comparatively cheap to make and has an artistic appearance," which leaves one wondering what the comparison group (or artwork) was.[5]

The human-powered engineering movement of the late nineteenth century might be mostly known for perfecting the bicycle. In 1896, R. L. Boulter crossbred a canoe and a bike to come up with a bicycle boat, or boats, depending on how you looked at it. Perhaps it was a distant relation to the paddleboats of the twentieth century.

*Courtesy of the U.S. Patent and Trademark Office.*

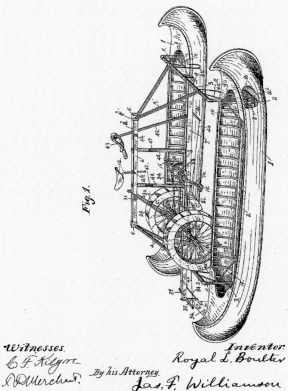

(No Model.)                                    3 Sheets—Sheet 1.

R. L. BOULTER.
BICYCLE BOAT.

No. 557,647.                        Patented Apr. 7, 1896.

Fig. 1.

Witnesses.                                    Inventor:
C. F. Kilgore                                 Royal L. Boulter
D. D. Merchant.        By his Attorney.
                       Jas. F. Williamson

With the construction of the *Vendenesse,* it was probably inevitable that the French navy would take an interest in aluminum boats. One result was *Le Foudre,* a torpedo boat tender (actually built in Britain) with a skin of sheet aluminum thicknesses varying from 1 to 5 millimeters. After about 1900, aluminum was abandoned by navies as a major construction material because of issues of corrosion in salt water.   *Courtesy of Bibliothèque nationale de France.*

While the French were struggling with the *Vendenesse* and *La Foudre*, a Swiss foundry crafted an aluminum-framed yacht for the German Prince William of Wied for his use on Lake Zurich and the Gulf of Genoa. The twin-masted *Aluminia* had a wooden deck and five watertight compartments below, and soon the *Susanne* and the *Luna* joined her in the German fleet. But the material did not catch on. "It cannot be said that the results have been satisfactory so far," wrote one contemporary commentator.[7] Part of the problem was that the aluminum ships were twice as expensive as a similar wooden boat, so the prince and Count Jean de Chabannes la Palice were two of a few who could afford to cruise in one. (Alfred Nobel, the inventor of dynamite and founder of the Nobel Prizes, was another. His boat, launched in 1892, was the *Mignon.*) Other makers, including at least one canoe builder, experimented with aluminum in the late nineteenth century; there is an account of a portable aluminum boat constructed for a trip to the interior of Africa.[8] But it would be nearly two generations before aluminum came into common use in boats.

Although aluminum is the world's most common metal, it is not found lying around by itself in huge veins, ready to be mined. It is almost always mixed in ores, such as bauxite; to be used efficiently, it must be separated from its ore and processed. This has been done more or less successfully since at least the 1850s, although the real breakthrough came in the 1880s, when American Charles Martin Hall and Frenchman Paul Héroult, working independently, devised a cost-effective extraction method based on electrolysis (eventually named the Hall-Héroult

Prior to the development of hard-topped automobiles, it was a bit of a problem to travel with a canoe on a soft-top car. One solution, which limited the use of all of the car doors, was to strap the boat on sidesaddle, as shown with this wood-and-canvas model. This photograph was taken in Milwaukee, Wisconsin, sometime before 1930.

*Photograph by J. Robert Taylor. Courtesy of the Wisconsin Historical Society, WHS-49483.*

process). Hall's company, Pittsburgh Reduction, was the forerunner of Alcoa, still one of the world's largest producers of aluminum.

World War I interrupted leisure-time activities, including bicycling and boating, and the industries that supported them. Canoe sales dropped during the war and then rebounded to prewar numbers in the 1920s before starting a slow decline. Working canoes for hunting and fishing, usually wood and canvas as opposed to all wood, continued to sell, but the canoe and motorcar did not cohabitate well until the 1930s, when car roofs were made strong enough to support a canoe.[9] (Canoe liveries, where boats could be rented rather than purchased, remained common.)

After World War I, the nascent aircraft manufacturing industry increasingly looked to aluminum parts because of their weight (one-third that of steel), pliability, and strength,

After World War II, Americans enjoyed an increase in leisure time (and more spending money) as the economy started to hum. Automobiles fitted with car-top carriers, such as this one from 1946 made by Berg's, held camping gear beneath the canoe and attached to the rain gutters along the roof of the vehicle. *Photograph by Arthur M. Vinje. Courtesy of the Wisconsin Historical Society, WHS-44704.*

especially at low temperatures. The Wright brothers had used aluminum engine parts in the early 1900s, and Count Ferdinand von Zeppelin's airship had aluminum frames in 1900.[10] But none of the early aircraft builders took to aluminum as readily as Leroy (Roy) Grumman, the principal owner of the Grumman Aircraft Engineering Corporation in Long Island, New York. He and his partners, who started the firm in 1929, kept the factory floor humming by welding aluminum truck frames while chasing government military contracts for airplanes, where "steel and aluminum

Leroy Grumman tests out his trademark aluminum canoe. Grumman's name is important in the history of canoeing owing to his company's development of the aluminum canoe as a way to keep his factories busy after World War II. The canoes were heavy, loud, hot in the summer and cold in the winter, and people loved them. Thousands of inexpensive and tough Grumman canoes still ply waters across the continent.

*Photograph courtesy of the San Diego Air and Space Museum, BIOG00431.*

alloys began to supplant wood and fabric in airframe construction."[11]

Meanwhile, in Britain, boatbuilders successfully used an aluminum-magnesium alloy, marketed under the name of Birmabright, that proved to be more corrosion resistant than earlier forms.[12] The author and adventurer Pierre Pulling, who promoted himself as "the dean of American canoeists," reports seeing an aluminum canoe in 1930 in Michigan but does not mention the builder.[13] Nonetheless, all nonmilitary uses of aluminum came to a sudden stop with the advent of another world war, and the alloy production went almost entirely into warplanes.

Canoes, along with many other types of small craft, were deployed in World War II, including at least one British-made model of a metal alloy construction and a late-war design that used Birmabright.

By the middle of World War II, Grumman was the major supplier of aircraft, such as the famed F4F Wildcat and F6F Hellcat, to the U.S. Navy. But it became clear as the war was winding down that Grumman needed to reduce its labor force—employment went from more than 20,000 to slightly more than 5,000—as well as find new markets as the demand for military aircraft nearly vanished. The company returned to commercial amphibian models and aluminum truck bodies and added private light planes. But perhaps its most well-known new product was the Grumman aluminum canoe.

The idea came from Grumman's chief tool engineer, William Hoffman. He was an avid fisherman and outdoorsman, and at the end of May 1944 he took a canoe trip into the Adirondacks. Hoffman's personal canoe was a 13-foot

Old Town that had seen some wear; his trip took him on a portage from Limekiln Lake to Squaw Lake, and, like many canoeists, he swore that his boat weighed more than its advertised 50 pounds when he reached the end of that haul. A lighter canoe might be possible with aluminum, he thought, so he took the idea to Grumman and Jake Swirbul, a manager at the aircraft company. "They liked the idea, particularly as a postwar project, and suggested I start some studies on it," Hoffman said.[14] A marketing survey was commissioned.

Grumman was convinced, and Hoffman's group went to work on a design. The bow and stern were heightened and watertight compartments added in each end. "Then we had to design the hull lines so that our aluminum stretch presses could form each of the two halves of the canoe out of one piece of aluminum sheet without any wrinkling," Hoffman recalled.[15] Two identical halves were riveted together and the keel and the gunwales produced from aluminum extrusions.

Alcoa designed and produced a special aluminum alloy for the Grumman canoes and sent along a canoe expert named Russell Bontecou, who had been working with aluminum boat prototypes for several years. Bontecou did not have Grumman's engineering expertise, or access to its big stretch presses, and he had been designing and building canoe prototypes in sections, which proved unworkable commercially. But he landed in the right spot, and his canoe knowledge was important to the project.

Hoffman, Bontecou, and their team built a 13-foot pilot model, using a maple die, based on an Old Town canoe

Grumman canoes, because of their low cost and nearly maintenance-free existence, became a common choice of canoe liveries by the 1950s. The boats could be stored outdoors year-round without much damage, and even the most inexperienced tenderfoot couldn't hurt one too much. *Photograph by Jon "ShakataGaNai" Davis.*

The Canadian artist and author Bill Mason did as much to popularize recreational canoeing as anyone. Through movies, instructional films, and writings, Mason (often seen with his family) became the face of Canadian canoeing to many people. Here they are shown shooting the rapids in a Grumman; his favorite boat was a red wood-and-canvas Chestnut Prospector. *Photograph courtesy of the Mason family.*

owned by Hoffman. The aluminum boat weighed 38 pounds, while the elderly Old Town tipped the scales at 64 pounds. More test models, this time 17 feet long, were ordered, and production of the longer prototypes was moved to the company's bowling alley in Plant Number 2 at the end of 1944. In the spring of 1945, the company sent a crew down the Allagash River in Maine in a prototype, and it survived the rocks and rapids without a problem, just like the birchbarks, dugouts, and wood-and-canvas boats before it. The marketing department took another prototype to Abercrombie and Fitch in New York City, where it sat in a display window and drew interested crowds.[16]

## ☙ Canoes in Wartime

Of the many uses to which Native tribes put
their canoes, perhaps the most important was
that of war. The canoe was the "principal means
of war" among North American woodlands
Indians because it was fast, silent, and light.[1]
The differences between the awkward elm-bark
canoes of the Iroquois and the maneuverable
birch-bark canoes of their opponents made
a difference in the famous battle on Lake
Champlain in 1609.

Dugouts were often used for raiding along
the North American coasts and between islands
in the Caribbean; in this way, canoes were as
useful as any other vehicle in wartime. The
Arawaks in the Caribbean were particularly skilled at making war in canoes and
expanded their territory accordingly. A force of eighty canoes repelled Ponce de León
in 1513 in what is now Florida.

In the same region more than three hundred years later, the U.S. government
and the Seminole tribe engaged in a "canoe war" that was "the only U.S. naval flotilla
ever engaged in an Indian campaign."[2] About 140 dugout canoes were involved in the
skirmishes by the end of what was called the Second Seminole War in 1842.

In North America, war canoes were usually long—perhaps 25 feet or more—
and eventually became known and used for other purposes, including freight hauling.

Canoes were used in wartime by Native tribes
for centuries, and sometimes by all sides, as
late as the Seminole War (1835–42) in Florida.

*Courtesy of the Defense Department Archives,*
*National Archives and Records Administration.*

**THEY CALLED THEM "CANOE COMMANDOS"!**

*– The Never-Before-Told Story of the Top-Secret Guys!*

COLUMBIA PICTURES presents A WARWICK Production

Jose FERRER · Trevor HOWARD

**COCKLESHELL HEROES**

*Reader's Digest*
*The true and tremendous Reader's Digest story that thrilled millions!*

CINEMASCOPE
Color by TECHNICOLOR

Screenplay by BRYAN FORBES and RICHARD MAIBAUM · Executive Producers IRVING ALLEN and ALBERT R. BROCCOLI · Directed by JOSE FERRER

The real-life story of a World War II canoe raid by the British military on an enemy base was made into *Cockleshell Heroes*, a 1955 movie starring José Ferrer and Trevor Howard.

In the late nineteenth and early twentieth centuries, war canoe races allowed clubs to get several members in a boat for a single contest and became a popular pastime.

As part of his fascination with Native peoples, Edward S. Curtis's 1914 movie *In the Land of the War Canoes* (also known as *In the Land of the Head Hunters*) described the painted canoes of the Kwakiutl tribe in Vancouver.

Small boats of all sorts were used in World War II, including canoes. The British Navy commissioned one canoe model of a metal alloy construction using Birmabright.

Perhaps the most famous canoe story from the war involving self-propelled boats was that of the British-run Operation Frankton, which was carried out in "cockleshell canoes," a curious hybrid of folding kayak and sailing canoe, with sponsons. Some had canvas spray skirts, keels, and rudders and were propelled by double-bladed paddles. The boats were aluminum-framed and canvas-sided with a flat bottom, mast, and short deck and could fold to fit in a submarine.[3] Six two-man folding cockleshells armed with limpet mines were delivered to the west coast of France in 1942 in a commando raid; several docked cargo ships were blown up, but only two men survived.[4]

The British, working with Australians, repeated a canoe operation in Singapore harbor in September 1943 and sank several ships after smuggling the canoes in an old fishing boat, but a third canoe-based operation in 1944 failed when all crew members were caught and executed.[5]

By the end of 1945, the war was over and Grumman had ninety-four orders for its aluminum canoe. The company made it in four lengths and in regular and lightweight versions at the aircraft plant in Bethpage, Long Island. The following year, 10,000 canoes were ordered and the plant was running three shifts per day. By 1947, Grumman was the nation's largest canoe maker.[17] It was undercutting Old Town on price—a new Old Town OTCA was $199 in 1947, while the Grumman went for $157 in regular trim. And the aluminum boat was 18 pounds lighter, and 32 pounds less in its lightweight version. Eventually a heavier "livery" model was added to the lineup.

Following the war, recreational canoeing rode the Grumman popularity to a rapid recovery, but the aluminum boats represented signs of trouble for the traditional builders. Wooden canoe makers did well in the 1950s, but the old-line manufacturers tended to ignore or downplay any new materials coming into use.[18] "New technologies and market sophistication did not mix well with traditional ways of doing business" was one analysis.[19]

Not everyone in a wood-and-canvas canoe resisted the change. The American physicist Homer L. Dodge, who grew up in upstate New York and acquired a lifelong love of canoes there, paddled Grumman canoes in races and on camping trips and remained active in the sport until his death at age ninety-five in 1983.[20]

The Korean conflict interrupted aluminum canoe production at Bethpage, and the Grumman line was moved to a plant in Marathon, New York.[21] More manufacturers

Low-maintenance aluminum means more time for fun.

## Aluminum...new champion on the water

Aluminum takes to water with the ease of a dolphin. From canoes to cargo ships, to luxury liners—designers and builders are using aluminum in more and more ways.

Light, strong aluminum decreases topside weight—increases cargo capacity, stability and potential speed. Special, high-speed welding techniques make aluminum particularly suitable for shipbuilding. Its resistance to corrosion cuts maintenance to a minimum.

Aluminum's ability to create better, longer lasting products has led to its expanded use in virtually every field. More and more businesses are finding that aluminum

solves design problems, cuts shipping costs, sells products faster. Many of them look to Aluminium Limited for an important part of the aluminum ingot essential to their operation.

Aluminium Limited sells no consumer products in the U.S. It specializes in supplying high-quality aluminum ingot as well as technical assistance to help its customers expand their markets.

**Aluminium Limited, Montreal:** *Canada's independent producer of aluminum ingot for U. S. industries.* In the U.S.: Aluminium Limited Sales, Inc., 630 Fifth Avenue, New York.

Abundant water power in Canada's river-rich northland makes possible the vast quantities of electricity needed to make aluminum to serve U.S. industry requirements.

## Aluminum from Canada

With Grumman's success, other companies involved in aluminum production saw an opening in a new market. The Canadian firm Aluminum Limited, which became Alcan, promoted its product in this 1958 advertisement featuring a group of boys at camp. The company didn't make canoes; rather, it sold aluminum to companies that did so.

Homer Dodge, with his wife and frequent canoeing companion, Margaret Wing Dodge, helped popularize canoeing in the United States; he was sponsored by Grumman for a time. Dodge was a longtime physics faculty member and administrator at the University of Oklahoma.

*Courtesy of the AIP Emilio Segrè Visual Archives, Dodge Collection.*

In 1967, Minnesota-based Alumacraft (shown here as Aluma Craft Apex Co.) was apparently shoveling canoes out the door as fast as they could be produced. The company, founded by Henry J. Neils, was a competitor to Grumman in the canoe business and made other boats as well.

*Photograph by Norton & Peel. Courtesy of the Minnesota Historical Society, NP 303047.*

jumped into the market, but none reached the national sales success of Grumman. Dow Chemical made a 12-foot canoe of magnesium in the late 1940s, but it cost $325.[22] In Minnesota, an ironworks magnate named Henry J. Neils began producing aluminum boats in 1945; a year later he founded the Alumacraft Boat Company. Alumacraft, which was sold to Hupp Corporation in 1960, made a range of aluminum boats, including well-designed canoes.

Aluminum canoes met the market at the right time; they were cheaper, lighter, and easier to care for than their wood-and-canvas brethren, and, in the words of Pulling, "they could take a punch."[23] They were also loud—how many sportsmen had game and fish startled by the banging of a paddle on a gunwale?—and needed an air chamber or flotation in the stem, stern, or under the seats to stay afloat properly when swamped. Depending on the weather, they were either too cold or too hot, and some were poorly riveted or badly designed. Buyers ignored the drawbacks and snapped up thousands of the metal boats in the 1950s and beyond.

Purists argued that there was no romance in an aluminum boat, unlike the beautiful handcrafted lines of a Peterborough, Rushton, Old Town, or Morris. Craftsmen, they said, were giving way to mere builders.[24] At the traditional maker Old Town, owner Sam Gray rejected a partnership deal with Grumman—Gray felt aluminum canoes were ugly, noisy, too hot or cold, and got stuck on the rocks too easily. But aluminum was as important as any material in the introduction and dispersal of the canoe as a cultural object in the twentieth century. By the early 1960s, Old Town was selling 200 wood-and-canvas canoes per year, while Grumman was selling 20,000 aluminum models.[25]

Grumman shipped canoes by truck, among other means, to retailers large and small across the United States from its plants in New York. A load of boats is ready for customers in Madison, Wisconsin, in 1946 at Madison Marine Service. The trailer carried twenty-eight canoes.

*Photograph by Arthur M. Vinje. Courtesy of the Wisconsin Historical Society, WHS-44838.*

**Almost as SMOOTH as...**
**the new kind of FORD**

Canoes, as popular as they were, became symbols for benefits like quiet, smooth rides—on calm days, of course. Advertising agencies picked up on the canoe's attributes and tried to transfer them to their products, in this case new Ford motorcars in the 1960s.

*Courtesy of the Outdoor Advertising Association of America (OAAA) Archives, 1885–1990s: Item ID BBB6261, John W. Hartman Center for Sales Advertising and Marketing History, David M. Rubenstein Rare Book and Manuscript Library, Duke University.*

From 1951 to 1976, Grumman was the leading canoe builder in the United States, churning out the lightweight .032-inch-thick hulls as fast as three shifts could work, surpassing 33,000 canoes annually in the mid-1970s.[26] (Standard hulls were .050 inches thick, while the livery model was a tougher .060 inches.) But the seeds of change had been planted again for canoe builders, even Grumman, and this time it was an ancient concept—spun glass—that signaled room in the canoe mass market for more than just aluminum.

### PLASTIC COMPOSITES

Wood composites—pre-plywood—were used in boats at the beginning of the twentieth century and before. In 1917, Henry Haskell made what naval architect William J.

Deed calls the "first one-piece canoe of lightweight material," which was wood veneer.[27] Haskell's company later made marine plywood.

Non-wood canoes were inevitable. Fiberglass, or at least its foundation, has been known for 3,500 years in the form of spun glass. Molten glass drawn into thin strands, or even threads, had been a decorative device used in ornamental glassmaking for centuries. By the late nineteenth century, inventors began experimenting with the use of fine glass fibers in the textile industry. In France, and later in the United States, glass fibers were woven with silk into fine women's gowns and dresses, but neither the process nor the fashion caught on.[28]

Commercial fiberglass production in the United States began as a partnership between Owens-Illinois and the Corning Glass Works. Michael J. Owens is credited with

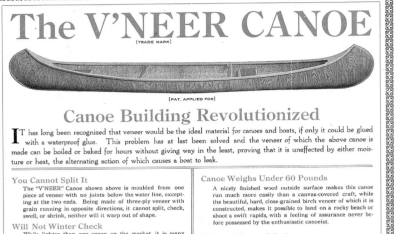

Around 1917, the Haskell Manufacturing Company of Ludington, Michigan, debuted a composite canoe called the V'neer. The boat was made of three-ply plywood with birch veneer on the faces and redwood in the center, held together with a waterproof glue that Henry Haskell had invented. The company claimed a weight of less than 60 pounds, but the construction technique did not catch on. *Courtesy of Daniel Miller.*

the invention of the automatic bottle-making machine in the early nineteenth century; Corning had been in the glass business under a few different names since 1851. Together, they formed Owens-Corning Corporation in 1935.

Like the aluminum entrepreneurs, the fiberglass makers were looking for a new material to be used in the aviation industry. The Owens-Corning product known by the trade name of Fiberglas (note the single "s") was stiffer than muslin or sisal, although all these materials needed a hardening resin before they could be used in manufacturing processes. DuPont stepped in with an early resin for such a purpose, followed by American Cyanamid with what became known as polyester resin in 1942. (Other resins, including vinyl ester, epoxy, and thermosetting types eventually came into use.) Owens-Corning began commercial production of fiberglass in 1939, just in time for World War II. A chemist named Ray Greene is credited with making a fiberglass dinghy in 1942.[29]

Early fiberglass canoes were a labor-intensive production; sheets of fiber were placed in a mold, soaked with resin, and left alone to cure. Mass production, if thought of as mechanization, was difficult. But the advantage of the fiberglass "lay up" came in its amenability to form the complex curves and shapes of a canoe created by the mold that held it. It did not require a heavy financial outlay for specialized equipment, as did aluminum, nor did the workers need extraordinary experience to do the job. As a result, many small manufacturers jumped into the small-boat business following the war, including the Beetle Boat Company of New Bedford, Massachusetts, which in some quarters gets credit for being the first to the market, in 1947, with a 9-foot glass-reinforced polyester dinghy.[30] Wizard Boats, a fiberglass boat company in Costa Mesa, California, in 1948 produced a 16-foot boat called the Plasticanoe that sold for a hefty $220. It was advertised as tough enough to be shot with a shotgun, hit with a sledge, run over by a car, and dropped from a roof.[31] Should any of those incidents happen to your Plasticanoe, a repair kit cost $6. In Binghamton, New York, the Linkanoe was made of cotton and Bakelite laminating resin, cured in a high-pressure hydraulic press. The 14½-foot canoe broke into ten pieces that fit into two canvas bags at 65 pounds and required a (sometimes) watertight canvas cover attached to the outside of the hull. "Goes in luggage compartment of car, by plane or pack horse," read the advertisements.[32] Its maker was yet another former aviation company.

A worker at Old Town Canoes puts the finishing touches on a fiberglass model. Fiberglass is applied from a sheet or off a roll onto a canoe mold, sometimes with other synthetic products to form a laminate. Manufacturers can also vary the resins used to harden it. The resins can be toxic, so workers wear protection when assembling a canoe. *Courtesy of the Gray Family Collections.*

Even though fiberglass canoes were labor-intensive compared to aluminum boats, they were much quicker to build than wood-and-canvas canoes. Some of the old-line makers were experimenting with fiberglass by the end of the 1950s, but not many stuck with it. Old Town was an exception. By 1971, Old Town came out with a model called the Rushton that was a 10½-foot fiberglass canoe designed from a plan found in a biography of Rushton.[33] Old Town, whose first fiberglass canoe came out in 1965, began to produce fiberglass kayaks in 1969.

The resin in a fiberglass canoe essentially made it a plastic craft, and it follows that other manufacturers were

The Linkanoe was another attempt, in the 1940s, at perfecting what was already a pretty perfectly designed boat. A sectional canoe, it was designed for ease of transport in the trunk of a car, the bed of a pickup truck, or an airplane hold. The company claimed it could be assembled in 10 minutes—no tools needed!—and stuffed into a canvas bag at the end of the day.

*Courtesy of the Edwin A. Link Collection, Binghamton University Libraries' Special Collections and University Archives, Binghamton University.*

experimenting with different types of plastic compounds at the same time. Scientists in the 1940s were looking for a substitute for rubber—like other natural materials, short of supply during the war—when they developed a copolymer of three ingredients: acrylonitrile butadiene styrene, or ABS.[34]

ABS is a hard, light, shiny thermoplastic that not only eventually worked in canoes but also became the basis for Legos, cheap plastic musical instruments like recorders, car bumpers, and golf club heads. Among its other early uses in the 1950s was for one-piece refrigerator liners and hard-sided luggage.[35] ABS had an advantage over early fiberglass production in that it could be molded by machine. Because it was seamless, leakage problems from poor rivets or welds were minimized, and those costly secondary assembly processes were not needed, either. That made it cheaper. A big drawback was its sensitivity to light; sunlight damages the material and early ABS products left sitting outside season after season faded badly, eventually cracking and failing from extended exposure.

On the plastic side of the market, canoe makers experimented with spray-up methods, wet hand lay-ups, vacuum bag molding, matched metal molding, heat curing, room-temperature curing, autoclaving, and layers after layers—"practically every fabrication process developed for rein-

The old-line canoe builder Old Town expanded into the fiberglass market in the 1960s. This advertisement for its Rushton model claimed a weight of 18.5 pounds on the 10½-foot solo boat, which cost $195. *Courtesy of the Adirondack Museum, 14681.*

forced plastics," according to one composite handbook.[36] Quality varied with the manufacturer, but almost all of them sold canoes on the basis of price, low maintenance, and ease of repair. "Plastic could easily be turned into surf boards, boat hulls, cute little kit cars, and all sorts of stuff

Among the synthetic materials that became important in the canoe market was ABS, or acrylonitrile butadiene styrene. The thermoplastic polymer made the basis of a tough, relatively inexpensive canoe that competed with the aluminum boats on the market. Here a Nova Craft Moisie model tackles the rapids on Ontario's Madawaska River.

*Photograph by Scott MacGregor/Canoeroots Magazine.*

being rhapsodized about by the Beach Boys," writes one author.[37]

ABS plastic was a key ingredient in one of the more popular laminates in the late twentieth century that became known by its trade name, Royalex. Developed by Uniroyal, Royalex in canoes consisted of a sandwich of a layer of vinyl, a layer of ABS, an ABS foam core, another layer of ABS, and then one more of vinyl. (A simple ABS boat eliminated the foam core. The vinyl layer helped protect it from the sun.) The company's first attempt at an ABS product was called Royalite, but it was not protected from ultraviolet rays and needed the added layer of a vinyl skin to keep it from deteriorating.

The Thompson Boat Company unveiled an ABS canoe in 1964 at the Chicago Boat Show,[38] and Old Town, which had tested and successfully marketed fiberglass canoes in the 1960s, experimented with what may have been the first canoe made by an old-line canoe manufacturer from flat sheets of Royalex, bringing it to the market in 1972.[39] The material proved nearly indestructible and critical for whitewater canoes, and led to a memorable PR stunt at the Old Town factory when the managers tossed a Tripper model made of Royalex (its version was called Oltonar) off the 35-foot-high roof of the factory. It was undamaged.[40] Uniroyal sold the formula in 2000; it was sold again in 2012; in 2013, PolyOne, the manufacturer, announced it was closing the plant that made the material.[41]

The Wichita, Kansas–based manufacturer Coleman, known for its lanterns and camp stoves, had expanded aggressively into the outdoor and camping market by

Sometimes canoe manufacturers went to extreme lengths to tout the quality of their synthetic canoes. In this case, Old Town dropped a Tripper model off the roof of its plant in Old Town, Maine, to show it could take a punch and more or less snap right back to straight again.

*Advertisement from* Backpacker *magazine, 1979.*

the 1960s. With the introduction of its RAM-X canoe, a vacuum-molded polyethylene model that was cheap, flexible, and tough, Coleman took over the bottom end of the canoe market. The boat had a .220-inch-thick hull and was heavier than Royalex, but at one-third the cost, most buyers did not care. The polyethylene skin needed to be stiffened with an aluminum frame, including gunwales and thwarts. The material is not buoyant, so a foam core or buoyancy chambers were added. Polyethylene boats were subject to abrasion and cuts but would knock back into their original shape if flexed.

At major discount stores, the canoes could be sold for a couple hundred dollars or less, and by 1974 Coleman was selling 20,000 canoes per year, by one estimate. Susan

**The Coleman Canoe: the first "family canoe" with guts enough to take on white water.**

Every canoe trip offers something special: like gliding up on a deer drinking from the stream. And there's never been a family canoe like this one. Or a white water canoe. Or a fishing canoe. It's so tough, so versatile, yet priced so it's reasonable for weekend outings.

That's because Coleman built a whole new kind of canoe. Not aluminum. Not fiberglass. It's molded in one piece (no seams, rivets) from a tough new petrochemical material, RAM-X.™

That tough hide springs back when you bang into a rock. It takes knocks that would crumple aluminum, puncture fiberglass.

It's quieter than an aluminum canoe too. It doesn't bang or clang when you run a gravel bar or accidentally drop a paddle. So on a wilderness stream, you see wildlife you wouldn't see otherwise. And on a quiet lake, you *catch* the fish instead of scaring them away.

The Coleman Canoe is a great addition to any family's fun in the great outdoors. (If you're a *camping* family, just pitch your tent right at the water's edge!) There's no motor. No gas. No noise. No trailer. It's easy for one person to load onto a simple car top carrier. Then you're ready for a great new experience.

Just look for our symbol... now at many Coleman Outing Products dealers.

**Coleman** MARINE
The Coleman Company, Inc., Wichita, Kansas

The Kansas-based outdoors company Coleman was a formidable competitor in the low-end canoe market by the 1970s. This advertisement from 1978 shows its polyethylene boats and touts their toughness and low price, comparing them favorably to aluminum boats. The company eventually sold the brand to Pelican International.

Audette, who wrote the definitive history of Old Town, says that Coleman's marketing genius lay in selling canoes to people who would have never otherwise owned one, although some of the RAM-X buyers moved up the price and quality ladder to better canoes.[42]

Benson Gray, who has made a close study of his family's former business at Old Town, says the low sticker price was the key to Coleman's success. "Recreational products are extremely price-sensitive," Gray says.

> When you have a product that the canoe has traditionally been, which requires a buyer to budget for it and plan for it—it's a big decision. If you get the price below a certain threshold, then it's no longer a big decision. People can say, "Oh, yeah, we're going on vacation. Why don't you go down to the mall? We need a cooler and we'll get some beer and some sleeping bags and get two or three of those kayak things, too. We'll throw 'em all in the back of the pickup truck and go off on vacation." When they're cheap enough, it's not as big a deal. Coleman was successful at getting below that threshold where it was no longer a big decision. That line moves but you can make a lot of money in the recreational market if you can get the price below it.[43]

Old Town eventually matched the RAM-X model in 1985 with its Discovery series, made of the same polyethylene material but in a different formula. Old Town used a layered roto-molded system with a foam core to help the canoe float and gain stiffness: the extensive aluminum frame of a RAM-X boat was not needed. By the mid-1990s, Old Town was selling nearly 15,000 plastic canoes per year and eventually claimed the Discovery was the number one–selling canoe in the world.[44]

Both models were of similar weight to aluminum canoes of the same length. Coleman remained in the market with its RAM-X canoe until 2000, when it cleaved off its "rigid hull canoe and fishing boat" operation and sold it to Pelican International, which continued to use the RAM-X name under license.[45] Old Town eventually tapped the plastic kayak market and by the early 2000s was selling more than 60,000 per year.[46]

A Wenonah Kevlar canoe glides through the Boundary Waters of northern Minnesota. By the turn of the twenty-first century, Wenonah was the largest Kevlar canoe manufacturer in the world, with an annual output of around 10,000 boats in a good year (the company also owns Current Designs kayaks). Canoe campers love these canoes for their light weight, sleek design, and durability.   *Photograph by Ray Goodwin.*

Grumman and the other aluminum makers responded to the flood of plastic boats with a number of marketing tricks. Perhaps the most unusual was borrowed from the grocery business; a purchaser of five boxes of Uncle Ben's Wild Rice in 1980 could turn in the box tops for about $150 off of a 17-foot Grumman canoe—the original price was $479—but even though several thousand Uncle Ben's fans became canoeists (or vice versa), it wasn't enough to reverse the market domination of the plastic boats.[47]

DuPont trotted out Kevlar for commercial use in 1972; it was lighter than fiberglass and more resistant to wear but more expensive than aluminum or other plastics and deteriorated in the sun. The company that became the leading maker of Kevlar canoes was Wenonah (also We-no-nah), based in Minnesota, and the high-school creation of Mike Cichanowski.

Cichanowski, who built his first boat as a student in 1965, doggedly stuck with composites from the late 1960s into the twenty-first century, adding kayaks to his line and trimming fiberglass boats from it when the market shifted. Wenonah also became expert at setting up a manufacturer-distributor-dealer network, adding a layer of geographic distributors to what had traditionally been either a direct-to-customer or a manufacturer-dealer system, allowing for a wider market. Wenonah's use of composites—from roto-molds to high-end carbon fiber—also allowed it to offer a larger lineup of boats, both in design and materials, than any aluminum maker could hope to produce. "This is not a high-margin business," says Cichanowski.[48]

## NEW MATERIALS, NEW USES

The growth of a new audience, inspired by cheap plastics, led to a different kind of canoe—fine lines, ease of entry, craftsmanship, and handling became secondary to stability, durability, and price. And canoes were used differently when their construction material changed from wood to aluminum to plastic, partly because people had more free time, but also because the boats were not a major investment.

The idea that leisure time is a 1950s phenomenon is overstated; Gary Cross, who has written a history of lei-sure, argues convincingly that free time has waxed and waned throughout history.[49] For example, in the Middle Ages, the leisure time of male elites was "dominated by physical training for combat and hunting." In Europe, hunting was a right reserved for the elites at least until the French Revolution. But as the European aristocracy moved from country estates into cities, the new urban cultures brought new interests, including fashions, and less interest in the outdoors.

In America, the colonists were hard at work surviving, but even the Puritans were fine with moderate exercise in the form of shooting, for example. American immigrants were not tied to elite European ways, however, and hunting and fishing in a land of plentiful, freely accessed game became a way of life even as it became democratic. "Leisure did not become a business in the 19th century, but the industrial economy made entertainment a more thorough and different sort of business," Cross writes.[50] Holiday "camps"—a forerunner to the resort—sprang up, almost always near water. Summer camps catering to children—think of the Camp Fire Girls, the Boy Scouts, and the Girl Scouts—taught thousands of kids how to paddle and provided a market for canoe makers.

More state and national parks were created in the early and mid-twentieth century, and a mass market for outdoor living experiences began to take shape, partially answering the question asked by President James Garfield two generations previous, when he said, "What shall we do with our leisure when we get it?"[51]

## ꙮ Square-Stern Canoes

My (coauthor Mark Neuzil's) parents invested in a square-stern canoe in about 1970, after an unfortunate incident involving the sinking of the Neuzils' World War II–surplus dinghy in a storm. The Dolphin fiberglass model, made in Wabasha, Minnesota, cost $100; it sold for $300 after forty years of service. A four-and-one-half-horsepower Ted Williams–model Sears outboard motor was its first power plant. That finicky motor became the source of an expanded vocabulary of the non-church-type for younger family members who listened to the grown-ups trying to get it pull-started in the middle of a lake on a hot day.

The balky motor led to us teenagers leaving it behind almost all of the time. We learned the ways of the canoe, with its very high, distinctive bow and its toughness as the only member of our fishing fleet. Eventually it developed a certain permanent aroma.

Fishing, and boating in general, were important in the development of the square-stern style. The invention of the gasoline-powered outboard motor in the early 1900s brought the new design with it. Electric outboards were tested in France in the 1870s by the inventor Gustave Trouvé, perhaps better known for building the first metal detector; an American "steam canoe" called

the *Nina* was featured in a *Scientific American* article in 1879.[1] But petroleum was used as the fuel of choice by the turn of the century, and Norwegian American inventor Ole Evinrude became the first successful outboard businessman with a three-horsepower gasoline model that sold by the truckload after its introduction in 1909. By the 1920s, Johnson, Elto, Atwater, Lockwood, and many more companies were in the market.

Square-stern canoes allowed for mounting a small outboard on the back of the boat; they were often used on large lakes by fishermen. Many of them were adapted from the Grand Laker models used by Maine fishing guides. Such craft could additionally be fitted with sailing rigs; the square stern lent itself to attaching a

Several companies made small, gas-powered outboard motors designed to work with square-stern canoes and other similar-sized craft. Evinrude, of Milwaukee, Wisconsin, was among the most successful of the manufacturers. Among its offerings was the Lightwin, a three-horsepower model that came with a rubberized-canvas carrying bag. The version shown here was built around 1952.
*Courtesy of the Minnesota Historical Society, 1988.211.1.A.*

rudder easily. Old Town introduced a square-stern model in 1917 and even became a distributor of Johnson outboards in the 1920s.[2]

Among the mid-century wood-and-canvas makers who built and sold square-stern canoes was Joe Seliga of Ely, Minnesota. Between 1938 and 1971, Seliga crafted thirty-three square-stern canoes; his very first form (for any canoe) was for a 16-foot, 40-inch beam, square-stern model called the Fisherman, clearly wide and flat and made for outboards.[3] Seliga, who built more than seven hundred canoes in his career, had looked at an Old Town catalog for his inspiration for that first form. Unlike the Old Town boats, however, Seliga's square-stern Fisherman did not have a keelson running along the inside centerline of the craft, although it did retain the outer keel.[4] His first effort, with a solid ash transom, was sold to a man from Missouri for $40; when he started up production again after missing three years because of the war, the price went up to $200. But increased restrictions on motors in Seliga's primary market of northern Minnesota and southern Ontario dried up square-stern sales, and he built only one more over the final three decades of his business.

The aluminum Grumman Sportboat (also branded SportCanoe), at 15 feet, 4 inches long, was a popular square-stern craft after the war despite having a weight of well over 100 pounds and too much width in the beam to paddle easily—it needed to be rowed. The original Sportboat went out of production in 1979.

Some canoeists prefer to use a side bracket to mount an outboard, after which the entire unit can be removed

Square-sterns were a popular style of Ely, Minnesota, canoe builder Joe Seliga, seen here in two photographs with his family in the early 1940s. *Courtesy of the Joe Seliga Family.*

and the canoe returned to its graceful original lines. Modern composite builders, including Mad River, Sun Dolphin, and others, make inexpensive square-stern canoes designed to be fitted with electric motors for anglers, duck hunters, and trappers.

Perhaps part of the interest in leisure-time activities came with the decline of Victorian-era repression; whatever the reasons, by the late nineteenth century, magazines devoted to the outdoor life—*American Canoeist* and *Forest and Stream* spoke for the paddlers—were firmly established in the marketplace, and newspapers added pages dedicated to sports, although in sports such as baseball and boxing, more people watched than participated. An exception to that, and related in a yet-to-be-explored way to canoeing, was the dramatic increase in the number of people who learned how to swim. Municipal beaches were jammed with people of all ages—and of both genders—in the 1920s and 1930s, as any remaining puritanism about the female form in a bathing suit in close proximity to its male counterpart mostly vanished. The American Red Cross's water safety program in the 1920s was the first major national attempt to teach everyone to swim.[52] The Red Cross also published "official minimum standards" for proficiency in canoeing, which became increasingly popular with youngsters during the interwar period as part of a renewed interest in all things Indian.[53]

The Great Depression and World War II interrupted what had been a period of expansion in almost all sports, but based on equipment figures, licenses, and permits, people returned to their recreational activities with renewed vigor when the soldiers and sailors returned home. After the war, canoe ownership became an affordable version of an upper-middle-class pleasure, made easier by postwar affluence and free time. By 1949, Cross estimates that nearly two-thirds of Americans took a vacation of ten

By the late 1950s, canoes represented the best in American outdoor life, appearing on the covers of magazines with regularity, such as this edition of *Field & Stream* from June 1959. There was more than a hint of nostalgia in the artwork by C. E. Monroe Jr.

Mark Hamel, *Canoe Livery, Lake Nokomis*, 2014. Oil on mounted linen, 40.64 × 50.8 cm.

*Printed with permission of the artist.*

days' time.[54] Throwing a canoe on top of a station wagon or camp trailer was little trouble. Fiberglass or aluminum canoes were easy to maintain and could be kept at home in a suburban garage or, in the case of aluminum, even left outdoors along a driveway. Square-stern canoes could handle a small outboard motor, which could be slipped on and off and stored in the garage, too.

Another phenomenon affecting canoe sales was the summer cabin (especially in Canada) or, in fewer cases, a second home in a rural area near water. Of course, the

Indians had built summer lodges for millennia. Americans were following in the path of the expert canoeist Henry David Thoreau, who built his cabin near Walden Pond, and others who have retreated to a "hut" to relax, recreate, and, in some cases, write or at least comment on modern society. (Playwright Arthur Miller wrote *Death of a Salesman* in a 10-by-12-foot cabin of his own construction.) The early-nineteenth-century minstrel song "Gum Tree Canoe" made a specific connection between a hut, a romance, and a canoe:

> On the Tombigbee River so bright I was born
> In a hut made of husks of the tall yellow corn
> It was there I first met with my Julia so true
> And I rowed her about in my Gum Tree canoe.[55]

Cabins passed through generations, along with their furnishings and recreational equipment, such as skis, snowshoes, fly rods, snowmobiles, and boats.

The canoe is as culture-bound as anything else found in a cabin, and it became very, very popular. *Life* magazine reported in 1953 that 8 million pleasure boats plied U.S. waters, including canoes, a figure it said was up from only 300,000 at war's end.[56] (Rowing and sailing also experienced a sharp increase with the rise in popularity of small, inexpensive crafts.) By 1979, the U.S. Census Bureau reported that 1.3 million canoes were in use in the United States.[57]

In 2005, the National Marine Manufacturers Association estimated that between 90,000 and 110,000 canoes

On Westport Island, Maine, the Writer's Block studio doubles as a boathouse. *Courtesy of Cheng + Snyder Architects.*

were sold annually.[58] A 2010 study conducted by Colorado State University estimated that, by 2020, 23.3 million canoeists will recreate in the United States, up from 20.7 million in 2000.[59]

Examining the cultural meaning of being able to call oneself a "boat owner" in the twenty-first century—even of a $300 plastic canoe—will be left to the sociologists or anthropologists. But as a popular pastime, canoeing has become well established.

## CHAPTER 7

# The Human-Powered Movement

**M**IKE CICHANOWSKI, the owner-founder of Weno-nah Canoe, is a fair representative of the human-powered movement that got kick-started in the 1960s. Not only is he of the right age, graduating from high school in 1965, but also his whole person seems to be constantly on the move. Tall and long-striding, Cichanowski dashes along through a tour of his two factories (one for canoes, one for kayaks) in Winona, Minnesota, at a pace that would cause

≺ The manufacture of synthetic canoes enjoyed a boost from the increased interest in human-powered outdoor recreation in the 1960s and 1970s, activities that also included bicycling and cross-country skiing. Canoes became more and more lightweight, which helped make them easier on the portages and on tops of vehicles; some of the new materials were also tough enough to run rapids.   *Courtesy of Wenonah Canoe, Inc.*

a short-legged person to get left in the ABS section while he had bounded ahead to the Kevlars.

The outdoor sports that we sometimes think of as being "rediscovered" in the 1960s—canoeing, bicycling, skiing, running, even snowshoeing—are familiar forms of recreation to the Cichanowski family. Mike Cichanowski still races canoes, winning his share of contests and keeping in good physical condition to do it; a snowy winter day finds him on the cross-country ski trails near his Mississippi River home, while a warm summer night has him in a boat. His daughters were state champions on the skinny skis.

His nearly fifty years in the canoe business tracks the human-powered sports renaissance. He began in high school with his first handmade canoe—a wooden model painted yellow that now sits in a local museum. Slowly his

company grew into the largest manufacturer of high-end Kevlar canoes in the world, and his expertise in composites is second to none.

"I wasn't that good in school, but I enjoyed building things," he recalls. "So I built one, made another, and sold a couple."[1] Eventually he attempted a fiberglass canoe that "was a total failure," but the Eagle Scout didn't give up. A canoe trip from the upper peninsula of Michigan back to Winona helped inspire him to work with canoes, and a job carrying groceries provided a source of steady income, however small.

Two phenomena of the era collided to give his career a shove. One was the increase in the popularity of fiberglass in all sorts of uses, and the second was the availability of small-business loans through an urban renewal program. As he took classes at a nearby college, Cichanowski ran a fiberglass repair business out of an old downtown building that he rented that took in more than just boats—fiberglass roofs were briefly popular. A small-business loan of $50,000 in 1968 enabled him to buy an acre of a tomato field on the edge of town and build his own facility.

"The first ten years were slow," he says. "We had to learn everything, and as an entrepreneur I was too stupid to call it quits. And racing was my hobby—there were always the boats." Cichanowski would paddle 1,000 miles during the short Minnesota summers in preparation for the canoe races.

Mike Cichanowski is founder and owner of Wenonah Canoes, which by the early twenty-first century had become the leading manufacturer of Kevlar canoes in the world.

*Courtesy of Wenonah Canoe, Inc.*

Canoe racing, with both professionals and Sunday cruisers competing, remains a popular form of outdoor adventure. At Lake Perez in Stone Valley, Pennsylvania, the Sy Barash Canoe Races—aluminum boats and all—drew hopefuls to the water during the 1980s. *Reprinted with permission from the Eberly Family Special Collections Library, Penn State University Libraries.*

Competitors—Mad River, Old Town, Sawyer, Bell, Mohawk, Lincoln—came and often went, but as the industry consolidated, Wenonah Canoe was a constant. When kayaks started to make inroads on the outdoor sports market, Wenonah partnered with and then purchased a Canadian brand, Current Designs, to meet that need. (Eventually Current Designs production was moved to Minnesota.)

As the owner of the company, Cichanowski remains heavily involved in designing and testing his boats. He tinkers constantly with hull shapes, seats, braces, and other elements. Cichanowski ships boats all over the world, and

## ✌ Paddles

Variations in canoe design can be hard to see with an untrained eye; differences in paddle design are at least as numerous but can be easier to identify. The position of the paddler—standing, seated, kneeling, resting on heels—influences the design, as do the type of stroke, freeboard of the canoe, and type of wood available, among many other factors.

The big breakthrough in canoe-paddle shape came in the 1970s, when racers looking for an edge created the bent-shaft paddle. From its beginning as a specialty racing tool with a somewhat radical look, the bent shaft has moved into the mainstream of canoeing, becoming as common as a padded yoke.

Just who came up with the idea remains an open question for canoe buffs, but veteran racer and canoe designer Eugene Jensen is often credited with the design. Jensen grew up on the Mississippi River in Minneapolis and was a marathon canoe racer, winning the 450-mile Bemidji-to-Minneapolis endurance test four times. In 1971, while paddling next to other canoeists, he began to watch the shape and motion of their endeavors. "They had to dig these enormous holes, and their paddles would really cavitate," he recalled in a 1993 interview. "They didn't seem to go as fast as they should. I decided, well, maybe the best thing to do is bend that shaft back a little so that the blade comes in at the beginning of the stroke rather than further back."[1] His first design had a 7-degree bend, and the idea evolved into shafts bent in 12-degree and 14-degree shapes. Jensen did not patent the idea, which led to conflicting claims about its origin.[2]

Native American paddle designs varied by tribe and geographic region.[3] Blades were wide or narrow, depending on their use, and

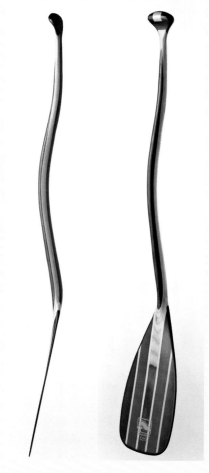

Bent paddles, such as these models made by Bending Branches, were first made for racing and came into popular use in the latter part of the twentieth century. *Photographs by Jerry Stebbins.*

grips (or handles) were also different. Still water might require a wider, flat blade, while hours-long trips in a river or large lake (think voyageurs) would be best with a light, narrow blade. West Coast Natives tended to craft a blade with a point on the end, while East Coast Indians favored a teardrop shape. A beavertail paddle is shaped just like its name, while an ottertail is its opposite, with the widest part of the paddle closer to the shaft, while it tapers to the tip. Materials were what was at hand, of course, but the best paddles were the lightest woods, such as cedar, spruce, or basswood. In shallow, swampy areas, poles of varying lengths and thicknesses replaced paddles as propulsion. Demand was such that by the late 1700s, paddles were mass-produced for the fur trade in Quebec.[4]

Like old canoes, paddles built in previous centuries deteriorated, broke, or were lost, making it difficult for scholars to research the origins of paddle making, design, and material.[5] A few drawings survive from the time of Champlain; Tappan Adney contributed about twenty paddle drawings from tribal sources in his work. Some paddles were highly decorated and probably ceremonial, while others were more workaday and contained personal markings or colors to tie them to an owner or a tribe. By the late twentieth century, modern materials such as aluminum and carbon fiber were in common use.

Paddles were all handmade in classic shapes at the Old Town Canoe Company factory. *Courtesy of the Gray Family Collections.*

The cultural significance of a canoe paddle and what it represents was illustrated at the funeral service for former Canadian prime minister Pierre Trudeau, who loved canoeing and the places it took him (and, it should be said, its role in making his public image). Leaning against his flag-draped coffin was a single canoe paddle.[6]

each market is slightly different. Skinny, high-end kayaks go to Norway, while canoes head to Finland. German canoes sport bright kayak colors, such as lime green and pink. In the twenty-first century, Wenonah showcases an extensive line of Kevlar, Royalex, polyester-fiberglass, and graphite canoes. Few companies have its range of experience with composite materials of all types. The company has a network of four hundred dealers to sell its boats.

Only 5 percent of Cichanowski's production was fiberglass in 2013, but he had 80 percent of the high-end Kevlar market in the United States. He can ship 1,000 boats per month if the demand is there. Wenonah tends to leave the low-end canoe and kayak market alone. "I saw an ad for an $89 kayak in Sunday's paper," he says. "I can't compete on that price. That [graphite] paddle over there"—pointing to a pile of them leaning on a filing cabinet—"costs $250."

Sales of low-end kayaks hurt the aluminum canoe market the most, Cichanowski says. "The aluminum canoe that sits alongside a cabin has been replaced by two kayaks." In addition, he notes that kayaks are easier for a child to learn to paddle, because they are easier to steer.

There aren't many of his generation left. "You look back and say, 'There is no way this is going to work,'" he recalls. "My wife was doing the books. My kids were working in the office.

One of the famous twentieth-century marathon canoe racers and designers was Eugene (Gene) Jensen, who made a name for himself racing on the Mississippi River. In this photograph he poses with his racing partner, Tom Estes (right), at the Minneapolis Aquatennial Canoe Race in 1950. His designs are still found on boats throughout the continent; he was said to have originated the bent-shaft paddle and the command "hut" to shift sides during races. *Courtesy of www.jensencanoes.com.*

And I'm about the last of the owner-founders." In 2013, Cichanowski was given the Howie LaBrant Award from the U.S. Canoe Association for outstanding contributions to the sport of canoeing, only the seventh person to be so honored since the award began in 1980. Previous winners include Cichanowski's friend Eugene Jensen, the canoe designer, racer, and builder; and the DuPont Kevlar Fibers Division.

≺ Wenonah continually experimented with new models, including this solo canoe called the Vagabond, seen on the shore of Abel Lake in Virginia. Solo canoes became popular for wilderness trippers and day paddlers alike. *Photograph by Edward S. Episcopo.*

Cichanowski, in both his business and personal life, represents the post-1960s environmentalist/entrepreneur who loved spending time outdoors and was the beneficiary, in his own way, of several dramatic events that focused national and international attention on the environment. Academics argue over which of the events "started" the modern environmental movement, but most agree that all played a part. Federal and state governments had a role as well, not only in responding to dramatic events but also in expanding the national and state park and wilderness systems to favor canoeists, hikers, and other human-powered recreation buffs.

### RACHEL CARSON AND *SILENT SPRING*

Certainly an important moment in the modern environmental movement was the publication of Rachel Carson's *Silent Spring* in 1962. British writer Conor Mark Jameson called the book's release a paradigm shift for the movement; environmental historian Mark Hamilton Lytle labeled the author "the gentle subversive."[2] Carson's book on the dangers of the unrestricted use of synthetic pesticides kicked off a national conversation about how humans were treating the world around them.[3] Carson (1907–1964) gained notice as a writer for the U.S. Bureau of Fisheries and had found success popularizing science in earlier books, including *Under the Sea Wind* (1941), the National Book Award–winning *The Sea around Us* (1951), and *The Edge of the Sea* (1955). Her fourth book was going to be titled *Man against the Earth* as the misuse of World War II–era

Rachel Carson's book *Silent Spring* has been credited with kicking off the "modern" environmental movement, although she died of breast cancer two years after publication and did not live to see the changes in American society in the late 1960s and 1970s. Carson, shown here with American wildlife artist Bob Hines, worked for the U.S. Fish and Wildlife Service. Hines illustrated Carson's book *Under the Sea Wind*.

*Photograph by Rex Gary Schmidt, U.S. Fish and Wildlife Service.*

chemical products, particularly DDT, captured her attention; she had enough of "a touch of the rebellious spirit" that drew her to authors such as Henry David Thoreau and John Muir to tackle the issue.[4] *Silent Spring* was serialized in *The New Yorker* and became a Book-of-the-Month Club selection; the author and editor E. B. White said in a letter to Carson that the stories were "the most valuable articles the magazine had ever published."[5] England's Prince Philip was reported to have purchased several copies for "influential friends" on a trip to the United States.[6]

National attention came to Carson and *Silent Spring* from President John F. Kennedy (he referred to "Miss Carson's book" at a press conference) and from congressional hearings in 1963 on the subject of pesticide use, human health, and the environment. But Carson herself was dying of breast cancer when she appeared at those hearings, and she did not live long enough to witness a string of dramatic environmental events that brought the movement into the forefront of American consciousness. William Souder, one of her biographers, wrote that Carson "can be credited not only with putting the movement into motion but for doing so in a way that would allow it to stand on its own."[7]

Carson was trained as a scientist, but worked as a writer and editor and never worked as a field biologist, although her public persona may have been as such. (It was not uncommon for cartoons and illustrations of Carson to place her in the bow of a boat, for example.) A lover of books and nature, Carson nonetheless "never became a competent swimmer and rarely ventured into water deeper than her ankles."[8] Souder said that Carson, who ironically helped launch a movement that led to more people enjoying the outdoors in pursuits such as paddling, "was not fond of boats. I am doubtful she was ever anywhere near a canoe."[9]

In 1964, the year that Carson died, the federal government authorized new rules on the use of pesticides on land managed by the Department of the Interior.[10] This began a decade or more of broader federal intervention into environmental issues, pushed along by a series of dramatic events that helped the movement gain political strength.

## EARLY PARKS AND RESERVES

The boom in outdoor sports in the 1950s coincided with concerns in the United States about the youth of the nation "growing soft" as a result of, in no particular order, juvenile delinquency, rock-and-roll music, comic books, hot rods, and general teen lust. Outdoor sports were seen as a cure, or at least a muscle hardener. The modern environmental movement cannot be understood without recognizing the role that human-powered activities had in getting people outside. The legislative rush to pass environmental laws that followed in the 1960s and 1970s was unparalleled in U.S. history.

The resurgence in interest in the environment, especially in outdoor activities such as canoeing, kayaking, hiking, and cross-country skiing, was assisted by new parks, wilderness areas, forest preserves, and other nature reserves. A number of legislative actions in the 1960s set the stage for more paddling opportunities. But the seeds of many water-based parks had been planted long before, with the creation of national park systems in Canada, the United States, and Mexico.

The roots of the Canadian park system date to at least 1885, when the government claimed 26 square kilometers of land around the hot springs in Banff. Not coincidentally,

Frank S. Nicholson, poster for the U.S. National Park Service, c. 1936–40.
This poster is from the NYC Art Project of the Works Progress Administration (WPA),
which sponsored artists of almost all stripes during the Great Depression. Nicholson was
among almost ten thousand artists who were supported by the WPA's Federal Art Project.

*Courtesy of the Library of Congress Prints and Photographs Division, LC-USZC2-1015.*

1885 was also the year that the transcontinental railway in Canada was completed, bringing thousands of young adventurers west and putting new pressures on the natural resources of the young nation. Along with the rise in wilderness appreciation came the growth of canoe clubs, which were centered in urban areas and, in the beginning, focused on racing.[11]

Once Canadians figured out that they liked the park idea, dozens of reserves followed. Because of the nature of the Canadian landscape, nearly all of the new parks contained water, and much of it was ideal for canoeing and canoe camping. Some of the areas, such as the Nahanni River, offered what many consider some of the most spectacular scenery on the planet.

In Ontario, the area that would become popularly called "canoe country" entered under the protection of the government in 1909 as a forest reserve, then as Quetico Provincial Park in 1913. On the U.S. side of the boundary, canoe country officially became known as the Superior National Forest, an example of "a little known but remarkably wise piece of international co-operation," according to one Canadian scholar.[12] Canoes had been in common use in the region for hundreds of years, as evidenced by their inclusion in pictographs on Crooked Lake, north of Basswood Falls. Roads cut into the region by 1954 increased its popularity, if decreasing its wilderness character.

Toward the East Coast, in New York State, what became the St. Regis Canoe Area in the Adirondacks proved popular among canoeists. Within the boundaries of Adirondack Park, established in 1892, there are 1,500 miles

The business of canoe liveries and outfitters in the lakes and rivers region of North America, including Ely, Minnesota, in 1958, allowed city dwellers to experience the joys of wilderness travel without actually owning a canoe. Trips of a week or two were common during the summer months for customers, who could also hire a guide for the journey.

*Courtesy of the Minnesota Historical Society, 60195.*

Evidence of travel by canoe exists in the form of pictographs hundreds of years old in the Quetico region of Canada. Scientists are not in agreement about who made the images—or even when—but the painting of people in a boat is unmistakable. *Photograph by Rolf Hicker, HickerPhoto.com.*

The Nahanni River in Canada became famous—and a popular destination for whitewater canoe adventurers— ➤ after the 1950s publication of the book *The Dangerous River* by R. M. Patterson, a hair-raising account of a trip into the wilderness region earlier in the century. *Photograph by Davin Martinson.*

Howard Zahniser was a significant figure in the American environmental movement in the 1950s and 1960s. His work on the Wilderness Act of 1964—he is credited with writing most of it—was instrumental in its final passage.

*Photograph by Ed Zahniser. Reprinted with permission.*

of river and 30,000 miles of streams, not counting lakes and ponds, in a public-private partnership.[13] In Florida, Everglades National Park was established in 1934 and dedicated in 1947. The Mexican park system dates to 1917 with Desierto de los Leones (Desert of the Lions) National Park, which had been a forest reserve since 1876.

### WILDERNESS ACT OF 1964

Shelagh Grant argued that by World War II, canoeing was on its way out in the Canadian north, as new interests at summer camps, new roads, motorboats, and seaplanes replaced it.[14] But the environmental movement that followed the war reinvigorated interest in all things human-powered, including canoes. By the late 1950s and into the 1960s, near the time of *Silent Spring*, park advocates, including canoeists, wanted more space. One of the most important pieces of legislation in the United States to give them that space was the Wilderness Act of 1964. Conservationists, led by Howard Zahniser of the Wilderness Society, had been working on a national wilderness bill since the 1950s, and a version of this idea was introduced in Congress in 1956. Zahniser owned a camp in the Adirondacks, and he and his wife, Alice, were expert and avid

Winslow Homer, *Adirondack Lake (Blue Monday)*, 1892. Watercolor on white wove paper, 30.1 × 53.5 cm (11⅞ × 21 1/16 inches).

*Harvard Art Museums/Fogg Museum, Bequest of Grenville L. Winthrop, 1943.302.*
*Photograph: Imaging Department. Copyright President and Fellows of Harvard College.*

canoeists. A 1937 trip down the Allegheny River from Olean, New York, to Howard's hometown of Tionesta, Pennsylvania, resulted in a journal of their experiences and made clear his love of the wild, stemming from his days as a boy: "The canoeing from Hickory on had the added interest of the faint recollection of familiar things," he wrote.[15]

Zahniser and his friends in the environmental community were opposed by a coalition of lumber interests, ranchers, mining companies, and other business groups, as well as by the U.S. Forest Service (which did not want national forests removed from timber harvesting), and, at least at first, by the National Park Service. By 1964, however, the environmental interests, with a series of compromises, had rounded up more than enough votes to pass the Wilderness Act (it passed in the Senate by 73–12 and in the House by 373–1). President Lyndon Johnson put his signature on it on September 3.

The key phrase in the legislation was the definition of wilderness, where "man himself is a visitor who does not remain."[16] Special mention was made of canoe areas in Section 3, grandfathering these regions of national forests into a wilderness system: "All areas within the national forests classified at least 30 days before September 3, 1964 by the Secretary of Agriculture or the Chief of the Forest Service as 'wilderness', 'wild', or 'canoe' are hereby designated as wilderness areas."

Special consideration for the needs of canoeists dated to the 1920s with Aldo Leopold's career in the U.S. Forest Service. Leopold, whose *A Sand County Almanac* was as important a book in the twentieth century as Thoreau's *Walden* was in the nineteenth, crafted a set of regulations adopted by the Forest Service in 1929 that were known as the L-20s.[17]

President Lyndon Johnson signs the Wilderness Act on September 3, 1964. The act created a legal definition of wilderness in the United States and protected millions of acres of federal land.

*Photograph by Abbie Rowe. Courtesy of the National Park Service Historic Photograph Collection.*

≺ Canoes and kayaks line the shore at Everglades National Park. The park's Nine Mile Pond Canoe Trail has long been a popular route for paddlers.    *Photograph by Miguel Vieira.*

## ↩ Canoe Packs

Canoe tripping—multiple-day traveling over and between waterways—requires a certain amount of gear that could be considered specialty equipment.

Consider, as an example, the canoe pack, which is not the same as a regular backpack. A canoe pack needs to fit snugly in the bottom of a canoe; if it is too tall and rides too high, the boat becomes less stable or the wind may catch it like a sail. Sitting in the bottom of the boat, a canoe pack often gets wet, and it is important to keep stuff inside it dry.

A canoe pack has to hold a lot of gear, including sleeping bags, pads, food, clothing, and tent. It needs to be lifted in and out of the boat, sometimes several times a day, so exterior flaps and zippers and hooks and draw cords and rings that all can catch on a thwart or a seat or a yoke are a potential problem.

Thus, the traditional canoe pack looks like a giant square envelope, though some can be box-shaped. It is short and squat and rides low in the boat. It has no frame, so it can conform to the shape of the canoe, nor does it ride above the wearer's shoulders, so a canoe can be portaged above it. Two packs can be smashed together, or stacked,

Arthur Carhart, next to a Morris canoe in the Superior National Forest in 1920, demonstrates how to stack and carry two canoe packs. Carhart, who worked for the U.S. Forest Service at the time of this photograph, was a tireless wilderness advocate who wrote two dozen books and hundreds of articles, helping to popularize ideas about conservation. *Courtesy of the Forest History Society, Durham, North Carolina, FHS3366.*

for a carry. The traditional canoe pack usually has one high-volume compartment, so more stuff can be crammed into it (a large pack may be 8,000 cubic inches) or taken out without emptying the whole darned thing. Older packs were made of waxed canvas, to shed water. An inner plastic liner can be used to make them watertight, sort of. The exterior is often unadorned, except for fasteners.

The flaw in the classic canoe pack design comes at the portage. A canoe pack is made for riding in a boat, and it is harder to portage than a frame backpack, which is made for hiking. Various attempts to improve on the design over the years have given us canoe packs lined with a wicker basket or foam (or just the wicker basket itself); packs with tumplines, hip belts, or other straps to take the pressure off the wearer's back; packs made from waterproof materials; and many more. An old-fashioned wooden box called a wanigan can still be seen from time to time in a canoe; it is used to haul cooking equipment or food and sometimes has a rounded bottom to conform to the shape of the hull.

Generations of military veterans and others made use of army and navy surplus packs. John McPhee recalled

The Poirier Pack Sack was the forerunner of the Duluth Pack, named after the city where it was manufactured. Duluth Packs are specially designed for canoe tripping.

a trip down the St. John River in Maine in the 1970s: "[Dick] Saltonstall got out his Uncle Sam's Canoe Bags, sold by Moor & Mountain—rubber, government surplus, and supposedly waterproof. He handed one to me, saying he was sure I would need it, less for the rain than for the river."[1] The pack kept McPhee's gear dry: "The Uncle Sam's Canoe Bag that Saltonstall gave me is authentically waterproof. I keep in it my change of clothes—the things I care most to keep dry—and in the night, in the interest of sleeping space, I toss it out in the rain, because not a drop will penetrate the bag."[2]

The Duluth Pack, often used as a synonym for a canoe pack, was patented by Camille Poirier in 1882 and has been produced by the same company since 1911. Today's green canvas-and-leather packs, familiar to generations of north woods travelers, still look much like the original models, down to the shiny copper rivets. Other manufacturers use the Duluth Pack size-based numbering system (#2, #3, #4). Writing about his Duluth Pack, Michigan outdoor writer Jerry Dennis compared it to discovering Shakespeare: "The realization took time to sink in, but eventually it occurred to me that classics become classics because they deserve it."[3]

These rules protected "primitive areas" for recreation. Bob Marshall, who was chief of recreation for the Forest Service and a founder of the Wilderness Society, crafted an even stricter definition of wilderness in 1939, called the "U" regulations. The U regulations, which superseded the L-20s, specifically identified canoe areas for wilderness protection.

Thus when the Wilderness Act became law, the regions under the U regulations, including canoe areas, were immediately protected. In fact, the Boundary Waters Canoe Area in northern Minnesota was mentioned by name for the purpose of maintaining the primitive character of the area, although some vague wording about timber and motorboats would cause paddlers indigestion over the coming years. Historian James Morton Turner writes, "The cam-

paign was not won with careful research briefs on the state of the nation's timber or petroleum supply or the diversity of wildlife in wilderness. Instead, it appealed to national values—patriotism, spirituality, outdoor recreation, and a respect for nature—and the responsibility of the people and the government to protect them."[18]

The legislation made millions of acres eligible for preservation in a wild state, which not only delighted canoeists across the country but also needed congressional action to create additional wilderness areas. One of the secondary criteria for wilderness protection was that it have "outstanding opportunities" for solitude or primitive recreation,[19] and canoeists liked to point out that their sport not only was older than the nation but about as primitive as water-based recreation can get. Zahniser, the

Biologist Aldo Leopold (center) accompanies his son Starker (left) on a canoe trip in Quetico waters in 1924. In *A Sand County Almanac* (1949), one of the seminal works of the environmental movement, Leopold advocated for the idea of a "land ethic," which held that people were responsible for the land they inhabited. The book is considered an inspirational text in popularizing the science of ecology.

*Courtesy of the Aldo Leopold Foundation, www.aldoleopold.org.*

Sigurd Olson, a biologist by training and a canoe outfitter in Ely, Minnesota, was among the important writers and political activists in the environmental movement. Olson's books were popular, though his work at the federal level in preserving a wilderness without roads or motors made him a controversial figure in his adopted hometown.

*Courtesy of the Wisconsin Historical Society, WHS-74065.*

able canoeist whose dedication to the recreation component of the law was foremost, sadly did not live to see its passage; he died of a heart ailment a few months earlier.

### THE NATIONAL WILD AND SCENIC RIVERS SYSTEM

President Johnson, who was not to be mistaken for a canoeist, nonetheless signed or enabled more pieces of environmental measures—three hundred by one count—than any other president, including the Clean Air Act of 1963, the Land and Water Conservation Fund of 1965, the Water Quality Act of 1965, and the Endangered Species Act of 1966. He was not finished protecting and setting aside

more of America's waterways, however. On October 2, 1968, as his presidency wound down, the Texan signed the National Wild and Scenic Rivers Act, which created a federal bureaucracy to protect rivers from development. The act classified rivers into three types—wild, scenic, and recreational—mostly related to their level of access or development. Goals for river protection were written into the legislation, including rivers that "possess outstandingly remarkable scenic, recreational, geologic, fish and wildlife, historic, cultural or other similar values, shall be preserved in free-flowing condition, and that they and their immediate environments shall be protected for the benefit and enjoyment of present and future generations."[20] By the

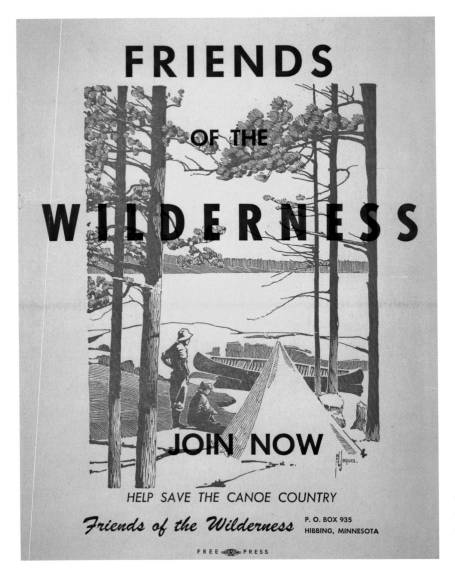

FRIENDS

OF THE

WILDERNESS

JOIN NOW

HELP SAVE THE CANOE COUNTRY

*Friends of the Wilderness*     P. O. BOX 935
HIBBING, MINNESOTA

FREE PRESS

second decade of the twenty-first century, the system covered 12,598 miles of 203 rivers in thirty-eight states and the Commonwealth of Puerto Rico.

On that same October 2, the popular canoe, camp, and hike destination of Ross Lake National Recreation Area in the northern Cascades, just south of the Canadian border in Washington State, was established.

### SANTA BARBARA OIL SPILL

More dramatic events were to take place to instill a sense of protection in the citizenry and its legislators as the 1960s came to a close. One happened off the coast of Santa Barbara, California, on January 28, 1969. Considering what was to take place in the coming hours, days, and weeks, there was no small irony to the fact that the city of 75,000 a few miles north of Los Angeles was named for Saint Barbara of Nicomedia, the patron saint of petroleum.[21] Tar from oil deposits in the region was so plentiful and easy to access that the Native tribes used it as a sealant for the seams of their canoes; records from one explorer in 1542 noted that the Natives' boats were caulked with the gooey substance.[22]

Shortly before 11 a.m. on January 28, Well A-21 on Platform A, 5½ miles from the shore of Santa Barbara, blew

Groups interested in preserving canoe country from development sprang up all over the continent. Canoes were often used as images of a free and quiet outdoors experience, as in this poster with artwork by Francis Lee Jaques, c. 1949.   *Courtesy of the Minnesota Historical Society, 51153.*

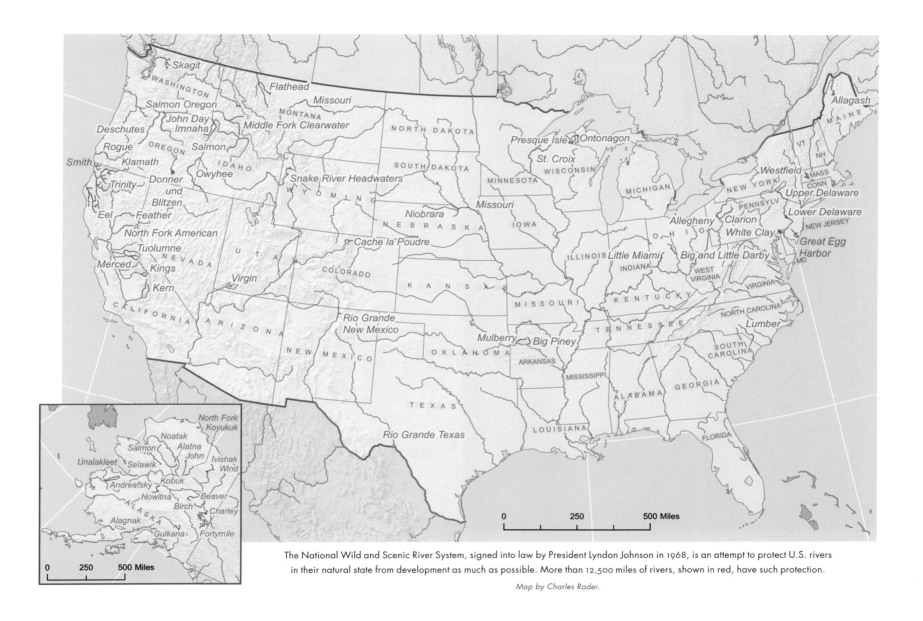

Skagit

WASHINGTON

Salmon Oregon

Deschutes

John Day
Imnaha

OREGON

Rogue

Klamath

Smith

Trinity

Donner
und
Blitzen

Eel

Feather

North Fork American

Tuolumne

Merced

Kings

Kern

CALIFORNIA

Owyhee

IDAHO

NEVADA

UTAH

Virgin

ARIZONA

Flathead

Missouri

MONTANA

Middle Fork Clearwater

Salmon

Snake River Headwaters

WYOMING

COLORADO

NEW MEXICO

Rio Grande
New Mexico

NORTH DAKOTA

SOUTH DAKOTA

MINNESOTA

Niobrara

NEBRASKA

Cache la Poudre

KANSAS

OKLAHOMA

Mulberry

Big Piney

ARKANSAS

TEXAS

Rio Grande Texas

LOUISIANA

MISSISSIPPI

Missouri

IOWA

Presque Isle Ontonagon

St. Croix

WISCONSIN

MICHIGAN

ILLINOIS

INDIANA

Little Miami

MISSOURI

KENTUCKY

TENNESSEE

ALABAMA

GEORGIA

FLORIDA

Allagash

MAINE

VT

NH

NEW YORK

Westfield

MASS

CONN

Upper Delaware

PENNSYLV

Lower Delaware

Allegheny

Clarion

White Clay

NEW JERSEY

Great Egg
Harbor

MD

Big and Little Darby

WEST
VIRGINIA

VIRGINIA

NORTH CAROLINA

Lumber

SOUTH
CAROLINA

North Fork
Koyukuk

Noatak

Salmon

Alatna

John

Unalakleet

Selawik

Ivishak

Wind

Andreafsky

Kobuk

Nowitna

Birch

Beaver

ALASKA

Charley

Alagnak

Gulkana

Fortymile

0       250      500 Miles

0       250      500 Miles

The National Wild and Scenic River System, signed into law by President Lyndon Johnson in 1968, is an attempt to protect U.S. rivers in their natural state from development as much as possible. More than 12,500 miles of rivers, shown in red, have such protection.

*Map by Charles Rader.*

The 1969 Santa Barbara, California, oil spill, seen from above the critical platform, was at the time the worst spill in U.S. history; it was later surpassed by the *Exxon Valdez* (1989) and *Deepwater Horizon* (2010) spills. An estimated 80,000 to 100,000 barrels spilled into the Pacific Ocean, affecting the shoreline from Santa Barbara to the Mexican border.

*Photograph by Dick Smith. Reprinted with permission by the* Santa Barbara News-Press.

out. Crews were removing 90-foot lengths of pipe from the shaft, which had just been bored, when drilling mud and gas shot into the air, beginning "the largest disaster of its kind in U.S. history."[23] The Union Oil Company, principal owner and operator of the platform, stumbled in its response to the crisis and downplayed its seriousness. In less than twenty-four hours, the spill was covering between 50 and 75 square miles of ocean and threatening the tourism-dependent beaches along the coast. Gas and oil were gushing not only from the well but also through cracks and faults on the ocean floor near the drill site. By the second day, a citizens' group called GOO (Get the Oil Out) was formed; by day three, oil had reached the city beaches and the first oil-soaked dead seabirds were found. The Santa Barbara oil spill became national news.

By day five, the government estimated that 200,000 gallons were leaking daily into the Santa Barbara channel. The *Los Angeles Times*, in a Sunday editorial, invoked Rachel Carson in critiquing the inept response of the company and the scientists employed by the federal government: "Rachel Carson was wrong. It is not the spring that is silent. It is the scientists and engineers—the one element in our society that really knows what is happening in the pollution of our environment."[24] Containment booms broke apart, dispersants did not disperse, and vacuuming the spill was ineffective.

Citizens of Southern California were outraged at the tardy response of the Nixon administration, although President Nixon had been in office only seven days before the spill hit. A congressional hearing on February 5 drew more attention than any subcommittee not concerned with the war in Vietnam. Union Oil boss Fred Hartley told Congress: "I am always tremendously impressed at the publicity that the death of birds receives versus the loss of people in our country in this day and age." Further, Hartley said, "It is not a disaster to people. There is no one being killed."[25]

Nixon, who did not tour the site until nearly two months after the blowout, temporarily suspended all drilling on federal oil leases in the channel the next day, except for a relief well. Meanwhile, locals had been taking their Union Oil credit cards to the beach, dipping them in the oil, and mailing them to company headquarters in Los Angeles. After nearly eleven days, as much as 2.3 million gallons of oil had been spilled. Among those hired by

Union Oil to clean the beaches were prisoners, who were paid pennies for their labor and $9.50 per day for living expenses.

Oil, as much as 3.3 million gallons, leaked into the area until 1970. Beaches as far south as San Diego and as far north as San Luis Obispo County were affected, and thousands of birds, fish, and other organisms died. Yet the most important long-term effect of the disaster—later surpassed in volume by the *Exxon Valdez* wreck in 1989 and the 2010 British Petroleum spill in the Gulf of Mexico—was a shift in attitude among citizens in favor of caring for the earth and a string of legislation urged on by the environmental movement.

More dramatic events followed and intensified the national mood. About five months after the Santa Barbara blowout, while crews were still mopping up the oil-soaked beaches in California, a river in Ohio caught fire and caught the nation's attention.

### CUYAHOGA RIVER FIRE

On June 22, 1969, the Cuyahoga River in Cleveland, Ohio, caught fire. The blaze, coming on the heels of the oil spill, caught the imagination of the mass media and the attention of the public, who asked questions such as: How does a river catch fire? Can water burn?

In Cleveland (and Baltimore, Buffalo, Houston, and

The dramatic oil spill off Santa Barbara in 1969 drew more interest to environmental issues. A tardy response by the oil company and politicians only made the matter worse. Cleanup came at the level of one waterfowl at a time, under a sink.   *Photograph by Mary Frampton. Copyright 1969, Los Angeles Times. Reprinted with permission.*

Detroit, to name five cities), the answer was that a river can catch fire if it is heavily polluted. In fact, fire was not uncommon on the filthy Cuyahoga—pollution in the river had burned as far back as 1868.[26] The 1969 Cuyahoga fire was not the worst blaze, nor was it even in the top tier. In 1912, an inferno killed five men; in 1952, an oil fire on the water jumped to the shore, causing $1.5 million in damage. In contrast, the 1969 fire near the Republic Steel mill burned parts of two railroad trestles, closing one because

Cleveland Mayor Carl Stokes enjoyed a high level of popularity among adults and children during his tenure; his advocacy for clean water extended beyond the Cuyahoga River controversy and included opening up neighborhood pools such as this one at Edgewater Park, on July 4, 1969. Utilities director Ben Stefanski (next to Stokes) joined the mayor for a swim.   *Photograph by John W. Mott, Cleveland Press Collection, Michael Schwartz Library, Cleveland State University.*

the heat warped the tracks, with total damages estimated at between $50,000 and $85,000. No one was killed; no one was injured.

Smoke billowed 50 to 60 feet in the air on a summer Sunday, when folks were off of work and perhaps out for a stroll. The fire department had the flames under control before the noon hour ended; the weekend news crews for local TV stations either missed the fire entirely or didn't bother. The town's two main newspapers showed up late. If not for Cleveland Mayor Carl Stokes, no one outside of northern Ohio would have even gotten wind of the fire.

Stokes, who in 1967 had become the first African American elected to the mayor's office in a major U.S. city, had been angry with the bureaucracy of the state of Ohio for months. The city had spent tens of millions of dollars attempting to clean up the Cuyahoga, but, in Stokes's view, the state government, the court system, and unfunded mandates from the federal government kept getting in the way of any effective change. With that in mind, he decided to use the burned trestles as a backdrop for a press conference on Monday, in which he ripped into state officials, polluters, and the U.S. Congress. He waved copies of letters he had sent that day to the governor and the head of the state department of natural resources.

Stokes's angry remarks got more press than the fire itself. Significant national coverage came from the weekly newsmagazine *Time*, although the magazine's story came a month after the blaze and featured a photograph of the much more serious 1952 fire. Other national media matched the *Time* story, and some tied the river fire to the

Santa Barbara oil spill.[27] Stokes testified before Congress, where his brother Louis was a representative, during the debate over what would become the Clean Water Act of 1972, and environmentalists took advantage of the dramatic event in their lobbying and public relations efforts.

### EARTH DAY

Ten months after the Cuyahoga River fire, students from Cleveland State University trailed behind a large banner in a protest march from their campus to the river, surrounded by newspaper reporters and television cameras. An activist dressed as city founder Moses Cleaveland floated along the Cuyahoga and met the marchers, only to turn away in mock disgust at the sorry ecological state he found in his community. The record is unclear on whether the fake Cleaveland traveled by canoe (the local newspaper said "boat")[28] as did the real one, but the point was made.

The occasion was Earth Day, April 22, 1970, a national teach-in that was the brainchild of Wisconsin Senator Gaylord Nelson and his staff. Congress recessed for the day; 20 million Americans took part—nearly 10 percent of the population of the United States. It was the most successful grassroots event ever seen in the United States. Nelson threw the idea out there, and a very small staff "oversaw" it; the entire Earth Day office budget was $185,000, according to Nelson. Its bipartisanship was telling. Outdoor adventurers, including canoeists, bikers, hikers, hunters, and fishermen, were a key part of the loose coalition that participated in Earth Day.

A cleanup of the Potomac River via canoe was one of the hundreds of activities featured on the first Earth Day in 1970. The brainchild of Wisconsin Senator Gaylord Nelson, Earth Day was called a "teach-in" and gained more attention for the environmental movement.  *Photograph by Thomas J. O'Halloran. Courtesy of the Library of Congress Prints and Photographs Division, LC-DIG-ds-00750.*

More legislation rolled through Congress in the months and years that followed, almost all of it directly or indirectly beneficial to the lovers of the outdoor life. A partial list includes the Clean Air Act of 1970, the aforementioned Clean Water Act of 1972, the creation of the Environmental Protection Agency in 1972, and a strengthening of the Endangered Species Act in 1973. One count showed that twenty-eight major environmental laws were

Wisconsin Senator Gaylord Nelson, seen here in the bow of a canoe on the Namekagon River in 1966, is considered the founder of Earth Day. The first Earth Day was celebrated in 1970.

*Courtesy of the Wisconsin Historical Society, WHS-56790.*

The Missouri National Recreational River, a national park, is made up of two free-flowing sections of river. The upper stretch is 39 miles long, ending at Running Water, South Dakota, and the lower stretch concludes its 59-mile reach at Ponca, Nebraska. The park is known as a challenging trip for paddlers because of high wind, strong current, and a shifting main channel.

*Map by Charles Rader.*

passed in the next decade.[29] When the public saw a brilliant photograph of Earth from *Apollo 17* taken on December 7, 1972 (known as the Blue Marble photograph), showing a fully illuminated and somehow small planet, the cultural circle of caring for the ecosystem seemed to be complete.

Parks and wilderness areas popular with canoeists were part of the 1970s wave of environmental preservation. The Ozark National Scenic Riverways in Missouri, created in 1964, was dedicated in 1971. The Eastern Wilderness Act, signed by President Ford in 1975, designated sixteen new wilderness areas in thirteen states.

Logging was banned in Quetico Provincial Park in Canada in 1971; a motor ban followed in 1979. Nearby, on the U.S. side of the border, Voyageurs National Park came into being in the mid-1970s, honoring the explorers and fur traders who paddled across the frontier centuries earlier; the main body of the 200,000-acre park is accessible only by boat. In 1978, the Boundary Waters Canoe Area Wilderness was created in northern Minnesota, which, along with the Quetico Park, became the most popular canoe destination in the world.

The inevitable backlash from big business, big agriculture, and other forces began in the late 1970s with names such as the Sagebrush Rebellion and the Wise Use Move-

Threats to canoe routes across the continent come (and sometimes go) as industry and government eye the land for other uses. In 2014, Amy and Dave Freeman paddled a canoe signed by hundreds of wilderness advocates from Ely, Minnesota, to Washington, D.C., in support of the Boundary Waters Canoe Area Wilderness in Minnesota. An area near the BWCA was being considered for a metals mine.    *Photograph by Nate Ptacek.*

ment. But for canoeists, government protection of their waterways, lakes, and shorelines had become the norm; the tools were in place for managing the resource through state and federal agencies, the court system, and established environmental groups.

Even more market-driven solutions to environmental problems of the twenty-first century could not slow the

The Northern Forest Canoe Trail covers parts of the northeastern United States and eastern Canada, running 740 miles. After its official opening in 2006, it was called a wetter version of the Appalachian Trail; there are thirteen sections and, unlike the Appalachian Trail, much of it moves through private property.   *Map by Charles Rader.*

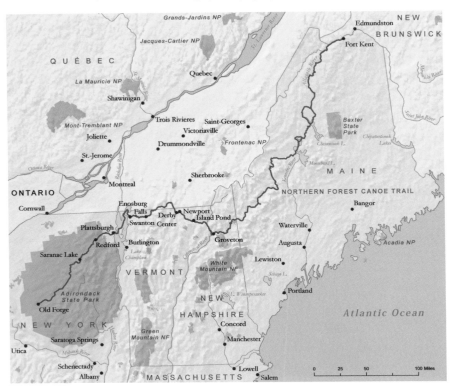

# Keep the BWCA open to Everyone

Support the

# Boundary Waters Conservation Alliance

## *Our goal . . .*

**1.** to preserve a 700,000 acre wilderness area in Northern Minnesota for the wilderness experience . . . for those who want to canoe, hike, backpack, and cross country ski.

**3.** to keep open 400,000 acres of lakes and forests for family camping, where a fisherman can take his boat and motor, where snowmobilers can venture.

**2.** to keep the forests healthy by fighting forest fires, insects, and disease.

**4.** to prevent additional government take-over of private property.

## *You can help!*

### *Support Congressman Oberstar's efforts to keep the BWCA open to everyone.*

Contribute to the
Boundary Waters Conservation Alliance
222 Phoenix Building
Duluth, Minnesota 55802

In the late 1970s, legislation to ban motors from canoe country in Minnesota was a controversial issue. Wilderness advocates wanted the motors out, and many outfitters and resort owners perceived a threat to their businesses. Feelings ran high on both sides, although wilderness supporters won in the end. Note that the canoe in this flyer is a square-stern model with a motor attached, so there is little doubt which side the underwriters of the material were on.   *Courtesy of the Minnesota Historical Society, 51152.*

recreational zeal of those who took to the water. A few open spaces were preserved early in the twenty-first century, including the Northern Forest Canoe Trail (from New York to Maine) in 2006, and additions to the National Wild and Scenic Rivers System, provided for in the Omnibus Public Land Management Act of 2009. Canoe culture had come a long way since the *Minneapolis Tribune* headline of 1914, which read "Girl Canoeists' Tight Skirts Menace Society."[30]

### CANOE RACING

Canoe racing rode the wave of its post–World War II popularity; by the 1970s, well-established competitions were held across North America and hundreds of participants competed in races on local lakes and rivers all the way up to the Olympic Games. Few, if any, were better than the Canadian racer Larry Cain, who won Olympic gold and silver as a twenty-one-year-old in 1984. He had been consistently winning races since he was thirteen.

"You need time to put some context to it," Cain said years later. "I remember thinking 'Yeah, I did it,' then sitting back and thinking, 'What the hell did I just do? Did I really just do what I wanted to do for the last eight years?' For eight years of my life, it's what I'd dreamed about. You pinch yourself. You try to figure out whether it's really happened or whether it's just another dream."[31]

Canada's Olympic heritage usually focuses on the Winter Games, but success at canoeing in the summer event dates back before World War II, when men's canoe and

The Canadian Olympic hero Frank Amyot at the Berlin Games in 1936, where he won his country's only gold medal in a custom-built canoe made to fit his 6-foot-plus frame. *Photograph courtesy of Canada's Sports Hall of Fame, sportshall.ca / Panthéon des sports canadiens, pantheonsports.ca.*

High-level racing, here featuring a women's C-4 race at the National Canoe/Kayak Championships in Sherbrooke, Quebec, has been a part of canoeing history since clubs were formed in the nineteenth century.   *Courtesy of Jessica Rando.*

kayak sprint racing was introduced at the 1936 Berlin games. Ontario's Frank Amyot won the first gold medal, in the 1,000-meter singles canoe race. Teammates Harvey Charters and Warren Saker took a silver and a bronze in tandem events.[32]

Cain, born in Toronto in 1963, was inspired to race by watching countryman John Wood win a silver at the 1976 Games in Montreal. "That's what I want to do," he told his family.[33] He also said, "A lot of kids my age had idols in the National Hockey League, but John Wood was my hero."[34] He joined the local canoe club at age eleven, but said he spent most of that first summer in the water after repeatedly falling out of a racing canoe. "It was kind of neat. After we were finished, we could splash around in the water and chase frogs," he recalled.[35]

In 1980, Cain, called "doggedly determined, tenacious" by his coach, notched Pan American Championship medals (gold and silver) and followed that up with two golds at the junior world championships the next year, to become Canada's first world champion since Amyot.[36] At the Los Angeles Games, his gold came in the C-1 500-meter race (1:57.01) and the silver was in the C-1 1,000 (4:08.67). He narrowly missed another Olympic medal in the latter race, finishing fourth at the Seoul Games in 1988. With partner David Frost, Cain made the finals in two tandem races at the 1992 Olympics.

There is no doubt Cain loved paddle sports. What did he seek to do after claiming Olympic gold and winning at the Canadian nationals? "I want to go on a canoe trip once the nationals are over," he said.[37]

He retired from international racing in 1996, after seventeen years as a member of the Canadian National Canoe Team. His career included teaching physical education at St. Mildred's-Lightbourn School in Oakville, Ontario, his hometown.

Canadian Olympian Larry Cain at the 1984 Games in Los Angeles, California. A sprinter, he was Canada's first gold medalist in canoeing since Frank Amyot, winning the C-1 500-meter race. Cain was also a silver medalist in the C-1 1,000 meters.

*Photograph by Canadian Olympic Committee, Crombie McNeil / The Canadian Press.*

## CHAPTER 8

# Canoe Tripping

HE HEART OF CANOEING is not necessarily the materials used to construct the craft; rather, it is the *experience* of paddling it.

We can drift quietly past a moose in Maine or under an osprey nest on the Selway River in Idaho. We can fish or hunt, or we can photograph a mother merganser and her brood of ducklings as they work upstream. Perhaps a river otter will suddenly appear ahead of the canoe, back-paddling and inspecting us, or a kingfisher will chatter while flying from tree to tree to keep us company. We can marvel at the glassy smooth water of a lake in Quetico surrounded by dark pines—as it has been for thousands of years—or we can paddle down a whitewater run in North Carolina so intense that we never notice the blooming wild rhododendron on the shorelines. More important, as many canoeists say, just being on the water is its own reward.

The experience of *canoe tripping*, especially as the term was used in the 1960s and 1970s, sounded like paddling under the influence of LSD. That's not what it means. The Canadian term simply means traveling in a canoe, usually overnight in provincial parks such as Algonquin or Quetico in Ontario, but it also contains hints of a certain shared experience.

◅ Winslow Homer (American, 1836–1910), *Shooting the Rapids,* 1902. Watercolor over graphite on off-white, thick, moderately textured wove paper with watermark, 35.4 × 55.4 cm (13$^{15}$/$_{16}$ × 21$^{13}$/$_{16}$ inches). *Brooklyn Museum, Museum Collection Fund and Special Subscription, 11.537.*

Sometimes canoe tripping reaches into the psyche of paddlers to suggest the fantasies of youth—following the routes of the voyageurs, or putting a canoe into a local stream and following confluence to confluence until reaching the Mississippi River and then paddling to the ocean— a kind of Huck Finn fantasy. Canoes figured prominently along with rafts in Mark Twain's *The Adventures of Huckleberry Finn*. Or we can think about following in the foot-

steps of Alexander Mackenzie, who paddled across Canada to the Pacific Ocean ten years before Lewis and Clark went overland on a similar journey. Henry David Thoreau paddled the Concord and Merrimac Rivers and spent a week in the Maine woods with an Indian guide. Eric Sevareid, who became one of the most noted twentieth-century journalists, took on a challenging adventure by paddling from Minnesota to Hudson Bay in Canada, partly on the

Wood-and-canvas canoes on a stop for provisions before a wilderness expedition prior to 1920.

*Photograph by Jule Fox Marshall. Courtesy of the Marshall family.*

Red River of the North, when he was a teenager. Putting all the gear you need in a Duluth Pack and paddling the length of the Connecticut River, or the Hudson, or the Missouri, or the Mackenzie, or going all the way to Hudson Bay—there's something truly North American about that.

What we experience in canoe tripping is inherent in the craft. Whether it be a dugout, birch-bark, or wooden canoe, or a modern craft made of aluminum, fiberglass, or foam—or even a Klepper, as we'll see below—the feeling of being on the water, of being part of nature, enriches our lives.

Expressing such an experience in words challenges any writer. John McPhee, who for decades worked for *The New Yorker* magazine and became one of the modern writers most associated with canoeing, wrote in 2013, "I grew up in canoes on northern lakes and forest rivers. Thirty years later, I was trying to choose a word or words that would explain why anyone in a modern nation would choose to go a long distance by canoe. I was damned if I was going to call it a sport, but nothing else occurred. I looked up 'sport.' There were seventeen lines of definition: '1. That which diverts, and makes mirth; pastime; diversion. 2. A diversion of the field.' I stopped there." In *The Survival of the Bark Canoe*, McPhee wrote: "A canoe trip has become simply a rite of oneness with certain terrain, a diversion of the field, an act performed not because it is necessary but because there is value in the act itself."[1]

McPhee went on. "If your journey is long enough in wild country, you change, albeit temporarily, while you are there. Writing about a river valley in Arctic Alaska, I was

1, Sleeping pocket; 2, Compass and pin; 3, Camping mattress; 4, 5, 6, Folding camp furniture; 7, Sleeping bag; 8, Folding baker; 9, Folding canvas cupboard; 10, Vacuum bottle; 11, Waterproof matchbox; 12, 13, 14, 15, Canvas water pails; 16, Army kit; 17, Axe with folding guard; 18, First aid kit; 19, Metal tent peg; 20, Folding lantern; 21, Kerosene stove; 22, Folding grate; 23, Cook kit; 24, Folding baker, canvas case.

Typical canoe camping equipment illustrated in the 1915 book *Canoeing and Camping*, by James A. Cruikshank.

Florence Page Jaques wrote *Canoe Country* (1945) and *Snowshoe Country* (1944), both illustrated by her husband, Francis. They were among the premier wildlife authors and illustrators during the 1940s and 1950s, often concentrating their work in what is now the Boundary Waters Canoe Area of Minnesota.

trying to describe that mental change, and I was searching for a word that would represent the idea, catalyze the theme. 'Assimilate' came along pretty quickly. But 'assimilate,' in the context, was worse than 'sport.' So I looked up 'assimilate': '1. To make similar or alike. 2. To liken; to compare. 3. To . . . incorporate into the substance of the appropriating body.'" In his book on Alaska, *Coming into the Country,* McPhee wrote of sighting a grizzly bear feeding on a nearby hillside: "It was a vision of a whole land, with an animal in it. This was his country, clearly enough. To be there was to be incorporated, in however small a measure, into its substance—his country, and if you wanted to visit it you had better knock."[2]

Paddlers have always used the canoe for necessary work and more recently for symbolic journeys, as a diversion of the field and to incorporate their substance into nature. Finding the source of the Mississippi or reaching the Pacific Ocean may have been necessary, but there was more to it. The narratives of canoe travel from Alexander Mackenzie, Henry David Thoreau, Edwin Tappan Adney, Eric Sevareid, and John McPhee contain personal, symbolic, cultural, and even political elements. Journeys link in important ways with the human-powered movement, with conservation, and with measuring our place in nature.

This book has explored the history of canoes in North America from dugouts to modern craft, from working boats to recreational canoes and the cultural and environmental movements that came with them. From the first canoes built by Natives on the North American continent until today, the canoe has endured. It has been transformed by

*Joe mell asleep in his Canoe*

Joe Mell, a Passamaquoddy Indian, sleeps under his canoe on Duck Lake, Maine, c. 1895.

*Photograph by William Lyman Underwood. 1994.91.186. Courtesy of the Smithsonian American Art Museum, Washington, DC/Art Resource, NY.*

new construction techniques, new materials, and new passions for things like sea kayaks and stand-up paddleboards. Throughout time, however, the experience of gliding away from shore over a glassy lake has not changed at all.

While writing this book, the authors have come upon many original documents written over the course of centuries by paddlers themselves—far more than can be reproduced here. Something wonderful can be heard in those original voices, something that conveys the feeling of the experience in canoes. Here we present in chronological order some of our favorite excerpts from canoeists who went tripping in canoes.

Among the fur traders, the mother of all canoe journeys belonged to Alexander Mackenzie.

### ALEXANDER MACKENZIE

Sir Alexander Mackenzie journeyed for commercial advantage, not so much for personal fulfillment or challenge. After England conquered French Canada on the Plains of Abraham in Quebec City in 1763, the North West Company and Hudson's Bay Company fur traders had less competition, yet they still used French voyageurs for westward journeys. Mackenzie wrote disapprovingly that some traders abused and took advantage of the Indians, tried to destroy their rivals, and spread smallpox in the wilderness.[3] Mackenzie had worked the fur trade in Detroit and in 1785 agreed to "proceed to the Indian country."[4] The fur trade had declined and did not recover for several

Thomas Lawrence, *Sir Alexander Mackenzie*, c. 1800. Oil on canvas, 76.3 × 64 cm. In 1793, Mackenzie became the first European to cross the Rocky Mountains and reach the Pacific coast. He was knighted in 1802.

*Courtesy of the National Gallery of Canada, Ottawa, transfer from the Canadian War Memorials, 1921. Photograph copyright NGC.*

years. Further exploration to the north and west, it was felt, would yield more furs. Following two epic journeys, he published *The Journals of Alexander Mackenzie, . . . In the Years, 1789 and 1793.*

Mackenzie's paddlers were French Canadian voyageurs and "pork-eaters"—those being employed from spring through fall and then returning home in the winter. At Grand Portage on Lake Superior, in what is now Minnesota, Mackenzie described the food eaten by as many as 1,200 voyageurs and company agents:

> The proprietors, clerks, guides, and interpreters, mess together, to the number of sometimes an hundred, at several tables, in one large hall, the provision consisting of bread, salt pork, beef, hams, fish, and venison, butter, peas, Indian corn, potatoes, tea, spirits, wine, &c. and plenty of milk, for which purpose several milch cows are constantly kept. The mechanics have rations of such provision, but the canoe-men, both from the North and Montreal, have no other allowance here, or in the voyage, than Indian corn and melted fat. The corn for this purpose is prepared before it leaves Detroit, by boiling it in a strong alkali, which takes off the outer husk; it is then well washed, and carefully dried upon stages, when it is fit for use. One quart of this is boiled for two hours, over a moderate fire, in a gallon of water; to which, when it has boiled a small time, are added two ounces of melted suet; this causes the corn to split, and in the time mentioned makes a pretty thick pudding. If to this is added a little salt, (but not before it is boiled, as it would interrupt the operation), it makes a wholesome, palatable food, and easy of digestion. This quantity is fully sufficient for a man's subsistence during twenty-four hours; though it is not sufficiently heartening to sustain the strength necessary for a state of active labour. The Americans call this dish hominee.*

> *Corn is the cheapest provision that can be procured, though from the expence of transport, the bushel costs about twenty shillings sterling, at the Grande Portage. A man's daily allowance does not exceed ten-pence.[5]

Mackenzie was born in Scotland in 1764 and came to New York at age ten. With the American Revolution raging in 1778, he was sent to Montreal, where he secured an apprenticeship with a fur trading company that later merged with the North West Company. In 1788, Mackenzie followed rivers flowing northwest from Lake Athabasca, which sits at the corner of northwestern Saskatchewan and northeastern Alberta. Mackenzie was looking for the Northwest Passage. He reached the Arctic Ocean. The river he followed—the longest and largest river in Canada—was later named the Mackenzie River in his honor.

Mackenzie used his 1789 and 1793 journals as a historical examination of the fur trade, the country, and the

Frances Anne Hopkins, *Voyageurs at Dawn*, 1871. Oil on canvas, 73.7 × 151.1 cm. Hopkins's paintings of voyageurs at work and rest are considered so historically accurate that researchers refer to them to add to their knowledge of the time period. Note all the detailed equipment—tools, clothing, food, gear—in the foreground and middle ground of this work.

*Courtesy of the Frances Anne Hopkins fonds, Library and Archives of Canada, R5666-0-8-E.*

Native peoples who inhabited it. He documented the loads carried by the voyageurs and the difficult portages required in the fur trade. He counted the paces needed to traverse each portage:

The Portage of Plein Champ, three hundred nineteen paces; the Décharge of Campion, one hundred and eighty-four paces; the Portage of the Grosse Roche, one hundred and fifty paces; the Portage of Paresseaux, four hundred and two paces; the Portage of Prairie, two hundred and eighty-seven paces; the Portage of La Cave, one hundred paces; Portage of Talon, two hundred and seventy-five paces; which, for its length, is the worst on the communication; Portage Pin de Musique, four hundred and fifty-six paces, next to this is Mauvais de Musique, where many men have been crushed to death by the canoes, and others have received irrecoverable injuries.[6]

Mackenzie returned in 1792 and this time followed the Peace River westward from Fort Chipewyan on Lake Athabasca, hoping it would lead toward the Pacific Ocean. He was accompanied by voyageurs who were of French and Indian descent as could be told by their names: Beaulieux, Bisson, Courtois, Beauchamp, along with Joseph Landry and Charles Ducette, who had been on his earlier trip, and two Indian hunters and interpreters. After wintering over, they loaded a 25-foot bark canoe that was so light two men could carry her for 3 or 4 miles without resting,

and headed west in May.[7] "The canoe, repaired again and again," writes Grace Lee Nute, "and only passably with the substances at hand, became more and more crazy as the journey progressed. Portages became a serious matter, 'for the canoe was now become so heavy, from the additional quantity of bark and gum necessary to patch her up, that two men could not carry her more than an hundred yards, without being relieved; and as their way lay through deep mud, was rendered more difficult by the roots and prostrate trunks of trees, they were every moment in danger of falling; and beneath such a weight, one false step might have been attended with fatal consequences.'"[8] They crossed the Great Divide on foot through snow and descended the western side of the mountains in July on the Bella Coola River in cedar dugout canoes built and paddled by the local Indians.

Near the end of his journal, Mackenzie recounted the events surrounding their historic arrival at the coast, the first of the Europeans to traverse the continent.

*Thursday, July 18 [1793].* At one in the afternoon we embarked, with our small baggage, in two canoes, accompanied by seven of the natives. The stream was rapid, and ran upwards of six miles an hour. We came to a weir . . . where the natives landed us, and shot over it without taking a drop of water. They then received us on board again, and we continued our voyage, passing many canoes on the river, some with people in them, and others empty. We proceeded at a very great rate for about

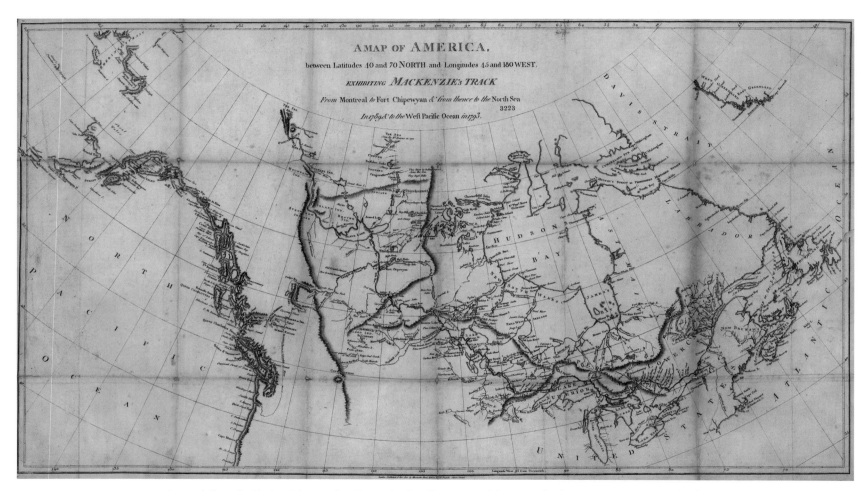

A map of Alexander Mackenzie's routes from Montreal to Fort Chipewyan and then onward to the Arctic Ocean in 1789 and to the Pacific Ocean in 1793. Published by Mackenzie in 1801. *Courtesy of the Library of Congress Geography and Map Division, G3401.S12 1801 .M2.*

two hours and an half, when we were informed that we must land, as the village was only at a short distance. I had imagined that the Canadians who accompanied me were the most expert canoe-men in the world, but they are very inferior to these people, as they themselves acknowledged, in conducting those vessels.

Some of the Indians ran before us, to announce our approach, when we took our bundles and followed. We had walked along a well-beaten path, through a kind of coppice, when we were informed of the arrival of our couriers at the houses, by the loud and confused talking of the inhabitants. As we approached the edge of the wood, and were almost in sight of the houses, the Indians who were before me made signs for me to take the lead, and they would follow. The noise and confusion of the natives now seemed to encrease, and when we came in sight of the village, we saw them running from house to house, some armed with bows and arrows, others with spears, and many with axes, as if in a state of great alarm. This very unpleasant and unexpected circumstance, I attributed to our sudden arrival, and the very short notice of it which had been given them. At all events, I had but one line of conduct to pursue, which was to walk resolutely up to them, without manifesting any signs of apprehension at their hostile appearance. This resolution produced the desired effect, for as we approached the houses,

the greater part of the people laid down their weapons, and came forward to meet us. . . .

The chief now made signs for us to follow him, and he conducted us through a narrow coppice, for several hundred yards, till we came to a house built on the ground, which was of larger dimensions, and formed of better materials than any I had hitherto seen; it was his residence. We were no sooner arrived there, than he directed mats to be spread before it, on which we were told to take our seats, when the men of the village, who came to indulge their curiosity, were ordered to keep behind us. In our front other mats were placed, where the chief and his counsellors took their seats. In the intervening space, mats, which were very clean, and of a much neater workmanship than those on which we sat were also spread, and a small roasted salmon placed before each of us. When we had satisfied ourselves with the fish, one of the people who came with us from the last village approached, with a kind of ladle in one hand, containing oil, and in the other something that resembled the inner rind of the cocoa-nut, but of a lighter colour; this he dipped in the oil, and, having eat it, indicated by his gestures how palatable he thought it. He then presented me with a small piece of it, which I chose to taste in its dry state, though the oil was free from any unpleasant smell. A square cake of this was next produced, when a man took it to the water near the house, and having thoroughly soaked it, he returned and, after he had pulled it to pieces like oakum, put it into a well-made trough, about three feet long, nine inches wide, and five deep; he then plentifully sprinkled it with salmon oil, and manifested by his own example that we were to eat of it. I just tasted it, and found the oil perfectly sweet, without which the other ingredient would have been very insipid. The chief partook of it with great avidity, after it had received an additional quantity of oil. This dish is considered by these people as a great delicacy; and on examination, I discovered it to consist of the inner rind of the hemlock tree, taken off early in summer, put into a frame, which shapes it into cakes of fifteen inches long, ten broad, and half an inch thick; and in this form I should suppose it may be preserved for a great length of time. This discovery satisfied me respecting the many hemlock trees which I had observed stripped of their bark.

In this situation we remained for upwards of three hours, and not one of the curious natives left us during all that time, except a party . . . of twelve of them, whom the chief ordered to go and catch fish, which they did in great abundance, with dipping nets, at the foot of their Weir. . . .

We were all of us very desirous to get some fresh salmon, that we might dress them in our own way, but could not by any means obtain that gratification, though there were thousands of that fish strung on cords, which were fastened to stakes in the river. They were even averse to our approaching the spot where they clean and prepare them for their own eating. They had, indeed, taken our kettle from us, lest we should employ it in getting water from the river; and they assigned as the reason for this precaution, that the salmon dislike the smell of iron. At the same time they supplied us with wooden boxes, which were capable of holding any fluid. Two of the men that went to fish, in a canoe capable of containing ten people, returned with a full lading of salmon, that weighted from six to forty pounds, though the far greater part of them were under twenty. They immediately strung the whole of them, as I have already mentioned, in the river. . . .

Near the house of the chief I observed several oblong squares, of about twenty feet by eight. They were made of thick cedar boards, which were joined with so much neatness, that I at first thought they were one piece. They were painted with hieroglyphics, and figures of different animals, and with a degree of correctness that was not to be expected from such an uncultivated people. I could not learn the use of them, but they appeared to be calculated for occasional acts of devotion or sacrifice, which all these tribes perform at least twice in the year, at the spring and fall. I was confirmed in this opinion by a large building in the middle of the village, which I at first took for the half finished frame of a house. The ground-plot

Frances Anne Hopkins, *Shooting the Rapids,* 1879. Oil on canvas, 91.4 × 152.4 cm. This is one of Hopkins's well-known later works; the rapids are at Lachine near Montreal. This may be a day trip because there are no packs, baggage, or cargo in the *canot du maître*.

*Courtesy of the Frances Anne Hopkins fonds, Library and Archives of Canada, R5666-0-8-E.*

of it was fifty feet by forty-five; each end is formed by four stout posts, fixed perpendicularly in the ground. The corner ones are plain, and support a beam of the whole length, having three intermediate props on each side, but of a larger size, and eight or nine feet in height. The two centre posts, at each end, are two feet and an half in diameter, and carved into human figures, supporting two ridge poles on their heads, at twelve feet from the ground. The figures at the upper part of this square represent two persons, with their hands upon their knees, as if they supported the weight with pain and difficulty: the others opposite to them stand at their ease, with their hands resting on their hips. In the area of the building there were the remains of several fires. The posts, poles and figures, were painted red and black; but the sculpture of these people is superior to their painting.

*Friday, July 19* . . . On my return to our lodge, I observed before the door of the chief's residence, four heaps of salmon, each of which consisted of between three and four hundred fish. Sixteen women were employed in cleaning and preparing them. They first separate the head from the body, the former of which they boil; they then cut the latter down the back on each side of the bone, leaving one third of the fish adhering to it, and afterwards take out the guts. The bone is roasted for immediate use, and the other parts are dressed in the same manner, but with more attention, for future provision. While they are before the fire, troughs are placed under them to receive the oil. . . .

I had applied several times to the chief to prepare canoes and people to take me and my party to the sea, but very little attention had been paid to my application till noon; when I was informed that a canoe was properly equipped for my voyage . . .

. . . I went to take the dimensions of his large canoe, in which, it was signified to me, that about ten winters ago he went a considerable distance towards the midday sun, with forty of his people, when he saw two large vessels full of such men as myself, by whom he was kindly received: they were, he said, the first white people he had seen. They were probably the ships commanded by Captain Cook. This canoe was built of cedar, forty-five feet long, four feet wide, and three feet and a half in depth. It was painted black and decorated with white figures of fish of different kinds. The gunwale, fore and aft, was inlaid with the teeth of the sea-otter.*

*As Captain Cooke has mentioned, that the people of the sea-coast adorned their canoes with human teeth, I was more particular in my inquiries: the result of which was, the most satisfactory proof, that he was mistaken: but his mistake arose from the very great resemblance there is between human teeth and those of the sea-otter.[9]

In 1967, these paddlers reenacted part of the 1793 Mackenzie Expedition, paddling from Fort St. John, British Columbia, to Expo '67 in Montreal, Quebec. *Courtesy of the Thunder Bay Museum, 981.39.638 F.*

After paddling with their Indian guides two more days down the rushing river, Mackenzie and company entered the braided channels that indicated the joining of the river with the ocean tides. "The tide was out," Mackenzie wrote,

and had left a large space covered with sea-weed. The surrounding hills were involved in fog. The wind was at West, which was a-head of us, and very strong; the bay appearing to be from one to three miles in breadth. As we advanced along the land we saw a great number of sea-otters. We fired several shots at them, but without any success from the rapidity with which they plunge under the water. We also saw many small porpoises or divers. The white-headed eagle, which is common in the interior parts; some small gulls, a dark bird which is inferior in size to the gull, and a few small ducks, were all the birds which presented themselves to our view.[10]

On the coast of what is now British Columbia, Mackenzie encountered more Natives, some friendly and others who had been mistreated during prior contact with

Europeans or Russians and were threatening. Before hastily departing one camp before more Indians could arrive, Mackenzie took measurements of the horizon to determine their latitude. He wrote, "I now mixed up some vermilion in melted grease, and inscribed, in large characters, on the South-East face of the rock on which we had slept last night, this brief memorial—'Alexander Mackenzie, from Canada, by land, the twenty-second of July, one thousand seven hundred and ninety-three.'"[11] He and his French-Canadian voyageur companions, aided by Native guides, had completed the first transcontinental crossing of North America north of Mexico, starting in birch-bark canoes and ending in cedar dugouts. Lewis and Clark would complete their overland journey more than ten years later.

Samuel Worcester Rouse, *Portrait of Henry David Thoreau,* 1854. Thoreau was thirty-nine years old at the time of this drawing.  *Courtesy of the Walden Woods Project.*

### HENRY DAVID THOREAU

Henry Thoreau, famous for his independence of mind and his cabin at Walden Pond, was a paddler. "Wherever there is a channel for water, there is a road for the canoe," he said in *The Maine Woods*. As he recounted in that book, he, a companion, and their Penobscot Indian guide, Joe Poulis, traveled north from Bangor in 1846, eventually reaching the end of lodges and civilization. "This was what you might call a brand-new country," Thoreau said, "the only roads were of Nature's making, and the few houses were camps. Here, then, one could no longer accuse institutions and society, but must front the true source of evil."[12]

Thoreau paddled on Webster Stream, which today is in

Baxter State Park along with Mount Katahdin, the highest mountain in Maine. Thoreau and his companion portaged around a rapid while their Indian guide ran the birch-bark canoe through the whitewater and picked them up below.

My companion and I carried a good part of the baggage on our shoulders, while the Indian took that which would be least injured by wet in the

Thoreau's canoe route through Maine included Pockwockamus Falls on the West
Branch of the Penobscot River, seen here in a 1915 photograph by Burt Call.

*Courtesy of University of Maine, Special Collections.*

canoe. We did not know when we should see him
again, for he had not been this way since the canal
was cut, nor for more than thirty years. He agreed
to stop when he got to smooth water, come up and
find our path if he could, and halloo for us, and after
waiting a reasonable time go on and try again,—and
we were to look out in like manner for him.

He commenced by running through the sluice-
way and over the dam, as usual, standing up in his
tossing canoe, and was soon out of sight behind
a point in a wild gorge. This Webster Stream is
well known to lumbermen as a difficult one. It is

exceedingly rapid and rocky, and also shallow, and
can hardly be considered navigable, unless that
may mean that what is launched in it is sure to be
carried swiftly down it, though it may be dashed to
pieces by the way. It is somewhat like navigating
a thunder-spout. With commonly an irresistible
force urging you on, you have got to choose your
own course each moment, between the rocks and
shallows, and to get into it, moving forward always
with the utmost possible moderation, and often
holding on, if you can, that you may inspect the
rapids before you. . . .

It was very exhilarating, and the perfection of travelling, quite unlike floating on our dead Concord River, the coasting down this inclined mirror, which was now and then gently winding, down a mountain, indeed, between two evergreen forests, edged with lofty dead white pines, sometimes slanted half-way over the stream, and destined soon to bridge it. I saw some monsters there, nearly destitute of branches, and scarcely diminishing in diameter for eighty or ninety feet.[13]

### EDWIN TAPPAN ADNEY

Tappan Adney went on a weeklong birch-bark canoe trip with a friend in New Brunswick and Quebec in 1888. A native of Ohio, Adney was then twenty years old and making one of his first visits to New Brunswick. Although he didn't know it at the time, he would later live and work in eastern Canada and marry a woman from New Brunswick; his interests would make him the world's leading expert on birch-bark canoes.[14]

Howard Chapelle, curator of transportation at the Smithsonian Institution, in 1964 published *The Bark Canoes and Skin Boats of North America*, which was co-authored by Adney, although he had died in 1950. This bible of birch-bark canoes relied heavily on Adney's drawings, canoe models, and papers, most of which were unpublished at that time. The book remains the main source for anyone researching birch-bark canoes, their var-

ied hull shapes, and their geographical and anthropological connections to Native peoples.

In 1888, all that was shrouded in the future. Adney and his friend Hum purchased a used birch-bark canoe from the local Indians for $3.50, including two paddles. "It could not be said to be a very fine canoe, but it was fairly good, though very old. It leaked some," Adney wrote with considerable understatement.[15]

Edwin Tappan Adney in the Yukon, 1897.

*Courtesy of the Provincial Archives of New Brunswick Travel Bureau Photographs, P155-1923.*

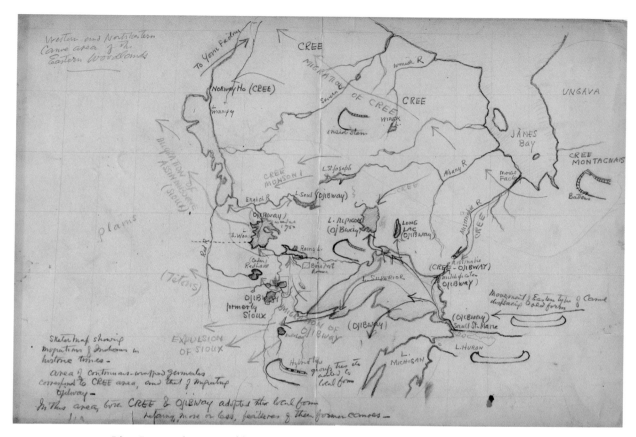

Edwin Tappan Adney's map of the eastern woodlands shows western migrations of Native peoples and the diffusion of their canoe types. *Courtesy of the Mariner's Museum, Newport News, Virginia.*

They went for the experience on a journey through the Squatook Lakes and down the Madawaska River, a route that took them through shallow sections of the river and over a couple of waterfalls that seriously scraped the bark.

This bit of their story starts across the lake from the village of Notre-Dame-du-Lac during a storm:

In the morning the wind had gone down but the seas were still running high. We ate the last of our fish and were entirely out of bread. We had to do something. It was a dangerous and foolhardy thing to attempt, but we had either to wait there hungry or get across to the village. It was like launching a lifeboat through the surf. The waves ran so high, that again and again we were tossed back. At length, wading far out, we got aboard and headed her into the teeth of the waves.

Our canoe was eighteen feet all over and thirty inches wide, loaded dangerously near the gunwales. Heading into the waves would not take us across. To turn across [the wind] was to instantly swamp. We headed therefore, quartering, but even then water came over the sides, and when we got endways I have seen the thin bows of the bark dip and the water pour over both ends. Hum was kept bailing [and] paddling hard a while till the water got too bad, then bailing again, and we kept up this, paddling just as hard as we could, for two miles when we got under a lee shore and made the village.

The first thing we did was to strike for a store. We went up the steps into a small store where a little of everything was kept, from a side of bacon to a sheet of writing paper or a piece of bed ticking or a fishing line. The storekeeper was French.

Everything is French up here, and English is not understood except by traders and those who have been to work in the lumber camps. Neither Hum nor I knew enough French to be understood, and we had to make our wants known by pointing and by signs. At length we got some groceries and then inquired for the baker's—*boulangerie*—we knew that much French.

"Have you bread?"

"Bread, bread, no compron, Oh yes, yes, pain pain oui, oui, boulanger, one mile," pointing down the lake. "Pain one mile."

We thanked him and bought a square yard of cloth for a sail. Then boiled the kettle on the beach and then paddled what we thought was a mile and went ashore.

I tended the canoe while Hum went after [the] *boulanger*. I waited and I think it must have been an hour when Hum got back with an arm full of bread.

"Where do you suppose that baker's was? Why, I had to go back all the way. It was only a little way from the other store. One mile. I suppose a Frenchman thinks that was a mile."

Hum hadn't a very good opinion of the ordinary Madawaska Frenchman. Raise a little buckwheat and then do nothing but fiddle and dance all winter.

We laughed a good deal about the Frenchman's "mile" but there was a mile we did not know about; that is, the Tobique Mile and they calculate it by starting a good healthy caribou and then running him to death. As no one has been known ever to run a caribou to death, the "Tobique Mile" must ever remain an unknown quantity. . . .

We had a week of much rain and hardship, but lots of excitement and [we] were anxious to get down the one hundred and forty miles of river that lay between us and home. The water was high in the Madawaska [River] and we made the voyage to Little Falls in short order. There we had a high mill dam to go around. It was noon when we arrived.

The dam was an apron dam with one slope of forty degrees, then it turns to about twenty and with a clear leap of four feet it was a drop shoot and a swish, then it left in a series of waves and masses of foam. On each side were eddies and there was a jam of logs in the right bank eddy. We looked at the dam and we says to ourselves, "We haven't stopped for anything yet—we ought not to stop for this."

We interviewed the mill man. "Oh yes, small boats often went over." He lied. They never dared to go over and every bateaux expected to take in water. "Suppose we try it," says Hum. "All right," says I.

As a precaution, we took our stuff out of the canoe and carried it around. Then we got into the canoe. It may be well to explain that instead of trimming level, I knelt in the compartment next to Hum so that the bow was high [out] of the water, for we expected that to go under.

Edwin Tappan Adney's sketch of a moose appeared alongside an 1893 article in *Our Animal Friends,* a publication of the American Society for the Prevention of Cruelty to Animals. Adney was a prolific illustrator and his work often graced the pages of *Harper's* and *Collier's* magazines in the late nineteenth and early twentieth centuries.   *Courtesy of Joan Adney Dragon.*

We went several rods up, to get a long start, and when we were ready, Hum and I called "Go!" simultaneously. Every man in the mill was at the window.

Our paddles struck the water and the canoe shot ahead. Our hope is to get over quick. We are ten feet from the brink when my paddle snaps. "Go ahead!" shout I.

We strike the pitch. The canoe upends and quick as a flash we drop like a toboggan and the water foams about our ears. The bow has gone under and the canoe is filling with water. Luckily, we struck the edge of the fall. A few strokes of Hum's paddle and my stick and we are almost in the eddy where we are borne against the logs and have just time to step ashore when the canoe goes under. We can see it between the logs. We are both wringing wet and we think our canoe is gone.

We fish around with poles and finally are able to work the canoe into the eddy and out clear of the logs. Then we haul it out of the logs, empty out the water, and I says to myself, I don't mean to be stumped with all those men there laughing at us. I'll show them something.

We still had to go around the logs. I stepped into the empty canoe and standing erect I put the canoe out into the rapids and [had] the canoe dancing under my feet, a trick I had learned, and I brought it around below the logs to a bit of beach where we drew the canoe out and found it twisted all ways. Every seam was open, and we had to go to the village and get a lot of tallow and rosin and linen cloth, and with the hot rosin pitch [we] pasted up every seam and crack.[16]

To protect the birch covering, they cut down straight cedar trees and split thin strips of wood. They lashed the strips to the bottom, which was called "shoeing the canoe."[17]

"A canoe with shoes does not paddle well," Adney said, "but it saves the bottom whenever it strikes a rock or when it is necessary to drag over bars. We ought to have thought of them from the start."[18] The "shoe keel" that later appeared on almost all wood-and-canvas canoes—a relatively flat keel designed to protect the bottom rather than to steer the boat—was a legacy from those cedar strips.

Every canoe paddler before and since has faced Adney's problem: how to protect the canoe from damage and keep the occupants from getting wet and spending three days on an island patching the exterior? Birch bark could be patched in the wild, but it was a sometimes difficult and time-consuming task that involved finding birch and preparing pitch and lashes. Patches were a temporary fix, as Adney and Hum discovered. All-wood canoes—made by many builders prior to the 1890s, such as Henry Rushton in New York and others in Peterborough, Ontario—required careful construction and maintenance to prevent leaks between the planks.

Canoes could be difficult to store. Native Americans

Winslow Homer (American, 1836–1910), *Young Ducks*, 1897. Watercolor on wove paper, 35.56 × 53.34 cm (14 × 21 inches).

often filled their bark canoes with rocks and submerged them under water for the winter. Modern materials gained an advantage in storage even while sometimes losing the graceful shapes of the original designs.

### PARE LORENTZ

Journeys are more important in the history of canoes than are materials. Boats of all kinds have permitted humans to spread across the globe. Canoes allowed Native Americans and fur traders to travel across North America in pursuit of their trade. With the arrival of the lapstrake and wood-and-canvas canoes, however, a diversion and a recreational activity were born.

Children growing up in the Midwest usually know one thing for certain about the streams and rivers in their region: they all eventually reach New Orleans and the Gulf of Mexico. Mark Twain's most famous character escaped the civilizing influences of school and society in *The Adventures of Huckleberry Finn* on a Mississippi River raft. Huck moved back and forth from islands to rafts and back to the shore using a stolen canoe. Put a canoe in almost any stream in the Mississippi River drainage, and you'll travel some portion of the route that Pare Lorentz wrote about in the prose poem narration for his great Depression-era documentary movie, *The River*:

From as far West as Idaho,
Down from the glacier peaks of the Rockies—
From as far East as New York,

Down from the turkey ridges of the Alleghenies
Down from Minnesota, twenty-five hundred miles,
The Mississippi River runs to the Gulf.

Carrying every drop of water that flows down
    two-thirds the continent,
Carrying every brook and rill, rivulet and creek,
Carrying all the rivers that run down two-thirds the
    continent,
The Mississippi runs to the Gulf of Mexico.

Down the Yellowstone, the Milk, the White and
    Cheyenne;
The Cannonball, the Musselshell, the James and the
    Sioux;
Down the Judith, the Grand, the Osage, and the Platte,
The Skunk, the Salt, the Black, and Minnesota;
Down the Rock, the Illinois, and the Kankakee,
The Allegheny, the Monongahela, Kanawha, and
    Muskingum;
Down the Miami, the Wabash, the Licking and the
    Green,
The Cumberland, the Kentucky, and the Tennessee;
Down the Ouachita, the Wichita, the Red, and Yazoo,
Down the Missouri three thousand miles from the
    Rockies;
Down the Ohio a thousand miles from the Alleghenies;
Down the Arkansas fifteen hundred miles from the
    Great Divide;
Down the Red, a thousand miles from Texas;

Down the great Valley, twenty-five hundred miles
from Minnesota,
Carrying every rivulet and brook, creek and rill,
Carrying all the rivers that run down two-thirds the
continent
The Mississippi runs to the Gulf.[19]

Children and quite a few adventuresome adults of the
Upper Midwest could also access another fantasy river
journey. Because of the height of land near the origin of
the Mississippi, some watersheds in upper Minnesota and
North Dakota actually flow north.

### ERIC SEVAREID

Eric Sevareid was born in North Dakota, where he lived
until his teenage years, when his family moved to Minneapolis. Later in life, from 1939 to 1977, Sevareid became a
distinguished CBS journalist and after 1964 served as a be-
loved commentator on the *CBS Evening News* with Walter
Cronkite. He was honored as one of only nine American
journalists who have appeared on U.S. postage stamps,
along with John Hersey, Martha Gellhorn, George Polk,
Horace Greeley, and Ernest Hemingway. When he graduated from high school in 1930 at age seventeen, he and a
friend, Walter Port, started north in a used canoe. Up the
Minnesota and Little Minnesota Rivers, through Browns
Valley to Lake Traverse and across the continental divide;
down the Bois des Sioux and the Red River of the North to
Lake Winnipeg; along the Nelson River, God's River, and

Hayes River, 2,250 miles from Minneapolis to York Factory on Hudson Bay. Sevareid recounted their epic journey
in *Canoeing with the Cree* (1935).

When they arrived at Winnipeg, they became guests at
the Canoe Club:

At the beautiful, spacious Canoe Club, we were
taken right into the "family" of more than a
thousand members. Sam Southern, the "skipper,"
we found to be very hospitable. Caretaker, canoe
builder and repairer, as well as unofficial father of
all troubles and fount of all wisdom about the place,
he immediately took charge of us, fixed up our boat
on a suitable rack and granted permission for us to

Eric Sevareid's nickel-plated, cased magnetic compass that guided the 1930 canoe
trip to Hudson Bay. *Courtesy of the Minnesota Historical Society, 1980.26.2.*

In June 1930, Eric Sevareid (left) and Walter Port started their canoe journey at Fort Snelling, Minnesota, and paddled 2,250 miles to Hudson Bay. *Courtesy of the Minnesota Historical Society, 95718.*

camp beside the club. . . . Sam showed us all the different types of canoes and paddles, which made our equipment look sick, although we refused to admit it. There were war canoes, which contain fourteen men, Peterboroughs, Sunnysides, Old Townes, like ours, and Chestnut freighters. One little canoe was only twelve feet long, a one-man trapper or prospector boat and had to be paddled from the middle.[20]

On the route to Hudson Bay, they met Ralph Butchart, the young clerk in the Hudson's Bay Company store at Norway House, and two Indians, Moses and Jimmy:

Ralph was a prince. At night when we were able to sit with our backs to a log and let the heat of the long fire the Indians made thaw us out, we had long talks together. Ralph was Scotch, like most Hudson Bay men. We were surprised to hear that he was a college graduate, extremely well read and, under the rough exterior one almost has to adopt in the far north, gentle and refined. He thought our trip was the greatest thing he had ever heard of, and told us so. Of course our hearts warmed toward the tall, slender, redheaded northerner more than ever.

Ralph had two more years of service with the company and then his term would be up. He told us he wanted to go back to Scotland and live in a city again, but constant reference to this thing and that thing which one must learn "to be a good bushman" showed us that he was growing closer and closer to the northland in his heart.

Each morning, when it was yet dark, the rough hand of Moses awoke us. There he would stand, shivering in the flickering light of the growing fire, wearing a childish skull cap which he always slept in. Breakfast for Moses and Jimmy usually was boiled rabbit. Jimmy caught a bunny nearly every night in a little snare of cord which he would loop over a rabbit trail.

We would paddle and portage steadily until noon, when we stopped to "boil the kettle." Then, until about five o'clock, we again labored, without a lull. After our supper at five, we took the trail once more and kept on until dark. Never did we camp except in a portage spot, where these Indians had spent many nights before. Sometimes we found supplies of fuel, already cut.

Our course followed a long chain of miniature lakes which lay close together and yet unconnected. Crystal clear, very cold, these gems of water lay deep in valleys of granite and row on row of pine and autumn birch reflected in their depths. Over these hills of rock we had to carry our outfits.[21]

### JOHN McPHEE

When John McPhee became old enough, his father, a physician for the Princeton University athletic teams, took him every summer to the Keewaydin canoe camp in Vermont. The Keewaydin canoe camp gave McPhee a lifelong love of paddling and the outdoors. References to canoeing wander throughout his work, including most prominently "Reading the River" (1970), "Travels in Georgia" (1973), *The Survival of the Bark Canoe* (1975), *Coming into the Country* (1977), and *The Control of Nature* (1989). The experiences of his formative years—interests developed before the age of twenty—shaped much of what McPhee would write about at *The New Yorker* magazine, including a portrait of a man who creates birch-bark canoes, profiles of people living in primitive conditions in New Jersey and in Alaska, and scientists arguing about the revolution that transformed geology. His home base for writing was Princeton, New Jersey, but his research took him all over the world.

In 1975, his destination was the Salmon River and the Kobuk River Valley in Alaska, in the company of four men paddling three boats. They were "a state–federal study team," McPhee said. "The subject of the study is the river."[22] Bob Fedeler, Stell Newman, Pat Pourchot of the federal Bureau of Outdoor Recreation, and John Kauff-mann, a National Park Service planner, paddled in the Brooks Range above the Arctic Circle. The Salmon River, McPhee said, has "the clearest, purest water I have ever seen flowing over rocks,"[23] through which the paddlers watched migrating salmon and Arctic grayling.

Two of our boats—the kayaks—are German. They can be taken apart and put back together. They were invented long ago by someone known as the

Mad Tailor of Rosenheim. The Mad Tailor, at the turn of the century, was famous for his mountain-climbing knickers and loden capes. It was in 1907 that he went into naval architecture on a diminutive scale. Every major valley in Bavaria had a railroad running through it. The forests were laced with small white rivers. It was all but impossible to get boats to them, because boats were too bulky to accompany travellers on trains. Wouldn't it be *phantastisch*, thought the tailor, if

John McPhee poling a canoe with his daughters Jenny (in the bow) and Martha (in the middle) in Ontario in 1978.   *Courtesy of John McPhee.*

a boat could fit into a handbag, if a suitcase could turn into a kayak? His name was Johann Klepper. He designed a collapsible kayak with a canvas skin and a frame of separable hardwood parts. In subsequent manufacture, the boat became an international success. Klepper might have stopped there. Not long after the First World War, he designed a larger version, its spray cover apertured with two holes. Where the original boat had been made for a single paddler, this one was intended for a team. We have with us a single and a double Klepper. The smaller one is prompt, responsive, feathery on the stream. The double one is somewhat less maneuverable than a three-ton log. Stell Newman, of the National Park Service, began calling it Snake Eyes, and everyone has picked up the name. Snake Eyes is our *bateau noir,* our Charonian ferry, our *Höllenfahrt.* Throughout the day, we heap opprobrium on Snake Eyes.

Pourchot and I have the double Klepper this morning. The ratio of expended energy to developed momentum is seventy-five to one. This is in part because the bottom of Snake Eyes at times intersects the bottom of the river, which is shallow at many of the riffles. The hull has become so abraded in places that it has developed leaks. The Grumman canoe is wider, longer, more heavily loaded. It carries at least half of all our gear. Nonetheless, it rides higher, draws less water, than Snake Eyes. Fortunately, the pools are extensive

here in the lower river, and are generally a little deeper than a paddle will reach. Pockets are much deeper than that. Miles slide behind us. A salmon, sensing the inferiority of Snake Eyes, leaps into the air beside it, leaps again, leaps again, ten pounds of fish jumping five times high into the air—a bravado demonstration, a territorial declaration. This is, after all, the salmon's eponymous river. The jumper moves on, among its kind, ignoring the dying. These—their spawning done—idly, sleepily yield to the current, their gestures slow and quiet, a peaceful drifting away.

We have moved completely out of the hills now, and beyond the riverine fringes of spruce and cottonwood are boggy flatlands and thaw lakes. We see spruce that have been chewed by porcupines and cottonwood chewed by beavers. Moose tend to congregate down here on the tundra plain. In late fall, some of the caribou that migrate through the Salmon valley will stop here and make this their winter range. We see a pair of loons, and lesser Canada geese, and chick mergansers with their mother. Mink, marten, muskrat, otter—creatures that live here inhabit the North Woods across the world to Maine. We pass a small waterfall under a patterned bluff—folded striations of schist. In bends of the river now we come upon banks of flood-eroded soil—of mud. They imply an earth mantle of some depth going back who knows how far from the river. Brown and glistening, they are

virtually identical with rural stream banks in the eastern half of the country, with the difference that the water flowing past these is clear. In the sixteenth century, the streams of eastern America ran clear (except in flood), but after people began taking the vegetation off the soil mantle and then leaving their fields fallow when crops were not there, rain carried the soil into the streams. The process continues, and when one looks at such streams today, in their seasonal varieties of chocolate, their distant past is—even to the imagination—completely lost. For this Alaskan river, on the other hand, the sixteenth century has not yet ended, nor the fifteenth, nor the fifth. The river flows, as it has since immemorial time, in balance with itself. The river and every rill that feeds it are in an unmodified natural state—opaque in flood, ordinarily clear, with levels that change within a closed cycle of the year and of the years. The river cycle is only one of many hundreds of cycles—biological, meteorological—that coincide and blend here in the absence of intruding artifice. Past to present, present reflecting past, the cycles compose this segment of the earth. It is not static, so it cannot be styled "pristine," except in the special sense that while human beings have hunted,

John McPhee's 1975 canoe trip to Alaska's Salmon River was featured in his book *Coming into the Country*. The river's headwaters pass through Kobuk Valley National Park.   *Courtesy of Western Arctic National Parklands.*

fished, and gathered wild food in this valley in
small groups for centuries, they have not yet begun
to change it. Such a description will fit many rivers
in Alaska. This one, though, with its considerable
beauty and a geography that places it partly
within and partly beyond the extreme reach of the
boreal forest, has been thought of as sufficiently
splendid to become a national wild river—to be set
aside with its immediate environs as unalterable
wild terrain. Kauffmann, Newman, Fedeler, and
Pourchot are, in their various ways, studying that
possibility. The wild-river proposal, which Congress
is scheduled to act upon before the end of 1978, is

something of a box within a box, for it is entirely
incorporated within a proposed national monument
that would include not only the entire Salmon
River drainage but also a large segment of the
valley of the Kobuk River, of which the Salmon is a
tributary. (In the blue haze of Interior Department
terminology, "national monument" often enough
describes certain large bodies of preserved land that
in all respects except name are national parks.)
The Kobuk Valley National Monument proposal,
which includes nearly two million acres, is, in
area, relatively modest among ten other pieces of
Alaska that are similarly projected for confirmation

by Congress as new parks and monuments. In all, these lands constitute over thirty-two million acres, which is more than all the Yosemites, all the Yellowstones, all the Grand Canyons and Sequoias put together—a total that would more than double the present size of the National Park System. For cartographic perspective, thirty-two million acres slightly exceeds the area of the state of New York.

Impressive as that may seem, it is less than a tenth of Alaska. . . .[24]

Starting off with precise sensory details of a balky watercraft on a splendid river, McPhee momentarily diverts us to the conservation of wild rivers. On December 1, 1978, a man with whom McPhee had paddled in Georgia, President Jimmy Carter, created the Kobuk Valley National Monument. The 70 miles of the Salmon River became a National Wild and Scenic River located within the Kobuk Valley National Park, which was designated in 1980. There are no roads within the park.

McPhee's story, part of *Coming into the Country*, first published in *The New Yorker* in 1977 and still in print today, may have influenced that legislation. He frequently showed up in a beautiful spot at a moment when it was endangered. Another book, *The Pine Barrens*, arrived in 1968 as a proposed airport threatened one of the most spectacular natural areas in New Jersey. In *Encounters with the Archdruid* (1971), McPhee convinced David Brower, head of the Sierra Club, and Floyd Dominy, commissioner of reclamation, to take a raft trip with him down the Colorado River in the Grand Canyon. Dominy wanted more dams built in Grand Canyon National Park and he had overseen construction of Glen Canyon Dam, the stopper that Brower considered an abomination. Brower opposed the idea of more dams, as did legions of Americans who may have never been touched by the Colorado River or seen the layered geological story in the walls of the Grand Canyon. McPhee brought these national treasures to life. One does not protect wild areas without creating an audience and a fan club for them.

Our feelings about the natural world—whether about spectacular places like the Boundary Waters and Quetico, the Grand Canyon, or more commonplace spots like a local stream—grow out of our cultural heritage and knowledge. Beliefs about what should remain natural or be developed change over time as a result of writers such as those represented here, and because of our own close contact with the world. The canoe has been a vehicle for experiences and for the development of cultural attitudes since its invention in the time before history. As Sigurd Olson writes, "When a man is part of his canoe, he is part of all that canoes have ever known."[25]

# Acknowledgments

We would like to thank several people whose special contributions made this book possible. Their assistance vastly improved the scope and accuracy of the manuscript, but those errors that always creep through are ours alone.

Thanks to Jenny Gavacs for helping get us started on this book, and to our editors, Erik Anderson and Kristian Tvedten at the University of Minnesota Press, along with former Pressman Todd Orjala, and Katie Lambright for her photo research. Charlie Rader's maps and Mark Hamel's paintings added greatly to the book.

Benson Gray, Kathy Klos, Tom Seavey, Dan Miller, Rollin Thurlow, Jerry Stelmok, Dan Lindberg, Ferdy Goode, and other members of the Wooden Canoe Heritage Association provided valuable assistance with historical questions and photos of birch-bark, all-wood, and wood-and-canvas canoes. Susan Audette, author of *The Old Town Canoe Company: Our First Hundred Years*, gave valuable historical information and personal stories.

Support and assistance on technical and personal topics came from a number of people. Donna L. Ruhl of the Florida Museum of Natural History helped with the anthropology of dugout canoes. Napolean Sanford of Salybia, Carib Territory, Dominica, West Indies, helped with stories of his personal experience building dugout canoes, as did Erik Simula of Finland, Minnesota, with his experiences with birch-bark canoes. Isabella Donadio provided tremendous assistance with the collection at the Harvard Art Museums. The brothers Alan, Everett, and Frederic Marshall provided assistance with the Jule Fox Marshall materials and photographs. Joan Adney Dragon was generous with her materials on Tappan Adney. Ken Brown, author of *The Canadian Canoe Company*, provided wonderful insights into the builders from Peterborough, Ontario. Others who helped include Alex Comb of Stewart River Boat Works, Jeanne Bourquin of Ely, Minnesota, Pam Wedd of Bearwood Canoes, Emily Schoelzel of Salmon Falls Canoe, Wenonah Canoe's Mike Cichanowski, and Northwest Canoe's Dennis Davidson, who offered able advice, as did the artist and builder Tom Schrunk of Minneapolis. Sig Olson's son Robert, as always, was helpful, as were all the folks at the North House Folk School in Grand Marais, Minnesota.

Museum curators and administrators provided information and photographs that are crucial for a book like this. Special thanks go to John Summers and Jeremy Ward of the Canadian Canoe Museum. At the Antique Boat Museum in Clayton, New York, extraordinary consultations were available with Emmett Smith, curator of watercraft; Claire Wakefield, curatorial assistant; Barton Haxall, volunteer librarian; and again with Dan Miller, former curator at ABM and proprietor of Dragonfly Canoe Works. At the St. Lawrence County Historical Association in Canton, New York, archivist JeanMarie Martello provided information on J. H. Rushton. At the Adirondack Museum in Blue Mountain Lake, New York, Doreen Alessi-Holmes, conservator and collections manager; assistant curator Angela Snye; and librarian Jerold Pepper provided assistance on multiple visits.

Norman would like to give special thanks to Diane deGroat for her support, suggestions, and patience while this book was taking shape. Thanks also to the late Priscilla Clarkson, dean of Commonwealth Honors College at the University of Massachusetts Amherst, for research support. And thanks to my boating friends who helped me learn canoeing and have been conservation and paddling colleagues for thirty years or more, including Rick Hudson, Tom Christopher, Jim Dowd, Bruce Lessels, Frank and Jennifer Mooney, Julia Khorana, Ken Kimball, Kristen Sykes, Charlie and Kathy Frazer, Joe Child, Jon Goodman, Connie Peterson, Jim Cooper, Deborah Rubin, Gordon Sims, and all my other friends from the Appalachian Mountain Club.

Mark would like to thank Amy Kuebelbeck and their three children, Elena, Maria, and Gabriel, as well as his parents, Jack and Fran Neuzil of Solon, Iowa, and siblings, Renee, Paul, and Beth. And thanks to friends in canoes over the years of tripping: Dodd Demas, Doug Glass, the late Dave Pyle, Michael Gaudio, Rich Braga, Bernie Brady, Michael Goodson, David Landry, Adam Heffron, Tom Connery, the late Steve Hoffman, Britain Scott, and Dave and Nancy Seaton.

# Notes

**FOREWORD**

1. From "Swimming with Canoes," in *The New Yorker*, August 10, 1998; reprinted as chapter 3 in *Silk Parachute* (New York: Farrar, Straus and Giroux, 2010).

2. From the foreword (copyright 2005 by John McPhee), in *Camp* by Michael D. Eisner (New York: Warner Books, 2005).

3. From "Encounters with the Archdruid: Part 3, A River," *The New Yorker*, April 3, 1971; reprinted in *Encounters with the Archdruid* (New York: Farrar, Straus and Giroux, 1971).

4. From "Farewell to the Nineteenth Century," in *The New Yorker*, September 27, 1999; reprinted as chapter 4 in *The Founding Fish* (New York: Farrar, Straus and Giroux, 2002).

5. From *The Founding Fish* (New York: Farrar, Straus and Giroux, 2002), 202–3.

6. From "The Keel of Lake Dickey," in *The New Yorker*, May 3, 1976; reprinted in *Giving Good Weight* (New York: Farrar, Straus and Giroux, 1979), 168–73. On November 25, 1981, the U.S. House voted to revoke authorization for the Dickey-Lincoln Dam, which would have drowned the St. John River, and a couple of years later the entire project ended.

7. From "The Orange Trapper," in *The New Yorker*, July 1, 2013.

8. From "The Patch," in *The New Yorker*, February 8, 2010.

**INTRODUCTION**

1. Paine, *Sea and Civilization*.

2. Ibid., 33.

3. *National Recreational Boating Survey*, 2011, http://www.uscgboating.org/assets/1/workflow_staging/News/614.pdf. The Coast Guard reported more than 2.5 million canoes in operation in the United States in 2011.

4. Portions of this story appeared in "From Branch to Lake: Clamps, Glue and Makeshift Steamers," *Outdoor News*, October 13, 2010, http://www.outdoornews.com/October-2010/From-Branch-to-Lake-Clamps-Glue-and-Makeshift-Steamers/.

## 1. DUGOUT CANOES

1. Paine, in *Sea and Civilization*, 27, noted that the Spanish conquistadors found South American Natives using sails on balsawood rafts. "*Balsas* were propelled by paddles and one or two triangular fore-and-aft or, more rarely, square sails."

2. McKusick, "Aboriginal Canoes in the West Indies," 8.

3. Kolbert, "Sleeping with the Enemy," 72.

4. Paine, *Sea and Civilization*, 25.

5. Ibid., 27–28. Note: "The Greater Antilles include the large islands of Jamaica, Cuba, Hispaniola, and Puerto Rico. The southward arc of the Lesser Antilles is divided into the northerly Leeward Islands, from the Virgin Islands to Dominica, and the southerly Windward Islands, from Martinique to Grenada." It seems likely, however, given the short distance, that Mayans may have paddled from the Yucatan to Cuba.

6. See Huth, *Lost Art of Finding Our Way*, 6, 21.

7. Paine, *Sea and Civilization*, 17–19.

8. McCanse, *Dominica*, 25–26.

9. McKusick, "Aboriginal Canoes in the West Indies," 3.

10. Jane, *Select Documents Illustrating the Four Voyages of Columbus*, 1:32.

11. McCanse, *Dominica*, 25.

12. Bourque, *Swordfish Hunters*, 66–67.

13. Transcript of comments by Dr. Arthur Spiess at the Monhegan Museum in November 1998, provided by the museum.

14. Bourque, *Swordfish Hunters*, 112.

15. Ibid., 113.

16. Ibid., 132.

17. Chapelle, "Migrations of an American Boat Type," 138; citing Henry Hall, *Report on the Ship-Building Industry of the United States* (Washington, [D.C.]: Government Printing Office, 1884), 29–32.

18. Diary of Reginald Drayton, 1871, in the Archives of Ontario, Toronto.

19. Kelly Smith, "New Tests Confirm Lake Minnetonka Canoe Is 1,000 Years Old," *Minneapolis Star Tribune*, April 9, 2014.

20. Milanich and Root, *Hidden Seminoles*, 1–5.

21. Chapel (error for Chapelle), "Seminole Canoe."

22. See Wheeler et al., "Archaic Period Canoes," and also Wheeler, "Ortona Canals."

23. Wheeler et al., "Archaic Period Canoes."

24. Ruhl and Purdy, "One Hundred-One Canoes on the Shore," 112.

25. Wheeler et al., "Archaic Period Canoes," 160.

26. Paine, *Sea and Civilization*, 20.

27. Kirch, *Unearthing the Polynesian Past*, 233.

28. Low and Estus, "The Navigators."

29. Dolin, *Fur, Fortune, and Empire*, 135.

30. An exception were the Europeans around Peterborough, Ontario, who built dugouts from basswood, rather than imitating birch-bark canoes.

31. Quadra Island is off northern Vancouver Island, British Columbia.

32. Stewart, *Cedar*, 48.

33. M. Reid, *Bill Reid*, 40.

34. Dolin, *Fur, Fortune, and Empire*, 139.

35. Ibid., 155.

36. John Ledyard, quoted in ibid., 144, from Ledyard's *A Journal of Captain Cook's Last Voyage to the Pacific Ocean, and in Quest of a North-West Passage* (1783), 70.

37. Kaplanoff, *Joseph Ingraham's Journal*, xii. Captain Ingraham's journey proved unprofitable because the Chinese for a brief time banned the import of sea otter fur as retaliation against the Russians. Ingraham was unable to trade his cargo of furs as had other captains, and returned to Boston unsuccessful. The import ban was lifted the next year.

38. Ibid., xi.

39. See, for example, Dolin, *Fur, Fortune, and Empire*, 156.

40. M. Reid, *Bill Reid*, 54.

41. Dolin, *Fur, Fortune, and Empire*, 142.

42. Sterba, "America Gone Wild."

43. Dolin, *Fur, Fortune, and Empire*, 158–60.

44. See, for example, Boas, "Art of the North Pacific Coast";

Boas, "Decorative Art"; and Boas, *Primitive Art*. See also Holm, *Northwest Coast Indian Art*.

45. Claude Lévi-Strauss, quoted in M. Reid, "Bill Reid," in *Bill Reid*, 109.

46. Shadbolt, *Bill Reid*, 13.

47. Quoted in ibid., 112.

48. Tippett, *Bill Reid*, 243.

49. Bill Reid, "Foreword" to Stewart, *Cedar*, 8.

50. Stewart, *Cedar*, 52–53.

51. M. Reid, *Bill Reid and the Haida Canoe*, 23.

52. Shadbolt, *Bill Reid*, 112, quoting Reid's unpublished paper "Haida Means Human Being," 1979.

53. Stewart, *Cedar*, 50.

54. M. Reid, *Bill Reid and the Haida Canoe*, 41.

55. B. Reid and Lawrence, *Totem*.

56. Tippett, *Bill Reid*, 241.

57. M. Reid, *Bill Reid and the Haida Canoe*, 82–86.

58. Guujaaw, "Man, Myth or Magic?," in Duffek and Townsend-Gault, *Bill Reid and Beyond*, 62.

59. Quoted in Gaines, "Dugout Canoes." See also "Tribes Use GIS."

60. See Oh, "How Canoes Are Saving Lives."

61. Quoted in Gaines, "Dugout Canoes."

#### NAPOLEAN SANFORD

1. Napolean Sanford, interview with Norman Sims, February 5, 2013.

2. McCanse, *Dominica*, 29.

#### 2. BIRCH-BARK CANOES

1. Erik Simula, interview with Mark Neuzil, Grand Marais, Minn., July 31, 2012. See also Arrowhead Journey: Erik Simula's Birch Bark Canoe Voyage, at http://arrowheadjourney.wordpress.com/.

2. "Canada Geography," Worldatlas, http://www.worldatlas.com/webimage/countrys/namerica/caland.htm.

3. Poling, *The Canoe*, 103.

4. Gidmark, *Birchbark Canoe*, 7.

5. Roy MacGregor, *Canoe Country*, 5.

6. Cook, *Voyages of Jacques Cartier*, x–xvi.

7. This quotation uses the language of the times, which to modern ears is offensive or worse; this and similar language is used only when quoting from original source materials.

8. Cook, *Voyages of Jacques Cartier*, 10.

9. Ibid.

10. See Roberts and Shackleton, *The Canoe*, 1; and Poling, *The Canoe*, 13–14. Several variants on the spellings exist. Samuel Johnson included the word *canoe* in his 1755 dictionary, restricting its meaning to a dugout "boat made by cutting the trunk of a tree into a hollow vessel." Later editions included an alternative spelling, "cannow."

11. Cook, *Voyages of Jacques Cartier*, 17.

12. Ibid., 24. A *sou* was a French coin of small worth.

13. Ibid., 25.

14. The Canadian Canoe Museum holds an eighteenth-century bark canoe of the Malecite/Abenaki type that was owned by a British soldier, Lieutenant John Enys, and rediscovered in a stone barn in Cornwall in 2010. It is believed to be one of the oldest surviving examples of the birch-bark canoe. See Vaillancourt, "Enys Birchbark Canoe," 72–79. In addition, the Peabody Essex Museum in Salem, Massachusetts, possesses a bark canoe that may be of a similar era and is in better condition.

15. The birch was important enough in later societies to be named the state tree of New Hampshire and the provincial tree of Saskatchewan and to be used as the raw material for Popsicle sticks.

16. Burns and Honkala, *Silvics of North America*, vol. 2.

17. Roberts and Shackleton, *The Canoe*, 71.

18. Hornell, *Water Transport*, 186.

19. The bracket fungus was particularly useful as an enema.

20. Tilford, *Edible and Medicinal Plants of the West*.

21. Burroughs, "A Taste of Maine Birch," 844.

22. Occasionally the boats were called birchrind canoes. See, for example, Heron, *Fort Garry Journal*, 10.

23. Evans, *Noah's Last Canoe*, 1.

24. Kidd, *Birch-Bark Scrolls in Archaeological Contexts*, 480.

25. Ahlgren and Ahlgren, *Lob Trees in the Wilderness*, 78.

26. Wingerd, *North Country*, 103.

27. Patterson, *Dangerous River*, 88.

28. Hubbard, *Woods and Lakes of Maine*, 62–63.

29. D.S. Davidson, "Folk Tales," 279.

30. Burns and Honkala, *Silvics of North America*, vol. 1.

31. Gidmark, *Birchbark Canoe*, 66.

32. Nute, *The Voyageur*, 235.

33. Gidmark and Alsford, *Building a Birchbark Canoe*, 2.

34. Jennings, *Bark Canoes*, 137.

35. Pinkerton, *The Canoe*, 97.

36. Roberts and Shackleton, *The Canoe*, 175.

37. Dickason, *Myth of the Savage*, 93.

38. "Algonquin Elder William Commanda."

39. Jennings, *Bark Canoes*, 137.

40. Poling, *The Canoe*, 22.

41. Kent, "Manufacturing of Birchbark Canoes for the Fur Trade in the St. Lawrence," in Jennings, Hodgins, and Small, *Canoe in Canadian Cultures*, 102.

42. Hornell, *Water Transport*, vi.

43. O. T. Mason, in *Pointed Bark Canoes*, reported in 1899 that, in a Kutenai tribe near the river of that name, women built the bark boats from start to finish in teams of two. Mason said they could complete a boat in four to five days.

44. Thoreau, *Canoeing in the Wilderness*, 60.

45. Ferdy Goode, interview, Northern Community Radio (KAXE), November 3, 2010.

46. Gidmark, *Birchbark Canoe*, 77.

47. Goode, interview.

48. Roberts and Shackleton, *The Canoe*, 168.

49. Penobscot chief Barry Dana and others building Penobscot-style canoes will smooth the ribs to a high degree. See Hennessey, "Entirely by Hand."

50. Goode, interview.

51. Rutstrum, *North American Canoe Country*, 23.

52. Adney and Chapelle, *Bark Canoes*, 96–98.

53. Poling, *The Canoe*, 42.

54. Young, *By Canoe and Dog-Train*, 71.

55. Traill, *Backwoods of Canada*, 258.

56. Adney, "How an Indian Birch-Bark Canoe Is Made" and "Building of a Birch Canoe."

57. Adney and Chapelle, *Bark Canoes*, 27.

58. Morison, *Samuel de Champlain*, 139.

59. Fischer, *Champlain's Dream*, 202.

### ELM-BARK CANOES

1. Adney and Chapelle, *Bark Canoes*, 8.

2. Ibid., 215.

3. Ibid., 15.

4. Bond, *Boats and Boating in the Adirondacks*, 26.

5. Strickland, "Correspondence," 141.

### THE OLDEST BIRCH-BARK CANOE

1. Enys, *American Journals*.

2. Fuhrmann, *Relic Canoe*.

3. Jeremy Ward, interview with Norman Sims, September 26, 2013.

4. Vaillancourt, "Enys Birchbark Canoe," 72. He added that the boat could have been made by Huron, Mohawk, or even French builders copying Native designs. "Expert Reveals Detail," 25.

5. Boswell, "Soldier's Journal."

6. Hadlock and Dodge, "Canoe from the Penobscot River," 301.

7. Boswell, "'Precious' Canadiana Rescued."

### 3. THE FUR TRADE

1. Thwaites, *Jesuit Relations*, 281.

2. Chief Black Hawk in his memoirs, published in 1833, describes a European who could only be Champlain.

3. Champlain, *Champlain's Voyages*, 248.

4. Interestingly enough, in French the word *verchères* is used as an adjective for a rowboat, the *chaloupe verchères*.

5. Champlain, *Champlain's Voyages*, 270.

6. Ibid., 279. About his only major error was to underestimate the size of the North American continent.

7. Thwaites, *Jesuit Relations*, 9:235.

8. Champlain, *Champlain's Voyages*, 248–49.

9. Fischer, *Champlain's Dream*, 627.

10. Ibid., 563.

11. Innis, *Fur Trade in Canada*.

12. Grant, "Symbols and Myths," 48.

13. The tradition continued into the mid-twentieth century. Queen Elizabeth received a beaver coat from the Hudson's Bay Company on the occasion of her wedding to Prince Philip in 1947.

14. Mansel, *Dressed to Rule*, xv.

15. Ribeiro, *Art of Dress*, 169.

16. Mansel, *Dressed to Rule*, 45.

17. Frazier, *Great Plains*, 20.

18. Linthicum, *Costume in the Drama of Shakespeare*, 229.

19. Morse, *Canoe Routes of the Voyageurs*, 34.

20. Five hundred years later, a wild beaver reappeared in England, on the River Otter in Devon. See Johnson, "Wild Beaver Sighted."

21. Dolin, *Fur, Fortune, and Empire*, 17.

22. Heidenreich, *Huronia*, 256.

23. Dolin, *Fur, Fortune, and Empire*, 84.

24. Grant, "Symbols and Myths," 48.

25. Young, *By Canoe and Dog Train*, 89.

26. Heidenreich, *Huronia*, 521. Priests also paddled when necessary.

27. Podruchny, *Making the Voyageur World*.

28. Ibid., 6, 18.

29. Beattie and Buss, *Undelivered Letters*, 293.

30. A French gold coin.

31. Beattie and Buss, *Undelivered Letters*, 296–97.

32. Ibid., 302.

33. By the early twentieth century, beaver populations were so exhausted that Quebec and Ontario closed the trapping season in 1903. The price of a pelt, which was about $1 in 1870, climbed to $8 by 1918 and then shot up in the 1920s to $17 to $20, leading to a mini-boom in trapping.

34. Dolin, *Fur, Fortune, and Empire*, 266, 273.

35. Ibid., 135. Dolin notes that coastal traders treated Natives more cruelly because they did not live among them as the land traders did. It may have also been because they were not repeat customers—many of the deals were onetime transactions.

36. Poling, *The Canoe*, 93.

37. Gibbon, *Romance of the Canadian Canoe*, 48.

38. Rutstrum, *North American Canoe Country*, 23.

39. Innis, *Fur Trade in Canada*, 226.

40. Ross, *Fur Hunters*, 198.

41. Roberts and Shackleton, *The Canoe*, 170.

42. Morse, *Canoe Routes of the Voyageurs*, 35.

43. Nute, *The Voyageur*, 26.

44. Podruchny, *Making the Voyageur World*, 35, 42.

45. David A. Armour, "Ducharme, Laurent," *Dictionary of Canadian Biography*, vol. 4.

46. Jane E. Graham, "Couagne, Jean-Baptiste de," *Dictionary of Canadian Biography*, vol. 4.

47. David A. Armour, "Bourassa, René," *Dictionary of Canadian Biography*, vol. 4.

48. Hélène Paré, "Ailleboust de la Madeleine, François-Jean-Daniel d'," *Dictionary of Canadian Biography*, vol. 4.

49. Moberly and Cameron, *When Fur Was King*, 104.

50. Podruchny, *Making the Voyageur World*, 106–7.

51. Ibid., 106.

52. Ibid., 100.

53. Bond, in *Boats and Boating in the Adirondacks*, reports that the word *portage* was seldom used in the Adirondacks; *carries* was used instead.

54. Roberts and Shackleton, *The Canoe*, 183.

55. Ibid.

56. Innis, *Fur Trade in Canada*, 226.

57. Ahlgren and Ahlgren, *Lob Trees in the Wilderness*, 29.

58. Pinkerton, *The Canoe*, 106.

59. Podruchny, *Making the Voyageur World*, 205.

60. Moberly and Cameron, *When Fur Was King*, 83–84.

61. Bigsby, *Shoe and Canoe*, 218–19.

62. Gibbon, *Romance of the Canadian Canoe*, 49.

63. Moberly and Cameron, *When Fur Was King*, 98.

64. Ibid., 147.

65. From the Cree words *pimmi* (meat) and *kon* (fat). That pretty well describes it.

66. Poling, *The Canoe*, 53.

67. As reported in Podruchny, *Making the Voyageur World*, 115.

68. Morse, *Canoe Routes of the Voyageurs*, 35.

69. Podruchny, *Making the Voyageur World*, 87.

70. Olson, *Listening Point*, 205–6.

### THE ALGONQUIN FUR TRADE

1. See http://www.birchbarkcanoe.net/algonquincanoes.html.

2. Adney and Chapelle, *Bark Canoes*, 114.

3. Jennings, *The Canoe*, 55.

4. See "Algonquins" at http://www.thecanadianencyclopedia.ca/en/article/algonquin/.

### FRANCES ANNE HOPKINS

1. Philip Shackleton, "Beechey, Frances Anne," *Dictionary of Canadian Biography*, vol. 14.

2. Ibid.

3. Huneault, "Placing Frances Anne Hopkins," 180.

4. Prakash, "Frances Anne Hopkins," 43.

### 4. ALL-WOOD CANOES

1. *Picturesque Peterboro' Souvenir Number 1901* at the Peterborough Museum.

2. John Summers, interview with Norman Sims, September 27, 2013, Canadian Canoe Museum. All quotations by Summers in this chapter are from this interview.

3. K. Brown, *Invention of the Board Canoe*.

4. Ibid., 5–7. In private correspondence, Brown said that *Mitchell's Canada Gazetteer and Business Directory for 1864–1865* listed Stephenson as a "boat builder," meaning that by 1863 he had a commercial operation.

5. K. Brown, *Invention of the Board Canoe*, 7.

6. Ibid., 10–11.

7. Ibid., 23.

8. K. Brown, *Canadian Canoe Company*, 13.

9. K. Brown, *Invention of the Board Canoe*, 8–9. See also Roberts and Shackleton, *The Canoe*, 238.

10. K. Brown, *Canadian Canoe Company*, 21–22.

11. Ibid., 102.

12. Ibid., 109.

13. Ibid., 25.

14. The traditional assumption was that the PCC bought OCC following the fire. But see K. Brown, *Canadian Canoe Company*, chapters 2 and 3. In correspondence with Norman Sims in 2013, Brown said, "I think that the correct story is that Rogers gave his blessing and support to a group of businessmen who were his friends and associates to start a new company before the fire. And the paperwork was in place for them to do so. It was after the fire that he actually sold what was left of the OCC to the PCC. This would have been some inventory, designs, moulds, and catalogue images. And the right to say that it was the successor company."

15. Roger MacGregor, *When the Chestnut Was in Flower*, 55, quoting from *The Daily Gleaner* newspaper on July 16, 1904.

16. Roger MacGregor, *When the Chestnut Was in Flower*, 101–10.

17. Ibid., 164–74.

18. Moores, "From Forest to Factory," 186–87.

19. K. Brown, *Canadian Canoe Company*, 122.

20. Ibid., 117–19.

21. Ibid., 121. See also Hoffman, "History of the American Canoe Association."

22. Manley, *Rushton and His Times*, chap. 2.

23. Sears, *Canoeing the Adirondacks*, 86.

24. Ibid., 75.

25. Ibid., 81.

26. Ibid., 76.

27. Ibid., 58.

28. Bond, *Boats and Boating in the Adirondacks*, 99.

29. Ibid., 126.

30. Manley, *Rushton and His Times*, 50.

31. J. Henry Rushton to Nessmuk [George Washington Sears], November 1, 1882, St. Lawrence County Historical Association, Canton, N.Y.

32. Rushton to Nessmuk, November 23, 1882, St. Lawrence County Historical Association, Canton, N.Y. Nathaniel H. Bishop paddled his "paper" canoe, the *Maria Theresa*, about 2,500 miles from Quebec City in Canada to Cedar Keys, Florida, in 1874–75. It was 18 feet long and 58 pounds, made of a wooden frame covered by thick waterproofed cardboard, by the Waters (later Waters & Balch) company of Troy, New York. The foremost manufacturers of paper boats, Waters used a thick cardboard, about ⅛ inch. The decks might have been varnished linen, as was commonly used on rowing shells, of which Waters was also a prominent builder.

33. Jerome, *Adirondack Passage*, 2.

34. Sears, *Canoeing the Adirondacks*, 34–35.

35. Jerome, *Adirondack Passage*, 4.

36. Sears, *Canoeing the Adirondacks*, 23; Rushton to Nessmuk, November 8, 1882, St. Lawrence County Historical Association, Canton, N.Y.

37. Sears, *Canoeing the Adirondacks*, 176.

38. Bond, *Boats and Boating in the Adirondacks*, 86.

39. Crowley, *Rushton's Rowboats and Canoes*, vii.

40. Bishop, *Voyage of the Paper Canoe*, 69–70.

41. Bond, *Boats and Boating in the Adirondacks*, 107.

42. Ibid., 108. The participant quoted in Bond is Florence Waters Snedeker, *A Family Canoe Trip* (1892), 86 and 97.

43. ACA details are taken from Hoffman, "History of the American Canoe Association." Wulsin's trip is described in Manley, *Rushton and His Times*, 31–43.

44. The 1926 ACA gathering, an exception to the string of meetings on Sugar Island, was held at Turtle Island in Lake George. See Hoffman, "History of the American Canoe Association."

45. Emmett Smith, interview with Norman Sims, November 4, 2013.

46. Bond, *Boats and Boating in the Adirondacks*, 108.

47. Ibid., 109.

48. Hoffman, "History of the American Canoe Association," 95, 97.

49. Summers, interview with Norman Sims, September 27, 2013.

50. Bond, *Boats and Boating in the Adirondacks*, 123.

51. "Modified Racing Canoe Proposed," *New York Times*, February 21, 1915.

52. Hoffman, "History of the American Canoe Association."

53. Moores, "From Forest to Factory," 178–79.

54. Rushton to Nessmuk, April 25, 1884, St. Lawrence County Historical Association, Canton, N.Y.

55. Rushton to Nessmuk, September 14, 1884, St. Lawrence County Historical Association, Canton, N.Y.

56. Bond, *Boats and Boating in the Adirondacks*, 147.

57. Manley, *Rushton and His Times*, 128–30.

### JULE FOX MARSHALL

1. Unless otherwise indicated, all quotations from Jule Fox Marshall came from interviews with Norman Sims or letters exchanged in 1980–81.

2. Zuk, "Cruising Class Sailing: 100 Year History, 1907–2006," in *Stories of a Century of Canoeing and Canoes*.

3. Hoffman, "History of the American Canoe Association," 182.

### 5. WOOD-AND-CANVAS CANOES

1. Crowley, *Rushton's Rowboats and Canoes*, 30–59. Catalog, Old Town Canoe Company (1903), 8; available from the Wooden Canoe Heritage Association (WCHA).

2. Catalog, B. N. Morris Canoe Company (1901), 10; available from the WCHA.

3. Manley, *Rushton and His Times*, 143.

4. Dan Miller, interview with Norman Sims, November 5, 2013.

5. Crowley, *Rushton's Rowboats and Canoes*, 43.

6. Ibid.

7. Manley, *Rushton and His Times*, 148.

8. Ibid., 149.

9. Ibid., 147–51.

10. *Peterborough Review*, July 26, 1878.

11. Quoted in K. Brown, *Canadian Canoe Company*, 19, from Stephenson's patent registration dated June 7, 1879.

12. Several canvas-covered canoes were made earlier. A man claimed in *Forest and Stream* magazine in 1910 that he had built one in 1858; *Forest and Stream* 60 (September 3, 1910): 385. Others gently disputed his claims and told how the heaviest grade of cotton duck was originally treated on such boats: "The canvas is treated on one or both surfaces with oil paint, the[n] stretched very tightly over the cedar hull and heavily filled with several coats of paint, each one of which is rubbed down when dry. The finishing coat is spar varnish"; *Forest and Stream* 60 (October 1, 1910): 546. Paint was not an adequate treatment, which helps explain why canvas did not catch on for a while. The Cree in northern Quebec and the Natives north of the St. Lawrence River pioneered the use of canvas for patching and as a canoe covering. But they used the same building techniques as with birch, meaning that the forms were spread on the ground and the ribs pushed down into the canvas; Moores, "From Forest to Factory," 180. Bond wrote in *Boats and Boating in the Adirondacks*, 151: "The inventor of the wood-canvas canoe was supposedly a Penobscot Indian guide. Dillon Wallace, a contributor to *Outing* magazine, who took wood-canvas canoes on several Labrador adventures, wrote that in patching his birchbark with a scrap of heavy canvas in the 1850s, the Penobscot had the bright idea of completely replacing the bark with canvas." Bond cites Dillon Wallace, "The Canoe Yesterday and Today," *Hunting and Fishing* (March 1929).

13. Quoted from Edward M. White, interview in the *Old Town Enterprise* newspaper in 1901, in Stelmok and Thurlow, *Wood and Canvas Canoe*, 25.

14. See "The Canoe Builders of Maine" at http://wcha.org/legacypages/maine-list.htm.

15. Catalog, B. N. Morris Canoe Company (Veazie, Maine: n.d.), 1; republished by the WCHA.

16. Morris details from Klos, *Morris Canoe*. Charlie was born in 1860 and Bert in 1866, before and after their father served in the Civil War as a member of the Maine Volunteers.

17. Audette and Baker, *Old Town Canoe Company*, 13.

18. Roger MacGregor mentions that the metal clinching bands were invented by Dan Herald and patented in 1871. Herald canoes were seen in Maine before Gerrish built his canoe, and the metal bands for clinching nails may have been copied from Herald's boats. Roger MacGregor, *When the Chestnut Was in Flower*, 68–71. The practice did not become standard in building all-wood canoes.

19. In 1890, the carriage industry was centered in Cincinnati, where eighty carriage companies produced 130,000 vehicles a year. The Studebaker carriage company was located in South Bend, Indiana, and Abbot, Downing & Co. in Concord, New Hampshire, produced the popular Concord Coach; see Fox, *Working Horses*, 3.

20. Catalog, Veazie Canoe Company, *Canvas Covered Canoes and Accessories* (Bangor, Maine: n.d.), 3; available in digital format from the WCHA.

21. See Moores, "From Forest to Factory." The *Annual Register of Maine* for the years 1887 and 1891 (pages 558 and 621, respectively) lists "Chas. Morris carriages" in Veazie, Maine. Charles Morris was Bert Morris's brother and eventually his partner in the canoe company.

22. Bond, *Boats and Boating in the Adirondacks*, 152, citing J. Henry Rushton, notebook no. 3, p. 64, St. Lawrence County Historical Association, Canton, N.Y.

23. Thanks to Jon Goodman for advice on early materials. For details on sizing and gesso, see Thompson, *Materials and Techniques of Medieval Painting*, 23–74; and Mayer, *Artist's Handbook of Materials and Techniques*, 241–75.

24. Depending on what one means by the term "wilderness," it may have been gone for thousands of years on the North

American continent. Some people think of wilderness as the land before people arrived. But North and South America were populated by large and sophisticated Native cultures for thousands of years before the Europeans arrived. What Europeans found—or imagined in the 1890s—was hardly wilderness by that definition.

25. Twain, *Autobiography of Mark Twain*, 1:96.

26. See James F. Kieley, "A Brief History of the National Park Service," U.S. Department of the Interior, 1940.

27. Benson Gray, WCHA forum, November 9, 2011, at http://forums.wcha.org/showthread.php?7166-Maine-Register-research. Gray is related to the family that founded the Old Town Canoe Company.

28. See the information on Gerrish at http://forums.wcha.org/knowledgebase/Manufacturers:E+H+Gerrish.

29. The date is uncertain, but Benson Gray places it in 1900 from family records. In a November 2013 WCHA forum, Gray wrote, "The first [*Old Town Enterprise*] newspaper reference to the Old Town Canoe Company is from October 13th, 1900 at http://oldtown.advantage-preservatio...0-10-13-page-1 titled 'CANOES BY THE HUNDRED' with the subtitle 'Another Factory to Be Added to Old Town's Busy Industries' with the conclusion that 'Since the organization of the company is not fully completed it is not possible at this time to name correctly the interested parties, but there is no question of doubt as to the ultimate success of the venture.' This is consistent with the other references listed at http://forums.wcha.org/showthread.php?10647 so there may not be much to work with." The first canoes may not have been built for a year or more.

30. Audette and Baker, *Old Town Canoe Company*, 116.

31. Gray, *Ancestry of Samuel Braley Gray*, 295.

32. All quotations from Benson Gray are from interviews with Norman Sims.

33. Audette and Baker, *Old Town Canoe Company*, 15–16.

34. According to legal documents held by Benson Gray.

35. Lena Dillingham Gray, letter to Sam Gray, December 8, 1900, in possession of Benson Gray.

36. K. Brown, *Canadian Canoe Company*, 40. The Old Town

website says, "our first wood and canvas canoe was built by A. E. Wickett in 1898 behind the local entrepreneur George Gray's hardware store." Dates for the first canoes vary. See "Heritage," at http://www.oldtowncanoe.com/craftsmanship/heritage/.

37. Audette and Baker, *Old Town Canoe Company*, 37, and interview with Benson Gray.

38. See Moores, "From Forest to Factory," 183.

39. Interview and written correspondence with Benson Gray.

40. Company records in the personal possession of Benson Gray.

41. The Chain of Lakes includes Cedar Lake, Lake Calhoun, and Lake of the Isles, which are connected and form part of the urban parks district in Minneapolis, and also Lake Harriet. For Canada, see McMullin, "Revolt at Riverside," 484.

42. Dan Miller, quoted from the WCHA website http://forums.wcha.org/showthread.php?8397-Please-Help-ID-the-Manufacturer.

43. Miller, interview.

44. Moores, "From Forest to Factory," 179.

45. Klos, *Morris Canoe*, 124.

46. Pollock, "Down by the Riverside."

47. Ode, "Canoe Craze." See also David C. Smith, "Canoe Jam on the Chain of Lakes," *Minneapolis Park History* (blog), March 20, 2012, http://minneapolisparkhistory.com/category/lake-of-the-isles/.

48. McMullin, "Revolt at Riverside," 482–94.

49. Audette and Baker, *Old Town Canoe Company*, 31; McMullin, "Revolt at Riverside," 484–85.

50. Quoted in "Post Cards from the Collection of the Newton Historical Museum," http://www.newtonma.gov/gov/historic/events/past/canoeing/essay.asp.

51. See "Kissing in Canoes," *Dateline: Boston 1905* (blog), July 29, 2008, http://boston1905.blogspot.com/2008/07/kissing-in-canoes.html.

52. McMullin, "Revolt at Riverside," 486, citing the *Boston Journal*, August 22, 1903; and *Boston Sunday Globe*, August 23, 1903, 8.

53. *Boston Sunday Globe*, August 23, 1903, 8.

54. McMullin, "Revolt at Riverside," 487, citing the *Boston Herald* on August 28, 1903.

55. McMullin, "Revolt at Riverside," 490.

56. The terms come from ibid., 482–94.

57. Ibid., 491.

58. Ibid., 492.

59. Dwight Eisenhower, *At Ease: Stories I Tell to Friends* (New York: Doubleday, 1967), 3–4, quoted in Woodruff, "Romancing with Ike in an Old Town," 6.

60. "Post Cards," http://www.newtonma.gov/gov/historic /events/past/canoeing/essay.asp.

61. The 1927 Old Town catalog cover was an exception that harkened back to the courting theme, but by that time it may have been seen as a nostalgic image.

62. *Printers' Ink: A Journal for Advertisers* 103, no. 2 (April 11, 1918): 111.

63. Quotations from Pam Wedd are from an interview with Norman Sims on July 18, 2014.

64. Quotations from Emily Schoelzel are from an interview with Norman Sims on October 20, 2014.

65. Quotations from Alice Zalonis Brylawski are from correspondence and an interview with Norman Sims on November 5, 2014.

66. Quotations from Rollin Thurlow are from an interview with Norman Sims on July 17, 2015.

67. For more information on contemporary birch-bark, all-wood, and wood-and-canvas canoe builders and suppliers, see the builder list at the WCHA website: http://www.wcha.org/build supply/.

## TOM SEAVEY

1. All quotations from Tom Seavey come from interviews with Norman Sims, including an extended one on November 20, 2012.

## CANOE SAILS

1. Bradshaw, *Canoe Rig*, 78.

2. Ibid., 22.

3. Unless otherwise noted, all quotations come from several personal conversations between Norman Sims and Todd Bradshaw.

## 6. SYNTHETIC CANOES

1. Information on Kwolek and her career is taken from D.E. Brown, *Inventing Modern America*, 62–65; and Ikenson, *Patents*, 126–27.

2. Kevlar is five times stronger than steel, heat resistant, and lighter than fiberglass. A bulletproof vest is made of many layers of Kevlar fibers; when a bullet strikes it, the force of the blow is distributed among the fibers, most of which do not break.

3. Hays and Hays, *Beauty, Health and Permanence*, 244.

4. *San Francisco Call*, April 26, 1896, 29.

5. Quoted in "French Aluminum Yacht Vendenesse," 406.

6. Ibid.

7. Kemp, *Yacht Architecture*, 543–44.

8. Dwight, *Aluminum Design*, 26.

9. Jennings, *The Canoe*, 210.

10. Dwight, *Aluminum Design*, 27.

11. Thruelsen, *Grumman Story*, 21.

12. Birmabright was also the material used in the bodies of the famous British Land Rover trucks. (There is an association of Land Rover owners called the Birmabright Brotherhood.) The Thunderbolt, a car successful in setting the land speed record in the late 1930s, had Birmabright panels on its chassis.

13. Pulling, *Principles of Canoeing*, 22.

14. Thruelsen, *Grumman Story*, 222.

15. Ibid.

16. Ibid., 223.

17. Jennings, *The Canoe*, 210.

18. Moores, "From Forest to Factory," 187.

19. Ibid., 189.

20. Henry, "Surprise Visitor."

21. The Grumman canoe line was sold to Outboard Marine Corporation (OMC) in 1990; it was sold again in 1996 to former Grumman managers and investors and renamed the Marathon Boat Group. The new owners licensed the Grumman name in 2000 and boats became known as Grummans again.

22. Spurr, *Heart of Glass*, 45.

23. Pulling, *Principles of Canoeing*, 32.

24. Benidickson, *Idleness, Water, and a Canoe*, 132.

25. Audette and Baker, *Old Town Canoe Company*, 87.

26. Riviere, *Open Canoe*, 100; also http://www.marathon boatstore.com/aboutus.asp.

27. Spurr, *Heart of Glass*, 7.

28. Knox, "Fiberglass Reinforcement," 136.

29. Spurr, *Heart of Glass*, 18.

30. Meikle, *American Plastic*, 158.

31. Spurr, *Heart of Glass*, 40.

32. "New Sectional Canoe," 216.

33. Manley, *Rushton and His Times*.

34. Freinkel, *Plastic*, 238.

35. Meikle, *American Plastic*, 191.

36. Graner, "Marine Applications," 701.

37. Fenichell, *Plastic*, 248.

38. Audette and Baker, *Old Town Canoe Company*, 97.

39. Riviere, *Open Canoe*, 120. Benson Gray states that Uniroyal was selling premade Royalex hulls to Thompson, Rivers & Gilman and many others in the 1960s. These firms would finish them and brand them as their own.

40. Mihell, "Royalex Revolution," 18. Early Old Town experiments with ABS boats had promise, Benson Gray said, but the ABS deteriorated very rapidly in sunlight. One of the Old Town designers said it was a good material for paddling at night. After a sun-induced fading experience, the company starting using a vinyl covering.

41. Pyette, "Royalex Is Dead." There was no immediate interest in a buyer for the line. In 2016, Canadian company Esquif International was developing a Royalex replacement called T-Formex.

42. Susan Audette, interview with Norman Sims, November 26, 2012.

43. Benson Gray, interview with Norman Sims, August 2, 2011.

44. "Old Town Wooden Canoe Production Estimates by Model," http://www.wcha.org/catalogs/old-town/models.html. See also Old Town promotional video.

45. Walzer, "Pelican International," 24.

46. "Old Town Wooden Canoe Production Estimates by Model," http://www.wcha.org/catalogs/old-town/models.html.

47. Riviere, *Open Canoe*, 100–101.

48. Mike Cichanowski, interview with Mark Neuzil, January 16, 2013.

49. Cross, *Social History of Leisure*.

50. Ibid., 124.

51. Dulles, *America Learns to Play*, 365.

52. Van Slyck, *A Manufactured Wilderness*, 83.

53. Ibid., 87.

54. Cross, *Social History of Leisure*, 205.

55. "Gum Tree Canoe," lyrics by S. S. Steele, in *Plantation Melodies* (Boston: J. H. Bufford, 1847).

56. Giordano, *Fun and Games*, 168.

57. Ibid., 176.

58. Wyatt, "Canoe Makers," 1.

59. Haas, *A Snapshot*, 3, 4.

## CANOE PATENTS

1. U.S. Patent Office Letters Patent #647,542, dated April 17, 1900. Serial number 732,387.

2. U.S. Patent Office Letters Patent #1,387,957, dated August 16, 1921. Serial number 423,792.

3. U.S. Patent Office Letters Patent #155,710, dated October 6, 1874.

4. U.S. Patent Office Letters Patent #234,164, dated November 9, 1880.

5. U.S. Patent Office Letters Patent #557,647, dated April 7, 1896.

## CANOES IN WARTIME

1. Poling, *The Canoe*, 75.

2. Roberts and Shackleton, *The Canoe*, 71.

3. The first order of these unique boats came from the Folbot Folding Boats Ltd., London. The practical use of the boats in small-scale raiding was demonstrated by a Lieutenant Courtney, who paddled under cover of darkness to a British carrier anchored in the Clyde estuary, stole a gun cover, and delivered it, dripping wet, to the ship's captain, who was attending an onshore conference.

4. Rees, *Cockleshell Canoes*. The story of the raid was retold in the 1955 movie *The Cockleshell Heroes*.

5. "Amphibious Operations, Evacuations, Invasions, Landings, Raids, Special Operations," http://www.naval-history .net/WW2CampaignsAmphibious.htm. The British had also fumbled around with canoes in planning the ill-fated Siege of Khartoum in Egypt in 1884, hiring Canadians to paddle and portage, but in the end the canoes proved ill-suited to the task.

## SQUARE-STERN CANOES

1. Roberts and Shackleton, *The Canoe*, 49.

2. Audette and Baker, *Old Town Canoe Company*, 67.

3. Stelmok, *Art of the Canoe*, 38–41.

4. Seliga expert Dan Lindberg reported that a thirty-fourth square-stern was built to order on a regular 17-foot form and the stern flattened. Email with Mark Neuzil, December 9, 2015.

## 7. THE HUMAN-POWERED MOVEMENT

1. Mike Cichanowski, interview with Mark Neuzil, January 16, 2013.

2. Jameson, *Silent Spring Revisited*, 35; and Lytle, *Gentle Subversive*.

3. Souder, *On a Farther Shore*; and Lear, *Rachel Carson*.

4. Lytle, *Gentle Subversive*, 199.

5. Lear, *Rachel Carson*, 420.

6. Jameson, *Silent Spring Revisited*, 36.

7. Souder, *On a Farther Shore*, 392.

8. Ibid., 84.

9. Souder, e-mail with Mark Neuzil, March 7, 2013.

10. Souder, *On a Farther Shore*, 393.

11. Grant, "Symbols and Myths," 15.

12. Coatsworth, *Indians of Quetico*, iv.

13. Lapping and Furuseth, *Big Places, Big Plans*, 143.

14. Grant, "Symbols and Myths," 22.

15. N.a., "Come Celebrate Pennsylvania's Wild Heritage and the 40th Anniversary of the Wilderness Act," *Friends of the Allegheny Wilderness* newsletter, 4, no. 2 (June 2004): 1.

16. Wilderness Act of 1964, Section 2, Part C.

17. Turner, *Promise of Wilderness*, 50.

18. Ibid., 18–19.

19. Ibid., 37.

20. Wild and Scenic Rivers Act of 1968, Section 1, Part B.

21. Easton, *Black Tide*, 6.

22. Ibid., 89.

23. Ibid., 8.

24. Ibid., 49.

25. Ibid., 89.

26. Neuzil, *Environment and the Press*, 192.

27. Ibid., 194.

28. McCann, "Hundreds Hike for Clean Land."

29. Nelson, Campbell, and Wozniak, *Beyond Earth Day*, 13.

30. Oatman-Stanford, "Love Boats."

31. Hunter, "Olympic Gold Generates Powerful Reaction."

32. Amyot's success was not without controversy. Canadian Olympic officials had refused to pay his way to Germany for the games; his boating club raised the money. Amyot was also coach and manager of the canoe team.

33. Oakville Sports Hall of Fame, http://oshof.com/vhof /cain_lao.html.

34. Millson, "Cain Raises Record Total."

35. Millson, "Canoeist Can't Get Enough."

36. Ibid.

37. Ibid.

### PADDLES

1. Weis, *Conversation with Gene Jensen*.
2. A patent issued in 1951 (#2,578,208) looks like a giant spoon, with the bowl of the spoon bent from the handle.
3. Stanley, "Know Your Paddles."
4. Roberts, "Lilly Dipping It Ain't," 117–18.
5. A good source is Gidmark and Warren, *Canoe Paddles*.
6. Roy MacGregor, *Canoe Country*, 72.

### CANOE PACKS

1. McPhee, *Giving Good Weight*, 140.
2. Ibid., 151.
3. Dennis, *From a Wooden Canoe*, 26.

### 8. CANOE TRIPPING

1. McPhee, "Draft No. 4," 34–35.
2. Ibid., 35.
3. Mackenzie, *Journals*, 18.
4. Ibid., 21–22.
5. Ibid., 42–43.
6. Ibid., 33–34.
7. Ibid., 220.

8. Nute, *The Voyageur*, 232–33.
9. Mackenzie, *Journals*, 352–60.
10. Ibid., 364–65.
11. Ibid., 371.
12. Thoreau, *Maine Woods*, 89.
13. Thoreau, *Maine Woods*, Allegash & East Branch—Part 7.
14. McPhee, *Survival of the Bark Canoe*, 117.
15. Adney, *Travel Journals of Tappan Adney*, 105.
16. Ibid., 117–20. On page 120 is a line drawing by Adney of their run over the falls.
17. See Adney and Chapelle, *Bark Canoes*, 80 for an illustration of shoes by Adney.
18. Adney, *Travel Journals of Tappan Adney*, 112.
19. This is the opening passage of *The River* by Pare Lorentz, produced for the Farm Security Administration, U.S. Department of Agriculture, in 1938.
20. Sevareid, *Canoeing with the Cree*, 67–68.
21. Ibid., 135–37.
22. McPhee, *Coming into the Country*, 6.
23. Ibid., 5.
24. Ibid., 14–17.
25. Olson, *Singing Wilderness*, 83.

# Bibliography

Adney, [Edwin] Tappan. "The Building of a Birch Canoe." *Outing* (May 1900): 185–89.

———. "How an Indian Birch-Bark Canoe Is Made." *Harper's Young People*, supplement, July 29, 1890.

———. *The Travel Journals of Tappan Adney, 1887–1890*. Edited by C. Ted Behne. Fredericton, New Brunswick: Goose Lane Editions, 2010.

Adney, Edwin Tappan, and Howard I. Chapelle. *The Bark Canoes and Skin Boats of North America*. 2nd ed. Washington, D.C.: Smithsonian Institution, 1964.

Ahlgren, C. E., and Isabel Ahlgren. *Lob Trees in the Wilderness*. Minneapolis: University of Minnesota Press, 1984.

"Algonquin." In *The Canadian Encyclopedia*, http://www .thecanadianencyclopedia.ca/en/article/algonquin/.

"Algonquin Elder William Commanda Was Honoured for Efforts to Bridge Cultures." *The Globe and Mail* (Toronto), August 3, 2011.

American Canoe Association. *Canoeing (Outdoor Adventures)*. Paper/DVD ed. Champaign, Ill.: Human Kinetics, 2008.

———. *Introduction to Paddling: Canoeing Basics for Lakes and Rivers*. 2nd ed. Birmingham: Menasha Ridge Press, 1996.

Anderson, Luther A. *A Guide to Canoe Camping: An Illustrated Manual for All Who Enjoy the Water-Wilderness of North America*. Chicago: Reilly and Lee, 1969.

Angier, Bradford, and Zack Taylor. *Introduction to Canoeing*. Mechanicsburg, Pa.: Stackpole Books, 1973.

Audette, Susan T., and David E. Baker. *The Old Town Canoe Company: Our First Hundred Years*. Gardiner, Maine: Tilbury House Publishers, 1998.

Baden-Powell, Robert Stephenson Smyth, Baron Baden-Powell of Gilwell. *Paddle Your Own Canoe*. Facsimile of 1939 ed. Dallas: Stevens Publishing, 1995.

Bartoo, William, Richard Butz, and John Montague. *Building the Six-Hour Canoe*. New York: Tiller, 2000.

Bearse, Ray. *The Canoe Camper's Handbook*. New York: Winchester Press, 1974.

Beattie, Judith Hudson, and Helen M. Buss, eds. *Undelivered Letters to Hudson's Bay Company Men on the Northwest*

Coast of America, 1830–57. Vancouver, British Columbia: UBC Press, 2003.

Bell, Patricia J. *Roughing It Elegantly: A Practical Guide to Canoe Camping*. 2nd ed. Eden Prairie, Minn.: Cat's-Paw Press, 1994.

Benidickson, Jamie. *Idleness, Water, and a Canoe: Reflections on Paddling for Pleasure*. Toronto: University of Toronto Press, 1997.

Bigsby, John Jeremiah. *The Shoe and Canoe: Or Pictures of Travel in the Canadas*. 1850. Reprint, New York: Paladin, 1969.

Bishop, Nathaniel H. *Voyage of the Paper Canoe: A Geographical Journey of 2500 Miles, from Quebec to the Gulf of Mexico, During the Years 1874–5*. Boston: Lee and Shepard, 1878.

Black Hawk. *Autobiography of Ma-Ka-Tai-Me-She-Kia-Kiak, or Black Hawk, Embracing the Traditions of His Nation, Various Wars in Which He Has Been Engaged, and His Account of the Cause and General History of the Black Hawk War of 1832, His Surrender, and Travels Through the United States*. Interpreted by Antoine LeClair. Edited by J. B. Patterson. Includes *Life, Death and Burial of the Old Chief, Together with a History of the Black Hawk War*, by J. B. Patterson. Cincinnati, Ohio: J. B. Patterson, 1833.

Boas, Franz. "Art of the North Pacific Coast of North America." *Science* 4, no. 82 (July 24, 1896).

———. "The Decorative Art of the Indians of the North Pacific Coast." *Bulletin of the American Museum of Natural History* 9 (1897).

———. *Primitive Art*. Mineola, N.Y.: Dover, 2010. Originally published in 1927.

Bolz, J. Arnold. *Portage into the Past: By Canoe along the Minnesota-Ontario Boundary Waters*. The Fesler-Lampert Minnesota Heritage Book Series. 1963. Reprint, Minneapolis: University of Minnesota Press, 1999.

Bond, Hallie E. *Boats and Boating in the Adirondacks*. Syracuse, N.Y.: Adirondack Museum, 1995.

Boswell, Randy. "Historic Canoe to Return to Canada." *Calgary Herald*, December 15, 2010.

———. "'Precious' Canadiana Rescued." *Edmonton Journal*, May 22, 2007.

———. "Soldier's Journal Uncovers 200-Year-Old Canoe." *Edmonton Journal*, December 28, 2010.

Bourque, Bruce. *The Swordfish Hunters: The History and Ecology of an Ancient American Sea People*. Bunker Hill, Ind.: Bunker Hill Press, 2012.

Bradshaw, Todd. *Canoe Rig: The Essence and the Art: Sailpower for Antique and Traditional Canoes*. Brooklin, Maine: Wooden Boat Publications, 2000.

Bridge, Raymond. *The Complete Canoeist's Guide*. New York: Scribner, 1978.

Brown, David E. *Inventing Modern America: From the Microwave to the Mouse*. Cambridge, Mass.: MIT Press, 2002.

Brown, Ken. *The Canadian Canoe Company and the Early Peterborough Canoe Factories*. Peterborough, Ontario: Cover to Cover, 2011.

———. *The Invention of the Board Canoe: The Peterborough Stories from their Sources*. Peterborough, Ontario: Canadian Canoe Museum, 2001.

Browning, Peter. *The Last Wilderness: 600 Miles by Canoe and Portage in the Northwest Territories*. 2nd ed. Lafayette, Ind.: Great West Books, 1989.

Bryce, George. *The Remarkable History of the Hudson's Bay Company, Including That of the French Traders of North-Western Canada and of the North-West, XY, and Astor Fur Companies*. 2nd ed. New York: B. Franklin, 1968.

Burns, Russell M., and Barbara H. Honkala. *Silvics of North America*. Washington, D.C.: U.S. Department of Agriculture, Forest Service, 1990.

Burroughs, John. "A Taste of Maine Birch." *The Atlantic Monthly*, June 1881.

Callan, Kevin. *Dazed but Not Confused: Tales of a Wilderness Wanderer*. Toronto: Dundurn, 2013.

———. *Gone Canoeing: Wilderness Weekends in Southern Ontario*. Erin, Ontario: Boston Mills Press, 2001.

Campbell, Marjorie Wilkins. *The Nor'westers: The Fight for the Fur Trade*. Calgary, Alberta: Fifth House, 2002.

Carter, Sarah Alexandra. *Man's Mission of Subjugation: The Publications of John Maclean, John McDougall and Egerton R. Young, Nineteenth-Century Methodist Missionaries in Western Canada*. Saskatoon, Saskatchewan: 1980.

Cary, Bob. *The Big Wilderness Canoe Manual: A Veteran Guide and Outfitter Tells You All about Camping, Paddling, and Voyaging in the Spirit of the New Outdoor Ethic*. New York: McKay, 1978.

Champlain, Samuel de. *Champlain's Voyages*. 1603. Reprint, Boston: Prince Society, 1880.

Chapel, H. [error for Chapelle]. "The Seminole Canoe." *Forest and Stream* 95, no. 5 (May 1922): 210.

Chapelle, Howard I. "The Migrations of an American Boat Type." *Contributions from the Museum of History and Technology*, Bulletin 228 (1961).

Chapman, Patrick F. *The Willits Brothers and Their Canoes: Wooden Boat Craftsmen in Washington State, 1908–1967*. Jefferson, N.C.: McFarland and Company, 2006.

Chittenden, Hiram Martin. *The American Fur Trade of the Far West*. 1902. Reprint, Lincoln: University of Nebraska Press, 1986.

Churchill, James. *Paddling the Boundary Waters and Voyageurs National Park. Regional Paddling Series*. Santa Fe: Falcon, 2003.

Coatsworth, Emerson S. *The Indians of Quetico*. Toronto: Published for the Quetico Foundation by University of Toronto Press, 1957.

Cook, Ramsay. *The Voyages of Jacques Cartier*. Toronto: University of Toronto Press, 1993.

Cross, Gary. *A Social History of Leisure since 1600*. State College, Penn.: Venture Publishing, 1990.

Crowley, William. *Rushton's Rowboats and Canoes: The 1903 Catalog in Perspective*. Blue Mountain Lake, N.Y.: Adirondack Museum, 1983.

Curran, David. *Canoe Trip: Alone in the Maine Wilderness*. New York: Hellgate Press, 2010.

Davidson, D. S. "Folk Tales from Grand Lake Victoria, Quebec." *Journal of American Folk-Lore* 41, no. 160 (1928): 275–82.

Davidson, James West, and John Rugge. *The Complete Wilderness Paddler*. New York: Knopf, 1976; 1st Vintage Books ed., New York: Vintage, 1982.

Dennis, Jerry. *From a Wooden Canoe: Reflections on Canoeing, Camping, and Classic Equipment*. New York: St. Martin's Griffin, 2000.

Dickason, Olive Patricia. *The Myth of the Savage: And the Beginnings of French Colonialism in the Americas*. Edmonton: University of Alberta Press, 1984.

*Dictionary of Canadian Biography*. Toronto: University of Toronto Press, 1991. http://www.biographi.ca/en/index.php.

Dolin, Eric Jay. *Fur, Fortune, and Empire: The Epic History of the Fur Trade in America*. New York: W. W. Norton, 2010.

Drabik, Harry. *Spirit of Canoe Camping*. Minneapolis: Nodin Press, 1981.

Duffek, Karen, and Charlotte Townsend-Gault, eds. *Bill Reid and Beyond: Expanding on Modern Native Art*. Vancouver, British Columbia: Douglas and McIntyre, 2004.

Dulles, Foster Rhea. *America Learns to Play: A History of Popular Recreation, 1607–1940*. New York: D. Appleton-Century, 1940.

Dwight, John. *Aluminium Design and Construction*. London: E and FN Spon, 1999.

Easton, Robert Olney. *Black Tide: The Santa Barbara Oil Spill and Its Consequences*. New York: Delacorte Press, 1972.

Edwards, Robert. *Aboriginal Bark Canoes of the Murray Valley*. London: Robert Hale, 1973.

Ellis, Alec R. *Canoeing for Beginners*. 4th ed. Glasgow: Brown, Son and Ferguson, 1971.

Enys, John. *The American Journals of Lt. John Enys*. Edited by Elizabeth Cometti. Blue Mountain Lake, N.Y.: Adirondack Museum, 1976.

Evans, Doug. *Noah's Last Canoe: The Lost Art of Cree Birch Bark Canoe Building*. Winnipeg: Great Plains Publications, 2008.

Evans, G. Heberton. *Canoeing Wilderness Waters*. Lancaster, England: Gazelle Book Services, 1975.

"Expert Reveals Detail on Canoe's Origins." *The Western Morning News* (Plymouth, England), February 5, 2011.

Farmer, Charles J. *The Digest Book of Canoes, Kayaks, and Rafts: The How-To of Canoeing, Kayaking, and Rafting*. New York: Follett, 1978.

Fenichell, Stephen. *Plastic: The Making of a Synthetic Century*. New York: HarperBusiness, 1996.

Ferguson, Stuart. "Ancient Artifacts: A Vessel of Indian Culture." *Wall Street Journal*, August 3, 2011.

Fillingham, Paul. *The Complete Book of Canoeing and Kayaking*. New York: Drake Publishers, 1974.

Finkelstein, Max, and James Stone. *Paddling the Boreal Forest: Rediscovering A. P. Low*. Toronto: Dundurn Press, 2004.

Fischer, David Hackett. *Champlain's Dream: The European Founding of North America*. New York: Simon and Schuster, 2008.

Fisher, Ron, and Sam Abell. *Still Waters, White Waters: Exploring America's Rivers and Lakes*. Washington, D.C.: National Geographic Society, 1977.

Folsom, Randy. *Strip Built Canoe: How to Build a Beautiful, Lightweight, Cedar Strip Canoe*. New York: BookSurge Publishing, 2007.

Fowle, Otto. *Sault Ste. Marie and Its Great Waterway*. New York and London: G. P. Putnam's Sons, 1925.

Fox, Charles Philip. *Working Horses: Looking Back 100 Years to America's Horse-Drawn Days*. Whitewater, Wis.: Heart Prairie Press, 1990.

Franchere, Gabriel, and Milo Milton Quaife. *A Voyage to the Northwest Coast of America*. 1854. Reprint, Chicago: Lakeside Press, 1954.

Franks, C. E. S. *Canoe and White Water: From Essential to Sport*. Toronto: University of Toronto Press, 1977.

Frazier, Ian. *Great Plains*. New York: Farrar Straus Giroux, 1989.

Freinkel, Susan. *Plastic: A Toxic Love Story*. Boston: Houghton Mifflin Harcourt, 2011.

"The French Aluminum Yacht Vendenesse." *Scientific American*, June 30, 1894.

Frost, Robert, and Ed Young. *Birches*. New York: Henry Holt, 1988.

Fuhrmann, Mike. "Relic Canoe from 18th Century a 'Stunning Find.'" *Winnipeg Free Press*, August 18, 2012.

Furtman, Michael. *Canoe Country Camping: Wilderness Skills for the Boundary Waters and Quetico*. Minneapolis: University of Minnesota Press, 2002.

Gaines, Leslie, director. "Dugout Canoes: Tribal Canoe Journeys—Paddle to Suquamish, Washington." Video. Florida Museum of Natural History, August 2009, https://www.flmnh.ufl.edu/exhibits/limited-time-only/dugout-canoes/english-videos/.

Gibbon, John Murray. *The Romance of the Canadian Canoe*. Toronto: Ryerson Press, 1951.

Gidmark, David. *Birchbark Canoe: Living among the Algonquin*. New York: Diane, 1997.

Gidmark, David, and Denis Alsford. *Building a Birchbark Canoe*. Mechanicsburg, Pa.: Stackpole Books, 1994.

Gidmark, David, and Graham Warren. *Canoe Paddles: A Complete Guide to Making Your Own*. Toronto: Firefly Books, 2001.

Gilpatrick, Gil. *Building a Strip Canoe: Full-Sized Plans and Instructions for Eight Easy-to-Build, Field-Tested Canoes*. 2nd ed. East Petersburg, Pa.: Fox Chapel Publishing, 2010.

Giordano, Ralph G. *Fun and Games in Twentieth-Century America: A Historical Guide to Leisure*. Westport, Conn.: Greenwood Press, 2003.

Glazier, Willard W. *Down the Great River: Embracing an Account of the Discovery of the True Source of the Mississippi, Together with Views, Descriptive and Pictorial, . . . from Its Head Waters to the Gulf of Mexico*. San Francisco: Hubbard Brothers, 1891.

Gordon, I. Herbert. *The Complete Book of Canoeing*. 3rd ed. Santa Fe: Falcon, 2001.

Gough, Barry M. *First across the Continent: Sir Alexander Mackenzie*. Norman: University of Oklahoma Press, 1997.

Graner, William R. "Marine Applications." In *Handbook of Composites*, 699–721. New York: Van Nostrand Reinhold, 1982.

Grant, Shelagh. "Symbols and Myths: Images of the Canoe and North." In *Canexus: The Canoe in Canadian Culture*, edited by James Raffan and Bert Horwood, 5–25. Toronto: Betelgeuse Books, 1988.

Graves, John. *Goodbye to a River: A Narrative*. New York: Knopf, 1960.

Gray, Benson. "How to Start a Canoe Company: The Founders of the Old Town Canoe Company." *Wooden Canoe* 195 (June 2016): 5–7.

Gray, Ruth. *The Ancestry of Samuel Braley Gray and His Wife Bessie Pendleton Benson*. Boston: Ashburton Press, 2007.

Gregorich, Joseph. *The Apostle of the Chippewas: The Life Story of the Most Rev. Frederick Baraga, D.D., the First Bishop of Marquette*. Chicago: Bishop Baraga Association, 1932.

Grinnell, George James. *Death on the Barrens: A True Story of Courage and Tragedy in the Canadian Arctic*. Berkeley, Calif.: North Atlantic Books, 2010.

Gruchow, Paul. *Boundary Waters: The Grace of the Wild*. Minneapolis: Milkweed Editions, 1999.

Gullion, Laurie. *Canoeing (Outdoor Pursuits)*. Champaign, Ill.: Human Kinetics, 1993.

Haas, Glenn E. *A Snapshot of Recreational Boating in America*. Fort Collins: Colorado State University, 2010.

Haddon, Alfred C., and James Hornell. *Canoes of Oceania*. Honolulu, Hawaii: Bishop Museum Press, 1975.

Hadlock, Wendell S., and Ernest S. Dodge. "Canoe from the Penobscot River." *The American Neptune* 8, no. 4 (1948): 289–301.

Harmon, Daniel Williams. *A Journal of Voyages and Travels in the Interior of North America*. 1905. Reprint, New York: Allerton Book Co., 1922.

Harrison, David. *Sports Illustrated Canoeing*. San Francisco: Sports Illustrated, 1988.

Hays, Samuel P., and Barbara D. Hays. *Beauty, Health, and Permanence: Environmental Politics in the United States, 1955–1985*. Cambridge: Cambridge University Press, 1987.

Hayward, John D. *Canoeing with Sail and Paddle*. New York: Frederick A. Stokes, 1893.

Hazen, David. *The Stripper's Guide to Canoe-Building: With Drawings*. 5th ed. Novato, Calif.: Tamal Vista Publications, 1982.

Heidenreich, Conrad. *Huronia: A History and Geography of the Huron Indians, 1600–1650*. Toronto: McClelland and Stewart, 1971.

Hennessey, Tom. "Entirely by Hand . . . from the Ground Up." *Bangor Daily News*, September 8, 2007, http://archive .bangordailynews.com/2007/09/08/entirely-by-hand-from -the-ground-up/.

Henry, Dick. "A Surprise Visitor, A Different Name." *Фyast Флyer* (Homer L. Dodge Department of Physics and Astronomy newsletter, University of Oklahoma), 14, no. 1 (Autumn 2005): 1–8.

Heron, Francis. *Fort Garry Journal*. Montreal: Hudson's Bay Company, 1825.

Hitchcock, Don. "Canoes of the First Nations of the Pacific Northwest." *Don's Maps*, http://donsmaps.com/canoesnwc .html (accessed May 16, 2014).

Hodgins, Bruce W., and Gwyneth Hoyle. *Canoeing North into the Unknown: A Record of River Travel, 1874–1974*. Toronto: Dundurn Press, 1997.

Hoffman, Ronald. "The History of the American Canoe Association, 1880–1960." Ph.D. diss., Springfield College, June 1967.

Holling, Clancy. *Paddle-to-the-Sea*. Boston: Houghton Mifflin, 1941.

Holm, Bill. *Northwest Coast Indian Art: An Analysis of Form*. Seattle: University of Washington Press, 1965.

Hornell, James. *Water Transport: Origins and Early Evolution*. 1946. Reprint, Devon, England: David and Charles, 1970.

Hubbard, Lucius L. *Woods and Lakes of Maine: A Trip from Moosehead Lake to New Brunswick in a Birch-Bark Canoe, to which Are Added Some Indian Place-Names and Their Meanings, Now First Published.* Boston: J. R. Osgood, 1884.

Huneault, Kristina. "Placing Frances Anne Hopkins: A British-Born Artist in Colonial Canada." In *Local/Global: Women Artists in the 19th Century,* 179–200. Burlington, Vt.: Ashgate, 2006.

Hunter, Paul. "Olympic Gold Generates Powerful Reaction." *Toronto Star,* July 24, 2012.

Huth, John Edward. *The Lost Art of Finding Our Way.* Cambridge: Harvard University Press, 2013.

Ikenson, Ben. *Patents: Ingenious Inventions: How They Work and How They Came to Be.* New York: Black Dog and Leventhal, 2004.

Innis, Harold Adams. *The Fur Trade in Canada: An Introduction to Canadian Economic History.* 1930. Reprint, New Haven, Conn.: Yale University Press, 1962.

Jacobson, Cliff. *Basic Essentials Solo Canoeing.* Basic Essentials Series. 2nd ed. Santa Fe: Falcon, 1999.

———. *Boundary Waters Canoe Camping.* 2nd ed. Guilford, Conn.: Globe Pequot, 2000.

———. *Canoeing and Camping beyond the Basics.* How to Paddle Series. 30th Anniversary ed., 3rd ed. Santa Fe: Falcon, 2007.

———. *Expedition Canoeing: A Guide to Canoeing Wild Rivers in North America.* Falcon Guides Canoeing Series. 20th Anniversary ed., 4th ed. Santa Fe: Falcon, 2005.

James, William C. "The Canoe Trip as Religious Quest." *Studies in Religion* 10, no. 2 (1981): 151–66.

Jameson, Conor Mark. *Silent Spring Revisited.* London: Bloomsbury, 2012.

Jane, Cecil. *Select Documents Illustrating the Four Voyages of Columbus: Including Those Contained in R. H. Major's Select Letters of Christopher Columbus.* Vol. 1. London: Hakluyt Society, 1930.

Jaques, Florence Page. *Canoe Country.* Minneapolis: University of Minnesota Press, 1938.

Jennings, John. *Bark Canoes: The Art and Obsession of Tappan Adney.* Toronto: Firefly Books, 2004.

———. *The Canoe: A Living Tradition.* Toronto: Firefly Books, 2002.

Jennings, John, Bruce W. Hodgins, and Doreen Small. *The Canoe in Canadian Cultures.* Toronto: Natural Heritage/Natural History, 1999.

Jerome, Christine. *An Adirondack Passage: The Cruise of the Canoe* Sairy Gamp. New York: HarperCollins, 1994.

Jessup, Elon Huntington. *The Boys' Book of Canoeing: All about Canoe Handling, Paddling, Poling, Sailing, and Camping.* New York: E. P. Dutton, 1926.

Johnson, Daniel. "Wild Beaver Sighted for First Time in 500 Years." *London Telegraph,* July 18, 2013, http://www.telegraph.co.uk/news/earth/wildlife/10187252/Wild-beaver-sighted-for-first-time-in-500-years.html (accessed July 31, 2013).

Kaplanoff, Mark D., ed. *Joseph Ingraham's Journal of the Brigantine* Hope *on a Voyage to the Northwest Coast of North America 1790–92.* Barre, Mass.: Imprint Society, 1971.

Keating, William Hypolitus, and Roy P. Johnson. *Narrative of an Expedition to the Source of St. Peter's River, Lake Winnepeek, Lake of the Woods, etc.* 1825. Reprint, Minneapolis: Ross and Haines, 1959.

Kemmer, Rick. *A Guide to Paddle Adventure: How to Buy Canoes, Kayaks, and Inflatables, Where to Travel, and What to Pack Along.* New York: Vanguard Press, 1975.

Kemp, Dixon. *Yacht Architecture: A Treatise on the Laws Which Govern the Resistance of Bodies Moving in Water, Propulsion by Steam and Sail; Yacht Designing; and Yacht Building.* 3rd ed. London: H. Cox, 1897.

Kent, Timothy J. *Birchbark Canoes of the Fur Trade.* 2 vols. Ossineke, Mich.: Silver Fox Enterprises, 1997.

Kidd, Kenneth E. "Birch-Bark Scrolls in Archaeological Contexts." *American Antiquity* 30, no. 4 (1965): 480–83.

Kimber, Robert. *A Canoeist's Sketchbook.* Camden, Maine: Countrysport Press, 2004.

Kirch, Patrick Vinton. *Unearthing the Polynesian Past:*

*Explorations and Adventures of an Island Archaeologist.* Honolulu: University of Hawaii Press, 2015.

Klos, Kathryn Hilliard. *The Morris Canoe: Legacy of an American Family.* Middletown, Del.: Wooden Canoe Heritage Association, 2015.

Knox, Charles E. "Fiberglass Reinforcement." In *Handbook of Composites,* 136–59. New York: Van Nostrand Reinhold, 1982.

Kolbert, Elizabeth. "Sleeping with the Enemy: What Happened between the Neanderthals and Us?" Annals of Evolution, *The New Yorker,* August 15 and 22, 2011.

Kraiker, Debra, and Rolf Kraiker. *Cradle to Canoe: Camping and Canoeing with Children.* Erin, Ontario: Boston Mills Press, 1999.

Kuhne, Cecil, and Cherie Kuhne. *Paddling Basics Canoeing. Paddling Basics.* 1st ed. Mechanicsburg, Pa.: Stackpole Books, 1998.

Kulczycki, Chris. *The Canoe Shop.* New York: McGraw-Hill, 2001.

Landry, Paul A., Matty L. McNair, and Robert E. McNair. *Basic River Canoeing.* Rev. ed. Martinsville, W.Va.: American Camping Association, 1985.

Lapping, Mark B., and Owen J. Furuseth. *Big Places, Big Plans.* Aldershot, Hampshire, England: Ashgate, 2004.

Lear, Linda J. *Rachel Carson: Witness for Nature.* New York: H. Holt, 1997.

Lent, D. Geneva. *West of the Mountains: James Sinclair and the Hudson's Bay Company.* Seattle: University of Washington Press, 1963.

Leuven, Susan Van. *Illustrated Guide to Wood Strip Canoe Building.* Lancaster, Pa.: Schiffer Publishing, 1998.

Linthicum, M. Channing. *Costume in the Drama of Shakespeare and His Contemporaries.* New York: Russell and Russell, 1963.

Long, J. *Voyages and Travels of an Indian Interpreter and Trader.* 1904. Reprint, Toronto: Coles Publishing, 1974.

Longfellow, Henry Wadsworth. *The Song of Hiawatha and Other Poems.* Pleasantville, N.Y.: Reader's Digest Association, 1989.

Lorentz, Pare (director). *The River.* Sandy Hook, Conn.: Video Yesteryear, 1985.

Lovelace, Maud Hart. *Early Candlelight.* 1932. Reprint, St. Paul: Minnesota Historical Society Press, 1992.

Low, Sam, and Boyd Estus. "The Navigators, Pathfinders of the Pacific." DVD. Original film released 1983. Watertown, Mass.: Documentary Educational Resources, 2014.

Lytle, Mark H. *The Gentle Subversive: Rachel Carson, Silent Spring, and the Rise of the Environmental Movement.* New York: Oxford University Press, 2007.

MacGregor, John. *A Thousand Miles in the Rob Roy Canoe on Rivers and Lakes of Europe.* London: S. Low, Son, and Marston, 1866.

MacGregor, Roger. *When the Chestnut Was in Flower: Inside the Chestnut Canoe.* Lansdowne, Ontario: Plumsweep Press, 1999.

MacGregor, Roy. *Canoe Country: The Making of Canada.* Toronto: Random House Canada, 2015.

Mackenzie, Alexander. *The Journals of Alexander Mackenzie. Voyages from Montreal, On the River St. Laurence, Through the Continent of North America, To the Frozen and Pacific Oceans; In the Years, 1789 and 1793. With a Preliminary Account of the Rise, Progress, and Present State of the Fur Trade of That Country.* Santa Barbara, Calif.: The Narrative Press, 2001. Originally published in 1801.

Makens, James C. *Makens' Guide to U.S. Canoe Trails.* New York: Le Voyageur, 1971.

Malo, John W. *Midwest Canoe Trails.* Chicago: Contemporary Books, 1978.

———. *Wilderness Canoeing.* New York: Collier Books, 1974.

Mancall, Peter. "Algonquin." In *Encyclopedia of Native American History,* 21–23. New York: Facts on File, 2011.

Manley, Atwood. *Rushton and His Times in American Canoeing.* Syracuse, N.Y.: Syracuse University Press, 1968.

Mansel, Philip. *Dressed to Rule: Royal and Court Costume*

*from Louis XIV to Elizabeth II*. New Haven, Conn.: Yale University Press, 2005.

Mason, Bill. *Canoescapes*. Erin, Ontario: Boston Mills Press, 1995.

———. *Song of the Paddle: An Illustrated Guide to Wilderness Camping*. Toronto: Firefly Books, 2004.

Mason, Bill, and Paul Mason. *Path of the Paddle: An Illustrated Guide to the Art of Canoeing*. Rev. ed. Toronto: Firefly Books, 1999.

Mason, Otis Tufton. *Pointed Bark Canoes of the Kutenai and Amur*. Washington, D.C.: U.S. Government Printing Office, 1899.

Mason, Paul, and Mark Scriver. *Thrill of the Paddle: The Art of Whitewater Canoeing*. Toronto: Firefly Books, 1999.

Mayer, Ralph. *The Artist's Handbook of Materials and Techniques*. 1940. 4th ed. New York: Viking, 1970.

McCann, William D. "Hundreds Hike for Clean Land." *Cleveland Plain Dealer*, April 23, 1970.

McCanse, Anna. *Dominica*. Durham, N.C.: Other Places Publishing, 2011.

McCarthy, Henry "Mac." *Featherweight Boatbuilding: A Woodenboat Book*. Brooklin, Maine: Wooden Boat Publications, 1996.

McDonald, Archibald, and Malcolm McLeod. *Peace River: A Canoe Voyage from Hudson's Bay to Pacific, by Sir George Simpson (Governor, Hon. Hudson's Bay Company) in 1828; Journal of the Late Chief Factor, Archibald McDonald (Hon. Hudson's Bay Company) Who Accompanied Him*. 1872. Reprint, Rutland, Vt.: C. E. Tuttle Co., 1971.

McGuffin, Gary, and Joanie McGuffin. *Paddle Your Own Canoe: An Illustrated Guide to the Art of Canoeing*. Erin, Ontario: Boston Mills Press, 2003.

McKenney, Thomas Loraine. *Sketches of a Tour to the Lakes*. 1827. Reprint, Minneapolis: Ross and Haines, 1959.

McKusick, Marshall B. "Aboriginal Canoes in the West Indies." *Yale University Publications in Anthropology* 63 (1960): 3–11.

McMullin, Thomas A. "Revolt at Riverside: Victorian Virtue and the Charles River Canoeing Controversy, 1903–1905." *The New England Quarterly* 73, no. 3 (September 2000): 482–94.

McPhee, John. *Coming into the Country*. New York: Farrar, Straus and Giroux, 1977.

———. "Draft No. 4." *The New Yorker*, April 29, 2013.

———. *Giving Good Weight*. New York: Farrar, Straus and Giroux, 1979.

———. *The Survival of the Bark Canoe*. New York: Farrar, Straus and Giroux, 1982.

Mead, Robert Douglas. *The Canoer's Bible*. Doubleday Outdoor Bibles. Rev. ed. San Francisco: Main Street Books, 1989.

Meikle, Jeffrey L. *American Plastic: A Cultural History*. New Brunswick, N.J.: Rutgers University Press, 1995.

M'Gillivray, Duncan, and Arthur S. Morton. *The Journal of Duncan M'Gillivray of the North West Company at Fort George on the Saskatchewan, 1794–5*. Toronto: Macmillan Co. of Canada, 1929.

Middleton, Harry. *Rivers of Memory*. Boulder, Colorado: Pruett Publishing, 1993.

Mihell, Conor. "Royalex Revolution." *Canoeroots*, Fall 2011.

Milanich, Jerald T., and Nina J. Root. *Hidden Seminoles: Julian Dimock's Historic Florida Photographs*. Gainesville: University Press of Florida, 2011.

Millard, Candice. *River of Doubt: Theodore Roosevelt's Darkest Journey*. New York: Doubleday, 2005.

Millson, Larry. "Cain Raises Record Total for Canada." *The Globe and Mail* (Toronto), August 11, 1984.

———. "Canoeist Can't Get Enough." *The Globe and Mail* (Toronto), August 11, 1984.

Moberly, Henry John, and William Bleasdell Cameron. *When Fur Was King*. London and Toronto: J. M. Dent, 1929.

Moores, Ted. *Canoecraft: An Illustrated Guide to Fine Woodstrip Construction*. 2nd ed. Toronto: Firefly Books, 2000.

———. "From Forest to Factory: Innovations and Mass Production." In Jennings, *The Canoe: A Living Tradition*, 162–93.

Morison, Samuel Eliot. *Samuel de Champlain: Father of New France*. 1st ed. Boston: Little, Brown, 1972.

Morse, Eric W. *Canoe Routes of the Voyageurs: The Geography and Logistics of the Canadian Fur Trade*. Toronto: The Royal Canadian Geographic Society, 1962.

———. *Freshwater Saga: Memoirs of a Lifetime of Wilderness Canoeing in Canada*. Toronto: University of Toronto Press, 1987.

Nelson, Gaylord, Susan Campbell, and Paul R. Wozniak. *Beyond Earth Day: Fulfilling the Promise*. Madison: University of Wisconsin Press, 2002.

Neuzil, Mark. *The Environment and the Press: From Adventure Writing to Advocacy*. Evanston, Ill.: Northwestern University Press, 2008.

"The New Sectional Canoe." *Popular Science,* April 1946.

Niemi, Judith, and Barb Wieser. *Rivers Running Free: Canoeing Stories by Adventurous Women*. 1st Seal Press ed. Berkeley, Calif.: Seal Press, 1992.

Nute, Grace Lee. *The Voyageur*. Reprint, St. Paul: Minnesota Historical Society, 1955. Originally published in 1931.

———. *The Voyageur's Highway: Minnesota's Border Lake Land, 1941*. Reprint, St. Paul: Minnesota Historical Society, 1965. Originally published in 1941.

Oatman-Stanford, Hunter. "Love Boats: The Delightfully Sinful History of Canoes." Collectors Weekly. http://collectorsweekly.com (accessed March 27, 2013).

Ode, Kim. "Canoe Craze Marked by Romance, Ribaldry." *Minneapolis Star Tribune,* July 27, 2013.

Oh, Leslie Hsu. "How Canoes Are Saving Lives and Restoring Spirit." *Smithsonian Magazine,* January 6, 2016, http://www.smithsonianmag.com/smithsonian-institution/how-canoes-are-saving-lives-and-restoring-spirit-180957712/?no-ist.

Olson, Sigurd F. *Listening Point*. New York: Knopf, 1958.

———. *The Singing Wilderness*. New York: Knopf, 1956.

Osler, Sanford. *Canoe Crossings: Understanding the Craft That Helped Shape British Columbia*. Victoria, British Columbia: Heritage House, 2014.

Ovington, Ray. *Canoeing Basics for Beginners*. Mechanicsburg, Pa.: Stackpole Books, 1984.

Paine, Lincoln. *The Sea and Civilization: A Maritime History of the World*. New York: Knopf, 2013.

Patterson, R. M. *The Dangerous River: Adventure on the Nahanni*. New York: W. Sloane Associates, 1954.

Perry, Ronald H. *The Canoe and You*. London: J. M. Dent, 1948.

Pettingill, Marc. *Building Sweet Dream: An Ultralight Solo Canoe for Single or Double Paddle*. New York: Tiller, 1996.

Pinkerton, Robert E. *The Canoe: Its Selection, Care and Use*. London: Outing Publishing Co., 1914.

Podruchny, Carolyn. *Making the Voyageur World: Travelers and Traders in the North American Fur Trade*. Lincoln: University of Nebraska Press, 2006.

Poling, Jim, Sr. *The Canoe: An Illustrated History*. Woodstock, N.Y.: Countryman Press, 2001.

Pollock, Robert F. "Down by the Riverside." In *Historic Auburndale*. Booklet, rev. ed. Auburndale, Mass.: Auburndale Community Association, 1996.

Prakash, A. K. "Frances Anne Hopkins." In *Independent Spirit: Early Canadian Women Artists*, 42–44, 242–45. Richmond Hill, Ontario: Firefly Books, 2008.

Pulling, Pierre. *Canoeing the Indian Way: Straight Talk for Modern Paddlers from the Dean of American Canoeists*. 1979. Reprint, Mechanicsburg, Pa.: Stackpole Books, 1989.

———. *The Elements of Canoeing*. Ann Arbor, Mich.: Duke Publishing, 1933.

———. *Principles of Canoeing*. New York: Macmillan, 1954.

Pyette, Kaydi. "Royalex Is Dead." Rapid Media. http://www.rapidmedia.com (accessed September 6, 2013).

Raffan, James. *Fire in the Bones: Bill Mason and the Canadian Canoeing Tradition*. 1st HarperPerennial ed. New York: HarperCollins, 1999.

———. *Wild Waters: Canoeing North America's Wilderness Rivers*. Toronto: Firefly Books, 1997.

Raffan, James, and Bert Horwood, eds. *Canexus: The Canoe in Canadian Culture*. Toronto: Dundurn Press, 1988.

Rees, Quentin. *The Cockleshell Canoes: British Military Canoes of World War Two*. Stroud, Gloucestershire, England: Amberley, 2008.

Reid, Bill, and Gene Lawrence. *Totem*. Documentary film. Vancouver, British Columbia: CBC Television, 1963. Originally shown as *Rescue Mission* (1959).

Reid, Martine. *Bill Reid: A Retrospective Exhibition*. Vancouver, British Columbia: Vancouver Art Gallery, 1974.

———. *Bill Reid and the Haida Canoe*. Madeira Park, British Columbia: Harbour, 2011.

"Restoration Work Begins at Maritime Museum on Canoe Built 250 Years Ago." *The Western Morning News* (Plymouth, England), January 7, 2011.

Ribeiro, Aileen. *The Art of Dress: Fashion in England and France, 1750 to 1820*. New Haven, Conn.: Yale University Press, 1995.

Rich, E. E. *The Fur Trade and the Northwest to 1857*. Toronto: McClelland and Stewart, 1967.

Richardson, John. *Arctic Expedition. Copy of a Report from Sir John Richardson, Dated Fort Confidence, Great Bear Lake, 16th September 1848, Reporting His Proceedings in Search of Sir John Franklin's Expedition*. London: HMSO, 1849.

———. *Arctic Searching Expedition: A Journal of a Boat-Voyage through Rupert's Land and the Arctic Sea, in Search of the Discovery Ships under Command of Sir John Franklin*. 1851. Reprint, New York: Greenwood Press, 1969.

Riviere, Bill. *The Open Canoe*. New York: Little Brown, 1985.

Rizetta, Sam. *Canoe and Kayak Building the Light and Easy Way*. New York: McGraw-Hill, 2009.

Roberts, Kenneth G. "Lilly Dipping It Ain't." In *Canexus: The Canoe in Canadian Culture*, edited by James Raffan and Bert Horwood, 107–122. Toronto: Betelgeuse Books, 1988.

Roberts, Kenneth G., and Philip Shackleton. *The Canoe: A History of the Craft from Panama to the Arctic*. Camden, Maine: International Marine, 1983.

Ross, Alexander. *The Fur Hunters of the Far West*. 1855. Reprint, Norman: University of Oklahoma Press, 1956.

Ruhl, Donna L., and Barbara A. Purdy. "One Hundred-One Canoes on the Shore: 3–5,000 Year Old Canoes from Newnans Lake, Florida." *Journal of Wetland Archaeology* 5, no. 1 (2005): 111–27.

Russell, Peter, Andrew F. Hunter, and E. A. Cruikshank. *The Correspondence of the Honourable Peter Russell, with Allied Documents Relating to His Administration of the Government of Upper Canada during the Official Term of Lieut.-Governor J. G. Simcoe while on Leave of Absence*. Toronto: Ontario Historical Society, 1932.

Rutstrum, Calvin. *North American Canoe Country: The Classic Guide to Canoe Technique*. 1964. Reprint, Minneapolis: University of Minnesota Press, 2000.

Schade, Nick. *Building Strip-Planked Boats*. Camden, Maine: International Marine/Ragged Mountain Press, 2009.

Schoolcraft, Henry Rowe, and Douglass Houghton. *Henry R. Schoolcraft: Expedition into the Indian Country. Letter from the Secretary of War, Transmitting . . . Information in Relation to an Expedition of Henry R. Schoolcraft into the Indian Country. March 7, 1832*. St. Paul: Minnesota Historical Society, 1967.

Schoolcraft, Henry Rowe, and Philip P. Mason. *Expedition to Lake Itasca: The Discovery of the Source of the Mississippi*. East Lansing: Michigan State University Press, 1958.

Sears, George Washington. *Canoeing the Adirondacks with Nessmuk: The Adirondack Letters of George Washington Sears*. Edited by Dan Brenan. 1962. Reprint, Blue Mountain Lake, N.Y.: Adirondack Museum/Syracuse University Press, 1993.

Selkirk, Thomas Douglas. *Lord Selkirk and the North West Company*. Ottawa: National Library of Canada, 1977.

Sevareid, Eric. *Canoeing with the Cree*. 75th anniversary ed. Minneapolis: Borealis Books, 2005.

Shadbolt, Doris. *Bill Reid*. Seattle: University of Washington Press, 1986.

Siggins, Lorna. "'Iconic Canoe' Returned to Canada." *The Irish Times* (Dublin), June 29, 2009.

Simmons, Walter J. *Building Lapstrake Canoes*. 2nd ed. Lincolnville Beach, Maine: Duck Trap Press, 2003.

Sivertson, Howard. *The Illustrated Voyageur: Paintings and Companion Stories*. 2nd ed. Duluth, Minn.: Lake Superior Port Cities, 1999.

Souder, William. *On a Farther Shore: The Life and Legacy of Rachel Carson*. New York: Crown Publishers, 2012.

Spears, Borden, and Bruce M. Litteljohn. *Wilderness Canada*. Toronto: Clarke, Irwin, 1970.

Spurr, Daniel. *Heart of Glass: Fiberglass Boats and the Men Who Made Them*. Camden, Maine, and New York: International Marine / McGraw-Hill, 2000.

Standfield, Don, and Liz Lundell. *Stories from the Bow Seat: The Wisdom and Waggery of Canoe Tripping*. Erin, Ontario: Boston Mills Press, 1999.

Stanley, Beth. "Know Your Paddles." *Canadian Woodworking*, June–July 2011, https://canadianwoodworking.com/get-more/know-your-paddles (accessed July 17, 2013).

Stelmok, Jerry. *The Art of the Canoe with Joe Seliga*. St. Paul: MBI, 2002.

———. *Building the Maine Guide Canoe*. New York: Lyons Press, 2003.

Stelmok, Jerry, and Rollin Thurlow. *The Wood and Canvas Canoe: A Complete Guide to Its History, Construction, Restoration, and Maintenance*. Gardiner, Maine: Tilbury House Publishers, 1987.

Steltzer, Ulli. *The Spirit of Haida Gwaii: Bill Reid's Masterpiece*. Vancouver, British Columbia: Douglas and McIntyre, 1997.

Stephens, William Picard. *Canoe and Boat Building: A Complete Manual for Amateurs*. New York: General Books, 2010.

Stephenson, Gerald F. "John Stephenson and the Famous 'Peterborough' Canoes." Occasional Paper No. 8. Peterborough, Ontario: Peterborough Historical Society, 1987.

Sterba, Jim. "America Gone Wild." *Wall Street Journal*, November 3–4, 2012.

Stewart, Hilary. *Cedar: Tree of Life to the Northwest Coast Indians*. Vancouver, British Columbia: Douglas and McIntyre, 1984.

Strickland, H. F. "Correspondence." *The American Canoeist*, September 1885.

Summers, John. *Can I Canoe You up the River?: The Story of Paddling and Romance*. Peterborough, Ontario: The Canadian Canoe Museum, 2014.

Swenson, Allen A. *L. L. Bean Canoeing Handbook*. New York: Lyons Press, 2000.

Taylor, Douglas. *The Caribs of Dominica*. Washington, D.C.: U.S. Government Printing Office, 1938.

———. "The Island Caribs of Dominica, B.W.I." *American Anthropologist* 37, no. 2 (1935): 265–72.

Thompson, Daniel V. *The Materials and Techniques of Medieval Painting*. New York: Dover, 2012. Originally published in 1956.

Thoreau, Henry David. *Canoeing in the Wilderness*. 1916. Reprint, New York: General Books, 2010.

———. *The Maine Woods*. In *The Portable Thoreau*, edited by Carl Bode. New York: Viking Press, 1964.

Thruelsen, Richard. *The Grumman Story*. New York: Praeger, 1976.

Thwaites, Reuben Gold. *The Jesuit Relations and Allied Documents: Travels and Explorations of the Jesuit Missionaries in New France, 1610–1791*. Vol. 9. Cleveland: Burrows, 1897.

Tilford, Gregory L. *Edible and Medicinal Plants of the West*. Missoula, Mont.: Mountain Press, 1997.

Tippett, Maria. *Bill Reid: The Making of an Indian*. Toronto, Ontario: Vintage Canada, 2004.

Traill, Catherine Parr Strickland. *The Backwoods of Canada: Selections*. 1836. Reprint, Toronto: McClelland and Steward, 1966.

"Tribes Use GIS in Time-Honored Canoe Journeys." *Esri News for Federal Government*, Spring 2015.

Turner, James Morton. *The Promise of Wilderness: American*

*Environmental Politics since 1964*. Seattle: University of Washington Press, 2013.

Twain, Mark [Samuel Clemens]. *Autobiography of Mark Twain*. Vol. 1. Reader's ed. Berkeley and Los Angeles: University of California Press, 2012.

Vaillancourt, Henri. "Algonquin Canoes." Birchbark Canoes, www.birchbarkcanoe.net/algonquincanoes.html (accessed May 23, 2013).

———. "The Enys Birchbark Canoe: A Late-1700s Treasure Rediscovered in a Stone Barn in England." *Wooden Boat*, September–October 2011.

Van Slyck, Abigail Ayres. *A Manufactured Wilderness: Summer Camps and the Shaping of American Youth, 1890–1960*. Minneapolis: University of Minnesota Press, 2006.

Vaux, C. Bowyer. *Canoe Handling: The Canoe, History, Uses, Limitations and Varieties, Practical Management and Care and Relative Facts*. New York: Forest and Stream, 1885.

Walbridge, Charlie. *The Nuts 'n' Bolts Guide to Outfitting Your Canoe or C-1*. Birmingham, Ala.: Menasha Ridge Press, 1996.

Walzer, Emily. "Pelican International." *Sporting Goods Business*, July 14, 2000.

Warren, Graham. *Making Canoe Paddles in Wood*. Norris, U.K.: Raven Rock Books, 1997.

Warren, Graham, and David Gidmark. *Canoe Paddles: A Complete Guide to Making Your Own*. Willowdale, Ontario: Firefly Books, 2001.

Weis, Chuck. "A Conversation with Gene Jensen." *Paddler Magazine*, August 1993, http://jensencanoes.com/articles-news/paddler/ (accessed July 17, 2013).

Wheeler, Ryan J. "The Ortona Canals: Aboriginal Canal Hydraulics and Engineering." *Florida Anthropologist* 48 (1995): 265–81.

Wheeler, Ryan J., James J. Miller, Ray M. McGee, Donna Ruhl, Brenda Swann, and Melissa Memory. "Archaic Period Canoes from Newnans Lake, Florida." *American Antiquity* 68, no. 3 (2003): 1–19.

White, William Chapman. *Adirondack Country*. New York: Knopf, 1967.

Wingerd, Mary Lethert. *North Country: The Making of Minnesota*. Minneapolis: University of Minnesota Press, 2010.

Woodruff, Jim. "Romancing with Ike in an Old Town . . . Or Was It a Morris?" *Wooden Canoe* 103 (February 2001).

Wyatt, Charles. "Canoe Makers Hope to Sink Competition." *Business Edge*, May 26, 2005.

"A Yacht Built of Aluminum." *The San Francisco Call*, April 26, 1896.

Young, Egerton Ryerson. *By Canoe and Dog-Train among the Cree and Salteaux Indians*. London: Charles H. Kelly, 1890.

Zuk, Larry. *Stories of a Century of Canoeing and Canoes: Canoeing in the American Canoe Association*. N.d., http://canusail.org/Zuk_Papers/index.html#p0011.

# Index

Page numbers in **bold** refer to illustrations.

## MARK NEUZIL

is a professor in the Department of Communication and Journalism at the University of St. Thomas in St. Paul, Minnesota. He is the author or coauthor of several books, many of them with environmental themes, including *Views on the Mississippi: The Photographs of Henry Peter Bosse* (Minnesota, 2001), and is a frequent speaker on environmental subjects. A former wilderness guide and summer park ranger, he is an avid outdoorsman who began canoeing in the 1960s with his family. He is a past board member of the Society of Environmental Journalists, the Minnesota chapter of the Society of Professional Journalists, and Friends of the Mississippi River. He lives in St. Paul, Minnesota.

## NORMAN SIMS

is a retired professor from the University of Massachusetts Amherst. His scholarly research focused on literary journalism, and he has been president of the International Association for Literary Journalism Studies. He served for twelve years on the Appalachian Mountain Club board of directors and has represented the AMC in several hydropower relicensing cases that resulted in improved releases for whitewater. He's been paddling for fifty years. An active member of the Wooden Canoe Heritage Association, he has a small collection of antique Morris wood-and-canvas canoes. He lives in Winchester, New Hampshire.

## JOHN McPHEE

is the author of nearly thirty books, including *Encounters with the Archdruid* (1972), *The Survival of the Bark Canoe* (1975), and *Coming into the Country* (1977). He received the Award for Literature from the Academy of Arts and Letters in 1977 and was awarded the Pulitzer Prize for *Annals of the Former World* in 1999. He lives in Princeton, New Jersey.

PRODUCED BY WILSTED & TAYLOR PUBLISHING SERVICES

*Project manager* Christine Taylor
*Production assistant* LeRoy Wilsted
*Copy editor* Nancy Evans
*Designer and compositor* Nancy Koerner
*Proofreader* Lynn Meinhardt
*Printer's devil* Lillian Marie Wilsted